HONG KONG: THE END OF AN EMPIRE

Jan Morris, who is Anglo-Welsh by parentage, divides her time between her library-house in North Wales, her *dacha* in the Black Mountains of South Wales, and travel abroad. She has been to Manhattan every year since 1954, makes an annual visit to Venice, and spends much of her life wandering and writing for (mostly American) magazines.

Among her best-known books are the *Pax Britannica* trilogy (*Heaven's Command, Pax Britannica* and *Farewell the Trumpets*, the autobiographical *Conundrum* and six other volumes of travel essays, *Venice, Oxford, Spain, The Matter of Wales, Among the Cities* and *Manhattan '45*. She has also edited *The Oxford Book of Oxford* and two Welsh anthologies. Her first work of fiction, *Last Letters from Hav* (Viking 1985, Penguin 1986), was shortlisted for the Booker Prize. Many of her books are published by Penguin.

JAN MORRIS

HONG KONG

香港

XIANGGANG

THE END OF AN EMPIRE

PENGUIN BOOKS

PENGUIN BOOKS

Published by the Penguin Group
27 Wrights Lane, London w8 5TZ, England
Viking Penguin Inc., 40 West 23rd Street, New York, New York 10010, USA
Penguin Books Australia Ltd, Ringwood, Victoria, Australia
Penguin Books Canada Ltd, 2801 John Street, Markham, Ontario, Canada L3R 1B4
Penguin Books (NZ) Ltd, 182–190 Wairau Road, Auckland 10, New Zealand

Penguin Books Ltd, Registered Offices: Harmondsworth, Middlesex, England

First published by Viking 1988
Published in Penguin Books 1990
10 9 8 7 6 5 4 3 2 1

Copyright © Jan Morris, 1988
All rights reserved

An extract from W. H. Auden's 'Hong Kong' is reprinted by
permission of Faber and Faber Ltd, from *Collected Poems* by W. H. Auden

An extract from Noël Coward's 'Mad Dogs and Englishmen' is reprinted,
by permission of Methuen London, from *The Noël Coward Songbook*

Filmset in Baskerville
Made and printed in Great Britain by
Richard Clay Ltd, Bungay, Suffolk

香港

CONTENTS

CHINESE NAMES ARE GENERALLY IN THE
PINYIN ROMANIZATION, BUT NOT ALWAYS

PICTURES

PEOPLE'S REPUBLIC OF CHINA

Shenzhen

Shao Chan R.

Sheung Shui

Hou Hoi Wan (Deep Bay)

Lau Fau Shan

Yuen Long

Shek Kong

250m.

250m.

N   E   W

Tuen Mun

250m.

250m.

Sham Tseng

Tsuen Wan

Tsing I.

Discovery
Bay

Green I.

Peng Chau

Mui Wo

Tai O

LANTAU ISLAND

750m.

500m.

250m.

250m.

Cheung Chau

Lamma I.

West Lamma Channel

Sha Tau Kok

Ping Chau

250m

250m

250m

Taiping Wan

(Mirs Bay)

150m

100m

Plover Cove
Reservoir

250m

Tolo Channel

Tap Mun Chau

250m

Tai Po

Tolo Harbour

250m

250m

250m

E   R   R   I   T   O   R   I   E   S

250m

250m

Sai Kung

High Island Res.

500m

Sha Tin

250m

wai Chung

250m

250m

500m

Kowloon
Peak

Kai Tak
Airport

am Shui Po

Hang Hau Town

ecutters I.

KOWLOON

Lei Yui
Mun

m Sha Tsui

Junk
Bay

Victoria Harbour

Central
District

Chai Wan

ictoria
Peak

250m

Tathong Channel

HONG KONG   ISLAND

erdeen

250m

Shek O

e Lamma Channel

Deep Water Bay

Repulse Bay

Stanley

Po Toi Islands

HONG KONG and
the New Territories

0   5 km

0   5 miles

I PROLOGUE

THE TRAVELLER IN CHINA SEES MANY MARVELS. FROM Harbin in the bitter north to Urumqi among the deserts of Xinjiang, from the frontiers of the Soviet Union to the marches of India, the way is marked everywhere by spectacle and anomaly. There are landscapes fragile or colossal, climates of infinite range, hideous cities, magnificent rivers. There are pagodas and porcelain bridges, mighty dams, acrobats, camels, flaming red banners, unimaginably dismal hamlets and glitzy tourist hotels. Venerable junks sail by, steam engines snort at railway stations, black limousines sweep through portentous gateways towards offices of incalculable power. The most astonishing thing of all, though, lies at the southern edge of the Chinese land mass, just below the Tropic of Cancer, where the Zhu Jiang or Pearl River debouches through Guangdong Province into the South China Sea.

Every night at ten a ship called *Xinghu* sails down the estuary from Guangzhou (Canton as it used to be transliterated), and taking passage on it suggests to me an evening in the theatre. Within sight of its wharf stands one of those smart tourist hotels, the White Swan, a convenient place to dine before the performance, and at the dock gates officials dispassionately gesture you through like ushers in the aisle. The formalities are brief, and hardly have you checked into your brown-panelled cabin (flowered thermos flask of hot tea comforting beside the bunk) than you feel the pulse of the engines vibrating the ship, and see through your porthole the lights of the city slipping away.

You are likely to be the only European on board, and your Chinese fellow-passengers look altogether of a kind. Pushy old ladies in high-collared black, exquisitely wide-eyed children, worn-looking mothers and robust anxious fathers – all are buried beneath similarly shambled baggage, move about at a kind of uniform trot, and seem less like real people than statistics on the move. Most of them settle below deck to gossip, gamble at cards, eat or sleep, and if you go up above as the ship steams down-channel you will find yourself almost alone in the dark. There is hardly a sound up there, only the swish of the wind and the beat of the turbines far below, but all round you unexplained lights go swimming by, lights of sampans or of freighters, fishermen's lights, torch-beams out of nowhere, the forty-watt lights of the towns and villages that line the estuary on either side, growing more faint and more distant as the river broadens towards the sea.

It is like the hush in the theatre that succeeds the overture. The dark grows darker, a few shadowy figures lean over the rail here and there along the decks, and you may feel, as you feel in the dress circle at another kind of show, a frisson of expectancy. Perhaps you may be tempted to go to your cabin and sleep, but if you happen to be writing a book you will prefer to stick it out on deck, huddling yourself against the cold until the first light dawns.

You nod off, of course, despite yourself, but after what seems no more than a moment or two suddenly it strikes you that the engines have stopped, and the ship is lying motionless and silent in a thick white mist. Fog-horns sound now and then. There is nothing to be seen now, unless out of the obscurity a solitary sampan comes chugging by, or you can just make out the dim shape of a freighter passing. The ship *Xinghu* seems to be dead. The water is quite still. The mist is of a swirling stagey kind, like mists in TV videos. You might be anywhere, or nowhere at all.

But then like the rising of the theatre's curtain the fog begins to lift, rolling slowly upwards from the sea, and you realize that you are already at anchor off another port. First the ships show, one beyond the other, hundreds of ships, ships of all sizes, ships of all shapes, cluttered about with lighters and apparently floating not in the water but in the mist itself. Then on each side of you buildings start to appear, speckled still with the lights of the night before – not those pale lights of the estuary, but bright, extravagant lights, in buildings of concrete, steel and mirror-glass, with advertisements on them, and forests of aerials.

Up goes the mist, taller and taller those buildings turn out to be, each higher than the one before – pressing upon one another, looking over each others' shoulders, immense clean buildings of white, or silver, or even gold, with masses of portholed windows, or great cross-girders, with jagged rooflines and spiky towers – up the city heights until green mountainsides appear behind, and there are white villas everywhere, and snaking roads, and white domes alone on summits, and the rising sun, shining clean through the windows of an apartment block on a high ridge, suddenly seems to set the whole structure afire, blazing all white and red above the sea.

So like a fanfare, as the vapours are burnt away, a last phenomenon of China is revealed to you; a futuristic metropolis, like something from another age or another sensibility, stacked around a harbour jammed fantastically with ships – the busiest, the richest and the most truly extraordinary of all Chinese cities, identified in the new orthography as Xianggang.

It is more than a city actually, being an archipelago of some 235 rocks and islands attendant upon a squat mountainous peninsula. Humped or supine, silent in the haze, to the south and west the islands seem to lie bewitched along the dim blue coast of China, and to the north a line of mainland hills stands like a rampart – the hills of Kowloon, or Nine Dragons. With luck the sea, when the mist disperses, will be a tremendous emerald green, and if one looks with a sufficiently selective eye it is easy enough to imagine the place as it was when it first entered world history 150 years ago.

In those days the Ladrones or Pirate Islands, together with the neighbouring peninsula, formed part of the San On district of Guangdong Province. This was not a very important corner of the Qing or Manchu Empire, which believed itself to be uniquely and divinely supreme among all the kingdoms of the earth, but whose capital was 1,500 miles away in Beijing – at least a fortnight's travel by the fastest messenger. The original inhabitants of the district had probably not been Chinese at all, but aboriginals of the stock called Yao, allegedly descended from miscegenation between a dog and a princess, who had left mystic monoliths here and there. Neither on the archipelago nor on the peninsula had there ever been a settlement larger than a small market town or a prudently fortified village.

The place had few resources, and some 80 per cent of the land, whether insular or mainland, was too mountainous to farm. The all-but-tropical climate was trying. At its best, especially in the autumn, it could be perfection, but it could also be terribly hot and humid, and sometimes the sky was overcast for weeks at a time. Typhoons were fierce and frequent, and besides malaria, cholera, typhoid and bubonic plague, the people were subject to a more particular horror called Xhu Mao Bing, the Bristle Disease, whose victims found spiky bristles like pig-hairs (sometimes apparently fish-scales, too) sprouting through their skin.

An esoteric wildlife roamed the hills and frequented the waters. There were leopards, tigers, badgers, Chinese otters, pangolins, wild cats and boars; but there were also crab-eating mongooses, an unusual variety of newt, 200 kinds of butterfly and thirty-two kinds of snake, including the Flower-Pot Snake, the White-Lipped Viper and the Rock Python, which grew up to sixteen feet long and could swallow a dog. There were fish like the Golden Thread, the Lizard-Fish, the Big-eye and the Croaker, together with several varieties of venomous water-serpent. The bird life was rich and varied (the black-and-white pied kingfisher was found nowhere else), the wild-flowers included many species of orchid, and among the shrubs of the mountains grew the rare and profitable Incense Tree.

Only two moderately momentous historical events had ever occurred in these parts. One was the Great Evacuation of the seventeenth century, when during a war against Taiwan the Manchus removed inland all the inhabitants of the San On coastal regions, some 16,000 people, and ordered the destruction of all sea-shore crops and properties – an early example of 'scorched-earth' tactics which was to be remembered for many generations in the local folklore. The other was the flight to the Kowloon Peninsula, in 1277, of the child-emperor Duan Zong, the penultimate ruler of the Song dynasty: driven south by usurping Mongols he spent a year in the district with his fugitive court and his half-starved army before being harried to his death at the age of nine, and an inscribed boulder on a hilltop commemorated his pathetic passage.

Remote and inconsequential though the territory was, in the first decades of the nineteenth century scattered communities existed throughout the islands, and in the fertile flatlands of the peninsula. There were rice-farmers, salt-producers, fishermen, quarrymen, incense-gatherers. There were not a few pirates, who found convenient retreats among the myriad islands at the mouth of the great estuary (hence the name Ladrones, which means 'pirates' in Portuguese) and who sometimes operated in great force – when the pirate leader Zhang Bao-zi capitulated to the authorities in 1810, he surrendered 270 junks and 1,200 guns.

The inhabitants were of four Chinese races: the Punti or Cantonese, the Hoklos, the Hakkas or 'stranger families', and the outcast people called Tankas or 'egg people' (perhaps because their boats had egg-shaped canopies). They lived for the most part in segregated communities, speaking their own languages and generally antipathetic towards one another. The powerful landowning families of the region, however, were all Cantonese, and they were grouped into the Five Great Clans, Tang, Hau, Pang, Liu and Man, each dominating its own villages and possessing its inherited lands in common.

The area was governed from Nam Tan, on the shores of Deep Bay to the north-west. There the district magistrate ('the father–mother official') had his *yamen* or seat of authority. He was responsible, through several gradations of hierarchy, to the Viceroy of Guangdong, and he was sustained by troops and warships. There was a fortified headquarters at Kowloon City near the southern tip of the peninsula, and among the islands were several small forts and naval bases, part of the coastal defences of the Guangzhou Delta, beneath whose guns the rotund war-junks anchored, and around whose walls the camp-followers deposited their shacks. Set against the bare green hills, too often washed in humid drizzle, all these outposts must have seemed very emblems of far-flung dominion, so lonely there among that half-charted archipelago; in old pictures, in fact, the main fort at Kowloon City looks just like a frontier stronghold in hostile territory, a stronghold on a hillock from which a ramshackle street runs like an escape route to the nearby quay. Government seems to have been sketchy at best, officials seldom visiting the more isolated settlements, and was also notoriously corrupt. There were frequent clan wars and feuds between villages, some of which had armies of their own, uniformed and equipped with artillery.

Nevertheless, though the territory was often turbulent, and was remote indeed from the exquisite subtleties of the Chinese Establishment, at a local level the people seem to have organized their lives competently enough. The class of scholar-gentry, which had for centuries set the tone of Confucianist civilization, was thin on the ground in these parts, and there was not much education; but the village headmen and elders were influential, residents' associations were active, local tradition was strong, and the people, while venerating an eclectic range of Buddhist and Daoist divinities, not to mention countless spirits and totems of animism, were united in honouring the Confucian ethic. Records were kept, on slabs in temples and ancestral halls. Lineages were maintained. Elaborate rules of land tenure were enforced. The laws of *feng shui*, 'wind and water', the ancient Chinese geomancy of location and design, were scrupulously obeyed. Travelling theatre companies made their circuits of the villages, and as a district magistrate recorded in surprise in 1744, 'culture has spread even to this remote place near the sea – the Book of Poetry is read here as early as sunrise . . .'

Many of the people, especially the Tankas whom everyone else despised, lived on boats. Many more lived clan by clan in the dozen or so walled villages which were characteristic of the region – the local Cantonese dialect was known as 'the dialect of the walled villages'. Blue-tiled, moated, sometimes towered, with narrow symmetrical streets around temple and ancestral hall, these were apparently sufficiently well administered by the clans' own leaders and associations. So long as they paid their taxes, the Imperial Government generally left them alone. At night the village watchman beat his reassuring gong every half hour, ending at dawn with a long roll of reveille. In the daytime the workers went out, nearly all of them landowners in one degree or another, to work the communal fields around. On the hills above, sheltered by correctly planted trees, the ancestral graves looked down from positions meticulously calculated by the geomancers.

So the territory was by no means primitive or deserted when, in the first half of the nineteenth century, it became known to the wider world. Nor was it unvisited. On the contrary, a constant sea-traffic moved through the archipelago, or anchored in the magnificent deep harbour which lay at the foot of the peninsula. Raggety sails of sampans, proud banners of imperial warships, skulking pirate masts and the high superstructures of cargo junks – all these were to be seen perpetually moving among the waterways. Much of the commerce of the Pearl River Estuary passed this way to the northern Chinese provinces, Taiwan or Japan, and by the 1830s the indigenes had become familiar too with an alien category of shipping; shipping of another technology, another culture – schooners, brigs and lofty full-rigged ships, bringing to the archipelago fateful intimations of another world to the west.

*

Guangzhou was the one port of China which maintained links with that other world. The Celestial Empire in Beijing officially classed all foreigners as Barbarians – Outer Barbarians, in fact – and all foreign States as mere tributaries, so that there was no diplomatic contact between China and other Powers, and very little intercourse. The Manchus themselves were not Chinese by origin, having come from Manchuria in the seventeenth century, but this did not inhibit their xenophobia, and they treated all other non-Chinese with an ineffable mixture of contempt and paternalism.

Guangzhou in the south, however, as the chief port of China, had for centuries been in touch with the countries of south-east Asia, with India and with the Arabs. Since the sixteenth century, when the Portuguese had been allowed to establish a trading colony at Macao on the western shore of the Pearl Estuary, the city had also been in touch with Europe. All the nations of the west dreamed of tapping China's fabled resources, and for many years several of them had been permitted to operate 'factories' or warehouses on the waterfront at Guangzhou, the only Chinese city where foreigners were allowed to live. They sold woollens, cottons, furs and a few manufactured goods, they bought silks, works of art, the emetic rhubarb and huge quantities of tea. During the winter trading-season they lived in a closely confined waterfront enclave outside the city walls – around the site of our White Swan Hotel, as it happens. In summer they withdrew to more comfortable quarters in Portuguese Macao. The officials of the Dragon-Emperor treated them at best with condescension, at worst with a kind of ritual contumely, calling them Devils and Demons.

At the end of the 1830s the merchants of four foreign Powers maintained factories at Guangzhou – the British, the Americans, the French and the Dutch. Of these businessmen much the most numerous, truculent and successful were the British, to whom China seemed a putative extension, if only in commercial terms, of their highly profitable Indian Empire. They were in a mood of dynamic confidence. The power of new technology was behind them, and they felt themselves to be on a winning streak. In particular, victory in the Napoleonic wars had made their nation indisputably dominant in the East, both the French and the Dutch competition having been largely eliminated, and the establishment of Singapore as an outpost of the British East India Company had seemed to promise the opening of all the China seas to their trade and influence.

The Company had lately abandoned its official monopoly of Anglo-

Chinese trade, and there were now some thirty British firms operating from the Guangzhou waterfront. In theory at least they were supervised by a Chief Superintendent of Trade, appointed by the British Government and known to the Chinese as 'The Barbarian Eye'.[1] By now the pattern of their trade had shifted, and they depended largely upon illicit dealings in Indian opium – 'foreign mud' as the Chinese called it, eagerly lighting their pipes, for though it was banned in China it was enormously in demand.

The growth and sale of opium was officially organized in British India, and traders brought vast quantities of it up the Pearl River, selling it at handsome profit to Chinese entrepreneurs. As a matter of fact there was not much else British traders *could* sell to the Chinese, who were self-sufficient in most things and scornful of western innovations, so that the opium traffic was developed with relentless energy. The drugs illegally sold to China were worth twice as much as all the legal commodities put together, and without them Britain's imports of China tea could have been paid for only in specie. Opium became, so it is said, not only the principal export of the Indian Empire, but actually the largest single article of international commerce anywhere in the world.

Much skulduggery was involved, since the trade was forbidden even in Guangzhou; but opium or no opium, in any case relations between the Chinese and the foreigners, especially the British, were equivocal. The drug trade was only a symptom. These were the early years of a fateful confrontation, between east and west, between empires, between cultures, and each side was antagonized by the alien ways of the other. The westerners were intent upon expansion, commercial, political, even spiritual: the Chinese were determined to preserve their own status quo. One side was profoundly conservative and lethargic, the other vigorously radical and aggressive.

Pinpricks, frustrations and anomalies abounded. On the one hand the traders were strictly circumscribed by Chinese Government regulations, forbidding them for instance to learn any Chinese language, or to bring their wives to Guangzhou, or to arm themselves, or to enter the walled city proper, or to ride in sedan chairs, or to deal with any Chinese merchants other than those officially appointed, or to go boating for pleasure without express permission. On the other hand the whole relationship was riddled with mutual corruption, and the

[1] Or in the case of its first incumbent, Lord William Napier of Maristoun, by a convenient ideographic transcription of his name which meant 'Laboriously Vile'.

Chinese generally turned a venal blind eye not only to infringements of the residential rules, but also to the all too obvious trade in narcotics. The traders constantly agitated for greater commercial freedom, the Chinese reiterated their reminders that the Outer Barbarians were there purely on sufferance, and should be humbly grateful for what they had – 'Tremble and Obey', as the imperial rescripts used to say, 'Oppose not!' British attempts to open diplomatic relations, and to establish normal trading practices throughout China, were haughtily rebuffed. Fortunes were made on both sides; enmities and friendships too.

Matters had been more or less like this for half a century, give or take a crisis or two. There was growing anxiety in China, though, about the debilitating effects of opium on the populace, and in 1839 a mandarin of unaccustomed probity, Lin Ze-xu, arrived in Guangzhou as Imperial High Commissioner of the Court of Heaven. He had specific instructions to stamp out the opium trade, and the sly old equilibrium was now shattered. Besides banning all opium imports, Lin demanded the surrender of the 20,291 chests of the drug the merchants had in stock.

He little knew what historical forces he was unleashing. The Chief Superintendent of Trade, Captain Charles Elliot R.N.,[1] decided to the contempt of the merchants that the chests must be handed over, and they were publicly destroyed. This was, however, by no means the end of the affair. The infuriated businessmen withdrew from Guangzhou to emergency headquarters on their vessels anchored at the mouth of the estuary (their 'devil-ships', as the Chinese called them). Lin forbade any Chinese citizen to supply them with food and water, Elliot responded by having the Royal Navy open fire on three Chinese war-junks, and so a *casus belli* was provided.

It was welcome in London. Lord Palmerston, Foreign Secretary in Lord Melbourne's Whig Government in London, viewed the rest of the world rather as the Chinese did themselves, and his chief political purpose was the furtherance of British trade wherever the British wanted it. The two principal British Guangzhou merchants, the Scots-men William Jardine and James Matheson, had long pressed him for action to force the Chinese into the comity of international trade – a 'forward policy', as the jargon of the day had it, to be sustained by the

[1] Previously commander of a hospital ship and Protector of Slaves in British Guiana.

threat of military violence. Jardine had now retired to Britain and had been elected to Parliament, and seizing upon the affair of the opium chests he drew up for Palmerston a battle-plan for the humiliation of the Celestial Kingdom.

Palmerston obliged. Gunboat diplomacy was authorized. Gladstone, in Opposition, warned that going to war with China on such pretexts would cover Great Britain in permanent disgrace – 'we . . . are pursuing objects at variance both with justice and religion' – but he was isolated even within his own party. British naval squadrons stormed the forts guarding the approaches to Guangzhou, and at the same time seized the islands of Zhoushan, at the mouth of the Yangtze far to the north. The Chinese were forced into negotiation, and acting without authority from London, the sensible Captain Elliot achieved a suspension of hostilities with a convention of his own design.

His chief purpose was to acquire out of the fracas physical possession of a piece of China – a territorial base, under British sovereignty, where British traders could arrange their Chinese profits well away from Beijing's preposterous dictates or the equivocations of Guangzhou. This was not a new idea. The British made much use of Macao, the only foreign foothold on the China coast, and had often coveted a similar enclave for themselves. A permanent British military presence, it was argued, would soon bring the Chinese to their senses, and open up their country to all the blessings of Free Trade and Christianity. Palmerston himself had demanded the acquisition of 'one or more sufficiently large and properly situated islands' off the Chinese coast – Taiwan had been suggested, or Zhoushan – while a few extremists had their eyes on Guangzhou itself.

Elliot's ideas were more modest. Among the scattered islands of the Ladrone chain there was a small, hilly, treeless granite island known to the British as Hong Kong. The name was variously interpreted as meaning Incense Port, Fragrant Harbour, or Aunty Heung, commemorating a legendary female pirate; the way the British pronounced and transliterated it is said to reflect the pronunciation of the Tanka people, who first identified the island for them – when other Chinese people said the name, it sounded to western ears more like Hernkong, or even Shiankang. The place was familiar to British seamen because a cataract on its south-western shore, easily seen from the sea, was a useful source of fresh water. This island, at 114°10′E, 22°15′N, the Chief Superintendent of Trade now demanded, and the humiliated Chinese agreed to surrender.

Its area was twenty-six square miles, and it was separated from the Kowloon mainland only by a mile-wide strait. It was shaped rather like a multi-clawed and corrugated crab. Its landlords were of the Tang clan, and it supported no more than six or seven thousand inhabitants, many of them living on boats. The island was less than 100 miles from Guangzhou; the Kowloon strait provided a superb deep-water harbour. From here, Elliot thought, the British Empire and its merchants could safely conduct all their business with the Chinese Empire, service and supervise their trade along the China coast, and establish a permanent outpost of British authority in the Far East. On 26 January 1841, a British naval party landed on the north-west shore of the island and raised the Union Jack. Jardine, Matheson and several other Guangzhou firms presently followed, land auctions were held, and the new possession was declared a Free Port. All British and foreign subjects were to be afforded the security of British law; Chinese were to be governed according to the laws and customs of China, 'every description of torture excepted'.

Unexpectedly, Palmerston was not pleased. He thought Elliot should have followed up a British victory with far more exciting demands, opening up all China, perhaps, to western activities. Who had ever heard of Hong Kong? It was no more than a barren rock with hardly a house on it. Queen Victoria and her husband, though surprised at the 'unaccountably strange conduct of Chas. Elliot', were rather amused by the acquisition, and thought their daughter 'ought to be called Princess of Hong Kong in addition to Princess Royal'; but the Royal Navy considered its victories wasted and the British merchants of the China trade, deploring the lost chance of trading concessions all over China, sarcastically belittled the new possession. 'A street on a gigantic scale is already far advanced,' sneered their newspaper the *Canton Press*, 'leading from an intended public office to a contemplated public thoroughfare; and we now only require houses, inhabitants, and commerce to make this settlement one of the most valuable of our pos-sessions.' Elliot left the China seas in ignominy, and was packed off to be British Chargé d'Affaires in the brand-new Republic of Texas.'[1]

But the thing was done. Actually both sides presently repudiated the convention, and fighting broke out again; but in 1842 the Treaty of

---

[1] Although he later became Governor successively of Bermuda, Trinidad and St Helena, and died (in 1875) an admiral, he is uncommemorated still in the colony that he founded, and his entry in the *Dictionary of National Biography* makes no mention of Hong Kong.

Nanking, ending the First Anglo-Chinese War, in a much more Palmer-stonian way, accepted the Hong Kong *fait accompli*. Besides extracting trading rights and privileges for British merchants in five Chinese ports (the so-called Treaty Ports), and arranging compensation for all the lost opium, and scrupulously ignoring the matter of future drug trading, which the British Government maintained was none of its business, and establishing, in principle anyway, conventional official relations between the two nations – besides all this, the treaty confirmed the transfer of Hong Kong from the Chinese Empire to the British:

> It being obviously necessary and desirable that
> British subjects should have some Port whereat
> they may careen and refit their Ships, when required,
> and keep stores for that purpose, His Majesty the
> Emperor of China cedes to Her Majesty the Queen of
> Great Britain the Island of Hong Kong to be possessed
> in perpetuity by Her Britannic Majesty, Her Heirs
> and Successors and to be governed by such Laws and
> Regulations as Her Majesty the Queen of Great Britain
> shall see fit to direct.

Except for Macao, which had never been formally ceded to Portuguese sovereignty, and some frontier strips transferred to Russia in the far north, it was the first segment of Chinese soil ever to be handed over to Outer Barbarians. It is said that before signing the document of accession the Emperor Dao Guang ('Glorious Rectitude') was seen by courtiers incredulously wandering his palace in the night, murmuring 'impossible, impossible', and repeatedly sighing.

Gladstone's 'disgraceful' war had done it, opened a few more doors into the Middle Kingdom and planted a British colony on its edge. Hong Kong formally became a British possession on 26 June 1843, and its founding Governor, Sir Henry Pottinger, declared his conviction that the island would very soon become 'a vast emporium of commerce and wealth'. The British China merchants soon came to see its possibilities too. 'Hong Kong', exulted an editorial in their newspaper now – 'deep water and a free port for ever!'

Twenty years later, after another and still fiercer conflict with the Manchus, the British enlarged their property. The Convention of Peking, ending the Second Anglo-Chinese War in 1860, brought them the southern tip of the Kowloon Peninsula (which they knew well because they liked to play cricket there) and the nearby islet called Stonecutters Island, three square miles in all which gave them secure control of the harbour and its sea-approaches. At first a perpetual lease was extracted from the Chinese, later this became absolute cession – absolute except only that, we are told, the British undertook not to damage or remove the boulder honouring the poor little Song Emperor on its hill beside the sea.

Forty years on again, and they made further demands. By now it was the heyday of imperialism, and several other Powers were grabbing parts of China for themselves. The French leased Qinzhou Bay in the south. The Germans established a protectorate over Jiaozhou Bay, on the coast near Beijing. The Russians seized Lushun, in the north, renaming it Port Arthur. The Japanese acquired Taiwan. Professing to fear attacks from these rivals, in 1898 the British extracted two new concessions for themselves. Far to the north they got a lease on the territory of Wei-hai-wei, to be held as long as the Russians occupied Port Arthur; and at Hong Kong they acquired the rest of the Kowloon Peninsula and its immediate hinterland, together with all the rocks and islands of the archipelago which lay immediately around Hong Kong. These extensions to the colony they called at first the New Territory, later the New Territories.

This time they did not demand outright cession, and it was agreed that the New Territories should be leased by the Chinese Empire to the British for a period of ninety-nine years, beginning in 1898 and ending in 1997. So at a stroke the subsequent history of Hong Kong was decreed, for as the twentieth century proceeded, and the colony developed, it became clear that without the New Territories Hong Kong itself could not long survive. It thus became a finite possession – the only such thing in the British Empire – with a terminal date already fixed. Just as the last Viceroy of India, Lord Mountbatten, counted off on his calendar the days that remained for the Raj, so in 1898 British Hong Kong, had it realized the truth, might have started ticking off the years to extinction.

For the time being the New Territories gave substance and security to the colony, increasing its total land area from thirty-two square miles to 390 – rather bigger than Madeira, considerably smaller than the Faeroe Islands – and adding all those Tangs, Pangs and Lius, all those clannish villagers and boat-people to its population. Even so, for many years Hong Kong never lived up to Pottinger's prophecy, and it sometimes seemed that Lord Palmerston had been right in the first place. The colony plodded along. Though great fortunes were made there by enterprising merchants, after the abolition of the opium trade China was never quite such a cornucopia again, and anyway the cosmopolitan treaty port of Shanghai, at the mouth of the Yangtze, developed into a far richer and livelier place than Hong Kong. Visitors in the 1920s and 1930s found the colony rather a bore, and the Japanese, who occupied it during the Second World War, never did much with it.

What finally brought Hong Kong into its own was the Chinese Communist Revolution of 1949. The revolution itself sent an influx of refugee industrialists into Hong Kong, and when in the following year the revolutionary Government went to war against the United Nations in Korea, the consequent interruption of all western trade with China transformed the colony's functions. Until then the territory had seen itself, as its founders had always seen it, primarily as an entrepôt, through which commerce with China could conveniently and efficiently pass. The free port of Hong Kong was one of the world's busiest, but the place produced very little itself, and though governed as a Crown Colony, and proudly listed in the imperial rosters ('Our Easternmost Possession'), was essentially an economic appendage of China proper. In 1950 however the western boycott of all things Chinese temporarily put an end to the old purpose, and obliged Hong Kong to find other ways of earning a living.

It did so spectacularly, and turned itself over the next decades into the immense manufacturing and financial centre whose towers, ships and lights so astonished us when we arrived from Guangzhou a few pages back. An endless flow of refugees out of the Chinese mainland provided cheap and willing labour, and European, Chinese and American enterprise combined to create a new kind of Hong Kong: a staggeringly productive City-State, only just a British Colony at all, into whose banks and investment houses funds flowed from every corner of the capitalist world, and from whose harbour was dispatched an amazing flow of products manufactured within its own small, crowded and improbable confines. The colony's population, estimated at 2.4 million in 1955, was 5.6 million by 1988 – 98 per cent of it Chinese, the rest a kaleidoscopic hodgepodge of races and languages. It was a phenomenon unique in history. In the twelfth century a magician-poet called Bai Yue-shan had mystically foreseen a Hong Kong ablaze 'with a host of stars in the deep night, and ten thousand ships passing to and fro within the harbour'; and as every morning voyager on the *Xinghu* knows, by the end of the 1980s it had all come true.

In 1898, the year Hong Kong signed away its future, the British Empire was at its apogee. Queen Victoria's Diamond Jubilee, the year before, had been celebrated as a colossal celebration of her inter-continental sovereignty; another year was to pass before the calamities of the Anglo-Boer War cracked the imperial certainty. In 1898 the British ruled nearly a quarter of the land mass of the earth, governed a quarter of its population and commanded all its seas. It was the widest dominion the world had ever known, and its confidence was overweening.

No doubt, at such a time of insolent assurance, the British regarded the lease of the New Territories as tantamount to a cession. 1997 was so far away, the Chinese were so generally addled, and the British Empire was not in the habit, as Victoria trenchantly observed when Heligoland was ceded to the Germans, of 'giving up what one has'. What the Empire had created in Hong Kong seemed impervious to Chinese intentions: it was not a Briton, but the Chinese revolutionary Sun Yat-sen who presently wondered aloud at how much Englishmen could achieve in seventy-five years upon a bare ocean rock, when Chinese could not do so much in millennia!

Nor did the notion of self-government, soon to transform the nature of the Empire, ever attach itself to Hong Kong, which remained into our own times a colony of the most archaic kind, with no democratic institutions whatever. Nevertheless as the years passed, as China sporadically revivified itself with revolution and reform, and brooded over the injustices of foreign intervention, as the power of the British themselves weakened, so the approach of 1997 was to give an extra paradox and uncertainty to a place already uncertain and paradoxical enough. By the 1980s the British Empire was, in a generic sense, dead and gone. Hong Kong was a last posthumous prodigy, its population being some thirty-five times greater than the population of all the other remaining overseas possessions put together, and the run-down to its denouement came to assume a symbolic fascination. It was like a race against time – as though in some ill-defined way Hong Kong might prove something, accomplish some definitive act, before it passed out of the hands of the capitalist west into those of the always unpredictable Chinese. It might prove something about capitalism itself, or it might offer a valedictory testament to the meaning of the lost Empire.

Today, as I write, the moment has almost come. We have entered Hong Kong's last decade as a British possession, and we are already watching its metamorphosis, in identity as in spelling, into Xianggang. In 1984 a new agreement was reached between Great Britain and the People's Republic of China, decreeing the return of the whole of Hong Kong to Chinese sovereignty in the fateful year 1997:

1. The Government of the People's Republic of
   China declares that to recover the Hong Kong area
   (including Hong Kong Island, Kowloon and the New
   Territories, hereinafter referred to as Hong Kong),
   is the common aspiration of the entire Chinese people,
   and that it has decided to resume the exercise of
   sovereignty over Hong Kong with effect from 1 July
   1997.
2. The Government of the United Kingdom declares that it
   will restore Hong Kong to the People's Republic of
   China with effect from 1 July 1997.

The British agreed to withdraw not merely from the New Territories, about which they had no choice, but from Hong Kong Island and the Kowloon Peninsula, which had theoretically been ceded them for ever. The Chinese agreed to give Xianggang a semi-autonomous status as a Special Administrative Region, allowing it to continue in its capitalist ways for another half-century after its return to the Chinese motherland – 'One Country, Two Systems', as they said with their fondness for symbolic numericals. In the meantime they would evolve a new constitution, the Basic Law, to come into force in 1997, and the two Powers would work together in regular consultation towards an amicable handover. It was an accord specifically between London and Beijing. The people of Hong Kong took no part in the negotiations, as they had taken no part in any of the previous compacts between the Empires that ruled their destinies.

So the end draws near, and Hong Kong awaits it nervously, not knowing what to expect. Everything it does now is subject to the overwhelming fact of 1997, and to the dominant scrutiny of the People's Republic. Start to finish, the British colony of Hong Kong will have existed for 156 years. It was said of it long ago that by its acquisition the Victorians had cut a notch in the body of China, as a woodman cuts a notch in a great oak he is presently going to fell. But the oak has never fallen, and actually Hong Kong no longer feels an alien mark upon the coast of China: it has been notched there too long, it is too Chinese itself, its affairs have been too inextricably linked with those of China, and its return to the great presence, however ominous or bewildering the circumstances, seems only natural.

I have been writing about Hong Kong on and off for thirty years, and I come back to it now primarily as a student of British imperialism. Hong Kong is an astounding epilogue of Empire, and it is piquant to note that its return to China will occur almost exactly a century after that climactically imperial Jubilee celebration of 22 June 1897. In this book I set out to portray the last of the great British colonies as it is in its last years, and by alternating chapters of theme or analysis with chapters of historical description, I also try to make a whole of the imperial connection, to evoke something of Hong Kong's past as well as its present, and to explore how such an imperial anomaly came to survive so long.

The symbolism of the place and the moment, however, goes beyond Pax Britannica – Hong Kong seldom was a very characteristic British possession. In its affairs we see reflected not only the decline of a historical genre – it is the last great *European* colony, too – but the shifting aspirations of communism and capitalism, the resurgence of the new Asia, the rising power of technology. As it prepares to withdraw at last from the British imperium, it is like a mirror to the world, or perhaps a geomancer's compass.

For whatever happens to Hong Kong, in its present incarnation it is about to come to an end, and like the departure of ancestors its passing poses some last, lingering, ambiguous questions. Is there more? Is anything proved? How was the wind and water? Is the image of those ships and stars all that British Hong Kong leaves to history, or are there other messages?

The waterfall on Hong Kong Island, 1845

Mid-Victorian Hong Kong: *above*: the signal station; *below*: Happy Valley racecourse

CHRONOLOGY

British Empire	Hong Kong	China
1841 British flag raised over Hong Kong Island	**1841** British flag raised	**1841** Hong Kong occupied by British
1842 Hong Kong Island acquired under Treaty of Nanking	**1842** Hong Kong Island ceded by China under Treaty of Nanking	**1842** Hong Kong ceded to Britain under Treaty of Nanking
1842 First Afghan War ends	**1843** Governor, Sir Henry Pottinger	**1842** Treaty Ports opened to foreign trade
1843 Sind annexed	**1844** Governor, Sir John Davis	
1843 Natal annexed	**1848** Governor, Sir George Bonham	
1845–8 Sikh wars	**1849** Voyage of *Keying*	
1851 Great Exhibition, London	**1850** Population 33,000	**1850–64** Taiping rebellion against Manchus
1856–60 Second Anglo-Chinese War	**1854** Governor, Sir John Bowring	**1856–60** Second Anglo-Chinese War
1856 Oudh annexed	**1859** Governor, Sir Hercules Robinson	
1857 Indian Mutiny	**1857** Poisoned Bread Case	
1858 East India Company ended		
1860 Kowloon and Stonecutters Island	**1860** Population 94,000	**1860** Beijing occupied by British and French
	1860 Kowloon and	

British Empire	Hong Kong	China
acquired under first Convention of Peking **1867** Dominion of Canada founded **1867** Malayan Straits Settlement annexed	Stonecutters Island acquired from China under first Convention of Peking **1865** Hongkong and Shanghai Bank founded **1856** Governor, Sir Richard MacDonnell **1869** Visit of Prince Alfred	**1860** Kowloon and Stonecutters Island ceded to Britain under first Convention of Peking **1860** Frontier territory ceded to Russia **1861–72** Creation of arms industry
1874 Ashanti War **1874** Fiji annexed **1877** Queen Victoria proclaimed Empress of India **1878–81** Second Afghan War **1878** Cyprus occupied	**1870** Population 124,000 **1872** Governor, Sir Arthur Kennedy **1877** Governor, Sir John Pope-Hennessy	**1872–94** Growth of industry **1876** Korea declared independent **1877** Ryuku Islands ceded to Japan
1880–81 First Boer War **1882** Egypt occupied **1884** New Guinea annexed **1885** Gordon dies at Khartoum **1886** Upper Burma annexed **1887** Zululand annexed **1887** Queen Victoria's Golden Jubilee	**1880** Population 160,000 **1881** Visit of King Kalakaua of Hawaii **1883** Governor, Sir George Bowen **1887** Governor, Sir William Des Voeux **1888** Peak tramline opened	**1881** Ci-xi becomes sole regent of China **1887** Macao formally ceded to Portuguese
1890 Zanzibar declared a protectorate **1893–6** Ashanti Wars **1895** East African Protectorate established **1895** Jameson Raid **1896–8** Reconquest of the Sudan **1897** Queen Victoria's Diamond Jubilee	**1890** Population 198,000 **1891** Governor, Sir William Robinson **1894** Bubonic plague **1898** Governor, Sir Henry Blake **1898** New Territories leased from China under second Convention of Peking	**1894–5** War against Japan **1895** Taiwan and the Pescadores ceded to Japan **1897–8** Jiaozhou Bay acquired by Germany, Lushun (Port Arthur) by Russia, Quizhou Bay by France,

British Empire	Hong Kong	China
1898 Hong Kong New Territories leased from China under second Convention of Peking **1899–1902** Second Boer War		Wei-hai-wei by Britain **1898** New Territories leased to Britain under second Convention of Peking
1900–1903 Northern Nigeria annexed **1901** Ashanti annexed **1901** Queen Victoria dies, is succeeded by Edward VII **1901** Commonwealth of Australia founded **1907** New Zealand becomes self-governing Dominion	**1900** Population 263,000 **1904** Governor, Sir Matthew Nathan **1907** Governor, Sir Frederick Lugard	**1900–1901** Boxer rising: western Powers intervene **1904** Japanese besiege Port Arthur **1905** Russians surrender Port Arthur to Japanese **1908** Ci-xi dies
1910 Edward VII dies, is succeeded by George V **1910** Union of South Africa established **1914–18** First World War **1919** Amritsar massacre	**1910** Population 436,000 **1912** Governor, Sir Henry May **1912** University of Hong Kong opened **1912** Kowloon–Guangzhou railway completed **1919** Governor, Sir Reginald Stubbs	**1911** Revolution abolishes Manchu dynasty **1912** Kuomintang Party founded **1915** Japanese seize Jiaozhou Bay **1917** War with Germany **1919** New Culture Movement
1920 British East Africa becomes colony of Kenya **1920** Palestine, Iraq, Tanganyika become mandated territories **1921** Gandhi's non-cooperation movement begins **1922** Washington Naval Treaty **1926** General Strike in Britain **1928** Indian strikes	**1920** Population 600,000 **1922** Seamen's strike **1925** General strike **1925** Governor, Sir Cecil Clementi	**1920** Chinese Communist Party formed **1925** Sun Yat-sen dies **1926** Civil war begins against Communists **1928** Chiang Kai-shek becomes President

British Empire	Hong Kong	China
1932–4 Civil disobedience movement in India	**1930** Population 840,000	**1930** British withdraw from Wei-hai-wei
1936 Kipling dies	**1930** Governor, Sir William Peel	**1933** Japanese occupy Manchuria
1936 George V dies, is succeeded by Edward VIII	**1935** Governor, Sir Andrew Caldecott	**1934** Communist Long March
1936 Edward VIII abdicates, is succeeded by George VI	**1937** Governor, Sir Geffry Northcote	**1937** Japanese take Beijing, move southwards
1939 Second World War begins		**1938** Japanese take Guangzhou, set up puppet Government at Nanking
		1939 Japanese occupy Hainan
1940 Dunkirk evacuation	**1940** Population 1.6 million	**1943** Treaty port concessions renounced by western Powers
1940 Battle of Britain	**1941** Governor, Sir Mark Young	**1945** Civil war resumed between Communists and Kuomintang
1941 Japanese seize Hong Kong	**1941** Japanese seize Hong Kong	**1949** Communist Republic established under Mao Zedong and Zhou Enlai. Chiang Kai-shek withdraws to Taiwan
1942 Battle of Alamein	**1945** Hong Kong liberated from Japanese	
1944 Normandy invasion	**1945** Population, 610,000	
1945 Hong Kong liberated	**1947** Governor, Sir Alexander Grantham	
1945 End of Second World War	**1949** Chinese border sealed by Communists	
1947 India independent		
1948 Burma independent		
1948 Ceylon independent		
1948 Britain withdraws from Palestine		
1950 Britain enters Korean war	**1950** Population 2 million	**1950** Communist regime recognized by Britain
1952 George VI dies, is succeeded by Elizabeth II	**1951** UN embargo on trade with China	**1950** Treaty of friendship with USSR
1956 Suez intervention	**1952** Riots in Kowloon	**1950** Tibet occupied
1956 Sudan independent	**1953** Public housing programme begun	**1950–53** China fighting in Korean War
1957 Ghana independent	**1956** Wave of immigrants	**1958** Great Leap Forward
	1958 Governor, Sir Robert Black	
	1959 Kai Tak extension opened	

British Empire	Hong Kong	China
1960–68 Cyprus, Uganda, Tanganyika, Kenya, Zanzibar, Nyasaland, Malta, Gambia, British Guiana, Mauritius, Nigeria independent	**1960** Population 3 million **1962** Influx of Chinese immigrants **1964** Governor, Sir David Trench **1965–75** Hong Kong a rest and recreation centre for US troops **1966** Lion Rock tunnel opened **1967** Pro-Communist riots	**1966** Cultural revolution **1967** British Embassy sacked
1973 Britain joins European Common Market	**1970** Population 4 million **1971** Governor, Sir Murray MacLehose **1972** Cross-harbour tunnel opens **1973** First New Town completed **1974** Anti-corruption commission established **1974** Godber sentenced **1979** Mass transit railway opens	**1971** China admitted to UN **1973** US recognizes China **1975** Gang of Four come to power **1975** Chiang Kai-shek dies **1976** Zhou Enlai dies **1976** Mao Zedong dies **1978** Deng Xiaoping comes to power **1978** First foreign tourists admitted since 1966
1982 Falklands War **1982** Negotiations open with China about Hong Kong **1984** Anglo-Chinese Agreement on Hong Kong	**1980** Population 5.2 million **1982** Governor, Sir Edward Youde **1984** Anglo-Chinese agreement on Hong Kong **1985** First elected members to Legislative Council **1987** Governor, Sir David Wilson	**1980** Gang of Four imprisoned **1982** Shenzhen Special Economic Zone opened **1982** Talks on Hong Kong open with Britain **1984** Agreement with Britain on future of Hong Kong **1989** Massacre in Tiananmen Square
1997 Britain withdraws from Hong Kong	**1997** Hong Kong returns to Chinese sovereignty	**1997** China regains Hong Kong

3   IMPACTS AND IMAGES

I

HONG KONG IS IN CHINA, IF NOT ENTIRELY OF IT, AND after nearly 150 years of British rule the background to all its wonders remains its Chineseness – 98 per cent if you reckon it by population, hardly less if you are thinking metaphysically.

It may not look like it from the deck of an arriving ship, or swooping into town on a jet, but geographically most of the territory is rural China still. The empty hills that form the mass of the New Territories, the precipitous islets and rocks, even some of the bare slopes of Hong Kong Island itself, rising directly above the tumultuous harbour, are much as they were in the days of the Manchus, the Ming or the neolithic Yao. The last of the leopards has indeed been shot (1931), the last of the tigers spotted (1967, it is claimed), but that recondite newt flourishes still as *trituroides hongkongensis*, there are still civets, pythons, barking deer and porcupines about and the marshlands abound with sea-birds. The predominant country colours are Chinese colours, browns, greys, tawny colours. The generally opaque light is just the light one expects of China, and gives the whole territory the required suggestion of blur, surprise and uncertainty. The very smells are Chinese smells – oily, laced with duck-mess and gasoline.

Thousands of Hong Kong people still live on board junks, cooking their meals in the hiss and flicker of pressure lamps among the riggings and the nets. Thousands more inhabit shanty towns, made of sticks, canvas and corrugated iron but bustling with the native vivacity. People are still growing fruit, breeding fish, running duck-farms, tending oyster-beds; a few still grow rice and a very few still plough their fields with water-buffaloes. Village life remains resiliently ancestral. The Tangs and the Pangs are influential. The geomancers are busy still. Half-moon graves speckle the high ground wherever *feng shui* decrees, sometimes attended still by the tall brown urns that contain family ashes. Temples to Tin Hau, the Queen of Heaven, or Hung Shing, God of the Southern Seas, still stand incense-swirled upon foreshores.

But the vast majority of Hong Kong's Chinese citizens live in towns, jam-packed on the flatter ground. They are mostly squeezed in gigantic tower-blocks, and they have surrounded themselves with all the standard manifestations of modern non-Communist Chinoiserie: the garish merry signs, the clamorous shop-fronts, the thickets of TV aerials, the banners, the rows of shiny hanging ducks, the washing on its poles, the wavering bicycles, the potted plants massed on balconies, the canvas-canopied stalls selling herbs, or kitchenware, or antiques, or fruit, the bubbling cauldrons of crab-claw soup boiling at eating-stalls, the fantastic crimson-and-gold façades of restaurants, the flickering television screens in shop windows, the trays of sticky cakes in confectionery stores, the profusion of masts, poles and placards protruding from the fronts of buildings, the dragons carved or gilded, the huge elaborate posters, the tea-shops with their gleaming pots, the smells of cooking, spice, incense, oil, the racket of radio music and amplified voices, the half-shouted conversation that is peculiar to Chinese meeting one another in the street, the ceaseless clatter of spoons, coins, mah-jong counters, abaci, hammers and electric drills.

It can appear exotic to visitors, but it is fundamentally a plain and practical style. Just as the Chinese consider a satisfactory year to be a year in which nothing much happens, so their genius seems to me fundamentally of a workaday kind, providing a stout and reliable foundation, mat and bamboo so to speak, on which to build the structures of astonishment.

2

What the West has provided, originally through the medium of the British Empire, later by the agency of international finance, is a City-State in its own image, overlaying that resilient and homely Chinese style with an aesthetic far more aggressive. The capitalists of Hong Kong have been terrific builders, and have made of the great port, its hills and its harbours, one of the most thrilling of all metropolitan prospects – for my own tastes, the finest sight in Asia. More than $5\frac{1}{2}$ million people, nearly twice the population of New Zealand, live here in less than 400 square miles of land, at least half of which is rough mountain country. They are necessarily packed tight, in urban forms as startling in the luminous light of Hong Kong as the upperworks of the clippers must have been, when they first appeared along its waterways.

The Tangs and the Lius may still be in their villages, but they are invested on all sides by massive New Towns, started from scratch in starkly modernist manner. All over the mainland New Territories, wherever the hills allow, busy roads sweep here and there, clumps of tower-blocks punctuate the skyline, suburban estates develop and blue-tiled brick wilts before the advance of concrete. Even on the outlying islands, as Hong Kong calls the rest of the archipelago, apartment buildings and power stations rise above the moors. Flat land in most parts of Hong Kong being so hard to find, this dynamic urbanism has been created largely in linear patterns, weaving along shorelines, clambering up gullys or through narrow passes, and frequently compressed into almost inconceivable congestion. Some 80 per cent of the people live in 8 per cent of the land, and parts of Kowloon, with more than a quarter of a million people per square mile, are probably the most crowded places in all human history. An amazing tangle of streets complicates the topography; the architect I. M. Pei, commissioned to design a new Hong Kong office block in the 1980s, said it took nine months just to figure out access to the site.

There is not much shape to all this, except the shape of the place itself. Twin cities of the harbour are the vortex of all Hong Kong, and all that many strangers ever see of it. On the north, the mainland shore, the dense complex of districts called Kowloon presses away into the hills, projecting its force clean through them indeed by tunnel into the New Territories beyond. The southern shore, on the island of Hong Kong proper, is the site of the original British settlement, officially called Victoria but now usually known simply as Central; it is in effect the capital of Hong Kong, and contains most of its chief institutions, but it straggles inchoately all along the island's northern edge, following the track worn by the junk crews when, before the British came at all, adverse winds obliged them to drag their vessels through this strait. Around the two conglomerates the territory's being revolves: one talks of Kowloon-side or Hong Kong-side, and on an average day in 1987 more than 115,000 vehicles passed through the underwater tunnel from one to the other.

Once the colony had a formal urban centre. Sit with me now in the Botanical Gardens, those inescapable amenities of the British Empire which have defied progress even here, and still provide shady boulevards, flower-beds and a no more than usually nasty little zoo almost in the heart of Central. From this belvedere, fifty years ago, we could have looked down upon a ceremonial plaza of some dignity, Statue Square. It opened directly upon the harbour, rather like the Piazza d'Italia in Trieste, and to the west ran a waterfront esplanade, called the Praya after its Macao original. The steep green island hills rose directly behind the square, and it was surrounded by structures of consequence – Government House where the Governor lived, Head Quarter House where the General lived, a nobly classical City Hall, the Anglican cathedral, the Supreme Court, the Hongkong and Shanghai Bank. The effect was sealed by the spectacle of the ships passing to and fro at the north end of the square, and by the presence of four emblematically imperial prerequisites: a dockyard of the Royal Navy, a cricket field, the Hong Kong Club and a statue of Queen Victoria.

It has all been thrown away. Today Statue Square is blocked altogether out of our sight by office buildings, and anyway only the spectre of a plaza remains down there, loomed over, fragmented by commercialism. Even the waterfront has been pushed back by land reclamation. The surviving promenade is all bits and pieces of piers, and a three-storey car park obstructs the harbour view. The cricket ground has been prettified into a municipal garden, with turtles in a pond. Government House and the Cathedral are hardly visible through the skyscrapers, the Hong Kong Club occupies four floors of a twenty-four-floor office block, Queen Victoria has gone.

This is the way of urban Hong Kong. It is cramped by the force of nature, but it is irresistibly restless by instinct. Except for the harbour, it possesses no real centre now. As we shall later see, the territory as a whole has lately become a stupendous exercise in social design, but no master-plan for the harbour cities has ever succeeded – Sir Patrick Abercrombie offered one in the heyday of British town planning after the Second World War, but like so many of his schemes it never came to anything. Proposals to extend that promenade were repeatedly frustrated down the years, notably by the military who would not get their barracks and dockyards out of the way; all that is left of the idea is the howling expressway that runs on stilts along the foreshore.

Today beyond Statue Square, all along the shoreline, across the harbour, far up the mountain slopes, tall concrete buildings extend without evident pattern or logic. There seems to be no perspective to them either, so that when we shift our viewpoint one building does not move with any grace against another – just a clump here, a splodge there, sometimes a solitary pillar of glass or concrete. Across the water they loom monotonously behind the Kowloon waterfront, square and Stalinesque; they are limited to a height of twelve storeys there, because the airport is nearby. On the sides of distant mountains you may see them protruding from declining ridges like sudden outcrops of white chalk. Many are still meshed in bamboo scaffolding, many more are doomed to imminent demolition. If we look down the hill again, behind the poor Governor's palace immolated in its gardens, we may see the encampment of blue-and-white awnings, interspersed with bulldozers and scattered with the labouring straw-hatted figures of construction workers, which shows where the foundations of yet another skyscraper, still bigger, more splendid and more extravagant no doubt than the one before, are even now being laid.

3

If there is no civic diagram to Hong Kong, no more is there a Hong Kong style of architecture – even the standard forms of Britain's eastern empire found only precarious footholds in this colony. The old Chinese buildings here and there are, for the most part, just old Chinese buildings, while except for a few recent surprises the Euro-American blocks are standard modernist mediocrity.[1]

[1] Five exceptions are worth recording for architectural enthusiasts: The Shui Hing Building, Nathan Road, Kowloon, by Gio Ponti; the head office of the Hongkong and Shanghai Bank, Central, by Norman Foster; Exchange Square, Central, by Remo Riva; the Bond Centre, Central, by Paul Rudolph; the Bank of China, Central, by I. M. Pei.

The British first raised the flag at the north-western end of Hong Kong Island, at a spot they called Possession Point. Today it is well inland, and is occupied by indeterminate Chinese tenements, apartment houses and offices, with no plaque to mark the spot, only the name Possession Street on a lane nearby. Somewhere here, we may assume, the colonists put up their first temporary buildings – the shanties which are still called in Hong Kong mat-sheds, walled with bamboo poles and roofed with matting. The first permanent European building in Hong Kong, however, was very properly a granite warehouse built without official permission by Jardine, Matheson, while the first proper European house was James Matheson's verandahed bungalow nearby, cattily described at the time as being 'half New South Wales, half native production', and surrounded by a plantation of sickly coconuts.

Presently buildings went up in a neo-Mediterranean mode copied from Macao. Along the island waterfront arose offices and warehouses with tiled roofs and arcades, awnings and jalousies, which becoming fretted and peeling as the years passed at least give the place an authentically hot-weather look. The traveller Isabella Bird, in 1879, thought it looked like Genoa. The young Kipling, arriving ten years later, was reminded of the Calcutta style. Very few of these buildings are left intact, but embedded among the tower-blocks one may sometimes see the half-blocked remains of a colonnade, with balconied windows above it, perhaps, as of a *piano nobile*, and sagging jalousies.

The later Victorians built Victorianly, regardless in their confident way of climate or precedent. They built some grandiosely classical buildings, and some engaging examples, with balustrades and pointed arches, of the style they used to call Indo-Saracenic. They erected no prodigies in Hong Kong, like their masterpieces in India, but for a time they did give the place some monumentalism. The buildings around Statue Square, the shipping offices with their tiers of Venetian arches, the pompous banks, the properly Gothic university – when the globe-trotters of *fin-de-siècle* sailed into Hong Kong these buildings made them feel they were entering an outpost of the great imperial order. 'A little England in the eastern seas', dutifully but unconvincingly wrote the future King George V, at the instruction of his tutor, when with his brother Eddy he visited Hong Kong in 1881.

But it never acquired majesty, or real elegance, or cohesion, or even an assured identity. A reporter for the *Illustrated London News*, surveying the Anglican cathedral when it first went up, called it 'an unsightly pile, quite disturbing the oriental appearance of the place', while *The*

Encyclopedia of the British Empire, *c.*1900, remarked coolly that 'the architecture of Hong Kong is of a somewhat mixed character'. Mixed it has decidedly remained, and a tragic lesson in wasted opportunity – for what a miraculous city could have been built upon this site, backed by hill and island, fronted by the China seas! Too late: as it approaches its end as a City-State Hong Kong is more than ever a topographical marvel, an architectural hodgepodge.

4

The fundamentals then are plain and practical, the design is inchoate, the architecture of a somewhat mixed character; yet Hong Kong is astonishingly beautiful. It is made so partly by its setting, land and sea so exquisitely interacting, but chiefly by its impression of irresistible activity. It is like a cauldron, seething, hissing, hooting, arguing, enmeshed in a labyrinth of tunnels and flyovers, with those sky-scrapers erupting everywhere into view, with ferries churning and hoverfoils splashing and great jets flying in, with fleets of ships lying always off-shore, with double-decker buses and clanging tram-cars, with a car it seems for every square foot of roadway, with a pedestrian for every square inch of sidewalk, and funicular trains crawling up and down the mountainside, and small scrub-faced policemen scudding about on motor bikes – all in all, with a pace of life so unremitting, a sense of movement and enterprise so challenging, that one's senses are overwhelmed by the sheer glory of human animation.

Or perhaps by the power of human avarice. The beauty is the beauty, like it or not, of the capitalist system. More than a usual share of this city's energies goes towards the making of money, and nobody has ever pretended otherwise: as a *Hong Kong Weekly* writer calling herself 'Veronica' frankly put it in 1907, in this colony 'plenty of money and plenty of push will always ensure you a seat in High Places, supposing you are desirous of the same'. It was the prospect of wealth, more than the exertion of pride or power, that brought the British here in the first place, in a classic reversal of the dictum that trade follows the flag. Even in times when evangelical improvement was a powerful motive of imperialism, the merchants of Hong Kong abided by the principles of *laissez-faire* at their most conscienceless – 'We have every respect', as James Matheson himself wrote, 'for persons entertaining strict religious principles, but we fear that very godly people are not suited to the drug trade.'

Today only a solitary bronze financier stands in Statue Square, but even in the prime of Empire, when Queen Victoria was still on her plinth and the offices of Authority stood lordly all around, the most imposing of the central buildings were those of the Hongkong and Shanghai Bank, the Chartered Bank next door and the Hong Kong Club, storeyed stronghold of the business classes. The merchants and financiers have always aspired to be top dogs in this city, and have never been afraid to show it, in a conceit that is notorious, a histrionic flair and a legendary hospitality to strangers. James Pope-Hennessy, writing about Hong Kong in the 1960s, waspishly dubbed it Half-Crown Colony, and used as the text for his book [1] the one famous poem ever written in English about the place, W. H. Auden's '*Hong Kong*':

> Its leading characters are wise and witty,
> Their suits well-tailored, and they wear them well,
> Have many a polished parable to tell
> About the mores of a trading city.
>
> Only the servants enter unexpected,
> Their silent movements make dramatic news;
> Here in the East our bankers have erected
> A worthy temple to the Comic Muse. [2]

To the comic muse perhaps, at least in the eyes of iconoclastic 1930s poets, but to the epic muse too, for there has frequently been something heroic to the ostentation of Hong Kong. In its early days the crews of Hong Kong clippers earned far more than other sailors, and splendidly proclaimed the fact in the polish, the gleaming paint-work, the scrub-white decks and elaborate decoration of their ships. Today's rich are much the same, and as a matter of fact the wealth is remarkably widely distributed. Its impact upon the temper of the place is by no means confined to the business centre and the expensive residential areas, where the prevalence of high finance sometimes makes everything feel like Conglomerate City, an international settle-ment of the plutocracy. On the contrary, a sense of satisfied avarice is pervasive nearly everywhere, because almost everybody makes *more*

---

[1] *Half-Crown Colony*, London 1969.
[2] From *Journey to a War*, London 1939. Auden, with Christopher Isherwood, was on his way to observe the war in China and wrote of their stay in Hong Kong that they were perpetually in a hurry, struggling into dinner-jackets and racing off in taxis to keep overdue appointments.

money here: the Chinese taxi-driver gets far more than his comrade in Guangzhou, the Australian journalist makes far more than his colleagues in Sydney. Chinese dollar-millionaires, though difficult to pin down, can certainly be numbered in their scores of thousands, while a foreigner can spend a few years in Hong Kong and retire home rich – in 1987 a British lawyer threw a party to celebrate the earning of his first £1 million from a single protracted court case.

The most showy of the plutocrats are the Chinese. That pink Rolls-Royce could only belong to a Chinese magnate.[1] That young man so loudly quoting multi-digital investment terms over his cellular telephone in the coffee-shop is inevitably a Chinese broker. Chinese tycoons own all the most exuberantly exhibitionist of the mansions, the ones with the palace gardens, the ceremonial gateways and the great red dragon sentinels. But irrespective of race a deliberate display of wealth characterizes all the upper ranks of the business community, and unavoidably affects the general atmosphere.

For example every Sunday morning you may see, bobbing offshore beside Queen's Pier at Central, or in the harbour at Aberdeen on the island's southern coast, the launches, yachts and shiny motorized junks that take the well-off to their Sabbath pleasures. Some fly the flags of great banks or merchant companies, some belong to lesser concerns – even law partnerships maintain pleasure-junks in Hong Kong. Some are just family craft, or love-boats. Whatever their ownership, they are likely to have trimly uniformed Chinese boat crews, and awnings over their high poops, and probably white-clothed tables already laid with bottles, coolers and cutlery. Off they go, one after the other, towing speedboats sometimes, with laughter ringing out across the water. Girls are stretched out for sunbathing on the prow, owners in blazers and white slacks are already sharing a first Buck's Fizz with their guests, who are very likely visitors from overseas, and look at once jet-lagged, red-faced from the sun and elated by the lavishness of it all.

The rich of Hong Kong, if they do not live in plush apartments, tend to live in Marbellan or Hollywoodian kinds of houses, all marble pools and patios on hillsides, and love to show themselves at

[1] There are more Rolls-Royces per head in Hong Kong than anywhere else on earth, more in number than in any other country except the United States, Britain and Saudi Arabia. When the Peninsula Hotel bought a fleet of eight it was the largest single order ever placed for the marque: the cars have since been replaced three times, and the present Silver Spirits, which cost $HK12m. in 1987, have room-service telephones enabling arriving guests to place their orders on the way from the airport.

public occasions – looking bronzed and well-diamonded at cocktail parties, vulgarly furred at the races (Hong Kong shamelessly declares itself the fur-buying capital of the world), bidding effervescently at charity auctions or most characteristically of all, perhaps, sailing into the Sunday morning on those yachts and varnished junks. All this is faithfully recorded in the pages of the *Hong Kong Tatler*, which supplements its portraits of successful financiers, its property pages advertising attractive well-converted farmhouses in the vicinity of Grasse or fabulous golfing environments on the coast of southern Spain, with well-illustrated reports of the social goings-on.

I thumb my way through a few typical issues of the late 1980s. Dr and Mrs Henry Li, Sir Y. K. Pao, Lady Kadoorie, Mr Simon Keswick and Mr Hu Fa-Kuang celebrate the recent elevation of the Hon. H. M. G. Forsgate to his Commandership of the Order of the British Empire. Mr Stanley Ho, Mr Teddy Yip and Dr Nuno da Cunha e Tavora Forena welcome Mr Henry Kissinger to a dinner party. Who are these lovely people enjoying their drinks aboard the yacht *Bengal I*? Why, they are members of the 100 Elite of Hong Kong, the magazine says, being entertained by the Japanese billionaire Masakazu Kobayashi in Repulse Bay. 'He came, he saw, he cocktailed', quips the *Tatler* of a visit by the Chinese People's Republic Director of Hong Kong Affairs, and here he is doing it, wearing a very large boutonnière. M. and Madame François Heriard-Dubreuil, of Remy-Martin Cognac, present the Remy X.O. Cup to Mr Wong Kwoon Chung and his fellow owners of Champion Joker (trainer Kau Ping Chi, jockey B. Raymond): and sure enough, here on a back page associates of Beresford Crescale (Far East), enjoying a party aboard the brigantine *Wan Fu*, are to be seen upon the quarterdeck toasting the world with frosted drinks in the sunshine.

There are always visiting swells to grace these occasions. To many fashionable transients Hong Kong is hardly more than a distant extension of the New York–London–Paris round of profitable socializing, and everyone grand and famous comes to Hong Kong at one time or another. I was once strolling in the Botanical Gardens when Bernhard Prince of the Netherlands appeared with a brisk retinue of courtiers, all of whom looked like elderly English colonels in a British movie of the Second World War. Startled by their sudden arrival, and not at first recognizing the royal features, I stopped dead in my tracks and demanded of this impressive brigade who they all were; but they took me for an Extremist, and hurried by.

5

Of course it is not all pleasure – it soon becomes apparent to the stranger that few smart events in Hong Kong are pure pleasure. They are nearly always viewed with an eye to the main chance, and in fact half the parties recorded in the *Tatler* are really commercial functions, to woo clients, to cherish business associations or even frankly to plug a product. Business life is a gamble, and both the British and the Chinese have always enjoyed gambling (the Chinese used to run books on competing candidates for the Imperial Civil Service Examinations); so since the early days of the Crown Colony one of the chief places for combining business with pleasure, and thus exhibiting the plutocratic style of Hong Kong, has been the racecourse.

Since 1871 gambling in the colony has been legal only if you are gambling on horses. The Chinese have always assiduously evaded this puritanical decree, betting incessantly on mah-jong behind closed doors, crossing the border to clubs and casinos in more tolerant places – in former times to Kowloon City or the village of Shenzhen across the Chinese border on the mainland, nowadays to Macao, whose casinos are Hong Kong-owned. They will gamble on anything, and are obsessed with omens and numbers; rich Chinese will happily pay $HK 250,000 for lucky car numbers, when the Government auctions them for charity.

And Ring-a-Rolls will send you, if you ask them, a lucky-numbered Silver Shadow or Silver Spur to take you to the Happy Valley racecourse on Saturday afternoon – even the price, $HK 668, will be in well-omened digits, both double sixes and eights being famously propitious. Several million citizens would rent one, if they could afford it, for the races grip the Hong Kong masses as nothing else: when, in 1986, 300 detectives in forty squads simultaneously cracked down on drug-traffickers and loan-sharks all over the territory, they chose that moment of universal distraction, the start of the three o'clock race at Happy Valley.

The course is almost as old as Hong Kong itself. It occupies a valley in the island hills which the early settlers thought especially desirable, but which was later found to be unhealthy for European residence and reserved instead for recreation (and for burial, in cemeteries on the slopes around). There is a second racecourse now at Shatin in the New Territories, but Happy Valley, still overlooked by its burial-grounds, remains the headquarters of the Royal Hong Kong

Jockey Club and thus one of the symbolical assembly points of Hong Kong.

They used to say that the colony was ruled by the Jockey Club, the Hongkong and Shanghai Bank and the Governor,[1] and the club remains immensely influential still. Its twelve stewards invariably include leading members of the old British merchant companies, who have been racing their ponies and horses at this track for 140 years, and representatives of the newer but equally powerful Chinese plutocracy. Its secretary nowadays is usually a retired British general. Legally the Jockey Club is obliged to hand over its profits to charitable purposes: it largely paid for the Hong Kong Polytechnic, and all over Hong Kong you may see clinics, schools and other worthy bodies financed by its totalizers.

But Happy Valley on a race day (twice a week throughout the season) does not feel a charitable place. For a start its arrangements are exceedingly lavish. Even the horses at their training stables beyond the course have air-conditioned quarters and swimming-pools. In the middle of the track a vast video screen shows the whole of every race, so that no punter need miss a single foot of the action, and throughout the grandstands computers are clicking and screens are flashing. Nothing feels cheap or makeshift, and this is only proper, for I have been told that as much money is often laid during an afternoon at Happy Valley as is staked on one day in all the racecourses of England put together.

The Jockey Club's own premises are very splendid. Up in a hushed elevator one goes, and on every floor there seems to be a different restaurant – each with a different name, each jam-packed with race-goers Chinese and European, scoffing *coq au vin* with Chambertin in one, bird's-nest-soup with brandy at another, while keeping watchful eyes flickering between race cards and the closed-circuit TV screens dotted around the walls. Hong Kong's palpable aura of money is everywhere – scented as always with perfumes, cigar smoke and the smells of rich food, and accentuated by the small groups of men who, standing aside from the bars and restaurants, are here and there to be seen deep in distinctly unfrivolous (and patently uncharitable) conversation.

Other clubs have their own quarters in the stands – the Hong Kong Club, the American Club, the Lusitano Club – and high above it all are the private boxes of the very, very influential, where the greatest

---

[1] 'In that order'.

merchants and their guests, a visiting Senator from the United States perhaps, a TV star from London, a couple of Italian tycoons, some Japanese bankers and a Scottish earl eat magnificent luncheons, discuss terms, conclude deals, swap innuendos, savour nuances and adjourn now and then to watch the races in an atmosphere of impregnable exclusivity, heightened into excitement partly by alcohol, partly by the prevailing sense of power. Once I lunched myself in such a box, feeling shamelessly privileged; more often I have glimpsed these occasions through half-open doors, as I have prowled the corridors outside, and this is a far more suggestive experience.

Like Hong Kong itself, Happy Valley on race day is a bitter, brilliant, grasping place, not in the least blasé or world-weary. The tension which grips any racecourse towards the end of a race seems to affect Happy Valley with an extra *frisson*, sweeping through the stands like a gale out of the hills. The Chinese proletariat below may take it stoically, and the rich Chinese above them, too, preserve for the most part their smooth self-control, but the Europeans are different: eminent financiers and women in silks leap to their feet with the thrill of a finish, the men shouting meaningless exhortations like 'Come on, Champion Joker', the women sometimes jumping up and down like participants in an American TV quiz.

It is a curious spectacle, in a city that spends all its working days so assiduously in the pursuit of profit – who would think a casual bet could mean so much? – and it leaves in more dilettante minds a disturbingly fanatic impression. If you are of this temperament, better not look through your binoculars at the faces of the winning owners or the successful trainer, when the victorious horse is led into the ring below, and the big gold cup is presented – occasionally one can get a nasty shock, from the malevolent satisfaction their expressions seem to convey, as they look triumphantly round them at their rivals.[1]

6

We are talking of impacts, and undeniably an impression of the unscrupulous, paling into mere shadiness, has always struck observers to Hong Kong. Few outsiders have ever thought this a *nice* place. The mid-Victorian Colonial Secretary Bulwer-Lytton said that his dispatches from Hong Kong revealed 'hatred, malice and uncharit-

[1] But then as a Hong Kong resident observed, upon reading this passage in typescript, 'ugliness is in the eye of the beholder'.

ableness in every possible variety', while in 1859 *The Times* observed that the very name of the colony 'may be not inaptly used as a euphonious synonym for a place not mentionable to ears polite'. The place was fostered, after all, by the narcotics trade, and problems of law and order, mayhem and immorality have plagued its rulers always.

Piracy was the first basis of Hong Kong crime, together with smuggling, and was for years a local way of life. Pitched battles between the Royal Navy and pirate fleets were not uncommon, and while pirate commanders could be unbelievably bloodthirsty, sometimes they saw themselves in a romantic light – 'Chief of the Sea Squadron', proclaimed the banner flying from the masthead of one such nineteenth-century bravo, 'who takes from the rich and not from the poor'. As late as the 1930s the steamers for Guangzhou and other China ports went to sea with their superstructures fortified with barbed wire, machine-guns mounted on their bridges and passengers locked in their cabins. The last pirates were driven from these waters only when the Communists took over the mainland harbours, and by then the tradition had diversified: it was in the skies between Hong Kong and Macao, in 1948, that a Hong Kong-owned Catalina flying-boat became the first aircraft to be hijacked – four armed pirates took it over, but in a struggle the pilot was shot, the aircraft crashed, and twenty-six people were killed.

Some of the territory's best-known crime stories have been wonderfully piratical. There was the occasion in 1878 when a gang of toughs sealed off a whole city block, fought off armed police, ransacked a store and escaped across the harbour in a steam launch. There was the mass escape, in 1864, of 100 convicts from the prison hulk *Royal Saxon* – nearly half its inmates, some of whom were never caught. There was the discovery in 1921 of eight and a half tons of Persian opium, guarded by an armed sampan in a cliff cave on the uninhabited island of Kau Yi Tsai. There were the robbers who, in 1865, spent several weeks tunnelling into the vaults of the Central Bank of Western India, getting away with a fortune in gold bullion. There was the attempted shooting in 1912 of the new Governor, Sir Henry May, when having at that moment disembarked from his ship from Fiji to take up his office, His Excellency was attacked at point-blank range while riding along the quay in his sedan-chair, carried by eight bearers in white gaiters and feathered hats and escorted by Sikh policemen through ranks of saluting soldiers. Best of all, there was the celebrated Poisoned Bread Case of 1857.

This was a dramatic realization of that favourite Victorian chiller, the Yellow Peril. A Chinese patriot named Cheong Ah Lum, responding to the wave of xenophobia then sweeping China, decided to exterminate the principal British residents of Hong Kong. Since he was the most respected baker of the island, he was in a strong position to achieve this, and by slipping arsenic into his loaves he did indeed give some 400 Britons very severe indigestion (though by putting in too much, and thus making them vomit, he did not succeed in murdering them). Panic understandably seized the colony, the British Empire having only just been plunged into the horrors of the Indian Mutiny, but the plot was discovered and Cheong Ah Lum, though acquitted of murder for lack of evidence (by a judge and jury all of whom had swallowed some of his arsenic) was deported to China. With a shudder British society returned to normal, the Governor, Sir John Bowring, himself composing a hymn of thanksgiving to be sung in the Cathedral. For years afterwards visitors were shown Cheong Ah Lum's bakery as a Chamber of Horrors, and a chunk of the poisoned bread, well-preserved by its arsenic, was kept in a cabinet in the Chief Justice's office until the 1930s.

7

Pick up any local newspaper, and you will see that Hong Kong crime today, though generally less spectacular, can be just as surprising. The tang of it is always in the air, like the sting of profit; often the two merge, confirming I suppose the belief of idealistic Marxists that capitalism is a misdemeanour in itself.

Though by international standards the rate of serious crime is remarkably low, the streets are generally safe and vandalism is rare, there is all the general chicanery one expects of a great city, especially a port-city so volatile as this: protection rackets, pornography, prostitution, illegal gambling, smuggling, violence of one sort or another. Every few months the Tactical Unit of the Hong Kong police force mounts an intensive anti-crime sweep, setting up road blocks, stopping and questioning thousands of citizens, raiding night-clubs, dance-halls and mah-jong schools, but though a few dozen arrests are always made the great body of organized crime is scarcely affected.

The drug trade in particular is always on the boil. Until the 1930s the Hong Kong Government still leased out an opium farm, or agency, and the smoking of opium was legal here until 1940 – extraordinary survivals of old imperial mores. The subsequent banning of all narcotics has led to an inexpungable black market in heroin, cocaine and marijuana. In 1987 fifty-seven people were prosecuted for murder and manslaughter, 570 for rape and indecent assault, but more than 10,000 were charged with drug offences, whether with trafficking or with simple possession – an average of forty for every day the courts sat. At the other end of the crime market, ever and again the predictable cases of crooked dealing emerge from the affairs of big business.

Much of the crime is organized by the Triads, secret societies which began as subversive political organizations in Manchu China, but developed into huge ramifications of skulduggery. Triads have been at work in Hong Kong almost since the start of the colony, and as 1997 impends are apparently intensifying their activities while the going is good. There are said to be at least fifty separate gangs in the city now, with at least 100,000 members, binding themselves together with secret oaths and rituals, and engaged like the Mafia in many kinds of criminal enterprise. They are supposed to number in their ranks many a well-educated and professionally respectable citizen, but they can be primitively brutal: a businessman stabbed to death by Triad hit-men in 1987 had been sent in warning, a few days earlier, the severed head of a dog.

The largest Triads are far too prominent to be entirely clandestine, and play a more or less open part in Chinese community affairs, rather like the IRA in some parts of Northern Ireland. They are said to have infiltrated many schools, and young men join them as a demonstration of their manhood, or are trapped into complicity by their own dependence on drugs. The largest society of all, the Sun Yee On or 14K Triad, which moved to the colony from China after the Communist Revolution, is believed to have at least 25,000 members. Some Hong Kong Triads have become internationally powerful too, especially in the heroin business, with branches in the Netherlands, Belgium, Canada and the United States, and agents in every overseas Chinese community: one of the most active along the drug routes is said to be the Tai Huen Chai Triad, the 'Big Circle People', which was set up in Hong Kong by former Chinese Army soldiers disgraced during the Cultural Revolution of the 1960s.

The Triads are seldom entertaining, but the small-time misbehaviour of Hong Kong can be wonderfully picaresque. The Hong Kong newspapers devote whole pages to the local court news, in the manner of English or American provincial newspapers half a century ago, and by monitoring them just for a few days I culled the following cases more or less at random:

A house agent, pretending to be the owner of two premises, rents them out to twelve separate clients, taking deposits from each.

A brothel manager is caught by the police hiding on an external second-storey ledge of his premises with an entirely naked employee.

A woman police inspector, charged with stealing five cosmetic items and a birthday card from a store, says she was thinking about an important case she was involved in, and forgot to pay.

A sixty-nine-year-old caretaker, charged with indecently molesting small girls, says that fondling children brings him good luck in gambling.

Two men are fined for smuggling giant-panda furs on a sampan out of China.

Undercover policemen posing as construction workers are caught gambling on the building site by other undercover policemen.

A man advertising his Mercedes for sale is invited to bring it to a Kowloon hotel, where he is obliged to sign the papers of sale and is left bound and gagged while the villains sell the car to someone else.

Most notoriously, Hong Kong has specialized in criminal venality. When it comes to corruption the territory has always sailed as close to the wind as possible, and bribery, variously euphemized as *'cumshaw'*, 'squeeze', tea money, steak fees, kickback or entertainment expenses, has always been a fact of life, whether it is a street-vendor bribing the local constable to let him stay on his pitch, or a building contractor slipping a few thousand dollars to an appropriate Government department. Ever since the days of the compradors, the Chinese intermediaries who interpreted and negotiated for the early British merchants, Hong Kong has been run very largely by brokers, agents and go-betweens, and it is a small enough step from commission to graft. Besides, it is a dazzling, tempting city in itself – just the place to seduce those who are, as Conrad once wrote of corrupt officials in the East, 'not dull enough to nurse a success'.

If you find all this difficult to imagine, as you stroll home through a balmy summer evening from some agreeable function, where Mr X, the well-known investment broker, has been so very charming, Mr Y, the property millionare, has inquired so kindly if he can be of any help to you in your work, and that perfectly delightful trainer from Happy Valley has invited you out on his junk next Sunday, lift your eyes beyond Statue Square, between the Supreme Court and the Hilton

Hotel, to the top floor of the Murray Road multi-storey car-park. There is sure to be a light burning up there, however protracted your dinner has been, because it is the headquarters of the Independent Commission Against Corruption, a body established in 1974, rather in desperation, to fight squeeze, *cumshaw* and tea money in the colony.

Its powers are immense – it can act without higher authority to inspect any institution, public or private, it can hold suspects without trial indefinitely, and it receives an inexhaustible flow of intelligence about the private lives of everyone, from the Governor down. In 1988 its agents arrested the chairman of the Stock Exchange itself, on suspicion of corruption. Its interrogations are said to be severe, and quite likely some poor devil is being questioned up there at this moment. Brokers and property developers are likely suspects of course, but you would be surprised how many Jockey Club trainers have been invited to the Murray Road car-park too.

8

Many foreigners, especially perhaps Japanese and Americans of a certain age, think of Hong Kong primarily as a place of sexual licence, where a business trip is easily lubricated by adventures on the town, and painted girls in topless bars are always ready to ease the tension after dark.

Indeed it is a louche and lascivious city. Sexual gossip abounds. A judge is observed in a red-light district, a well-known Chinese lady is seen in Macao with an influential administrator. Illicit relationships true or imaginary are staples of conversation, and several thousand people, including Heaven-knows-who, are said to be on a secret police list of homosexuals. It was always so. From the beginning Hong Kong seems to have been more prurient even than most such colonial settlements, partly because of the climate perhaps, partly because European males have always been attracted by nubile Chinese females, partly because the early settlers were often men of vigorous appetite and flexible morals, and partly because the air of Hong Kong somehow seems to suggest that in sex, as in most other things, anything goes.

Even in High Victorian times, it appears, English gentlemen might acceptably flirt with Chinese women, as they certainly might not with Africans or Indians. The London *Graphic* reported with amusement, in 1872, the response of an Englishman disembarking in Hong Kong when a pretty Chinese girl asked if she could wash his clothes for him: 'Yes! and me too, if you like, my duck of diamonds!' Many nineteenth-century Europeans took Chinese mistresses. From their liaisons sprang a Eurasian community which still survives, though nowadays its members tend to think of themselves simply as Chinese, and which has produced some distinguished citizens – notably Sir Robert Ho Tung, said to be Hong Kong's first millionaire.

Very early in the colony's history we read of brothels flourishing in the area off Hollywood Road, west of Central, staffed sometimes by Chinese, but often by Europeans and Americans. 'Clouds and rain' was the Chinese slang for sexual intercourse, but the English equivalent was 'honey'. The Beehive Inn, a well-known bordello of the mid nine-teenth century, hung out a sign saying:

> Within this hive, we're all alive,
> And pleasant is our honey;
> If you are dry, step in and try,
> We sells for ready money.

And when in 1851 an Australian 'actress' opened an establishment in Lyndhurst Terrace she advertised it thus in the Press: 'At Mrs Randall's – a small quantity of good HONEY in small jars.' Church-going colonists, leading merchants, senior Government officials, were not ashamed to visit these houses, and visitors were often shown them. Kipling, when he visited Hong Kong in 1888, spent a night inspecting the stews, and wrote about it freely in *From Sea To Sea*. He declared it 'Life with a Capital Hell', being especially perturbed by his discovery of Englishwomen among the whores.[1] Even in the 1930s the best-known of the contemporary madams, the Russian-born Ethel Morrison, was a familiar figure of Hong Kong society, and when she died there was a memorial service for her at the Anglican Cathedral.

The grander brothels presently moved to the Happy Valley area, the rougher ones further west, so that the area called Kennedy Town entered the naval vocabulary for a generation or two (though Her Majesty's ships were also served by a peripatetic corps called The Midnight Fairies, who used to climb their hulls at dead of night). Later the red lights shifted again, and for a time made the name of Wanchai,

---

[1] Innocent that he was, he was shocked by their colourful use of language – 'very many men have heard a white woman swear, but some few, and among these I have been, are denied the experience. It is quite a revelation . . .'

a hitherto seedy district surrounding Lockhart Road, a soldiers' and sailors' synonym for roister:

> Way down in Wanchai there is a place of fame
> There stands a street, and Lockhart is its name.
> Slant-eyed Chinese maidens all around I see,
> Calling out 'Artillery man, abide with me'.[1]

During the wars in Korea and Vietnam, when Hong Kong became a centre for Rest and Recreation ('R and R') for the United States forces, Wanchai was like a wildly liberated Las Vegas. All along Lockhart Road and down the dimmer side-alleys, girls offered their wares at the doors of bars, music pulsed across the sidewalks, soldiers and sailors staggered drunkenly along the pavements, whistled the wolf-whistle which was the contemporary signal of *machismo*, and were skilfully fleeced by bartenders, restaurateurs, madams and whores alike. To this day there are many Americans to whom the name of Hong Kong suggests first of all *The World of Suzie Wong*, Richard Mason's novel about a golden-hearted Wanchai prostitute in a waterfront hotel: it was made into a famous film,[2] and can still bring a nostalgic look into the eyes of veterans far away.

Today Hong Kong's night-life is concentrated over the water in Kowloon, and a relative peace has fallen upon Wanchai – even Suzie Wong's hotel, the Luk Kwok, has been reborn as a popular family hostelry. It is the area of Nathan Road that now more often summons the end-of-day businessmen, mostly Japanese nowadays, and the visiting seamen (though there is still no shortage of Midnight Fairies among the sampan people). There the topless bars are the most topless, and the honey is most overtly for sale.

A vast panoply of neon advertisements casts the whole area into a gaudy glow, like a nightmare disco, their huge signs Chinese and English marching one behind the other far up Nathan Road towards the mountains. Like all advertising displays in Hong Kong they are obliged by law to be motionless, to avoid confusing the navigators of ships and aircraft, and this unwinking stillness of them, their reds and golds and purples staring so gigantically sterile down the street, seems to emphasize the calculated nature of the pleasures to be found below.

---

[1] Quoted in Paul Gillingham's *At The Peak*, Hong Kong 1983.
[2] 'Dull set-bound romantic melodrama without much gusto,' says *Halliwell's Film Guide*.

9

Yet heartless and loveless though it may sometimes seem, Hong Kong by and large is a remarkably festive place, and a general sense of having a good time is shared by all races, at all levels of wealth and poverty.

The principal Chinese contribution to the common delights has unquestionably been food. Willing as they are to eat almost anything and to cook it in every conceivable way, the Chinese have made of Hong Kong a permanent gastronomic celebration. There are said to be some 30,000 eating-places, licensed or un-licensed, or one for every 200 citizens. You can eat here in European styles, of course. You can eat elegantly French in the great hotels, predictably Italian among the usual fishing-nets and prints of Vesuvius, all-American with fried chicken-legs in plastic trays, and you may find a fair imitation of the Old English manner at restaurants like Bentley's, a loyal scion of its London original, or Jimmy's Kitchen, where the Chinese waiters in their black ties look almost like chop-house retainers.

You can eat much more merrily, though, Chinese – and with infinitely more variety, because immigrants from every part of China pursue their own regional cuisines, delicate or hefty, spiced from Szechuan or sizzling out of Mongolian hotpots. There are Chinese restaurants of subtle discretion, appreciated only by gourmets or valetudinarians, where they cook abalone, snake or shark's fin in manners all their own, and make sure elderly customers are served only the bear's left front paw – thought to be the best for rheumatism because it is the one the bear most often licks. There are restaurants which take especial care of foreigners, and restaurants which are more or less clubs, and trendy restaurants that offer a kind of *nouvelle Cantonese*, and famously expensive restaurants where plutocrats like to show off their wealth. For me though nothing can be much more fun than to walk blind into one of the great popular Chinese eating-places, places like carnival railway stations, emporia of eating, palaces of gourmandcy, which flourish in every part of the territory.

We will choose one of the largest, one of the loudest, one of the most brazen, at one of its busiest moments – Saturday lunchtime, say. Its ground plan is confusing, because there are restaurants on several floors, rooms opening one into another, rooms square and rooms circular, with balconies and staircases leading here and there, huge chandeliers like a gaming-hall, mock junks piled high with victuals. There seem to be a couple of thousand tables, and at them in uproarious enjoyment sits a vast multitude of Chinese, in families running the gamut from infancy to old age. Nobody is alone. Nobody is silent. The noise is deafening, all that talk and laughter mingling with the clanking of plates, the shouts of waiters from one side of the room to the other, the occasional cries of babies, the sizzling of woks and the Chinese music blaring from hidden loudspeakers.

In we go, *extremely* European, all by ourselves, speaking scarcely a word of any Chinese tongue, hardly knowing the difference between a *dim sum* and a Peking Duck, certainly quite impotent to identify the Five Great Grains (wheat, sesame, barley, beans, rice) which offer a proverbial Chinese test of the palate. It is like sitting on the edge of a maelstrom, as we vacantly study the enormous menu (bound in gold and scarlet), offered encouraging nods and explanations perhaps from our neighbours at the next table, and smiling ourselves in a baffled and innocuous way across the Chinese mass. In a dumb daze we order, the waiter speaking no English, and as by a miracle our food arrives, piping hot and indefinable, green wriggly vegetables, sea-things in sauce, wicker baskets of dumplings, haunches of some greasy but delicious bird. In no time at all we are slurping it happily away, all inhibitions lost, as to the Chinese manner born.

Sex apart, such is the one universal Chinese pleasure to which the Europeans of Hong Kong have found their entry, mah-jong still remaining beyond them. On the other hand there is scarcely a European indulgence which has not been avidly adopted by the Chinese. They have been for the most part outdoor indulgences, for here as everywhere the imperial British threw themselves with a hardy enthusiasm into sports and exercises, if only as a prophylactic against sickness.

Even in the 1840s, we read, when Hong Kong was scarcely a town, its British merchants habitually went for two-mile walks before breakfast, to get the system working. Forty years later Kipling found himself dragged on a ten-mile hike in horrible wet weather from one side of the island to the other ('behind, rose the hills into the mist, the ever-lasting mist . . .'). Horse-riding was never popular in the precipitous landscapes of Hong Kong Island, but after the New Territories became available the inevitable colonial hunt was founded – the Fanling Hunt, which chased the civet cat and the South China Red Fox across the stony wastelands with full paraphernalia of cap, horn, stirrup-cup and imported English hound.

The British went sailing, of course – they had done that since the days of the Guangzhou factories. They went trekking, climbing and bird-watching in the empty islands. They played golf. They shot snipe and teal on the marshlands of the peninsula. They swam from the bathing-beaches of Hong Kong Island, which they eventually turned into small resorts of vaguely Mediterranean ambience. They played cricket on the cricket pitch between the Supreme Court and the Hong Kong Club. In short they did everything that Britons were expected to do, to keep themselves properly British in foreign parts.

An old tale tells of the Chinese gentleman who, watching a pair of Englishmen sweating away at a game of tennis, inquired why they did not hire coolies to play it for them. Certainly we may imagine Chinese residents observing the early colonists with a bewildered air, as the foreign devils hurled themselves around tracks on ponies, clambered up unnecessary gradients or disturbed the water-spirits by diving in cold wet seas. Presently, though, Chinese were not only gambling on, but actually riding ponies at Happy Valley, and in the end all those imperial pastimes, except possibly cricket and rugby, were to be pursued at least as vigorously by the indigenes. Today there can be no spectacle more redolent of *mens sana in corpore sano* than the sight of a group of young Hong Kong Chinese hiking somewhere in the outlying islands. They go there in their hundreds, every fine weekend, wearing spotless anoraks and neat clean boots, all spick and span, all gleaming, all smiles, all Walkman radios, all *mens sana*, swinging boisterously along the country tracks, waving flags sometimes and singing. They look like figures in a propaganda poster; and though in fact this particular enthusiasm came to Hong Kong out of China proper, and the real inspiration for that hearty gait was probably Mao's Long March, still one cannot help thinking that the old British colonists, as they set out for their two-mile walk before the morning kedgeree, would have liked to think of it as a legacy of their own.

10

And talking of two-mile walks, for myself there is still no greater pleasure of Hong Kong than the most familiar of all such promenades: the walk around Victoria Peak, crowning massif of Hong Kong Island. The British Empire was expert at pleasaunces, and a classic example is the circular path around the Peak, through its bowers of jasmine and wild indigo, daphne, rhododendron and shiny wax trees. Part of it is called Harlech Road, part of it Lugard Road, but it is really hardly more than a bridle-track, and though here and there along it villas lie half hidden in shrubberies, cars are parked discreetly in lay-bys and the little red Suzuki Royal Mail van sometimes trundles by, for the most part it is to this day a secluded country walk of the sub-tropical imperial variety, a languorous ramble on a Sunday afternoon, or better still a marvellous stimulant before breakfast.

Sometimes it is true the walk is all but obliterated by those mists, everything drips with damp and there seems to be nobody alive up there but you. More generally all is fresh and dewy in the early morning. Butterflies waver about your path, kites and long-tailed magpies swoop, among the trees the racket of the cicadas seems to fall as a torrent all about you. As you progress terrific vistas reveal themselves below. Now you see the island-studded blue-green southern reaches, and the ships coming stately through the Lamma Channel. Half a mile later you are looking towards the Pearl River Estuary, and there lie the fleets of merchantmen at their moorings in the outer anchorage, and a jetfoil is streaming away towards Macao or Guangzhou, and the hills of Guangdong stand blue in the distance. Then, just as you are beginning to pant a little perhaps, through a sudden gap you see the city itself precipitously below you, stirring in the morning. The early sun catches the windows of Kowloon across the water, the ferries are coming and going already, and the traffic hurries to work over flyover and highway far below. Seen from this high eyrie it is like somewhere in another country.

And even better than the prospects are the people, for on a fine morning soon after daybreak Harlech Road and Lugard Road are full of exercisers like yourself. There are joggers in headbands panting rhythmically by, trim and muscular young Chinese, lanky indefatigable Americans. There are courteous Chinese gentlemen with walking-sticks, who smile and bow slightly as they pass, and elegant European ladies exercising dogs, and portly Englishmen, sweating rather too much, who look as though they are there under doctor's orders. Sometimes I have encountered a tough and stocky Japanese, elderly, stripped to the waist and holding a long thin cane like a wand.

The Peak path follows the 400-metre contour line, and follows it discreetly, as though its old British engineers were obeying, consciously or unconsciously, the precepts of *feng shui*. It never disturbs the character of the hillside. It never seems to intrude. So it is only proper that the most numerous and dedicated of its morning pilgrims are the scores of Chinese men and women, mostly elderly, who go up there to practise Tai Ji Quan, the Great Ultimate Fist – the measured position of the limbs, the controlled silent contortions, the expression of inner deliberation, which sometimes seem to me the most haunting of all symptoms of the Chinese mystery.

II

That it is a mystery, most Europeans in Hong Kong would concede. The vast majority speak no Chinese language, and are almost completely in the dark about Chinese attitudes and intentions. As was once written by A. A. S. Barnes, a British officer with long service among Chinese soldiers: [1]

'The Chinee [sic] is unlike any other man on earth, and can therefore be judged from no known standpoint, and not even from his own, if it can be found.'

Nevertheless in Hong Kong today there is an inescapable overlap of the cultures, which is partly simply an aspect of the general familiarization of east and west, but is partly specific to the place. Here more intimately than anywhere else, Chinese and Barbarians have been thrown together. The Chinese have never been exactly subservient, thinking of themselves at least as equals. The British have never been very adaptable, assuming their own ways to be a priori the best. Yet the result has been, in certain parts of Hong Kong society, an ironic blend of manners, usages and even appearances.

An unbalanced blend, one has to say, few Europeans of Hong Kong ever having 'gone Chinese', or even been noticeably orientalized, except perhaps in business method. Ordered British colony that it is, the place was never on the multi-ethnic hippie trail of the 1960s, and no young devotees found their gurus in the Daoist temples of Hong Kong. As for the expatriate residents, so different of build, so alien of mentality, they find it awkward to adopt Chinese ways – witness any solid European housewife in a *cheong-sam*, the tight split skirt that elegant Chinese women wear so delightfully. However most of them have mastered the use of chopsticks, nearly all of them have mastered the use of Chinese food, the more cultivated among them have acquired taste for Chinese art, and not a few have acquired Chinese husbands or

---

[1] Composer indeed of the bugle-call *Oh Chinamen, come and serve the Queen, come, Chinamen, serve the Queen!*

wives. The principles of *feng shui* are accepted, if a little bashfully, by many European residents, and a few Chinese words have entered the local English vernacular: for example taipan (literally top class, hence great manager or company head), hong (a merchant house), gweilo (literally a ghost or a devil man, hence a foreigner), or cumshaw (which is thought however by some philologists to have been itself derived from 'Come ashore', the cry that used to entice foreign sailors to temptation). Only the very crudest of redneck expatriates nowadays expresses any racial bigotry towards the Chinese.

For their part the Chinese, especially Chinese of the educated classes, deftly and shrewdly absorb Europeanisms. At the end of the nineteenth century the Chinese reformer Zhang Zi-dong enunciated the precept 'Chinese learning for essentials, western learning for practicalities,' and it is still honoured. As a college song at the Chinese University of Hong Kong has it:

> China's still evolving culture, grateful, we retain
> East and West, through fully sharing, further strength obtain.

At least 400 practical English words have been adopted by the local Cantonese vocabulary, and many a western influence has been assimilated to perfect naturalness. I was walking one day down one of the most tumultuous shopping streets of Tsim Sha Tsui, Kowloon-side, amidst the tireless pandemonium of your archetypal Chinese market, when I heard familiar music coming from a record-player in one of the shops. It was the allegro movement of Mendelssohn's violin concerto, and there amidst the crimson banners and the neon ideographs, the jostling Chinese crowds and the unforgiving Chinese traffic, its exuberant confidence sounded absolutely right.

Nobody is more at home in a Rolls-Royce than a rich Hong Kong Chinese woman, reclining with such befurred complacency in its back seat, all cash and condescension, while her chauffeur drives her stately up the hill to her mansion on the Peak – an almost Victorian match, like the wife of a self-made Lancashire millionaire going home to her country house in the back of a landau. Nobody can look much more ineffably Ivy League than a young Chinese merchant banker home from Harvard Business School, with his hands in his trouser pockets, his head held back, a signet ring on his finger and an air of unassailable certainty. Chinese judges look very well in the wigs and ermine of the High Court, and there is something about the British naval uniform, with its trim jerseys and jaunty round ribboned caps, which exactly suits the Chinese physique. I once watched a Chinese family absorbing a minor facet of westernization right before my eyes – for the first time in their lives they were eating oysters with a fork, in the coffee-shop of a Holiday Inn.

Chinese magnates of Hong Kong have never been slow to accept British titles, so that the names of exotic-sounding knights – Sir Robert Ho Tung, Sir Sik-nin Chau, Sir Run-Run Shaw – have long entered the ranks of the imperial chivalry. Western given names, too, are very common, originally bestowed by European schoolteachers unable to tell one Chinese name from another: idly scanning the noticeboard at Hong Kong University one morning I discovered Chinese students named Angela, Philomene, Karen, Belinda, Selina, Jackie, Denise, Silvia, Cindy, Tracey, Ivy and Queenie.[1]

Not long ago European culture in the exacter sense hardly showed itself in Hong Kong, so that Chinese citizens were almost as ignorant about western arts as westerners were about theirs. Books were scarce, music was scarcer, there was no proper theatre until 1962, and the only museum was hidden away inside the City Hall.[2] Hong Kong was never on the imperial round of professional actors, writers and musicians who found their way to India, to Singapore and even to Shanghai. By any reckoning it was a dismally Philistine colony. The painter Luis Chan says that when he was a young man in the 1930s nobody in Hong Kong knew about any art more modern than the Impressionists, and when the composer Ravel died in 1938, the *South China Morning Post* commented: 'A writer of many excellent works, Ravel's name came much before the Hong Kong public recently because of the popularity of *Bolero* following its incorporation into a film starring George Raft.'[3]

Today, almost at the end of the colony's career as an outpost of the West, things are different. Philistinism is still alive and well in Hong Kong – the territory's highly profitable television services seem to me on the whole the worst I have ever watched – but nowadays the

[1] They were being advised that copies of '*The Love Song of J. Alfred Prufrock*' could be picked up at the General Office.

[2] In 1937 a Carnegie Foundation report said that Hong Kong had the worst museums in the British Empire, 'with the exception of the smaller islands of the Pacific and the more backward African territories'.

[3] 'It is hardly conceivable', bravely wrote Harold Ingrams in his officially published *Hong Kong*, 1952, 'that a colony of any Power except Britain could show such indifference to culture.'

Britons in Hong Kong: *left*: William Caine,
Lieutenant-Governor, 1850s; *below*: celebrants
at the Club, 1930s

China in Hong Kong: *left*: bun towers at the festival of Ta Chiu, 1980s; *below*: stone of the Song Emperor, Kowloon, 1930s territory is at least on the frontiers of western civilization. It has always been an exhibition of capitalist economics: now it provides its Chinese citizens with a potted version of western culture – force-fed culture, as the writer David Bonavia has described it.[1]

The Hong Kong Philharmonic is Government-supported, and so is the Academy of the Performing Arts, dedicated equally to western and to Chinese forms. The Hong Kong Arts Festival has brought famous performers from all over the world; scarcely a week goes by without some cultural opening, a play, a concert, an exhibition – a parade of Henry Moore sculptures brought out at colossal expense and displayed along the Kowloon waterfront, a visit from Michael Jackson or the Swiss Mime Mask Theatre, a performance by the St Louis Symphony Orchestra. Exchange Square, home of the Hong Kong Stock Exchange, is decorated with pictures by Sidney Nolan and larger-than-lifesize bronze buffaloes by Elisabeth Frink, and the Cultural Centre at Tsim Sha Tsui occupies the most desirable stretch of the whole Kowloon waterfront.[2] Many Chinese visual artists express themselves in western modes as well as oriental. There are of course innumerable Chinese concerts, exhibitions and operas too, more every year, but few are the Europeans who attend them: look though at the bemused earnest faces of the young Chinese at the City Hall or the Hong Kong Arts Centre when Kiri Te Kanawa sings Mozart, or the Manhattan Ballet comes dancing![3]

And among the tycoons, the richest of Hong Kong's rich, it some-times seems to me that a kind of osmosis has set in. Foreigners and Chinese share the uppermost ranks of business and finance, and it is a back-handed tribute to the personality of the place, honed by so many generations of astute commercial practice, that whatever their private attitudes, in public the descendants of the Celestial Empire behave so like the Outer Barbarians.

Those suits help of course – those beautifully cut English-style suits, figuratively admired by Auden so long ago, which are worn by rich Chinese and European alike, and which proclaim all their wearers in some sense members of a club. Then there is the language. Few of the foreigners are likely to speak Chinese, but the Chinese all speak Oxford-

---

[1] In *Hong Kong 1997: The Final Settlement*, Hong Kong 1985.
[2] It is described in a Government handout as 'a high-technology nail in the coffin of the long-dead cliché that Hong Kong is a cultural desert'.
[3] Read the reviews, too, for authentic cultural transplants: 'There were moments in the Beethoven and the Schumann when the pictures seemed to lack a firm frame in which they could stand for best enjoyment . . .'

or Harvard-accented English, the lingua franca of business Hong Kong. The mannerisms of the two sides are curiously alike – self-deprecatory, restrained. The same jokes may not always amuse both parties, but common to both is the jovial tolerant laugh with which they make allowances for each other's inadequate sense of humour.

Most tellingly of all, they seem to share a sense of permanently watchful calculation. By heredity at least they have all been making money on this China coast for a long, long time. They are wise to all ruses of profit, cognizant of all legal loopholes, and they are wary not only of every supplier, customer, diplomatic innovator or Government inspector, but not least, Chinese or gweilo, of themselves. They understand each other very well, and this makes a subtle community of them.

12

Whether there are underlying racial prejudices and dislikes, waiting for events to unleash them, I cannot tell. I can only say that I have never myself felt any inkling of ethnic ill-will from a Chinese in Hong Kong, while most of the Europeans I know profess admiration, if often baffled admiration, for the Chinese. In most Hong Kong homes the races never mix, but it is usually because of lack of opportunity, the language gulf, varying boredom thresholds, plain shyness or the restraints of 'face' – the Chinese reluctance, so pervasive in all circumstances, either to lose it oneself, or to make others lose it.[1]

It was not always so. For much of Hong Kong's history a profound mutual suspicion divided the two communities, and was crossed only by the very rich, the holy or the truly innocent – the good-natured entertainer Albert Smith, visiting Hong Kong in 1858, made friends so easily among the Chinese that when he left they saw him to the quay with anti-demon music and banners emblazoned with his praise.[2] A

[1] For example, a teacher invites a pupil to ask a question; the pupil at first declines, because he might lose face by asking a silly one, or make the teacher lose face by not knowing the answer, but eventually complies because it would make the teacher lose face if he doesn't. (From an essay by Joseph Agassi and I. C. Jarvie in *Hong Kong: A Society in Transition*, London 1969.)

[2] Recorded in Nigel Cameron's *Hong Kong: The Cultured Pearl*, Hong Kong 1978. Surgeon, dramatic critic, satirist, pantomimist, lyricist, novelist (*The Struggles and Adventures of Christopher Tadpole at Home and Abroad*), Smith had achieved prolonged success with an entertainment based upon his ascent of Mont Blanc, which he performed at the Hong Kong Club, but alas, a sequel concerned with his visit to the colony was short-lived, for he died in 1860, aged forty-four.

Governor of the 1850s could describe social intercourse between the races as 'wholly unknown'; a Governor of the 1860s said it was his constant concern to preserve Europeans and Americans from the injury and inconvenience of mixing with Chinese; a Governor of the 1920s said the Chinese and European communities moved in different worlds, 'neither having any real comprehension of the mode of life or ways of thought of the other'. The very jargon by which the races conversed, when they conversed at all, was a barrier between them. Pidgin English really meant no more than 'business English', and was devised in Guangzhou in the days when miserable foreigners were forbidden to learn Chinese, but its comical and child-like phrases – 'Missee likee more tea? Massa likee whisky now?' – paradoxically made the British feel all the more contemptuous, and put Chinese at a permanent disadvantage.

Even when I first went to Hong Kong, in the 1950s, I noticed that Britons habitually spoke to Chinese in a hectoring or domineering tone of voice: a few years before, during the Japanese occupation, British civilian internees had been reluctant to dig sewers in their camp, despite the appalling risks of disease, because as the Camp Health Officer put it, 'the typical Hong Kongite still regarded menial work as being the birthright of the Chinese . . .' These attitudes were deeply ingrained – even institutionalized because for generations the races were kept apart by administrative system, besides being estranged by personal preference.

The more prejudiced British thought the Chinese irredeemably dishonest. The simple Chinese thought the British daemonically evil. British doctors, it was whispered during the plague of 1894, scooped out the eyes of Chinese babies to compound them into medicine, while the decennial census of 1921 was no more than a means of finding suitable children to bury under each of the ninety-nine piers of a proposed harbour bridge. As late as 1963 rumour said that the Government was looking for infants to sacrifice beneath the foundations of the new Plover Cove dam.

The fear and loathing is not apparent now, but occasionally the association between the two races still strikes me as unnatural, or forced. Sometimes the symptoms are merely endearing. How pleasant for instance to discover that the Journal of the Royal Asiatic Society in Hong Kong has been printed by Mr Y. F. Lam of Ye Olde Printerie! How entertaining to recognize the Hong Kong derivative of London Underground's 'Mind the doors, please' – 'Mylerdoors, Central next stop, mylerdoors!' What an agreeable surprise to hear the children of a Lantau elementary school, housed in a venerable Manchu fort, singing dutiful Chinese words to the tune of *Red River Valley* – '*Remember the Red River Valley, and the cowboy that loved you so true . . .*'!

But sometimes the sense of jar or anomaly can be perturbing. Sad but scary, for example, is the spectacle of an Anglicized young Chinese financier in his cups, talking in London upper-class slang, speaking of old times in England, of racehorses at Newmarket, balls at Oxford, but now and then, if crossed in argument, allowing his face to reset in the stylized convention of malice that we recognize from Chinese villains in old movies – or from photographs of the Cultural Revolution. And disconcerting can be the contrast, still often experienced, between westernized appearance and oriental reality.

Not far from that school in the old fort, I was once held up on a sea-shore track by the unloading of live pigs from the Chinese mainland. This is a familiar ugliness of Hong Kong. The pigs are conveyed in narrow cylindrical cages of wire or wicker, into which they must be jammed so tightly that the mesh often catches them cruelly, sometimes crushing a folded ear, or cutting into a leg, so that they lie there grotesquely squashed and distorted, and frequently in pain. On Lantau that morning the pigs were squealing heart-rendingly as they were bumped in barrows at speed towards their slaughter, and I stood helpless and grieving beside the track. At that moment there came in single file in the opposite direction, on their way home from school, a line of small girls in almost exaggeratedly English uniforms, crested blazers, pleated white skirts, small neat knapsacks on their backs. Demure and dimpled they filed past, their faces exuding school pride and team spirit: and they took not the slightest notice, as they walked daintily by, of the doomed animals screaming in their torture-chambers.

Such moments of culture shock can still upset the westerner in Hong Kong. For all that mergence of the races, the impact of the place can still be traumatic, and it often takes time for foreign residents to adjust. The American Chamber of Commerce has published a book for the benefit of newcomers,[1] and in it Dr Mildred McCoy, a psychologist at the University of Hong Kong, suggests the four stages of reaction that foreigners may expect. First they feel a fine euphoria, so exciting and interesting is the spectacle of Hong Kong, so reassuringly familiar are many of its aspects. Next they became tense and bewildered, as they

[1] *Living in Hong Kong*, Hong Kong 1986.

realize how vastly foreign the territory really is, and experience a growing feeling of isolation. Then, sensing their own ethnic identities challenged, they endure a period of irritability, grumbling a lot and being hostile to Chinese. And if all goes well, finally they relax into the environment, accepting its essentially alien nature, developing new tolerance, greater objectivity and, says Dr McCoy, 'appropriate coping skills'.

13

Coping skills are undoubtedly required. The pressures of Hong Kong are violent: another handbook of guidance for newcomers is subtitled *How To Survive In Tough City*.[1] There is something at once invigorating and exhausting to the relentless opportunism of the territory, expressing itself constantly in new astonishments – huge new shopping centres, powerful new tunnels, enormous power stations or wide blue reservoirs, ever more expensive apartment blocks, hotels, offices – the new Hongkong and Shanghai Bank building, claimed to be the most expensive office building ever constructed – the new Bank of China nearby, the tallest skyscraper outside America – Discovery Bay on Lantau, nicknamed 'Disco Bay', described as the world's first billion-dollar concept living scheme and designed to house 25,000 residents with their own hovercraft services to Central!

Almost nothing seems built to last. It is said that no city in history has grown so fast as has Hong Kong in the past thirty years, and the place has little time for posterity. The anguished efforts of conservationists have failed to preserve any but a handful of historic structures: the look of the territory changes kaleidoscopically from one year to the next, and generation by generation the landmarks disappear into the dust – the Victorian and Edwardian buildings have nearly all gone by now, and the nemesis of demolition fast approaches the proud new skyscrapers of a decade ago.

For years a showpiece of the town was a house called Euston, one of three Gothic mock-castles built in the 1930s by the eponymous millionaire Eu Tong-sen. Every visiting grandee used to be taken to Euston, every picture-book showed it, and it stood lordly above Bonham Road like another Governor's Palace, furnished with turrets and castellations, and backed by hanging gardens at various levels on

[1] *Coping with Hong Kong*, by Brian Apthorp, Hong Kong 1984.

the rising ground behind. In 1985 I set out to explore the state of this famous folly, and found it vanished. The World Development Co., in association with Metro Realty Co., had just completed its demolition, and nothing was left but fragments of its garden grottoes – a classical pediment here, a plinth there, a lonely nymph or goddess holding an urn. Big trucks rumbled dustily in and out of the ruined gateway, and when I spoke of the mansion at a nearby shop the people seemed almost to have forgotten the existence of Euston already, as though by some Daoist precept they had deliberately expunged it from their consciousness.

When old buildings do survive, they seem sometimes pathetically, sometimes ridiculously anachronistic. In Tsim Sha Tsui stands Signal Hill, from which until 1933 the dropping of a hollow copper ball from a mast signalled one p.m. to the ships lying in the harbour – a token of order and efficiency in an up-to-date imperial seaport. Today the signal-station is still there, with its white lattice mast beside it, but all is hemmed in and landlocked. The hillock has a quaint backwater air. Chinese boys birdwatch in the woods that have grown up around its flanks, Chinese lovers dally in the little pavilion near its summit. There are two guns on a rampart, posted to command the harbour long ago: but one of them now finds itself aligned upon the New World shopping centre, and the other, if fired, would demolish the lobby of the Regent Hotel (five-star de luxe).

Sometimes it seems that only the temporary is permanent here. Nothing is rooted. Everyone is trying to move on – to bigger apartments, to better-paid jobs, to classier districts, often enough out of the territory altogether. The national flower of Hong Kong is the Bauhinia, a sterile hybrid which produces no seed.

14

As I write there is a Chinese living on the sidewalk at Sung Wang Toi Road, near the airport. Everyone in the neighbourhood knows him, a tall, very brown, handsome but emaciated man with a short black beard and a high forehead, always carrying a stick, who strides incessantly around his patch of pavement with a stylish strut. His name is Tse Pui-ying, and he is mad. Everyone knows him, but nobody can get near him – make the slightest attempt to approach, and he will threaten you with his stick, swear at you, or throw stones. He has no identity card, he has no address. He spends all his days scavenging the gutters for food, and watching the aircraft come and go deafeningly above his head.

He is one poor citizen alienated for ever, from his kind and from his own humanity, by the relentless personality of Hong Kong. Another was the wife of an itinerant goldfish hawker who briefly entered into the news when, faced with imminent eviction from her miserable tenement flat, suffering from protracted post-natal depression and the aftermath of an abortion, she hanged her two children, cut her own wrists and jumped to her death from a fifth-floor window.

There are days when I feel that it is all too much, that the place has become a cruel parody of itself. The day of that woman's death was one, and another occurred less heart-rendingly soon afterwards, when two items dominated the local news. First Mr Rupert Murdoch, controller of newspapers, magazines, television and radio stations throughout the world, bought what would soon develop into control of the *South China Morning Post*, 'the most profitable newspaper company in the world, using the world's most modern computer system' – for in Hong Kong, sagely observed the *Post* itself, 'everything is for sale . . . everything has its price'. Then the daughter of the chairman of the Hongkong and Shanghai Bank married an Australian theatre manager at the Cathedral of the Immaculate Conception, and all the rich of Hong Kong, all the powerful, all the fashionable ('Government officials, judges, business leaders and other celebrities') were driven beflowered and grey-toppered in mini-buses to a reception at Skyhigh, the chairman's residence on a high pinnacle of the Peak, which has a gatehouse like a Spanish castle, and can be seen like a fortress from far away. Thrust into obscurer columns by these great events were all the everyday occurrences and preoccupations of the City-State, the suicides, the pitiful petty crimes, the seizures of smuggled heroin, the scandals about insurance rates or housing conditions, the sad prevalence of traffic accidents at Tuen Mun, the debates about 1997 . . .

These are familiar provocations of Hong Kong, which has repelled visiting liberals for generations. Successions of reformers have sought to disturb the conscience of the world, and especially of the British, about the state of this colony – about its reactionary political system, its social inequities and its unlovely motives. Everyone feels that way sometimes – there are far more compassionate people in Hong Kong than you might guess from first impressions – and nearly everyone is intermittently chilled by the contrast between the splendours of mansions like

Skyhigh, the spilling of money by billionaires, and the hardships of Hong Kong's poor living in such fantastic congestion down the hill.

It is an abnormal city. Until our own times it has been predominantly a city of refugees, with all the hallmarks of a refugee society – the single-minded obsession with the making of money, amounting almost to neurosis, and the perpetual sense of underlying insecurity, which makes everything more tense and more nervous. Only recently, as we shall presently discover, has the emergence of a new, educated Chinese middle class, born and bred in the colony, made one feel that Hong Kong is approaching some kind of social equilibrium, becoming a real, balanced city – and with 1997 closing fast, perhaps it is too late.

Yet for myself I find that in a place where for so long almost everyone, rich or poor, of every age and every race, has been frankly out for the main chance, a curious sense of liberation obtains. Hong Kong is not a place of pathos, not perhaps the right environment for very Godly people. It has always been the brazen embodiment of free enterprise, or as a Government official put it to me in the 1970s, of 'Victorian economic principles, the only ones that have ever really worked'. 'We are just simple traders,' said Sir Alexander Grantham, Governor of Hong Kong from 1947 to 1957, 'who want to get on with our daily round and common task. This may not be very noble, but at any rate it does not disturb others.' Nevertheless the foreigner's first response to this territory, Dr McCoy's phase of euphoria, is justified. There are few places in the world where such a large proportion of the population is at least doing what it wants to do, where it wants to be, and in a poll of Chinese residents in 1982 only 2 per cent admitted to any 'unmitigated dislike' of Hong Kong. I would have been among the 2 per cent myself then, but the years have changed my responses.

Sometimes in the early evening I like to walk down to one of the city waterfronts, to watch the lights of the ships go by, share the pleasures of the couples strolling along the piers, or eat fried chicken on a bench in the gathering dark. The air is likely to be rich and humid, the sky is lit with the brooding glow of a great city's lights, blotting out the stars. It does not matter where I am, Kowloon or Hong Kong-side; around me always, beyond the little pool of quiet I have made for myself on bench or bollard, the huge endless stir of the place, the roar of the traffic, the passing of the ships, the comings and goings of the ferries, combine into one gigantic sensation of communal energy. For the most part, I know very well, it is not energy expended in any very high-flown purpose, but still its ceaseless rumble and motion move me, and

I sit there gnawing my chicken, drinking my San Miguel beer from the can, more or less entranced.

Among all the mingled noises of the evening, one is generally inescapable, thump, thump, thump, somewhere or other along the waterfront, across the harbour, behind me in the recesses of the city or far away in the dark countryside beyond. It is the sound of a jack-hammer, the leitmotif of Hong Kong. It may be helping to pull a building down, it may be putting another one up, and in one guise or another it has been dictating the impacts and images of the place since the first developers settled on this foreshore 150 years ago.

4   1840s: ON THE FORESHORE

IN THE 1840s QUEEN VICTORIA'S EMPIRE WAS JUST GETTING into its stride. To the footholds in India and the Caribbean which it had inherited from the eighteenth century, to its settlements in Canada and Australia, since the end of the Napoleonic wars it had added new possessions in many parts of the world – Singapore (1820), Assam (1826), Aden (1839), New Zealand (1840), Sarawak (1841), Sind (1843), Natal (1843). The British had been engaged in wars victorious (against the Sikhs) and calamitous (against the Afghans), they had thrown their naval weight about from the Atlantic to the eastern seas, and they were beginning to accustom themselves to the heady romance of imperialism.

It was an excitement then, but hardly a surprise, when in the spring of 1848 the junk *Keying*, the first such vessel ever to round the Cape of Good Hope and visit the western world, sailed under the British flag up the River Thames and docked at Gravesend. She was a spectacular sight, very large and ornamented with painted eyes upon her bows, besides being so high of prow and poop, and so rounded of hull, that she seemed to lie almost semi-circularly in the water. The *Illustrated London News* said she looked 'aboriginal, or arkite', and reported that she carried as passenger 'a mandarin of rank'.

She had come (via as it happened New York, thanks to adverse winds and an uncooperative crew) from the new and still imperfectly conceived colony of Hong Kong, away beyond India somewhere, Hong Kong seemed an infinitesimal jewel indeed in the imperial diadem, and very likely paste at that. Its status was inexact, its reputation cloudy, its location, for most people, vague. It was not one of the great imperial fortresses, like Malta or Gibraltar, to which lordly captains of the fleet were proud to be posted. It was not one of your famous trading centres, like Bombay or the fast-emergent Singapore. It had been acquired in one of the more dubious of the colonial wars, and lived so it was said by disreputable means. Its infrequent appearances in the news colums were generally in contexts of squabble or disaffection. If, as know-alls argued, it was the key to vast new markets in the sequestered Chinese Empire, little showed for it yet, and in fact there had been recurrent rumours that the Government was planning to abandon the place – 'The Queen,' minuted Her Majesty on the subject to her Foreign Secretary in 1844, 'taking a deep interest in all these matters . . . begs Lord Aberdeen to keep her always well informed . . .'

Even the genesis of the junk *Keying* was unclear to most of the amused Britons, including Charles Dickens and the Duke of Wellington, who went aboard her down at the East India Docks, and might not have pleased them if they had known it. The vessel was named for a Chinese statesman, Qi-ying, who had been a signatory of the Treaty of Nanking six years before. Qi-ying had twice visited the new colony, had expressed himself overjoyed by what he had found, had bestowed fulsome compliments upon its colonists but had gone home to report to the Dragon-Emperor that all this was only persiflage, designed to keep the ignorant Barbarians under control.

The colonists in return, though they had been entertained by Qi-ying as a person (he was amiably described by the *Friend of China* as resembling a large boiled turnip), had certainly not been deceived by his diplomacy, and believed him to represent a thoroughly decadent and hopelessly inefficient civilization; so it was a measure of their cynical opportunism, not by and large what the British Empire preferred to admire in itself, that they had named their vessel after him, manned it with a crew partly British, partly Chinese, and sent it around the world on what was in effect a publicity cruise.

Which is to say that Hong Kong, 6,000 miles away at the other end of the Empire, was already sui generis: a distant and not altogether suitable maverick of the imperial order, like no other colony, and in some sense as much a part of the Manchus' Empire as it was of Queen Victoria's.

Seen from the sea, especially through painterly eyes, Hong Kong in the mid-1840s looked quite encouraging. The hills of the island were almost treeless in those days, and against their brown bareness the more substantial buildings of the infant colony stood white and cocky on the northern shore. A handful of warehouses and merchant offices were lined up along the quays, walls rising sheer from the water, with their own piers and their boats hung on davits. Here and there were comfortable-looking bungalows, built so a contemporary reporter said 'in an Anglo-something style, with verandahs', and a few quite charming villas had appeared on the waterfront and on the slopes of the hills behind, giving the scene a first inkling of that languid, easy-going look beloved of the imperial water-colourists.

There was always shipping in the harbour, too, to enhance the composition. Much of it was coastal shipping passing through, Chinese junks and sampans using the strait as they always had, but there were also warships, opium clippers, heavy Indian merchantmen, American whalers, gigs, the swift many-oared craft, nicknamed centipedes and looking like Venetian galleys, which maintained a passenger service to Macao, and by the middle of the decade the first few tall-funnelled paddle-steamers.

So from a distance it did not look too bad, and the artists, erecting their easels aboard their anchored ships, did their best to idealize it. It was only when you went ashore, expecting perhaps a trim and finished colonial seaport, that you realized how crude and straggly a place it was, and how infinitely remote from home. It was more like a gold-rush town than an imperial foundation. Victoria, the main settlement, extended sporadically for about a mile along the shoreline, in a muddle of the orderly and the haphazard – here a few pleasant houses or some well-organized offices, next door a wasteland or a shambles – at one corner a Baptist church or the Catholic Chapel of the Conception, at another a sleazy pub. Untidy mat-shed structures were all over the place. Camps and depots were deposited wherever the military authorities felt like it. Queen's Road, the settlement's main thoroughfare, was hardly more than a rough track still, in dry weather thick with dust, in wet ankle-deep in mud, and its spasmodic grandeur was interspersed with warehouses, mat-sheds and knock-about seamen's taverns.

More disconcerting still to the ingenuous new arrival, the streets of Victoria were full of Chinese – hawkers with pack-ponies, country boys riding water-buffaloes, coolies with long shoulder-poles, drunks, beggars and idlers. Only a few hundred yards along Queen's Road, Chinatown began, a muddle of sheds and squatters' huts, with ramshackle theatres, opium divans, schools, temples formal and improvised, duck-pens, pig-sties, gambling halls, eating-stalls, and all the tumbled accessories of Chinese life – a terrible shock to unaccustomed European sensibilities. By 1845 there was a shifting population of some 20,000 Chinese on the island, including not only merchants of substance, artisans and tradesmen of every kind, thousands of Tanka boat-people and Lamqua the well-known portraitist from Macao (whose sign proclaimed him Handsome Face Painter), but also, or so it sometimes seemed, half the riff-raff of Guangzhou.

The British thought the proximity of this motley crowd terribly unhealthy. The colony's first decade was full of ups and downs – typhoons, fires, shifts of confidence – but the colonists were chiefly troubled by disease. Quite apart from the toxic emanations of Chinatown, Hong Kong's climate was authoritatively defined, by the Hong Kong Directory itself, as 'about the most unhealthy upon the face of the globe'. Some said the very island rocks gave out pernicious influences. Malaria and dysentery were endemic, there were frequent epidemics of typhus and cholera, and among the military garrison, in particular, the death-rate was appalling. In 1842 one contingent of Scottish soldiers was described poignantly as being no more than 'a mass of emaciated dying lads', and in 1848 one in five of the European soldiers died.

No wonder few early observers had much good to say about the place. Robert Montgomery Martin, an early Colonial Treasurer, arriving in 1844, dismissed it almost at once as 'small, barren, unhealthy and valueless', and thought it ought to be handed back to China. Robert Fortune, author of *Three Years' Wanderings in China*, spoke disparagingly of its stunted trees, lack of birds and superfluity of wild goats, and feared that 'viewed as a place of trade' it was sure to be a failure. Orlando Bridgeman, a subaltern of the 98th Regiment, thought it 'a horrid place – inferior to Sierra Leone for the fact of its being less healthy, less amusing and less near England'. Undoubtedly Hong Kong had yet to prove itself as an asset to the Crown. It consisted still only of Hong Kong Island itself, and in 1845 fewer than 600 Europeans, including some ninety women, had yet decided to risk their fortunes or their lives in the colony.

It was not like other colonies: the presence of that far larger Chinese community, itself a community of settlers, with its smells and its noises, its disregard for privacy and its unsettling air of indifference, made the infant Hong Kong feel less than utterly British, in the way that most imperial towns were British. The Chinese were very different from flexible Bengalis, naïve Africans, charming Malays or frankly hostile Pathans. They infiltrated everything with a peculiar air of self-sufficient calculation, and seemed hardly like subjects at all. Several hundred million of their compatriots lived just across the water, and they had been brought up one and all in the conviction that every Chinese ever born was superior to every foreigner.

The British of course felt precisely the opposite, and were for the most part animated by a profound contempt for all things Chinese. The very purpose of the colony was to puncture the pretensions and delusions of the Celestial Empire, and the naming of its principal town after the Queen of England would, as was claimed by its first newspaper, the *Friend of China*, 'prelude a glorious victory over the superstition, pride and prejudice of the Chinese'.

The colonists accordingly, in their own sufficiently untidy enclave on this foreshore, set out to live very Britishly. For a start they symbolically renamed much else in Victoria after their monarch and her ministers. There was Victoria Peak, Victoria Harbour, Queen's Road, the Royal Battery, while the smaller settlements of the island's southern shore, reached by bridle-paths over the mountains, were named respectively for Lord Stanley, Secretary of State for the Colonies, and Lord Aberdeen, Foreign Secretary. Chinese residence was banned in the central part of Victoria, and the neighbouring bazaar quarter was reserved specifically for Chinese who had helped the British in the recent war – collaborators, in fact.

Standard institutions of colonial life were soon established, on the pattern of Crown Colonies like Jamaica, Bermuda or Mauritius. Hong Kong was ruled by a Governor, assisted by a three-man Council nominated by himself, and supported by a proper little hierarchy of official grandees – a general in command of the garrison, a commodore in charge of the naval establishment, a Colonial Secretary and a Colonial Treasurer and a Colonial Chaplain, a Chinese Secretary, a Registrar of the Supreme Court, a Chief Justice, an Auditor-General, an Attorney-General. (They were not always as stately as they sounded, though, there being no professional Colonial Service in those days: in Pottinger's administration the Chinese Secretary was a Pomeranian clergyman, the Treasurer a former ship's mate, while in 1849 the Registrar-General dropped everything and joined the Gold Rush to California.)

The Governor was absolutely in command. He was subject directly to the instructions of the British Government, indirectly to the decisions of Parliament at Westminster, and theoretically to the will of the Queen, but since it took anything up to a year for any message from Hong Kong to get an answer from London, in immediate matters what he said went. Moreover he was not merely a Governor. Once reconciled to the fact of Hong Kong, Palmerston had seen it chiefly as an off-shore station from which would be supervised the trade of the new Treaty Ports – Guangzhou, Amoy (now Xiamen), Foochow (Fuzhou), Ningpo (Ningbo) and Shanghai. By 1844 some fifty British firms were operating in the ports, and another twenty or so Indian, also of course entitled to the imperial attentions. Lord Aberdeen went further still, and envisaged Hong Kong, the only British possession east of Singapore, as a military and administrative centre for the entire Far East. The Governor was therefore, ex officio, also Her Majesty's Plenipotentiary and Envoy-in-Ordinary, whose authority embraced all matters of British concern in the Far East – 'accredited', recorded Sir John Bowring of himself with satisfaction, 'to a greater number of human beings (indeed no less than one-third of the human race) than any individual had been accredited before'.

His more responsible officials too, military or civilian, saw themselves as more than mere island functionaries, but as members of the wider imperial system. In general it was the example of India that they looked towards, like all British imperialists in those days. The three Governors of the 1840s were all Anglo-Indian by background – Pottinger's brother Eldred, 'The Hero of Herat', had entered the Anglo-Indian pantheon because of his exploits in the war against the Afghans – and the affairs of British India preoccupied the colonists. Indian reports figured prominently in the *Friend of China*, from entire pages about the The Situation in Afghanistan to foot-of-the-column reports about petty promotions in Madras. The East India Company rupee was legal tender in Hong Kong. Indian opium was the staple of its finance. Many Anglo-Indian words and phrases – tiffin, mullah, punkah, sepoy, verandah – entered its English vernacular. Many Indian merchants had followed the flag to the new colony, among

them rich and influential Parsees, and the Indian troops regularly stationed there, the constant comings-and-goings of ships from Calcutta or Bombay, added satisfactorily to the Anglo-Indian illusion.

There was as yet no Government House, such as provided the traditional focus of the imperial order in other colonies. Throughout the 1840s Governors variously inhabited rented accommodations and furnished rooms attached to the Record Office (also used for weddings). The slopes behind Central had however been nominated Government Hill, and around it an incipiently Establishment style was already becoming apparent. The first mat-shed premises of the Church of England gave way, by the end of the decade, to a properly Gothic cathedral of St John. The tents of the soldiers had metamorphosed into barrack blocks on the Indian pattern, arranged in elegant echelon down the hill. On the site of James Matheson's original 'half New South Wales, half native' bungalow arose Head Quarter House, the general's neo-classical official residence.

There was a court-house, and a gaol, and a post office, and a harbour-master's office, whose first occupant, Lieutenant William Pedder, ran a tight enough port – berths strictly allocated, top-gallant yards to be struck on entrance, jib and spanker booms rigged close when ordered. In 1846 the Hong Kong Club opened in a three-storey clubhouse, and in the same year the first races were run at Happy Valley. The Freemasons, who had come to the China coast with the East India Company, pursued their rituals in rented rooms in Queen's Road; the amateur dramatic society, that *sine qua non* of colonial content, performed in a series of mat-shed Theatre Royals. Ever and again the redcoats came tramping from their quarters to the parade-ground above the sea, bear-skinned, pipe-clayed, long bayonets on their muskets. British warships habitually lay in the harbour, and once a month a packet loaded the mailbags for the Overland Route, via Egypt, home to England.

The official classes were trying hard to achieve a proper colonial stance. For instance amidst all the makeshift the Club, by tradition the fulcrum of colonial identity, set out to be just as lofty as any of its Anglo-Indian progenitors, even down to coolie-energized punkahs. Rules of membership were strict, all foreigners, women and people of unsuitable social background being banned, and very soon the place became, according to one contemporary chronicler, 'the paradise of the select and temple of colonial gentility', whose members spent much of their time in its high-vaulted rooms, playing billiards, reading the newspapers, eating things like roast beef, game pie or suet pudding, and dressed from head to foot in white linen (though at some times of the year they wore flannel underneath).

Out of doors too, if we are to believe the old pictorialists, a suitable display was presented. Ladies in dainty bonnets, men in tall hats, are driven along those few rutted streets by liveried grooms. Officials are carried about in sedan-chairs, hanging their hats perhaps on hooks especially provided, and smoking their pipes complacently as they go. Military officers in plumed hats ride here and there on chargers, gallantly saluting passing barouches.

It is true that even in the water-colours the miscellaneous crowd of Chinese idlers, together with stray dogs and grazing donkeys, rather spoils the elegance of the Sunday afternoon promenade, on the parade-grounds beside the new Cathedral; but still a military band plays, and through the crowd one sees a sprinkling of decorous English families, gentlemanly-looking strollers with canes and boutonnières, pantalooned children with their Chinese nursemaids, and benevolently watching from his porch above, one likes to fancy, the newly appointed Right Reverend Bishop of Victoria, whose diocese also embraces Japan and the whole of China.

The flag flies over Head Quarter House. Turbanned Sikhs salute passing officers. Down in the harbour there is a flash of oars, perhaps, as the Commodore is conveyed in spendour from his flagship, the magnificent seventy-two-gun battleship *Blenheim*, to pay a call upon His Excellency the Governor. When the light was kind, when you looked the right way, Hong Kong was already recognizably Imperial; even Mr Robert Fortune was stirred by the knowlege that here 'lives and property were safe under the British flag, which has . . . braved a thousand years the battle and the breeze'.

But off-shore at the eastern end of Victoria there lay another kind of headquarters ship, looking distinctly less ceremonial than the *Blenheim*, and smelling in an odd way of rotting vegetables. It was the smell of opium, very familiar in these parts, and the vessel was the massive old Indian trader *Hormanjee Bormanjee*, in whose holds, during the first years of Hong Kong, Messrs Jardine and Matheson stored not only their bullion, but the drugs which their swift armed clippers would distribute up and down the China coast.

In a way the *Hormanjee Bormanjee* was more truly a colonial flagship than the Commodore's battleship, for Hong Kong frankly depended then upon the profits of the narcotic trade. 'In common with every Philanthropist,' piously proclaimed the *Friend of China* in its very first issue, 1842, 'we must deeply deplore the addiction of the Chinese to this fascinating vice,' but hardly anybody really believed it – even the Great Seal of the colony, designed in 1844 by the Queen's own medallist-in-chief, depicted beneath the royal crest a waterfront piled profitably with what might have been tea-boxes, but were generally assumed to be opium chests. In 1844 the Governor himself declared that almost anyone with any capital in the colony was either in the Government service, or else in the drug trade.

For every British warship in the roads, there were likely to be two or three opium clippers, as spendidly equipped, as confidently dressed as any frigate. The flag above the general's residence was no more assertive than the flag above the Jardine, Matheson headquarters at East Point, half a mile along the shore. Hong Kong's Government might be clothing itself in consequence; in cash it was far outshone by the merchant community, which brought to the colony all the insolent panache it had developed at Guangzhou. 'You will like to know', Robert Jardine wrote home in 1849, 'who have got the nicest houses here. As you are aware the Governor and the General have generally the finest, here it is not so, "Who then?" – Jardine's . . .'

Within a few years of the colony's settlement dozens of merchant companies had come to Hong Kong, together with European shop-keepers, physicians, publicans and miscellanous commercial men. Most of the companies were British or Indian, but they included American, German, Italian, Dutch and French concerns, and they were domin-ated by three old familiars from Guangzhou: Jardine, Matheson, the most famous or notorious of them all, with five partners and twenty European assistants; Dent and Company, their chief rivals, with five partners and eight assistants; and the American Russell and Company, with six partners and eight assistants.

Life in Hong Kong really revolved not around the Governor, but around these formidable hongs and their bosses the taipans. Not only were they the shipowners, the warehouse men, the accountants, the agents and the chandlers of the colony, but they also played the parts of insurers and bankers. It was they who had induced the British Government to acquire this island, and they considered themselves its true possessors. The historian G. R. Sayer [1] likened Hong Kong in

[1] In *Hong Kong, 1841–1862*, Oxford 1937.

these early years to the headquarters of a commercial expeditionary force, whose outposts were at the Treaty Ports along the China coast; if the Governor was its chief of staff, unquestionably its field commanders were the taipans.

For they were frontier merchants of the most shrewd and energetic kind. Their rivalry was fierce, their methods were no-holds-barred, and they all lived for the moment, in the happy knowledge that twenty years in this place would make most of them rich. Few intended to stay longer, and the taipans frequently came and went, often handing over dynastically to family successors. William Jardine himself, who never came to Hong Kong, had spent only twelve years on the China coast; his partner James Matheson presently went home after nineteen years; but other Jardines, other Mathesons and lateral descendants of both clans were to remain in Hong Kong for generations.

They lived in some style, influenced still by memories of the East India Company at Guangzhou. The independent merchants had loathed that immense and venerable establishment, but had caught some of its attitudes all the same. Thus those waterfront offices of Hong Kong were clearly descended from the EIC's old factories, and the manner of life among the merchants was distinctly John Company. Like the Anglo-Indians, they had their native surrogates, the go-betweens between rulers and ruled; the compradors were the interpreters, the middlemen of the hongs and often important men in their own right. Like the Anglo-Indians again, the merchants worked extremely hard, scorning the effete Latin notion of the siesta, as it was practised at Macao, and dressing for the office as they would dress for it in England, in high collars, thick suits and boots.

Like the Anglo-Indians, they sustained themselves amply in their exile. The assistants (nicknamed here, as in India, 'griffins') lived for the most part in messes, but the more senior men, who sometimes had wives and families with them, occupied sizeable houses; one advertised for sale in 1845 had two thirty-foot sitting rooms, five bedrooms with bathrooms *en suite*, two 100-foot verandahs closed by Venetian blinds, and 'commodious out-buildings for servants'. Dent's maintained a fine garden villa on the waterfront, prominent in those ship-deck pictures. Jardine's No. 1 House, the one Robert Jardine bragged about, was a mansion in the Grecian mode, where the partners of the day were attended by many servants and well-protected against the island fevers – David Jardine's London tailors, sending him a bill for a suit, expressed surprise at the increase in his measurements, and were 'pleased to infer that the climate of Hong Kong agrees with your constitution'.

It was not however the climate. Jardine's had imported a chef from London, just as Dent's had brought one from France, and the taipans and all their assistants were very well fed. Victuals as varied as Dublin stout, English hams, tripes and tinned oatmeal were regularly shipped from Britain, alcohol seems to have been unlimited – they drank claret with their breakfasts, beer with their midday tiffin, and in the evenings great quantities of claret, champagne and port. As for local provisions, the *Friend of China* tells us that as early as 1842 beef was cheap and there was plenty of milk and butter. One could get pheasant, partridge, venison and all kinds of fish familiar and unknown. Ice soon became available from a publicly subscribed ice-house, and there was a Sheep Club whose members clubbed together to graze Indian and Australian sheep for mutton (though a London *Times* reporter, George Wingrove Cooke, writing about the Hong Kong cuisine in the following decade, complained that because in summer the sheep had to be killed on the day of eating, their meat was 'as hard as death stiffened them').

The merchants were nearly all young men, even the taipans being seldom older than thirty, and whether they lived in houses or in company messes, pursued their lives with a boyish brio, larking about a lot, playing a great deal of billiards, smoking heavily and living it up at the Happy Valley races, which were like country race-meetings in Ireland, and were dominated by the hongs' own racing ponies. 'I never saw one of the young clerks with a book in his hands,' wrote the genial Albert Smith;[1] they had, he said 'a mind-mouldering time of it'. For the most part their jobs were office jobs, tedious enough labours of accountancy and stock-taking, but all around them was the excitement of get-rich-quick. Everything was urgent, everything was fast, not everything was above-board. The opium ships that sailed in and out of the harbour were ships made for speed and getaway, raked schooners built to the latest American pattern. The tea clippers that stopped by were the most powerful sailers of their day, engaged in perpetual thrilling races with each other on the long run to England. Hard, reckless, well-paid captains came and went, telling tales of hit-and-run battles with Chinese cruisers, or planning yet more sensational voyages home.

In the early years of the decade many businessmen regretted their

[1] In *To China and Back*, London 1859.

move to Hong Kong, and thought of returning to Macao or Guangzhou. Later confidence fitfully grew. Hong Kong had certainly not yet become the immense mart of trade that Pottinger forecast, partly because the China commerce was now funnelled also through the Treaty Ports, but it was not languishing. Its free-port status brought much traffic, there being at that time no customs dues at all. Apart from opium, still illicit in China but still immensely profitable, there was trade in cotton, sugar candy, rattans, salt and tea – much of it smuggled through the Chinese customs. Dent's, it was true, were getting into financial difficulties by the middle of the decade, their scheme to make Hong Kong the principal tea centre of the China coast having failed, but Jardine's compound at East Point, around and below No. 1 House, was thriving. Built upon a small promontory, looking across to the *Hormanjee Bormanjee*, its three-storey warehouse was surrounded by granite and brick workshops, stables and lesser houses, and it sponsored its own Chinese quarter, Jardine's Bazaar, on the higher ground behind. From its shipyard was launched the first foreign ship built in Hong Kong, the schooner *Celestial*.

Another mid-century observer, the civil servant Alfred Weatherhead, declared that the chief reason why people remained in Hong Kong was 'the powerful, all-absorbing love of gain'. So it was, and not least among the well-mannered but extremely hard-headed Scots who set the tone of Jardine, Matheson. When in 1850 a partner's daughter, a Miss MacLean, had her wedding breakfast at the East Point compound, with fifty guests and a merry dance, the company accountant wrote characteristically to a friend recently returned home, when the festivities were over: 'It was a capital chance for your Plate, which I began to despair of selling, and I got old MacLean to take it at your price of $200 . . .'

Inevitably these two societies, the official and the merchant, clashed. They mingled at weddings of course, they shared the Club and the racecourse, but their differences were fundamental. The best of the officials – only the best – were concerned with the imperial interest, the general extension of trade, Christianity and all else that went with the glory of England. The best of the merchants – even the best – were concerned with self-enrichment. Government sought to raise sufficient revenue to pay for the administration of the place. Merchants resisted all efforts to raise taxes, and they were perfectly ready to evade British authority altogether, if necessary, by becoming honorary consuls of foreign powers, or by sailing their ships under Danish or American flags. The two sides thus worked to different rules, all too often honoured different standards, and the life of the colony was punctuated by rows between them – the London *Times* once remarked in despair that Hong Kong seemed always to be racked by 'some fatal pestilence, some doubtful war or some discreditable internal squabble'.

In particular the merchants were antagonized by Governors of liberal tendencies, Governors who were thought to be too sympathetic to the Chinese, or Governors who showed insufficient respect for Free Trade in all commodities, especially opium. Pottinger the first Governor, a militant man, seemed at first to be just their kind, and when he posted an order (later rescinded anyway) that opium ships would not be allowed in the harbour, James Matheson commented knowingly: 'Sir Henry never means to act on it, and no doubt privately considers it a good joke.' Even he, though, upset nearly everybody in the end, and his successor Sir John Davis, who headed the administration for most of the 1840s, had nothing but trouble.

For Davis was not only a Protectionist, but also a Sinologue, having lived and worked on the China coast on and off for thirty years, mostly with the East India Company which the independent merchants had so detested. He was a man of fastidious if intrusive culture, had translated some of the Chinese classics into English, and was always saying 'That's not how the Company used to do it.' He was hardly the man to please the traders, and in return he frankly despised most of them. In no time at all he had infuriated them by reducing the terms of their land leases (they claimed they had been promised perpetual tenure), imposing a property tax, setting up Government opium and salt monopolies to be let at auction, and trying to make everyone, English or Chinese, register with the Government.

The merchants disliked everything about Davis. They were affronted when they discovered he had emblazoned his own armorial bearings, displaying three stars and a bloody hand, on the tower of the new Cathedral, whose foundation stone he had laid. They were irritated by his choice of street names for the growing town: he named Shelley Street after the later bankrupted Colonial Auditor, and he named Hollywood Road after his own family home at Westbury-on-Trym near Bristol, but 'not even a lane', wrote Alexander Matheson crossly, 'for a merchant'. They were so furious about the registration plan that

Davis was forced to withdraw the proposal, and impose the register only upon the Chinese.

Not only did the merchants stir their lobbyists in London into action against Davis, but they treated him with boorish incivility. A memorial of protest they once sent to him was so rudely worded that he refused to accept it, and when the unfortunate Governor was due to present the Plenipotentiary Cup at Happy Valley in 1848, not a single horse was entered for the race. 'It is a much easier task', wrote Davis querulously to Lord Stanley, 'to govern the 20,000 Chinese inhabitants of this colony, than a few hundreds of English.'

The temper of Hong Kong being what it was ('the land of libel and the haunt of fever'), Davis was also led into controversy with some of his own officials. He was at odds with his Colonial Treasurer, Robert Montgomery Martin, the man who thought the very possession of Hong Kong a mistake, and who once likened the island to a decayed Stilton cheese. Despite the street name he described his Colonial Auditor as dissipated and negligent. He was daggers drawn with his Chief Justice, John Walter Hume, whom he rashly accused, in a letter to Lord Palmerston himself, now the Prime Minister, of being a habitual drunkard.

When London unexpectedly responded by ordering an official inquiry into this charge, Davis lost his nerve and offered his resignation. It was, says E. J. Eitel, Hong Kong's first historian, 'unhesitatingly accepted',[1] and the delighted merchant community boycotted all the farewell ceremonials, when Davis sailed away from the quayside to 'the faint cheer of a few devoted friends'. The *Friend of China* cocked a last snook with the sarcastic valedictory: 'Never, surely, in the Heavens above, or in the earth beneath, did there ever exist, embodied or disembodied, such a pleasant little gentleman as Sir John Davis.'

His successor, Sir George Bonham, was much more to the merchants' taste. Since he concentrated on reducing official expenditure rather than raising more revenue, and since he spoke no word of any Chinese language, and indeed declared the mere study of Chinese 'warping to the mind', they thought him a capital fellow.

These unlovely conflicts at the heart of things, at the beginning of things, did not help to raise the moral standards of Hong Kong as a

[1] *Europe in China*, Hong Kong 1895.

whole, and already an insistent strain of villainy ran through its affairs, orchestrated by rumour, gossip, backbite, slander and intrigue.

At the top was the presiding dubiousness of the opium trade. At the bottom, every kind of vice flourished among the Chinese proletariat and the crowds of sailors, soldiers and miscellaneous beachcombers of the waterfront. In the middle was a floating population of European adventurers and confidence tricksters – 'Why did he leave home?' was the first question asked about any unannounced newcomer. Almost everything was tainted in one way or another. Official dispatches were often carried on opium schooners, and the equivocal cleric Karl Gutzlaff, Chinese Secretary, had previously acted as an interpreter on Jardine's drug-smuggling ships, distributing Christ's message to the heathen at the same time.

For all those burgeoning symptoms of the imperial order, this was a tough town. It was a seaport of the east, a garrison town, a smuggling centre, a haunt of pirates and racketeers, a drug market and already, with its admixture of Portuguese, Parsees, Americans and many other nationalities, among the most cosmopolitan of all Her Majesty's possessions. Triads from Guangzhou had very soon infiltrated the Hong Kong underworld, bringing to the colony every kind of hustler. Opium divans and gambling schools abounded, brothels flourished: the Chinese population of Victoria, it was estimated in 1842, supported 439 prostitutes in twenty-three houses, 131 opium sellers in twenty-four shops.

It was a great place for pubs, too, many of them kept by former seamen and pretty tough themselves: we read of the British Queen, the Britain's Boast, the Britannia, the Golden Tavern, the Caledonian, the Eagle, the Waterloo, the Commercial, and we hear frequently of drunken brawls outside them – the *Friend of China* reported one day in 1842 that two sailors from the *Blenheim*, drunk, stripped to the waist and streaming with blood, fought a boxing match outside Labtat's Tavern watched by a crowd that included half-a-dozen policemen.

Sharp dealing in currency was rampant: coins from Britain, China, India, Spain, Mexico and all South American States circulated legally and were ripe for manipulation. As for the profiteers who flocked to every nineteenth-century frontier town, every new settlement upon a foreign shore, they were in their element here: H. C. Sirr, newly arrived as Attorney-General in 1844, claimed that his boarding-house, through whose windows the rain dismally poured, was as expensive as a first-class London hotel (he was explaining, in the magistrate's court, why he had felt it necessary to assault its proprietor).

Hong Kong's tradition of enthusiastic crime reporting was already born, and many columns of the newspapers were filled with dastardly news. We are told of 'astounding rumours implicating certain Chinese residents . . . in dark deeds of piracy and crime'. We are told of the 'diabolic procedures' employed by the hordes of pirates infesting the Pearl River Estuary. We hear at length of 'the ruffian Ingood', who specialized in robbing drunken sailors, and who, having drowned one over-protesting victim, became in 1845 the first European to be hanged in Hong Kong. We read of a plot to poison twenty-five men of the Royal Artillery, of a battle in the harbour between junks and boats of HMS *Cambrian*, of an attempt to burn down the Central Market, of a reward offered for the Governor's assassination, of protection rackets, robberies with violence and incessant housebreaking. We hear of Mr Sirr fined $HK 10 for assault.

It was distinctly unsafe to wander the town after dark, and the nights were hideous with the watchmen's drumming of their bamboo tympani. It was dangerous to stray beyond the urban limits even in daylight; in 1849 two army officers out for a stroll near Stanley were murdered when they stumbled by mistake upon a pirate ammunition depot. The Government was haunted by problems of law and order – more than once the home of the Governor himself was burgled – and in 1845 Charles May, a London policeman, was brought out as Super-intendent of Police to stiffen the colony's constabulary (seventy-one Europeans, forty-six Indians and fifty-one Chinese, most of them corrupt, many habitually drunk and some too fond of boxing matches). Helplessly trying to clamp down on Chinese organized crime, the administration also issued a brave but totally ineffectual ordinance 'to Suppress the Triads and other Secret Societies, which Associations have Objects in View which are incompatible with the Maintenance of Good Order and constituted Authority . . .'

Penalties were fierce, especially for Chinese offenders. The Chinese who had followed the flag to Hong Kong, most of them Hakkas, did not much endear themselves to the British. The first Registrar-General, Samuel Fearon, described them as 'careless of moral obligation, un-scrupulous and unrespected'. They came and went as they pleased, many of them lived on their boats, and everyone agreed, even Sir John Davis, that they needed firm discipline. Before the registration system began they were obliged to carry lanterns if they went out between sundown and ten p.m., and after ten p.m. they were in theory forbidden to go out at all.

Chinese criminals were tried, as the Treaty of Nanking had stipulated, under Chinese forms of law, and suffered Chinese penalties (except where a Chinese precedent was 'repugnant to those immutable principles of morality which Christians regard as binding'). Punishment frequently started with the cangue, a wooden board clamped around the neck, or the cutting off of pigtails, said to be a particularly galling sign of humiliation. Members of secret societies might be branded, originally on the chest, later on the ear-lobe or under the arm, and deported. Pirates were sometimes hanged, often sentenced to long terms in irons, with hard labour. Floggings were frequent, not being repugnant to those immutable principles of morality – they were frequent everywhere under British rule. On a single day in 1846 fifty-four Chinese, arrested for not being in possession of registration tickets and unable to pay a $HK5 fine, were flogged in public; when in the following year the police rounded up diseased or decrepit destitutes in the streets, twelve of the poor vagrants were first flogged, then taken over the harbour and deposited on Chinese territory.

Thus there was no pretending that Hong Kong was a very gentlemanly place. Britons obliged to go there on duty, wrote Sirr, must have 'a stout heart, and a lively trust in God's mercy'. No wonder Donald Matheson, taipan of the greatest of the hongs, surveying the moral standards of his business, decided in 1848 that he could stomach it no more, and giving up all financial interest in the firm, went back to Scotland, home and good works.

So already, long ago near the start of the great enterprise, Hong Kong was definitively Hong Kong. For a century or more nothing that befell it would really change its character. The urge for profit, the taste for good living, the flair for the dazzling, the energy, the mayhem, the gossip – all were there. East and West merged kaleidoscopically in the city streets. Merchants' suits were well-tailored, and they wore them well.

And also apparent, it seems in distant retrospect, was an unfulfilled rootlessness behind the energy, blunting the sensibilities and making the place feel empty at the core. The circumstances were truly exciting, the chances of wealth were real, events moved at a tumultuous pace, there was a raffish and vagabond element that seemed a promise of adventure. Yet all too often Hong Kong depressed its visitors – 'like a beautiful woman with a bad temper', thought Lawrence Oliphant, who went there in the next decade. Was it just the climate? Was it the cramped and improvised environment? Was it the lack of any higher purpose or ideology, such as inspired the imperialists in other parts of their Empire – Raffles of Singapore, for instance, who hoped the British would leave a message for posterity 'written in characters of light'? Or were the colonists of Hong Kong even then, consciously or subconsciously, overawed by the presence of China beyond the harbour, so enervated and contemptible in the 1840s, but surely so certain, one day, to come mightily into its own?

Far away the junk *Keying* excited no such sensations. She was merely a curiosity to the rulers of the seas. After exhibiting herself around the British ports she was broken up at Liverpool, and her teak was used to build River Mersey ferry-boats. Almost certainly it was one of her Chinese complement – perhaps that 'mandarin of rank'? – who, attending the opening of the Crystal Palace by Queen Victoria in 1851, was mistakenly supposed to be an Ambassador from the Celestial Empire, and is to be seen in the official painting of the event standing composed and picturesque in the forefront of the diplomatic corps.

5 PEOPLES

I

FOUR HUNDRED AND TWENTY TIMES A DAY, IN THE
Hong Kong of the 1980s, from 6.30 in the morning until 11.30 at
night, the double-ended diesel ferries of the Star Ferry Company cross
the harbour between Tsim Sha Tsui, at the southern tip of the Kowloon
Peninsula, and Central, old Victoria on Hong Kong Island. They are
green-and-white boats of thirty-nine tons, travelling at an average speed
of twelve knots and all named for stars – *Lone Star*, *Morning Star*, *Meridian*, *Celestial*, *Northern*, *Shining*, *Day*, *Silver* and *Twinkling Stars*. They
and their predecessors have been making the trip since 1868, and they
are now among the most famous ferries in the world. Every visitor to
Hong Kong travels on them, thousands of commuters use them every
day, and when during a strike in 1925 the Royal Navy took over their
operation, there were many complaints about inferior boatsmanship.

The ferries certainly move into their wharf with a practised ease,
after so many years on so short a route (hardly more than ten minutes
even in choppy weather). Chinese sailors in blue cotton uniforms deftly
handle the ropes, the Chinese helmsman has all the time in the world
to move from one wheelhouse to the other for the return voyage, and
many of the embarking passengers too, when the iron concertina gate

is lifted to allow them to board, do so laconically, some of them reading the paper as they come, others carelessly reversing a wooden seat-rest in order to face the right direction. There are two classes, first on the upper deck, second below, but people of means often prefer to travel second class because they can get off the boat quicker when it docks.[1]

We ourselves will travel on the upper deck, on our initial voyage across the harbour of Hong Kong, its clientele being more useful for our purposes. We throw back our own seat with a casual clatter, as though we have been doing it all our lives, we settle in the shade of the canvas awning which is keeping the hot sun off the starboard side, and as the boat wallows away from the pier we prepare to inspect our fellow-passengers. We shall sacrifice the passing view of the harbour, one of the most interesting on earth, but the passengers are revealing too.

They are very different from the passengers on the *Xinghu*, being wonderfully varied in manner as in race. Beside us now, for instance, there sits a young Chinese woman, eighteen or nineteen years old, dressed with exquisite neatness in yellow track suit, sneakers and white cotton jacket, wearing a plastic hair-clip and horn-rimmed glasses and reading *Sister's Pictorial*. Beyond her four very large and red-raced European tourists -- Swedes? Germans? -- are comparing video cameras, and beyond them again an elderly Chinese man in a dark baggy jacket and high collar is staring short-sightedly into what ought to be a volume of Confucianist ethic, but is more probably a thesis on computer-aided investment.

Here come three Japanese businessmen -- young businessmen, very smooth, smooth of face, smooth of dress, carrying briefcases, hitching their trousers decorously when they sit down, after making sure the seat is clean, talking very earnestly to each other and examining sheaves of graph paper. Pallid by the rail sits an English couple, well out of the sun -- an army private and his wife perhaps, but recently arrived on station, for they are feeling the climate badly, and look rather cross and listless. Violently in contrast behind them, a couple of local toughs bear themselves like characters from a Kung Fu drama, long-haired, slit-eyed, heavily muscled around the shoulders.

A tall Briton in middle-age scorns a seat and leans against a stanchion. He is the very image of the English gentleman, erring if anything

[1] However I am told Noël Coward once regretted the choice – nobody recognized him down there.

towards caricature: now and then he peers over the top of his half-moon spectacles to inspect the rest of us, and as he does so the glimpse of a smile softens his face, and makes it look at once imperturbable, aloof, well-disposed and condescending. Americans, too, are scattered here and there around the deck – companionable groups of tourists from the cruise ship moored at the Ocean Terminal, a couple of plump bankers or brokers, tight-buttoned in tropical suits over the *Asian Wall Street Journal*, a solitary emaciated and scholarly looking young man on his way, we guess, to a seminar.

Who else? Half-a-dozen badged and blazered Chinese school-children, carrying satchels and tennis-rackets. A party of Filipina housemaids, all flounce, giggle and plastic bags. An Italian hotelier we happen to know, who grins and waves his hands in a floppy way to indicate extreme heat. And filling in all the interstices between these varied stereotypes, the less distinguishable mass of the general Chinese population, well-behaved, polite, mostly young, not at all sweaty, either very serious of expression or else it seems lost in dreams – solid but non-absorbent, like the rough-edged crinkly paper on which a water-colour is painted.

As on the ferry, so in the city: a small but prominent selection of gweilos leavening the overwhelming mass of Hong Kong's Chinese population. The first two names in the Roman-script Hong Kong Island telephone directory, 1987, were A. Young Kent and Abadi Ezra, the last two were Zur Tse Wen and K. M. M. Zuraek.

2

The oldest foreign hands are of course the British, of whom there are generally about 16,000, including soldiers of the garrison and their wives. Except in the city centre they are not especially visible these days, constituting as they do at most 0.003 per cent of the population, but one is reminded constantly of their long residence here if only by the place-names on the Hong Kong map. In 1997 these may all be swept away, but for the moment they are like a public roster of the old association – Elliot Crescent and Pottinger Peak, Mount Davis and Bonham Strand, Shelley Street of course, Lady Clementi's Ride and Aldrich Village and Hill Above Belcher's . . . Every Governor of Hong Kong has something named after him, and today Percival, Irving, Anton, Landale, Matheson, Paterson, Johnstone and Keswick Streets, not to mention Jardine's Lookout,

Jardine's Bazaar and Jardine's Crescent, all commemorate British taipans.

To eastern eyes, I dare say, the British used to look as indistinguishable, one from another, as the Chinese mass looked to westerners. But you have only to examine the roll-call of Hong Kong Britons to realize that innumerable different kinds of expatriate have sought their fortunes in the colony during the past 150 years. We see a prevalence of Scotsmen, for example, in the names of the traders – Jardines, Mathesons, Inneses, Mackays, McGregors. We see a plethora of Evanses, Joneses, Williamses and Davises, not only in the St David's Society and Welsh choirs of the colony, but also among academics and in Government. There were once five Anglo-Irish Governors in a row. And unmistakable are the signs that declare the presence here, down all the generations, of the lesser English gentry.

In particular that prime emblem of the English upper bourgeoisie, the double-barrelled name, has proliferated through the history of Hong Kong. Here are a few examples to be met in the records, old and new: Fairfax-Cholmondeley, Sawrey-Cookson, Peterson-Todd, Akers-Jones, Steele-Perkins, Hutton-Potts, Norman-Walker, Wesley-Smith, Norton-Kyshe, Webb-Peploe, Pennefather-Evans, Cave-Brown, Vaughan-Flower, Muspratt-Williams, Jackson-Lipkin.

They sound a picturesque company, whether street-eponymed, Celtic or merely hyphenated, but by no means every one has lived up to the hopes of his family, seeing him off to a new life in the East, or to the expectations of his schoolmasters. Power and profit equally corrupt, and the British in Hong Kong have displayed the imperial condition at its worst and at its best.

3

Nobody pretends that the British taipans and other business leaders have generally been very *nice* men. They have often been interesting, often courageous and generally enterprising, but not habitually overflowing with the milk of human kindness. In 1862 Louis Mallet, Under-Secretary at the Board of Trade in London, characterized the Britons then entering the China trade as 'unscrupulous and reckless adventurers who seek nothing but enormous profits' (though James Matheson, more cultured and affable than most of them, had been allowed by one contemporary 'suavity of manner and the impersonation of benevolence').

Late-Victorian Hong Kong: *above*: a harbour excursion; *below*: Queen's Road, with the Pedder Street clock tower

Victorian imperialists, at work and play

Today, though drug-smuggling is certainly not pursued by the big British merchant houses of Hong Kong, in many other ways they are still ready to cut profitable corners, and their top officials are still recognizably in the old tradition. They are a breed on the defensive, as Chinese, American, Japanese, Australian and other foreign businessmen challenge them for financial hegemony, and Beijing awaits their subjection in 1997; but you would hardly know it, for ironically they are in their element in the world of the late 1980s. Through all the permutations of socialism and conservatism in Britain, they have maintained in this far colony the spirit of free enterprise at its most absolute; now they have come home, as it were, into the congenial years of Thatcherism and Reaganism, of monetarism and privatization and takeover bid and conglomerate merger, years when the capitalist idea rises so high that it is half-respectable even within Communist China. Let us contemplate a group of these merchants (they like to be called merchants) meeting perhaps at a dinner party with wives elegantly in attendance, and see what 150 years has made of them.

The old hongs drew heavily upon family associations, recruiting cousins, nephews and marital connections as often as they could. 'I can never consent to assist idle and dissipated characters,' wrote William Jardine severely, 'however nearly connected with me, but am prepared to go to any reasonable extent in supporting such of my relations who conduct themselves prudently and industriously.' Today the big British banks and business firms rely hardly less, if not actually on blood-links, at least upon the extended family of class and background. These half-dozen men laughing over their coffees are of a kind, and a cool kind at that. Good-looking, some of them, alert every one, drinking moderately, probably not smoking, everything about them seems formidably under control.

The social historian Colin Cresswell, writing in 1981,[1] made a study of twelve such captains of the hongs. In six cases, he cautiously revealed, 'kinship could be said to have been a significant career factor'. Eleven had been educated at English public schools and at Oxbridge. Nearly all had done military service in one of the smarter regiments of the British army (more recently one has done service in the French Foreign Legion, too, and written a book about it). We can assume from our own researches, as our subjects move on to coffee and brandy (ladies seldom adjourn to the drawing room in contemporary Hong Kong)

[1] *The Taipans*, Hong Kong 1981.

that they all vote Conservative when they are home in Britain, and that they probably have middle-sized but extremely well-equipped country houses awaiting their retirement somewhere within reach of London.

Although they all represent different firms, they are closely connected professionally, for the old British companies of Hong Kong often share directors and frequently collaborate on projects, making the whole system sometimes feel like a semi-secret organization of mutual advantage. Also they are all likely to be on the same club committees, and they doubtless share the pleasures of Happy Valley and the Shatin racecourse, and sail against each other perhaps at the Royal Hong Kong Yacht Club, and go out in each others' pleasure-junks, and are frequently pictured accepting each others' hospitality in the pages of the *Hong Kong Tatler*.

When we add to all this the fraternity of wealth – they are all very rich men, by British standards – it comes as no surprise that they so obviously speak the same language socially, professionally, educationally and probably morally. If we eavesdrop upon their conversation we are likely to find it, for all its gaiety, larded with references to company mergers, Exchange Square rumours, someone's recent bankruptcy or joint projects to build nuclear power stations in China. It is also slightly Americanized, in vocabulary, in allusion, sometimes in pronunciation and almost indefinably in attitude.

4

Such are the men known generically, at least to novelists and visiting journalists, as the Hong Kong taipans – in the 1960s indeed, if we are to believe the novelist James Clavell,[1] they used the word a lot themselves, and actually addressed the head of a firm as 'Taipan', as in 'Unless the market drops, Taipan, Chase Manhattan will never come up with the other half billion . . .' Below them economically in the ranks of Hong Kong Britishry is a much larger class of the less plutocratic bourgeoisie, business executives, brokers, advertising men and women, lawyers, doctors, academics, journalists. They form a more heterogeneous community than the taipans and their wives, and besides a sizeable stratum of extremely civilized and kindly people, include a fair proportion of men one might prefer not to buy a used car from, a sufficiency of women one would rather not be stuck beside at a cocktail

[1] *Noble House*, New York 1981.

party, and some children one is grateful one's own family need not go to school with.

Their social origins vary, as do their accents, which range from the heartiest Scots or Yorkshire to half-strangled timbres of gentility. They often have foreign spouses, Chinese, Japanese or European, but they generally send their children to school in England. They live very agreeably, in pleasant apartments on the mid-Levels (half-way up the Peak), or sometimes in comfortable villas with gardens. If of independent disposition they may commute from the more accessible of the outer islands, or at least have weekend retreats there. One successful lawyer and his wife have an apartment in Central and a pretty cottage, full of flowers and English prints, high among the hills of Lantau, from where they can supervise their second business, the nearby tea-gardens and riding-stables. For they are seldom idle, either the husbands or the wives – even in 1940 300 British women managed their own businesses in Hong Kong, and today one seldom meets a wife without a job. They do not however always share the taipans' virtues of calculated self-control, running often to floridity and sometimes to sottishness.

All in all they are, at a generalization, rather less completely British than the taipans, and they live more free-and-easily. Earning as they probably do far more than they would in Britain, they are seldom in a hurry to go home, but often seem to be pursuing their careers in a pleasant state of half-speed-ahead, eating well, enjoying their friends, gossiping in the club bar, taking the junk out on Sundays – 'whatever you do,' they tell the visitor, 'don't go out with Bill (or Simon, or Ted), you'll be drunk before you get out of the harbour.' Many work hard for charities. Some grapple with the Cantonese language. Almost all leave the territory for an annual holiday somewhere, and they are familiar with much of the Far East, talking easily of Taiwan or the Philippines, Singapore or Tokyo, much as their relatives at home in Britain would speak of Tuscany or the Dordogne.

Nevertheless the lives of such people revolve around the intense goings-on of the territory itself, its coups and its scandals, its economic condition, its restaurants newly fashionable or in decline, and especially, as 1997 approaches, its future. What is to become of the territory has become an obsession of their conversation. They read every word of the *South China Morning Post*, the Hong Kong *Standard*, the *Far Eastern Economic Review*, all written or edited by people they are likely to know, and because many of them do business in China they are profligate with rumours out of Beijing.

There are always some mavericks in this community. A stockbroker named Noel Croucher, elder of the Hong Kong Club and well-known for his curmudgeonly attitudes and miserly ways, was found when he died in 1978 to have left the whole of his very large fortune to a trust for the educational advancement of Hong Kong Chinese – one of the most generous of private educational trusts anywhere in the world. And nobody could be more indomitably her own mistress than Mrs Elsie Tu (neé Hume, in Newcastle-on-Tyne, 1913), who has been for thirty years the voice of Hong Kong's liberal conscience, fearlessly championing the poor, defying Authority and exposing corruption. Most of the British bourgeoisie, however, feel no profound loyalty to Hong Kong. Some detest the place, and only a few of the most thoroughly assimilated are planning to remain after 1997. They are essentially transients anyway, and long ago many of them prepared for the future by buying one of those nice small properties in the vicinity of Grasse, where the food will still be good, the sun will shine a little like the eastern sun, and they can keep a boat in a marina somewhere.

5

There was a time when British companies in Hong Kong employed many Britons of a simpler kind. There were never poor whites living here, except in earlier years among the beachcombers and prostitutes, and few British manual workers of any kind, but especially between the two world wars an expatriate petit bourgeoisie flourished, as it did in many another colony. Lane Crawford's department store, for example, used to employ British shop assistants, and they are shown in old photographs lounging in topees on the verandahs of the company mess, or enjoying themselves decorously at Christmas parties, moustachioed figures like characters from H. G. Wells – the assistant manager of the footwear department, the deputy supervisor of soft furnishings.

There are a few contemporary echoes of this now all-but-vanished society. At its less genteel level scores of pubs still provide an authentic football-pool-and-spilt-beer flavour, spiced nowadays with juke-box and Australianisms. At its more refined, to this day the English-language newspapers are rich in pedantically ill-written letters from people signing themselves 'An Angry Customer', or 'True Brit', and until very recently also went in for a jolly variety of comic verse, often Jingo or at least reactionary in tone, which would well have suited the London penny press of fifty years before. Now however the lower ranks of commerce, as of Government, are filled almost entirely by Chinese, and if you identify a working-class Briton in Hong Kong he is likely to be a soldier from the British garrison which has been based here without a break (if for a time confined in Japanese prison camps) since the foundation of the colony.

In 1877 a sergeant from that garrison, apparently enraged by the advantages of the official and merchant classes, single-handedly attacked the Hong Kong Club with drawn sword, hacking away at lamps and chandeliers and threatening members with the dread phrase: 'You are one of them!' Today's off-duty British soldier seems at least as remote from club membership as poor Sergeant Shannon felt himself then. His hair is cropped, his face is flushed with sun, and he tends to walk around town with an air of long-suffering detachment. Unless he has a wife and family with him, he is attended by a bad reputation for drunkenness and boorish behaviour, and like all his predecessors down the generations, he is unlikely to have a high opinion of the Chinese population – 'they're no good,' as a corporal observed to me in the 1970s, 'they don't *want* to understand, and they smell.' Still, he is often to be seen in his leisure hours somewhat morosely celebrating in the bars of Kowloon and Wanchai, rather the worse for too much of the local beer, and entertained with patient distaste by tired ladies of the night.

6

On the other side of a metaphysical fence stands the British official in Hong Kong. He comes in all kinds, and nowadays he mixes freely with the commercial and professional classes, but he remains by the nature of his office consciously separate.

He has probably been recruited for some specialist skill, as an engineer or a port manager, a journalist, an accountant, a botanist or a meteorologist – even in 1987, when Chinese had succeeded to most Civil Service jobs, there were still some 3,500 expatriates on the Government payroll. He may however be a career member of the Foreign and Commonwealth Service, which absorbed the remains of the old Colonial Service in 1968 (there being by then a distinct shortage of colonies). Perhaps he reached the territory by way of other British possessions, now independent. Or perhaps he may be, if of a certain age, one of the last of the officers trained specifically for service in Hong Kong.

There was a time, and not so long ago, when very few British members of the Hong Kong administration spoke any Chinese language. Today they include a strong cadre of linguists, and a handful of men whose very passion is the civilization of China, in the old imperial tradition of the scholar-administrator. Since the senior administrator of contemporary Hong Kong is likely to be virtually the last of the line, let us accept an invitation to dine with one of these enthusiasts, and his no less enthusiastic wife, and drive out of the humid heat of Central, between the towering block of mid-Levels where the lights of evening are beginning to appear, up the winding twisting road to his white official house above the harbour.

'Did you know,' he says with a diffident shuffle of his feet, as we stand with our drinks on the terrace surveying the spectacular scene, 'did you know that last year 15,000 ocean-going ships came in and out of that harbour? What's that now, thirty-five, forty a day? Not too bad, is it?' He says it as a man might refer to the progress of his roses, in a gently proprietorial or even creational way. Up there on the slopes of the mountain, so far above the frenzies of the city, one does have a certain divine sensation, and God-like, he cannot resist a complacent rider, 'And that doesn't, of course, include small craft from China – another 80,000 or so of them . . .'

When we move inside for dinner we find his house, though colonially grand of architecture, furnished with restraint, English in décor with touches of Chinoiserie like wall-scrolls and dragon-decorated vases. Dinner too turns out to be an Anglo-Chinese meal. 'How do you like the fish?' asks our host urgently. 'It's carp from a pond you know, sent to us by old friends in the New Territories. Don't you think its taste is quite extraordinarily subtle?' 'What do you think of the tea?' asks our hostess. 'It's from Fujan, probably the very tea Li Yu referred to in the *Cha-jing*, very good for the digestion, too . . .' The bottle of Riesling seems an intrusion upon the cuisine, added especially for us perhaps, and we feel almost ashamed to decline that familiar of all Chinese gastronomy, a toothpick.

As for the conversation, it centres upon historical Chinese inscriptions on Lantau, a subject on which our host is an acknowledged expert, and on social arrangements in South China in the eighteenth century, upon which he has written a couple of monographs, while his wife intervenes now and then with comparisons and illuminations from her own rather superior command of the Tanka dialect, and her experiences as honorary president of five or six charitable societies.

I exaggerate, but only in the detail, and parody only in affection. It is a modest, kind and decent evening that we enjoy. Our hosts are very decent people. Before we leave we venture to ask where will they go on the day of the Great Denouement, 1997. 'Go?' they answer as one. 'We won't go anywhere. We'll stay at home in Hong Kong.' [1]

7

The British hardly even like to call Hong Kong a colony now, preferring to call it a territory. It plays no part in any wider British imperial system, and performs the statutory colonial rituals with perceptible embarrassment. But nostalgically, aesthetically perhaps, the British of Hong Kong do sometimes pine for the old sentiments. They show it particularly on Easter Day, when at the sound of the cathedral chimes (donated by the Hong Kong Club to commemorate Queen Elizabeth's coronation in 1953), a positive paroxysm of Anglican religiosity appears to seize the British community, as it used to seize such congregations across the Empire. All the pews are filled that morning with very British figures, together with properly Anglicized members of the subject races, and the expatriates revert to older forms. Hands are crossed meekly over paunches, as the executives line up to receive the Body and the Blood. Haughty eyes of *Tatler* wives are lowered in submission – even the ladies of the public-relations corps look maidenly.

Although there are, it is true, only two or three Easter bonnets to be seen (all worn, I suspect, by Australians), the whole scene is suggestively imperial. The louvred windows are open to the sun, as they used to be in Simla or in Freetown, the choir sings the old hymns, a Welshman preaches the sermon ('Far as we are from home, my friends, still on this holy day of rejoicing . . .'), the Chinese acolyte in his surplice looks properly respectful, and all is as it should be beneath the comfort of flag and Establishment.

It is one moment of the year when the British of Hong Kong frankly proclaim their identity. It is also one of the few moments when they seem to be united, because this community has always been split not only by the fissures of interest that we observed in the 1840s, but also by the differences of class and calling that we have just been examining. Almost from the start everyone looked down on everyone else. Henry T. Ellis, a naval officer in port in 1859, defined [2] the general social

[1] Preferably, cynics might add, with a company directorship or two to see them through.
[2] In *Hong Kong to Manila*, London 1859.

attitude of Hong Kong as one of 'purse-proud stuck-upism', and the definition has never been out-dated.

For many years, to a degree even now, the very attitude of one's house was an infallible guide to one's social status, and the position of a pew in the Cathedral was another indication of rank and self-esteem. Elaborate social protocols were upheld, involving precedence at dinner-parties, the leaving of cards and harsh dilemmas about who should first call upon whom; when in 1857 the warship *Tribune* put in to harbour, its captain never met any of the British taipans, so famous for their hospitality, because neither he nor they would so far demean themselves as to make the first visit. Officials looked down on businessmen. Wholesale merchants looked down upon retail merchants' clerks. 'The little community,' wrote Alfred Weatherhead, 'far from being a band of brothers, is split up into numerous petty cliques or sets, the members of which never think of associating with those out of their immediate circle.'

It was a familiar imperial phenomenon, and happened perhaps because the sea-change of empire made all classes more conscious of their own importance. The official became an aristocrat, when he was posted to the colonies. The dockyard foreman and his wife found themselves with underlings to command at work, servants to make the beds at home. Even the private soldier had a coolie to kick about. If the impulse sounds un-stylish, the truth is that by and large the Hong Kong British seldom were very stylish people. Once its rip-roar founding days were over, the colony cherished few outstanding men or women – no Orwells served in its administration, no Kiplings worked for the *South China Morning Post*. Even eccentricity was rare. It is a measure of this community that local historians like to record the birth in Hong Kong of P. G. Wodehouse's elder brother, and the death of Thomas de Quincey's second son.[1]

8

Every Sunday morning, throughout the year, Statue Square is taken over by the Filipina maids of Hong Kong, who assemble here in their thousands to meet friends, swap news, cook al fresco meals, sell things to each other, read the Manila newspapers and sometimes dance to the

---

[1] Wodehouse's father was a magistrate in the colony – 'Plum' himself went home to be born, in 1881, but worked for a time in the London office of the Hongkong and Shanghai Bank. Horace de Quincey, an officer of the 26th Cameronians, died of a fever in 1842.

music of transistors. It is an extraordinary occasion, and suggests to almost everyone an assembly of starlings. The women swarm upon the square in mid-morning, pouring out of the subway stations, streaming off the ferries, and settling upon every bench, every patch of ground in a great eddy of shopping bags. If it is wet they occupy arcades, pedestrian bridges and shopping centres for half a mile around. A high-pitched chatter of Tagalog echoes among the skyscrapers, rival musics clash across the gardens, a vast tide of litter is swept here and there by the wind. Sometimes the excellent Filipino Community Symphonic Band plays in the closed-off street, and long after dark has fallen small clusters of friends still laugh and prattle on, reading one another letters from home, strumming guitars and eating small bits of fish.

Captain Elliot, raising the flag in 1841, declared that in British Hong Kong protection would be given to all foreigners, and ever since Hong Kong has been an entrepôt for everyone's commerce, a port of call for everyone's merchant ships and airlines, a favourite haven for the navies of all nations, and a great place for anyone who can get there to make money. Today the British form a minority among the expatriate residents, and foreigners of all kinds, like traders in an ancient caravanserai, are forever coming and going. Some came virtually at the start, and among them were the Filipinos, from Hong Kong's nearest non-Chinese neighbour, whose numbers were greatly increased when the Philippines were freed from Spanish rule, in 1897, and who now form the biggest foreign community of all.

Jardine, Matheson employed Filipino guards back in the 1840s, and Filipino musicians have always played the part in Hong Kong that Goan musicians played in British India – minstrels by appointment. Philippine affairs figure largely in the newspapers, the Philippine Republic's Consul-General is always prominent among the consuls. The endearing mass of the Filipino community, however, is provided by those laughing, chattering, always good-humoured girls on Statue Square each Sunday, indentured labourers who often work cruel hours and live in bunk-rooms hardly more than cubbyholes, but who still come to Hong Kong year after year in their eager thousands, many of them leaving husbands and small children behind, to escape still worse circumstances at home.

The Portuguese were also fellow-pioneers in Hong Kong – indeed they were on this coast long before the British. They had an old association with the British merchants in Macao, and many of them, including some of ancient family, came across the estuary to Hong Kong after the Treaty of Nanking. They gave Hong Kong some of its early architecture, and some of its vernacular – praya, for example, meaning a promenade, mandarin, originally a giver of mandates, comprador, literally a provider, amah, a nurse, and even surprisingly joss, which comes from *deus*.

The Portuguese have always been prominent in the middle ranks of business and the law, and they were among the first Europeans to build themselves houses in Kowloon, when it became British, making themselves almost an enclave over there. Their club, the Lusitano Club, is one of the oldest in Hong Kong, and some of them live in an exquisitely civilized style: I think of one distinguished lawyer, whose grandfather came to Hong Kong from Macao in 1842, sitting in his lovely house in the rural New Territories – fronted by an islanded bay, backed by a green mountain – with his four big dogs, his three cats, his fastidious library, his flowers and rare works of Chinoiserie, showing me the scribbled diary he kept when a prisoner-of-war of the Japanese, together with mementoes of his annual climbing trip to Zermatt, and the famous stamp collection which has made his name known wherever philatelists assemble . . .[1]

The Indian association with Hong Kong was based upon alliances between the British taipans and their Bombay or Calcutta trading partners – alliances that predated the colony. Parsee merchants in particular were important in Hong Kong affairs from the beginning, several having bought land in Elliot's original auctions, and Indians, fragmenting into Sikhs or Bengalis or Pathans, branching out into Pakistanis, have always been familiar in Hong Kong. They used to be familiar as soldiers, policemen and ships' guards, they are familiar still as hotel doormen and security guards. The aristocratic-looking gentlemen often to be seen standing in the lobby of the Mandarin Hotel, as if waiting to join their fellow-directors for luncheon in the grill, are I am told strong-arm men from the north-west frontier; the police who guard the ammunition stores on Stonecutters Island, in the harbour, are always Sikhs, because their religion forbids them to smoke.

In the past at least they suffered from dual racial prejudices – unless they were rich or grand they were liable to be slighted by British and Chinese alike – but they have often prospered mightily all the same. It was an Indian who first operated a cross-harbour ferry service, in the

[1] It really was his grandfather who came: the grandfather was in his teens, the grandson is in his seventies, and so three generations of D'Almadas have experienced the entire colonial history of Hong Kong.

1840s, and another began the Star ferries, and for many years Indians were prominent in the hotel business. Two of the original Indian firms in Hong Kong, founded in 1842, flourish to this day. As manufacturers and agents, Indians and Pakistanis play a role in the Hong Kong economy wildly out of proportion to their numbers; they form less than 1/400 of the population, but they generate a tenth of the colony's export trade.

9

Look at the buses of the Japanese School, lined up head to tail on the road above Chung Hom Kok! Listen to the animated chattering noise of the pupils on the beach below! Bear in mind that just across the bay, on Stanley Beach in 1943, thirty-three British, Indian and Chinese citizens were beheaded for alleged High Treason against the Japanese occupying Power! The Japanese association with Hong Kong has been ambiguous indeed. On the one hand their armies were the only armies ever to invade the colony, on the other for many years their foreign trade was largely financed by the colony's banks. On the one shore the children merrily bathing, on the other the bloodied heads falling on the sand.

It was from Hong Kong that Jardine, Matheson moved into Japan in the nineteenth century, and except for the war years they have maintained thriving branches there since.[1] The Japanese in return established a large commercial and financial colony in Hong Kong, besides providing, for example, one of the best-known Hong Kong barbers of the 1930, the surgeons who, during a terrible epidemic in 1894, first isolated the plague bacillus, and that once ubiquitous Hong Kong vehicle, the rickshaw, whose name was really jin-riku-sha, 'man's strength cart'. Until the Second World War there was a thriving Japanese Residents' Association, with its own temple, and when the future Edward VIII came to the colony in 1922 its members greeted him with a volley of rockets, which upon exploding released a multitude of Union Jacks on parachutes.

The years of the Second World War cast a pall of horror over the relationship, mingled (on the British side anyway) with a profound puzzlement and a trace of reluctant respect, but soon the Japanese were back in full force and confidence. Today they have their own banks, investment firms, insurance companies, hotels, restaurants and

[1] 'I'm so sorry,' I was once told of a Jardine's executive's wife to whom I had been given a letter of introduction, 'but she's away in Japan, launching a ship.'

at least ten perpetually jam-packed department stores. The rickshaws have almost vanished, but the Toyotas and the Nissans, the Sonys and the Panasonics are everywhere. The Hong Kong finance market might be in trouble without its Japanese funds, the topless bars and massage parlours of the territory would languish were it not for the insatiable lusts of Japanese businessmen, and the 10,000-odd Japanese residents are likely soon to develop, I would guess, into the biggest foreign community of all.

In Victorian times there was also a prosperous German colony – rather too prosperous, British competitors thought. It had its Germania Club, complete with theatre, and the Berlin Ladies' Association ran a foundling hospital. Germans were personally popular in the colony, and an elaborate welcome was offered, by Germans and British alike, when in 1898 Prince Heinrich of Prussia arrived in the cruiser *Deutschland* on his way to the new German protectorate of Qingdao up the coast.[1] Two world wars dispersed the community, but anti-German feeling was never fierce in Hong Kong. During the First World War the exploits of the German raider *Emden*, sinking British ships all over the Indian Ocean, were much admired by the colonists, who had happy memories of the cruiser from pre-war visits, and during the Second World War Nazi Germany was remote from the anxieties of Hong Kong. The Club, closed in 1914, has never been revived, and the German presence remains unobtrusive – 1,600 souls in 1987: but as you might guess from the prevalence of Mercedes and BMWs, West Germany is a more important trading partner to Hong Kong than is Great Britain itself.

Russia, whether Soviet or Tsarist, has always been suspect in the colony, but Russians of one sort or another have repeatedly turned up. The future Tsar Nicholas II turned up in 1891, with a royal yacht and an escort of four warships, and was given a fairly frosty reception; nobody cheered him, and after a brief visit to Government House he sailed away again. Less eminent Russians turned up after the Soviet Revolution, and others again retreated to Hong Kong after successive alarms in Shanghai, a racier international settlement which in general they much preferred. Throughout the 1930s there were always White Russians knocking about, earning their livings as ships' guards, as prostitutes, as dance teachers, as photographers, as racehorse trainers

---

[1] Though the real purpose of his visit, as Kaiser Wilhelm himself expressed it, was 'to make clear . . . that the German [Saint] Michael has planted his shield firmly in the soil [of China]'.

(the last Russian trainer at Happy Valley retired in 1986). There were enough to form a Russian platoon of the Hong Kong Volunteers, and when Hong Kong fell to the Japanese in 1941 there were enough to form a thirty-member Cossack choir in their prisoner-of-war camp.

The French, now represented by some 1,400 people and at least 140 firms, are old *habitués* of the territory. In 1852 a French architect built Hong Kong's first City Hall, in 1865 a Frenchman was appointed first general manager of the Hongkong and Shanghai Bank, in the 1950s French engineers built the new Kai Tak airport runway, protruding dramatically into the harbour. The chief Canadian connection with Hong Kong is a tragic one, being (as we shall later learn) the needless obliteration of two Canadian battalions in the Japanese invasion; today however there is a sizeable Canadian community, and Canada is best-known in the colony as the most popular destination for Hong Kong Chinese seeking a haven before 1997.

The Australian link is full of verve, beginning with the importation of New South Wales ponies to race at Happy Valley, culminating in the bold investment of Australian entrepreneurs in the nervous Hong Kong market of the early 1980s. Australians are everywhere in the history of Hong Kong, from Mrs Randall with her Honey to Mr Murdoch with his newspaper. They are everywhere on the ground too, developing properties, managing shops, editing papers, and their accents permeate High Court and stock exchange alike, besides ringing convivially (stridently sometimes) across yacht club marinas on Sunday mornings.

The gypsies have never come to Hong Kong, but their wandering comrades the Jews have often fulfilled themselves by these remote and alien waters. Many have been refugees, often refugees twice or three times over – from Nazi Germany, from Soviet Russia, from Japanese occupation or Communist China. Others have come in the course of business, and some have established themselves in the classic line of the British imperial Jew.

They have never been a large community, and for generations they were, for example, excluded from membership of the Hong Kong Club. On the other hand some gained acceptance by being very rich, owning successful racehorses and giving splendid parties, and some were notably interesting: E. R. Belilios, for instance, who came to Hong Kong in 1862, defied convention by keeping a camel to carry his provisions up the Peak, while Morris 'Two-Gun' Cohen, who arrived in the 1940s and had once been Sun Yat-sen's bodyguard, was one of the most colourful *condottieri* of the Chinese civil wars. The first great Jewish merchants followed the flag from Bombay, but some of them had orginally come from Baghdad, and their families include some of the best-known in Hong Kong history.

Their white twin-towered synagogue, built in 1902 in a vaguely Dutch style, exhibits near its porch a list of subscribers, and there you will see some unexpected names, like Gezundhaji and Mackenzie. You will also find Jewish names, though, that were famous throughout the British Empire. The synagogue is named Ohel Leah, Leah's Tent, having been built in honour of his mother Leah ('Peace Be To Her') by Jacob Sassoon, whose family came by way of Iraq and India to provide the empire with generations of poets, country gentlemen and millionaires. And prominent still in the affairs of the synagogue are the Kadoories, whom we see in pictures of a century ago dressed in turbans and baggy pantaloons, but who in 1981 produced Hong Kong's first peer of the British realm – Lawrence, Baron Kadoorie, of Kowloon in Hong Kong and of the City of Westminster.[1]

10

But of all the foreigners who have taken advantage of Britain's presence in Hong Kong, pre-eminent from the first have been the Americans, whose Republic was rather more than sixty years old when the Crown Colony was established, and who have maintained a Consulate here since 1845. 'Many people out in carriages,' noted a visitor in 1858, 'and some Yankees in light iron four-wheeled trotting gigs.' We can see them now, with their tilted hats and their cheroots, and this is not surprising, for they have never gone away.

American ships had first come to the China seas in 1784, when because of the Revolutionary War most foreign ports were denied them, and an American factory was established at Guangzhou in 1803. American entrepreneurs, nearly all British by origin in those days, regularly bought opium in India and in the Middle East, distributing it along the China coast in their own fast vessels. An American figures in the very first printed British reference to Hong Kong – he was an interpreter, picked up at a rendezvous off the west coast of the island by Lord Amherst's mission to Beijing in 1816 – and among the original

[1] The synagogue is threatened by development schemes, but the builders of the two forty-two-storey tower blocks proposed for its site have offered to provide a brand-new replica.

hongs of the colony was Samuel Russell and Company; founded in Boston in 1811, with partners from New York, Connecticut and Massachusetts, it remained for thirty years one of the presiding institutions of Hong Kong.

Americans built the first Christian church in Hong Kong (the Baptist Chapel, 1842), and brought the first ice (1847), and financed the first 1,000-room hotel (1962 – originally to be called the America Hotel, it is now the Hong Kong Hilton). An American owned the first motor car (not surprisingly he was a dentist, J. W. Noble). An American was present at the very first Government House Christmas dinner (he was George Henry Preble, one of Commodore Perry's officers on the expedition to Japan). An American naval band led the Masons along Queen's Road to the opening of their new lodge in 1853. Americans ran the first steamer to Guangzhou (the *Midas*, 1845), and made the first Hong Kong parachute jumps (the Baldwin brothers, 1891). The rental sampans known as Walla-Wallas are supposed to be named after a small town deep in the interior of Washington State, because that is where their original operator came from.

Ex-President Grant dined at Government House in 1879 ('the most illustrious guest that ever sat at this table'). Admiral Dewey used Mirs Bay, debatably within Hong Kong's territorial waters, as a base during the Spanish–American war. Emily Hahn the writer was an outstanding personality of pre-war Hong Kong, boldly defying pretensions grandiose and petty, living in a cheerfully unmarried state with the chief intelligence officer of the British garrison, and announcing the birth of her child, in the *South China Morning Post*, with a defiant: 'To Major Boxer and Miss Hahn, a daughter.' Kipling, on his visit to the colony in 1889, thought the whole town 'dressed by America, from the hair-cutters' saloons to the liquor bars', while the girls of the bordellos talked in an American argot ('I stood appalled at the depth and richness of the American language'): he went on one of the American river-steamers, too, and thought it not at all like the British boats of the Irriwaddy flotilla, being composed 'almost entirely of white paint, sheet-lead, a cow-horn and a walking-beam', with a stand of loaded Sniders to repel pirates.

Whenever there has been a tragedy, a scandal, a financial coup or an adventure, there are likely to have been Americans somewhere about. Americans have kept pubs in Hong Kong, staffed brothels, married into Government House, fought pirates and for that matter *been* pirates. One of the most famous pirates of all was Eli Boggs, a renegade American matelot, who preyed upon the Pearl River traffic with a fleet of thirty armed junks. A reward offered for his capture by the Hong Kong Government was won in 1857 by another American, Captain 'Bully' Hayes, who took part in a Royal Navy raid on the pirate fleet and personally arrested its commander. The subsequent trial was a sensation of the time – Boggs, though almost tenderly good-looking, was alleged to have led his Chinese ruffians in the seizure of countless ships, murdering their crews or forcing them overboard. No witness could be found who had seen him actually kill a man, but he was found guilty of piracy and sentenced to transportation for life. (However although 'Bully' Hayes got his $1,000 all right, Boggs never went to the penal colonies, for after three years in a Hong Kong jail he was released because of ill-health, and disappeared, it seems, simultaneously from Hong Kong and from history.)

During the Americans' Asian wars, in Korea in the 1950s, in Vietnam later, their servicemen fell upon Hong Kong in their thousands as they had fallen upon Tokyo in the 1940s – it is no coincidence that the modern soubriquet for a Hong Kong madam is *mama-san*, as in Japan. A generation of American males was conditioned then to think of Hong Kong as a paradise of hedonism, just as their successors today, the tourists who arrive for their own R and R on package tours and cruises, stereotype the place as the greatest of all shopping centres. Except for those of protectionist views (people in the textile industry, for instance), most American visitors and residents eagerly embrace the mores of Hong Kong, seeing in the territory no doubt some esoteric mirror-image of their own ideology, and buying in their hundreds of thousands a succession of popular novels about the place.

As for the Chinese of Hong Kong, so readily do they adapt to American tastes in return that the busiest of all McDonald's hamburger joints are those in this territory, and recently almost 4,000 people ate pizzas in a single day at a Pizza Hut in Kowloon.

II

Today there are more American nationals living in Hong Kong, official statistics say, than there are Britons: but probably half of them are Chinese–Americans, many from Hong Kong in the first place, and are thus invisible.

This is very proper, for the Americans' stance in Hong Kong has not always been what it seems. On the face of it their residency has been straightforward enough. They have their Chamber of Commerce and their International School. They have a gloriously luxurious American Club on the forty-seventh floor of a waterfront skyscraper in Central, one of the best places in the world to enjoy a vodka martini to Cole Porter in the piano bar, together with a sumptuous country club. They have their State of Illinois Asian Office, their State of Michigan Agricultural Department Office, their Asian edition of the *Wall Street Journal*. There are American presenters on Hong Kong television, and American enterprise is active in everything from the generation of electrical power in gigantic power stations to the construction of model ships in upstairs Kowloon workshops. There is a very large Consulate-General in a prominent position half-way between Government House and the Hilton, and in 1987, to cap it all, an American became managing director of Jardine, Matheson itself.

But their presence in Hong Kong is more subtle than that. Some of the Consulate-General windows are eerily mirror-glassed, to prevent spying visual or electronic, and official American attitudes in the Crown Colony have often been similarly opaque. As recently as 1986 a senior American consular official was heard to tell a visiting bigwig from New York that there, right there in that Consulate-General, was where Hong Kong was really run. If the American financial interest in the territory is enormous, and growing fast, the Americans have also had powerful historical, political and ideological stakes in the place.

Early in this century they began to regard China as particularly their sphere of influence. Commercially their commitment was no more important than Britain's, but emotionally, largely because of the proliferation of American evangelical missions in the Chinese interior, they felt themselves to have a superior lien upon the country. This conviction came to a head during the presidency of Franklin D. Roosevelt, whose maternal grandfather Warren Delano had been a partner in Russell's, and who was interested in China all his life.

It was during his presidency that we first sense a growing American determination that the British ought not to be in Hong Kong at all. Roosevelt was against all Empires, as any self-respecting President had to be in the 1930s and 1940s, and just as he thought the British should leave India, so he thought they should hand back Hong Kong to the Chinese. Like Chiang Kai-shek, the Christian convert who ruled China from 1928 to 1949, he considered the Treaty of Nanking, under which the colony had become British, an 'unequal treaty', one of many forced upon the Chinese in the previous century by the overwhelming power of Europe. Most of those treaties were revoked by agreement in 1943, but the original Hong Kong cession, and the later lease of the New Territories, were both upheld by the British, and were regarded by Chiang and by Roosevelt as iniquitous.

The later stages of the Second World War, when Hong Kong had been lost to the Japanese, and Chiang's Kuomintang China was formally admitted into the ranks of the Big Five Powers, seemed the opportunity to set things right. Correspondence between Chiang and Roosevelt frequently proposes the return of Hong Kong to China after the war. To Stalin, at Yalta, Roosevelt suggested the internationalization of Hong Kong. To Eden, in Washington, he said Britain should give up the colony 'as a gesture of goodwill'. Another suggestion was that the British should sell Hong Kong to China, the price being lent by the US Treasury, or that the Chinese themselves should be enabled by the Americans to liberate Hong Kong from the Japanese. Whatever the means, Roosevelt was confident that the matter would be arranged. 'We are going to be able to bring pressure on the British to fall in line with *our* way of thinking,' he told his son Elliott. 'We're going to be able to make this the twentieth century after all, you watch and see!'

But the American attitude changed when, in 1949, the Communists acceded to power in China, and Chiang Kai-shek moved with his refugee Government to another off-shore island, Taiwan. Now the British were no longer urged to hand the colony back to Beijing. On the contrary, when in 1950 the Americans found themselves fighting the Chinese Communists over the issue of Korea, Hong Kong became an outpost of their own power. The Consulate-General was enormously enlarged, becoming for a time the biggest of all American overseas missions, and was supplemented by every kind of skuldug outfit operating under the umbrella of the Central Intelligence Agency. An embargo was placed upon trade with Communist China, and in Hong Kong American officials pedantically enforced it as if the territory were their own, drawing preposterous distinctions between timber grown in China and timber grown in Hong Kong, or banning the export of processed prawns on the grounds that they might have been caught in Chinese territorial waters.

Now the ships of the United States Seventh Fleet vastly outgunned the few remaining warships of the Royal Navy, and the antennae of American radar aerials and electronic watchposts sprouted from the ridges of Hong Kong. For the next twenty years, through all the traumas of Chinese hostility and gradual reconciliation, through the agonies of the Vietnam war fought a few hundred miles to the south, Hong Kong was America's lookout into China, swarming with American servicemen, political and economic analysts, journalists, academics and plain spies. And when diplomatic relations were re-opened directly with Mao Zedong's China, and the United States recognized Beijing rather than Taipei to be the legitimate Chinese capital, the colony may have lost some of its strategic value to Washington, but became a favourite place of American investment – the fifty US companies in Hong Kong in 1954 had become 800 by 1985.

Today the Americans officially welcome the impending return of Hong Kong to its motherland, while wondering like everyone else what will become of their money. Their concern nowadays is discreet, and in public at least they are taking no part in the approach to 1997: but their warships still often lie in the harbour of Hong Kong and to those of determinedly romantic tastes, like me, there is still a faint nostalgic stir to be gained from the sight of the Stars and Stripes flying there, as it was flown so long ago by the elegant opium clippers, by Russell and Co.'s chugging paddle-steamers, and even when the moment was propitious by Eli Boggs the pirate.

12

And so to the 98 per cent: first and last of the Hong Kong peoples, the Chinese.

I was walking one day along a track on the island of Lamma, which lies two or three miles to the west of Hong Kong Island, thinking as it happened of the seafood lunch I was planning to enjoy beside the waterfront, and thinking too how much the island reminded me of a semi-tropic Scotland, with its bare heathy hills and salt wind – I was progressing in an amiable distraction when rounding a grove of shrubbery beside the path I came across ten or twenty people dressed all in white hooded cloaks, heads bowed, chanting incantations over an open pit. Aromatic smoke came from the ashes of a fire, and beside it a man in a long black gown and wide hat stood silently, as in trance, holding a wand. It was like a macabre dream, on that sunny morning, and it was partly because I did not wish to intrude, but partly because I was slightly shaken, that I hurried shamefaced by towards my fried garupa with egg plant (the Lamma fish restaurants are among the best in Hong Kong).

Shamefaced because I knew very well that it was no more than a

Chinese funeral I had seen, conducted according to the old Daoist rites, and thus almost as natural a part of the local life as the wind off the sea itself. It is a disagreeable anomaly of Hong Kong that, thanks to the peculiar history of the place, the westerner thinks of the Chinese culture there as esoteric, something to be stared and wondered at, or hastened past, when it is of course the foundation of all else in the territory. The incidence of Europeans in Hong Kong is about one in every hundred persons, and what seems extraordinary to them, is of course overwhelmingly the norm.

It is however, in fairness to the ingenuous foreigner, even by Chinese standards a varied norm. Only rather more than half the population was born in Hong Kong, and even without counting its foreigners the colony is an ethnic hodgepodge. Its original Cantonese, Hakkas, Hoklos and Tankas are still here, the Hakka women still in their wide black-fringed straw hats, the Hoklas and Tankas still living by the sea, if not in their junks and sampans, at least very often in semi-amphibious huts or permanently grounded vessels. But there are also sizeable colonies of people from Shanghai – they used to call Hong Kong's North Point Little Shanghai, so crowded was it with Shanghai-occupied apartment blocks, factories, restaurants, shops and offices – besides scatterings of immigrants from many other parts of China. Unless they happen to speak Putonghua or Mandarin, the central and official Chinese language, none of these peoples share a tongue, though they all share a written script. Some of them have traditionally been enemies; until very recently no self-respecting Cantonese would marry a Hakka, while Hakkas and Hoklas, it was said in the 1930s, 'have little in common save mutual dislike'.

Nor is it anything like a settled populace. Like all else in Hong Kong, it is in a perpetual state of restlessness, and one of the most characteristic of all Hong Kong sights is that of a Chinese family on the move, deep with bags and baskets, with poles over its shoulders and multifarious tied parcels, with bewildered children and sharp-eyed crones, standing patiently in line for train or hovercraft, aircraft or ferry. Every day thousands of Hong Kong residents cross the border into China, by train, by boat or on foot over the border, and every day thousands more return, while there is a perpetual flow of emigrants to places far away – to join relatives in San Francisco, to start restaurants in Manchester.

Even within itself the Chinese community is never static. Nothing stays the same! Not long ago rice was the chief product of the New

Territories, now there is hardly a paddy-field left, and as the face of the land constantly changes, so the people too are on the move, changing their jobs, changing their names, changing the way they live. Tankas and Hoklas forsake crafts of the sea to become factory workers, Hakkas fight their way out of the construction sites, farmers become businessmen and people of all ranks and races move out of squatters' huts into tenements, out of tenements into apartment blocks, out of apartments into villas in the hills. I would guess there is no community in the world in such a state of ceaseless ferment.

But there is nothing remarkable to it. It is the norm.

13

The Chinese population of Hong Kong is young, a quarter of it less than twenty-four years old, and it exudes a curious mixture of fun and earnestness. In the New Town of Yuen Long I once came across a bubble-tent, with windows in it and a guard outside. An odd kind of whistling noise emanated from it, half-way between a hoot and a protracted squeak. I looked through the windows and found it to contain a trampoline, upon which a large number of very small Chinese children were bouncing up and down. They did it not casually, nor wildly either, but with a fierce concentration, as though they were undertaking some important family duty, but at the same time they were doing it with such extreme enjoyment that the peculiar noise I had heard outside turned out to be a kind of constant solidification of their laughter.

I spend a few minutes with my notebook at a Chinese café – not one of the well-known tea-houses, which are sometimes frowsty or aloof, but a common-or-garden, *ad hoc* kind of general café, not very new, not very old, and almost anywhere in Hong Kong outside the expensive centre. I sit in a corner below the television set, thus obliging other customers to show their faces as they peer at the picture above my head, and order a cup of tea as an excuse for observation. Nobody minds. On the contrary, almost everyone greets me with smiles, the men behind the counter with grave smiles, the young women at their bean-curd with comradely smiles, the small girls with smiles that entail a deliberate, stylized narrowing of the eyes, the boys in their school uniforms with very polite, diffident and prefectorial smiles (are they members of their class Triad group?).

Sickly is the music, chirpy the Cantonese dialogue that emerges from above me. Sometimes the whole café breaks into laughter, and nods cheerfully in my direction as though to say that I really am missing something hilarious. Only the man at the corner table, who wears a jerkin inscribed ROUTE SAISONAL GIRL CORRESPONDENCE, and is reading the *Jockey Daily News* in Chinese, takes no notice. The counter is piled high with packets of tissues, a tin of Ovaltine, and a cardboard box marked SHOWA SPAGHETTI which is waiting to be turned into Chinese noodles. A couple of rather sinister youths push through the door, have a dour word with the owner, and go out again. An old, old man, the very image of a sage, creeps in and finds himself a warm place; he has a long crinkled Confucianist beard, very beady eyes, carries a walking stick with an ivory handle and wears a baseball cap.

As time passes the noise increases. The schoolboys break into argument. The small girls play merry games with chopsticks. The women talk very loudly with their mouths full. Outside the door an electric drill starts up, and the café owner reaches over my head to turn up the volume of the TV. It does not matter in the least. Noise is endemic to the Chinese, is part of the texture of their lives, and the now-deafening variety of affairs in the café is a true microcosm of the Chinese city outside. The frank untidiness of the establishment, its free-and-easy way, the feeling that it has not been there very long anyway, and may well have moved somewhere else next time I pass this way, is Chinese Hong Kong all over.

14

Yet there are Chinese families that can claim twenty-seven generations of residence upon the soil of Hong Kong. If the western presence here has been radical in most ways, it has been conservative in others. Elsewhere in China, including even Taiwan, the ancient Daoist, Buddhist, Confucianist and animist ideas have been challenged by three revolutions. The revolution of 1911, which overthrew the monarchy, laid emphasis upon western logic and efficiency, discouraged many an old tradition, and deliberately cut ties of custom that linked the people with the imperial dynasties. The Communist revolution of 1949 suppressed Daoism and most of its manifestations, discredited Confucianism and Buddhism and disintegrated the entire social structure. The Cultural Revolution of the 1960s did its mad best to extinguish everything old and interesting altogether.

The one corner of China which has completely escaped these convulsions is paradoxically Hong Kong. The British promised from the start to honour Chinese custom, and by and large they did. Long after the abolition of the traditional marriage laws in China, for example, the Manchu laws prevailed in Hong Kong, so that into the 1930s married women could not sue for divorce and had no property rights whatever. Until quite recently the colony even allowed Chinese defendants the right to have their cases heard under Chinese customary law, a baffling prospect for young British magistrates who knew nothing whatever about it (though the writer Austin Coates, who was one of them, was quite happy when the Chinese system was invoked, knowing, he said, nothing whatever about English law either).[1] It is true that the predominant official language of Hong Kong has always been English, but this has only left affairs more firmly in the hands of local elders determined to preserve the status quo: even now the New Territories, for all their fantastically burgeoning townships, offer rich fields of research for anthropologists and social historians.

On the surface, and in the tourist brochures, all this means that Chineseness in its most fantastic forms is honoured in the everyday life of this British colony. Hardly a month goes by without the celebration of some effervescent festival. Wild dragon-boat races are rowed, the full moon is honoured with picnics in high places, the spirits of the dead are placated with five-course meals in cemeteries, flotillas of toy ships with candles on them are launched into the sea, immense dragontrains wind their way through shopping streets, and at the Chinese New Year the entire city gives itself up to eating, drinking, parading, lighting lanterns, exploding illegal firecrackers and saying to one another in Chinese in the best Hong Kong convention, 'Respectfully hope you get rich!'

Some of the shrines and memorials of tradition have long since become tourist attractions. Everyone climbs the 500 steps to the Buddhist Temple of Man Fat, above the New Town of Shatin in the New Territories, to see the gilded corpse of the holy monk Yuet Kai; he died in 1965, and now sits bolt upright for ever in a tall glass case, covered in gold leaf and looking alert but blotched with what I assume to be preservative. Then high among the hills of Lantau is the immensely rich and gaudy Buddhist monastery of Po Lin, which is besieged all day by tourist buses. Its large enclosure contains com-

[1] He writes about it in *Myself a Mandarin*, London 1968, and kindly says I may quote him.

puterized offices and a popular vegetarian restaurant, and beside its
gates they are preparing to erect, as I write, the largest of all images of
the Buddha; this is being made in China by the satellite and rocket
manufacturers China Astronomical Industry Scientific and Consul-
tative Corporation, and will soon loom copper-sheathed over the island
as a new wonder of the world.[1]

Since Victorian times every visitor has been taken to the Man Mo
temple ('the Civil and Martial temple'), which is about as old as the
colony itself, and is a dim-lit, smoky, gilded, cluttered and cheerful
distillation of everything one supposes a Chinese temple to be. And for
so long have sightseers frequented the Tang clan's walled village of
Kat Hing Wai, at Kam Tin in the New Territories, that it has become
hardly more than a permanent exhibition. Its inhabitants are descended from Tang Fu-hip, who settled in the district in the eleventh
century, but shoddy souvenirs now fill the shops within its narrow
geometric streets, children demand payment for having their photographs taken, and outside its gates dreadful old women in traditional
costume, smoking traditional pipes, pose beneath umbrellas for profitable effect.

Among all these spectacular public manifestations, let us choose one
to suggest the flavour of them all: the festival of Ta Chiu on the island
of Cheung Chau, which is not only among the most popular of Chinese
celebrations, but a red-letter event on the tourist calendar too, when
half the launches, ferries, sampans and private junks in Hong Kong are
pressed into service to take the gweilos to see the show. It is dedicated
to the Pacification of Departed Spirits, including those of animals, and
in former times during its celebration the people of Cheung Chau
forbore from eating any kind of flesh.[2] The festival happens every year
some time during the fourth moon, but the exact date is variable and
apparently unpredictable, making it an unsatisfactory occasion for the
organizers of package tours.

Cheung Chau is about two and a half miles long from end to end,
and used to be called Dumbell Island because of its shape. There are
no cars on it, and it consists largely of a single cramped and crowded
fishing-town, extending from one shore to the other. For the three days
of Ta Chiu it is entirely given over to the festival, as Rio de Janeiro
gives itself up to Mardi Gras. Chinese operas are performed in the

---

[1] Or, some think, as a declaration of religious freedom after 1997.
[2] Except only the flesh of soulless oysters.

town square, dragon-dancers display themselves, and on the afternoon of the third day a marvellous procession weaves its way through the sinuous streets. There are banner-men, lion-dancers, stick-dancers, percussion bands, all strangely dominated by elaborately dressed and heavily made-up small children, apparently balanced magically on the tops of poles or the handles of axes; stalking stately above the crowds, they are really held up there with wires and struts, but look so permanently immobile, so artificial and so rigid, that they are rather like the monk Yuet Kai in his container.

The grand climax occurs later that evening, in the compound of a foreshore temple. This is dedicated to the Daoist divinity Pak Tai, Supreme Emperor of the Dark Heaven, and is the island's chief institution. Before the Second World War, according to the District Officer of the time, its finances were 'inextricably mixed with those of the market, the ferry, and the electric light station', and it is still the focus of various social, charitable and community associations, and contains wonderful things like swordfish beaks, and ancient swords, and armour, and signed photographs of English royalty.

There at the sea's edge the procession is welcomed by some strange constructions – four fat pillars, half-illuminated in the twilight, sixty feet high and each made entirely of some 5,000 half-pound buns. No wonder Europeans call this the Bun Festival. The towers stand there enigmatic against the night sky, offering sustenance it is supposed to the spirits beyond; but when midnight comes, and a priest has inspected the pillars through a jade monocle to make sure the ghosts have done, young men climb up there and take all the buns down, one by one, like corn coming off the cob, for distribution to the villagers. People keep them in airtight jars, and bits of them soaked in tea or water are said to be remedies for several ailments.

15

Such are the more publicized signs of Chinese tradition in Hong Kong, but in fact no announcements are necessary. It must be obvious to the least sensitive foreign visitor that in this territory we are experiencing the presence of a culture all-pervasive, all-enduring; despite the symbiotic overlap we earlier observed, fundamentally it seems oblivious to history.

In a thousand ways old tastes, habits and techniques resist all challenge. Here in the heartland of the solar-powered calculator, where virtually every household has a television set, and every schoolboy can write a computer programme, the abacus is still a common commercial instrument. Skyscrapers go up in frameworks of bamboo scaffolding. Chinese harmonics easily withstand the assaults of rock and European classical music. The clatter of mah-jong, which the Chinese have been playing in one form or another since the Song dynasty, is still far more common a sound than the ping of electronic games. Side by side with the western calendar the lunar calendar is observed, and everyone in Hong Kong knows what Chinese year it is (1997 will be the Year of the Ox).

After 140 years place-names often resist westernization. To Chinese people Stanley is still Chek Chu, as it was before the British came, Aberdeen is still Hong Kong Tsai, Little Hong Kong, and Mount Davis Road is Moh Sing Ling To, the Hill From Which We Can Touch The Stars. Into our own times the Chinese have called the Governor of Hong Kong Ping Tao, 'Military Chief', and the Botanical Gardens, across the road from his palace, are still known as Ping Tao Fa Yuen, Military Chief's Flower Garden. As for Chinese personal names, they defy all western practice still, since in the course of a lifetime a Hong Kong Chinese may have five or six different aliases – milk name in babyhood, proper name in childhood, school name, class name, business name, marriage name . . .

The Chinese of Hong Kong have a powerful aptitude for belief. They believe in gods and ghosts, signs and auguries, and supernatural faiths of one kind or another permeate every facet of the territory, ranging from sophisticated theological dogma to everyday superstition – the small mirrors so often to be seen hanging outside shops and houses are not there for decoration, but to ward off evil spirits. Half a million Hong Kong Chinese are Christians or Muslims, but many, many more are Daoists, Buddhists or animists, and many pursue an eclectically layered combination of religions – what Peter Fleming once called 'the marzipan effect'.[1] The gods of their pantheon, not so much worshipped as supplicated for favours, are innumerable – monkey gods, sea gods, earth gods, kitchen gods, martial gods, water gods, gods of affluence, of mercy, of happiness, of justice, of long life, of wisdom, of literary aptitude and conversely of wealth. When in 1980 the New Territories village of Fanling held a festival, seventy-eight different divinities were honoured; houses and apartments have private shrines to their own hearth gods, and almost anywhere you may come across the gypsy-like little sanctuary of stones, ribbons, red paper and

---

[1] In *The Siege at Peking*, London 1959.

candle stumps which marks a holy site of animism, with a couple of elderly ladies perhaps fiddling around with joss-sticks, or pulling cabalistic papers out of carrier bags.

Nor are these mere rural archaisms. The most thoroughly urbanized parts of Hong Kong are among the most powerfully religious. Many small Buddhist hermitages, sometimes housing a single holy man, are actually on upper floors of high-rise blocks, and the best-known of the myriad urban temples are as thronged as supermarkets – look in at any time of day, and there will be the caretakers at their dusty desks, surrounded by holy texts and pictures, and before the gaudy altars women will be shaking the *chim*, the box of bamboo fortune-sticks, while incense smokes, bells tinkle and the blackened god-images peer down from their altars. The vivacious temple of Wong Tai Sin, rebuilt in the grand manner in 1973, serves the new residential quarters of eastern Kowloon, and is surrounded by tower-blocks. Used mainly as an oracle for the foretelling of the future, it is a positive powerhouse of the transcendental: bright with colour, attended by arcades of sooth-sayers and charm-sellers, with occasional flute-players too, haunted by beggars with tin cups and conveniently served by an adjacent station of the underground railway. The fortune-sticks that fall from your *chim* are interpreted for you by the soothsayers, and if they recommend a prescription for some ailment, you can get it made up at the temple's own clinic.

Not so long ago one of the hazards of driving in Hong Kong was the belief among elderly Chinese that if they stood close enough to a passing car any evil spirits at their heels would be run over. In 1960, when the Royal Hong Kong Jockey Club suffered a series of calamities, including the death of a jockey, a Buddhist service of exorcism was held for four days and three nights upon the Happy Valley racecourse, led by sixty-eight monks and forty-eight nuns and attended it was reported by 40,000 citizens. The Ratings and Valuations Department, then housed in a former barracks, was also exorcised of ghosts left there since the Japanese occupation; the Press was given a preview of the ceremony. Three times a month childless women make their way to the phallic boulder called Yan Yuen Sek, up a track above Bowen Road in mid-Levels, where against a backdrop of plush apartment blocks, with the harbour beyond and the distant roar of traffic muffled through the trees, they light their joss-sticks, say their prayers and consult their fortunes in the lee of the monolith, which has probably been since neolithic times a symbol of fertility. The airy substances which waver and float above the scene are sometimes fragments of burnt offering, and sometimes dragon-flies.

Hong Kong's mountains and outlying islands are positively impregnated with holy thought and practice. If you fly over the New Territories in a helicopter you will discover that throughout the rough hill country are strewn the omega-shaped enclosures of ancestral graves, all alone in propitious sites, giving the whole massif a suggestion of sacred dedication. The island of Ap Chau is coloquially known as the Jesus island, since it is inhabited entirely by Chinese adherents of the True Jesus Church, and hardly less holy is Lantau.

That all too well-known temple of Po Lin is only one of a dozen retreats strewn across this large, bare and beautiful island, from red-roofed Buddhist monasteries in the flanks of mountain valleys to a rest camp for Christian missionaries high in the hills (the village of Tai O, on the western shore, was reported by the London Missionary Society in 1917 to be 'a stronghold of idolatry'). Proud above the sea at the northern end of the island is the church of the Trappist Monastery, whose community came here from Communist China. Its thirty silent Chinese monks (together, in 1987, with one Englishman) run their estate as a dairy farm, and have for years provided the Hilton Hotel with all its milk. A most homely smell of hay and cow-dung greets the visitor to their ugly buildings, together with the text PAX IN-TRANTIBUS, SALUS EXUENTIBUS – 'Peace to those who enter, health to those who leave'.

And on a plateau in the south, reached only by footpaths, high and exquisitely lonely stands the Buddhist monastery of Tsz Hing. The clanging of its bells, the chanting of its monks at their devotions, floats magically on the wind above the empty grassland all around.

16

Often the old Chinese traditions are formally institutionalized within the structure of this British colony. There are many Buddhist schools, there is a flourishing Confucianist academy, and the Chinese Temple Society administers most of the temples. The charitable body called Tung Wah, founded in the nineteenth century specifically to run a Chinese hospital, became almost a tribune of the people, and is now a complex agency of Chineseness. The Triads themselves are extremely traditional: in the Sun Yee On Triad, for instance, senior officers have ritual names, like Dragon Heads or White Paper Fan, and a functionary called the Incense Master, straight from Manchu China, supervises the whole hocus-pocus of ritual, codes and cryptic signs.

In the New Territories especially ancient conventions are still formally honoured. Ancestral halls may be crumbling and rubbish-strewn, old architecture disappearing, but the heritage is far from abandoned. The native people of the New Territories are officially called indigenes, to distinguish them from immigrants to Hong Kong, and they have long memories. Some 6,000 clan organizations, officially recognized, own and administer ancestral or communal properties. At Tai O the village ferry is still run by the Kai Fong, the traditional residents' association which used to provide the village watchmen too. On Cheung Chau tenants still pay rents to 400 members of the family which owned the island before the British came. The descendants of Lin Tao-yi, a thirteenth-century citizen of Kowloon, are paid a share of the moneys collected at the temple he built on Joss House Bay.

The walled village of Kat Hing Wai may have been degraded into self-display, but near Shatin another example, the Hakka village of Tsang Tai Uk, though run-down and hemmed in by urban development, is recognizably what it always was. Its name means Mansion of the Tsang Family, and it is more like a medieval castle than a village. Within its high square towered walls is a cheek-by-jowl, jam-packed assembly of four parallel brick alleys, very private of feeling, with a neglected temple in the middle. It is strewn with the bicycles, potted plants, dogs, children and outdoor washing machines of domestic life, and seems to form one extended household to this day.

Further north, at the village of Wang Toi Shan, though a main road passes nearby and all the modern domestic conveniences are available, the Tangs still cling to their ancestral rights. They own 60 per cent of the village still, and each male has the legal right to build himself a new house there, perpetuating the clan's hold over its fortunes. Its members live very traditionally, I learned from a Chinese-language television programme in 1986. They are buried as they always were, in ancestrally approved locations. They scorn to educate their daughters, who are expected to marry outside the village to avoid in-breeding, and so are regarded as merely temporary residents. They gamble incessantly, and the men share all the profits of the clan-owned lands. As a young Tang of Wang Toi Shan told the television interviewer, 'We don't have to work here, we just have pleasure. Or we work for three years, rest for five.'

Chinese medicine, pithily summed up by a nineteenth-century British Medical Officer as 'empiricism and quackery', is practised assiduously still in Hong Kong. Many Chinese people distrust western cures and treatment, having far more faith in the efficacy of bear's gall, weasel's liver, and other old stalwarts of the Chinese pharmacopoeia. The herbalist's shop is a common sight of Chinese Hong Kong. Its remedies are meticulously stacked in files and boxes, and the most precious of its specifics, like deer horn or Bezoar, which comes from the stomachs of ruminants, are laid out reverently in the window, sometimes in big glass caskets, sometimes on cushions of cotton wool.

Chinese mortuary practices survive, too. It is customary still to exhume the bones of the dead from their original graves and transfer them to urns; though now that bones decompose less slowly than they used to, I am told, under the influence of antibiotics, they are generally left in their graves for eight years, instead of the traditionally lucky six.

17

Then there is *feng shui*, wind and water, the geometry of place and balance. You can hardly *not* come across *feng shui* in Hong Kong. Its grasp upon the Chinese mind is tenacious, and the annals are full of its influences. James Hayes the historian has given us [1] a letter, written in 1961 to a District Officer, which he describes as a classic statement of *feng shui* fixation. Here it is:

Sir,
The hillside behind my hut is known, in *feng shui* terminology, as the Dragon's Vein, and is therefore of great importance to our villagers.

This fact notwithstanding, an outsider has had the audacity to hire some workmen to dig up the earth there in an attempt to build a house on the site. In so doing he has neither obtained the consent of the village elders nor applied to your Office first for a survey. Thus no sooner had the work started than the villagers' livestock, such as cattle, pigs and dogs, were afflicted with disease and ceased to drink or eat.

Their condition has shown some slight improvement only after I had the holes filled up and after a charm was employed to invoke the gods to drive away the evil spirit.

However, this man has no respect for our native traditions and is planning to tamper with the earth again. As this lawless character is not likely to show the least concern for our safety, would you please send an officer over as soon as possible to prevent him from carrying out these activities.

[1] In *The Rural Communities of Hong Kong*, Hong Kong 1983.

Dr Hayes comments that 'the geomantic quality of the land in question, the adverse effect of the interference with it, the remedy applied, the lawlessness of the offender, are all essential ingredients to a *feng shui* scenario'. Certainly in the past *feng shui*, with its undertones of magic and animism, has proved itself in the colonial context variously constructive and obstructive, comforting and terrifying, grand and petty. On the one hand whole villages were sometimes abandoned because the local *feng shui* had been disturbed, upsetting the cosmic balance, and European miners had to be imported to build the first railway tunnels because Chinese would not risk disturbing the earth-spirits; on the other hand *feng shui* gave to the countryside, in particular, a grace and proportion not entirely obliterated even now. Often it also had rapscallion perspectives. When a ship went ashore at Lantau in 1980 some of the islanders demanded compensation from the Marine Department on the grounds that its violation of the local *feng shui* had caused the otherwise inexplicable deaths of many chickens.

Even today no Hong Kong employer, from the richest bank to the simplest corner store, can afford to ignore the precepts of Wind and Water. Just as the wrong siting of an ancestral grave could affect the fortunes of descendants for ever after, so faulty design in factory or office can antagonize the earth-forces or the spirit world and bring bad luck upon all its workers. The doors of the Mandarin Hotel in Central were placed at an angle to the street to discourage the entry of inimical influences. The fifth chimney of the power station of Aberdeen is said to be there purely for safety's sake – four chimneys would be unlucky because the Chinese world for four sounds like the word for death. *Feng shui* is inescapable in this British trading colony and financial centre: even the two-day tourist is likely to see, mysterious in the windows of antique shops, the dizzily complicated disks and rulers with which the geomancer practises his craft (guarding for instance against any conjunction of the measurement 43 with the measurement $5\frac{3}{8}$, or making sure that the Five Elements, the Ten Stems and the Twelve Branches are auspiciously aligned).

I called once upon an eminent geomancer at his headquarters at Tsuen Wan in the New Territories. He also runs an electronic manufacturing company, and his office was air-conditioned, and contained an aquarium full of extremely valuable carp. Wearing a brilliantly white shirt and striped tie, with a gold pen in his breast pocket, a gold watch and gold-rimmed spectacles, he made his points by tapping his cigarette lighter on his desk, and suggested to me a rather mature computer buff. In fact he was above all a devotee of *feng shui*. It was the first thing of his life, he told me, which he had learnt from an older master as all practitioners must.

True *feng shui* had nothing to do with magic, he said, although in the old China it used to be given an esoteric mystery by magicians in yellow robes. It was a matter of harmony between man and nature, and was concerned with location, with colour, with proportion. As he scribbled some illustrative diagrams in my notebook, and considered the question of whether *feng shui* was an art or a science (a philosophy, he rather thought), he told me that he was never short of geomantic business. Indeed his press cuttings showed him in an honoured place at the recent opening ceremonies of Hong Kong's most spectacular new skyscraper, the headquarters of the Hongkong and Shanghai Bank, to the design of which he had contributed his expertise.

Actually that building, he said in a technical tone of voice, occupied one of the twenty best *feng shui* sites in the whole territory – with its back to mountains, beside flowing ridges, at the very bottom of one spur in a group of seven, on a gentle sloping site, facing the sea. Even so, he had felt obliged to make certain recommendations to improve the good fortune of the place, in particular adjusting the angles of the escalators.

The sophisticated assurance of such men, the unquestioning acceptance of their skills by highly educated Chinese, half-convinces many Europeans, too, that *feng shui* makes sense. As long ago as 1926 Sir Cecil Clementi, the Governor of the day, suggested that it might be regarded in some contexts as 'at least an embryonic form of the town-planning idea', and undeniably the *feng shui* woodlands planted by the ancients are ecologically valuable today. It is hard to know whether the owners of that new skyscraper, when they agreed to shift the escalators, really believed it would be beneficial, or whether they simply wanted to keep their employees happy; but some expatriates certainly employ a geomancer to approve the siting, the architecture or even the furnishing of their new houses, 'just in case' – for they have caught from the Chinese the cheerful if fatalistic attitude that it is worth appeasing all gods, in case one of them exists.

18

If there was ever a time when the Chinese of Hong Kong were truly subject to the foreigner, it has long gone. Numerically so overwhelming, psychologically they have grown only stronger down the years. More

On the frontier, 1980s: *above*: the road along the frontier; *left*: the frontier crossing, Man Kam To

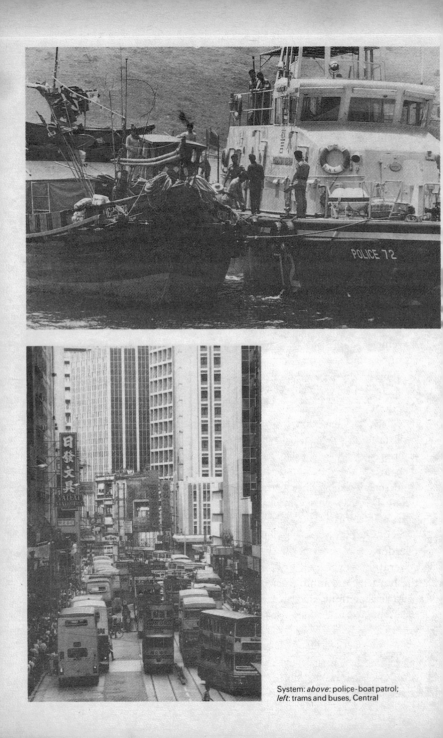

System: *above*: police-boat patrol;
left: trams and buses, Central

than half of them, and that the younger and more virile half, have been born in Hong Kong, and as the British prepare to leave the place already one can sense them dismissing the whole business of colonialism from their minds. They are Chinese first, after all, to whom the existence of this Crown possession has been no more than a fortunate convenience. Whoever their masters are to be in 1997, they will certainly not be Europeans, and I dare say even the most virulently anti-Communist of them, the most sympathetic towards the west, feels a certain satisfaction at the thought of Hong Kong returning to its roots.

We have glimpsed them rich and poor, but their great strength now lies in their young, educated, clever, modern and progressive middle class. This has been brought into existence by the British, during half a century of liberal education, and is unlike anything in China proper. You see its members everywhere. Consider for example this cluster of university students on the upper deck of an out-island ferry – a Saturday-morning ferry, say, taking them for a day's hiking and picnicking somewhere. They are extremely lively, extremely neat, extremely polite and engaging young people. Talking loudly, laughing a lot, with their bright blue rucksacks, their sneakers and their Walkman radios they look thoroughly modern, and if you engage them in conversation you will find that they are liberated in their emotions too. They may seem to think more practically, calculate more exactly than their counterparts in the west. They are still, as a rule, far more devoted to their families. But they are certainly not interested only, as the old Hong Kong canard has it, in money, and they are noticeably not respectful to the old Confucianist ideas of a rigid social order. They are just as idealistic, no more, no less, than young Europeans or Americans, just as concerned with a proper balance of life, between the necessary making of money and enjoyable ways of using it. Some are power-hungry, some drop-outs, some honest plodders, some dreamers. All in all, they are as likeable and normal a generation as you will find anywhere in the world, freed at last from the burdens and inhibitions of the Chinese condition.

At least I think they are. That is how they strike me, whenever I meet them, but history may prove me wrong. 1997 may find these young people returning to ancestral kind after all, or adapting to Communist requirements, for nothing is more flexibly resilient than Chineseness. When a New Town goes up in Hong Kong it feels at first utterly sterile and forbidding. All mass and concrete angles, it looks as though it will desiccate the humanity that comes to live in it, over-whelming ordinary lives by sheer size and functionalism.

But hardly have the first Chinese families moved into their apart-ments, still smelling of paint and cement, than everything changes. Almost overnight, that monolithic cheerlessness is dispelled. The first lines of washing appear, the first advertising signs go up, the first street-stall opens for business, the first restaurant announces its celebratory opening night – and next time you go back, all that cold new place is made real and vivid by the organic energy of Chinese life, its fructifying untidiness, its boisterous lack of privacy, its comforting pandemonium and its inescapable air of purpose.

The British Empire at its most tremendous failed to make much impression upon this down-to-earth genius, and the mass of the Chinese in Hong Kong today are not a jot less Chinese because they live beneath the Union Jack. A surprising number, after 150 years of British rule, still speak no English, and even those who enter the universities are often handicapped by an imperfect command of it.

For myself I find this stoic continuity obscurely comforting, and sometimes sailing not in a Star ferry across the harbour, but in a ramshackle sampan crab-like against the current from one island to the other, to the laboured chugging of diesel engines, and the creaking of timbers – old rubber tyres slung amidships, helmsman, though surrounded by talkative friends and relatives of all ages, ever-attentive in his little wheelhouse above – sometimes I feel I would like to be assimilated into Chineseness myself, and sail these waters under Chinese helmsmanship for ever.

The colonial masters of Hong Kong, though, have not always been so seduced by their subjects' ability to remain themselves. As was said in a querulous way by Sir William Robinson, Governor of Hong Kong in the very heyday of British imperialism, the reluctance of the vast majority of Chinese in Hong Kong to become in the least Anglicized was 'extraordinary, not to say discreditable . . .'

1880s: THE COMPLEAT COLONY

6

THE CHINESE OF HONG KONG MAY HAVE REMAINED unaccountably Chinese, but forty years after its foundation, as the British Empire approached its apogee of power, and Sir William Robinson his Governorship, the colony had become in British eyes The Pearl of the Orient, depicted at the head of its own coat of arms clasped between the paws of a lion rampant. The 1880s were high imperial years. Gordon was in Khartoum, Rhodes was in South Africa, Kipling was in India. The British Army went into action against Boers and Afghans, Sudanese and Burmese, and nations from Nigeria to New Guinea were newly embraced within the Pax Britannica.

In this atmosphere of mounting climax, Hong Kong found its own exotic place as the easternmost of all Her Majesty's dominions. It had greatly changed since our inspection of the 1840s. Wild and raffish no more, it had become in many ways the Compleat Colony, and looked the part perhaps more absolutely than it ever would again. The opening of the Suez Canal in 1869 had brought it closer to the sources of glory; the rising power of Empire illuminated it. To be sure the refulgence was partly illusory, like much else in the imperial show. Hong Kong's economic character had proved disconcertingly volatile, and the treaty port of Shanghai, not British at all, seriously challenged the colony as the most important entrepôt of the China coast. Also several foreign Powers had by now insinuated themselves into Chinese concessions. An explosion of railways in China, connecting other ports with the markets of the interior, seemed to mean that the island off the shore of Guangdong might one day be superseded, and the state of Hong Kong's founding hongs proved the point; Dent's had collapsed in 1867, Russell's had given up in 1879, and even Jardine, Matheson were concentrating their business in Shanghai. As for the Hong Kong Mint, set up in 1866, it had been closed within two years because it lost so much money.

But for the moment Hong Kong was booming – 'we have passed through our bad times', Jardine's taipan told Kipling, 'and come to the fat years.' Two million tons of ocean shipping entered and left its harbour annually, and it no longer felt remote; there were weekly sailings to Europe and Japan, monthly sailings to Australia, bi-weekly sailings to San Francisco (connecting with Pullman Palace Sleeping Cars for New York and New Orleans). There was also telegraphic communication with Britain, so that the Governor no longer made so many of his own decisions. The whole pace of life had been fiercely intensified by new technologies: as a local poet had it.

> Who can now a pleasant hour boast,
> With thirteen steamers daily up the coast –
> Sharebrokers pressing one to sell or buy –
> With telegrams each minute from Shanghai . . .?

Besides, for all those rival concessions Hong Kong was still the only foreign sovereign possession in China, and this gave it a status and a dignity all its own, satisfying to British self-esteem and important it was thought to British prestige. No longer did the colony seem to the British at home a mere barren rock of uncertain reputation, possibly to be abandoned; now they saw it as an exhibition of their splendour in the eastern seas.

'I sometimes imagine Britannia,' wrote a gentle and learned Sinologue, Rev. James Legge, who had come to Hong Kong in the 1840s and stayed there for thirty years, 'standing on the Peak and looking down with an emotion of pride upon the great Babylon which her sons have built.' Certainly Hong Kong no longer looked like a trading post upon the island shore. The Empire was immensely proud of its cities, translations in distant parts of the great commercial cities of Britain itself, and Hong Kong, though scarcely Babylon perhaps, since its total population was no more than 180,000, now stood recognizably in the pattern of Birmingham and Bombay. Since 1860 its limits had included the tip of the Kowloon Peninsula over the harbour, where an observatory upon a hillock, a police station, docks, go-downs and barracks had arisen, and this gave a new completeness and sense of permanence to the ensemble.

By now the few substantial buildings of forty years before had been absorbed into an urban mass. The waterfront was graced with an esplanade, the Praya, reclaimed from the sea, and all along it offices and warehouses stood in parade, each with its house flag flying, white launches on davits at every door and small craft jostling the water-steps. A city hall in French classical style, a handsome clock-tower and the twin-steepled Catholic cathedral gave a touch of romantic variety to the sea-shore silhouette, while up the hill the Anglican cathedral, which had once seemed so alien an intrusion, now looked almost venerably organic. Victoria had filled itself in, from Happy Valley in the east to Kennedy Town in the west, and rose in layers of villas and bungalows up the hills behind. Even the hills themselves had changed, for they had been planted with vast numbers of China pines and fourteen different species of Australian eucalyptus – by 1884, 714,000 new trees in all.

Pedder Wharf, named after the first harbour-master and crowded from dawn to dusk with launches, ships' boats and sampans, was where newcomers went ashore. Immediately they found themselves in the heart of commercial Hong Kong. No longer were its streets precarious with rutted mud and littered with mat-sheds; now they were proper Victorian thoroughfares, gas-lit and paved, such as the British had laid in commercial cities all over their Empire. 'If it were not for the sedan-chairs and palanquins,' wrote Lady (Anna) Brassey, in what was her highest category of commendation, 'one might fancy onself in dear old Gib!' [1] She was not stuck with the sedan-chairs, either, for though the horse had almost vanished from Victoria the black-hooded rickshaw, known colloquially as 'the rick', now made getting about much easier.

Pedder Street, which extended inland from the wharf, was really more a square than a street, and was the focus of business life. At its head stood that clock-tower, 150 feet high; its clock was said to suffer

[1] *A Voyage in the Sunbeam*, London 1878.

'fits of indisposition' owing to the climate, but was illuminated at night anyway, and acted as a beacon for boats coming into the wharf. The street itself was lined with a double row of trees, giving it rather a Mediterranean look. Sedan-chair men waited for their masters in the shade, and on each side were the arcaded premises of merchant houses, attended by Sikh doormen.

Beyond it Queen's Road, which we last saw in so patchy a condition, was now lined east and west with heavy business buildings and shaded here and there by fine banyan trees. A short way along the Praya stood the dignified but peculiar new building of the Hongkong and Shanghai Bank, one façade in totally different style from the other. The City Hall was a few yards beyond, and conveniently to hand was the six-storey Hong Kong Hotel, whose dining room overlooked the harbour, and whose smart white launches met all in-coming mail-steamers.

Gone, in short, was the old waterfront feeling of dubious adventurism; it was through a display of ample, well-established, rather pompous mercantile order that the stranger now entered the colony of Hong Kong.

Most of the appurtenances of modern life – the accessories of Empire – were available to such a newcomer. A Chamber of Commerce would advise him on prospects. Plenty of brokers, agents and insurers would accept his custom. The Post Office would sell him Hong Kong's own postage stamps, of which the 2¢ rose-lake was generally considered the prettiest. He could exchange his money drafts for the paper currency of four different issuing banks, or for the colony's own coinage which had a hole in the middle if of low denomination, a portrait of the monarch and the inscription VICTORIA QUEEN if more valuable.

If he was Anglican, the Bishop of Victoria was said to be famously hospitable. If he was Catholic, the Bishop of Acantho was in residence to bless him, and twenty-six nuns, mostly Italian, would pray for him at the Caine Road convent. If he was Jewish the synagogue on Hollywood Road would welcome his attendance, if a Mason, there were now nine chapters and lodges in the colony.

Six hundred policemen, 18 per cent of them European, 25 per cent Indian, the rest Chinese, were there to assure his safety (their officers could easily be distinguished, because they wore white topees and carried swords). Seventeen consulates were there to help (the German had its own Physician and Shipping Master). Three daily papers in

English would not only give him the news, but entertain him in the facetious style British colonial newspapers preferred.[1]

T. N. Driscoll, tailor by appointment to HIH The Grand Duke Alexis of Russia, would soon make a suit for our newcomer, and Mrs J. Rose Harmon, with the help of her assistants the Misses Ford, Carr and Woodford, would quickly run up a dress for his wife. G. Falconer, who also dealt in Patent Mechanical Fog-Horns, would mend his watch. G. Panati would give him piano lessons. A Portuguese barber, a German gunmaker, French bankers, Jewish brokers, English lawyers were all at his disposal, and you could hardly find, anywhere in the Empire, a more capable physician than Patrick Manson, MD.[2]

Until he found a house for himself he would be perfectly comfortable, we may be sure, at the Hong Kong Hotel: and if he was the sort of person we feel sure he must have been, it would not be long before he was fixed up with membership of the Club.

Several thousand Europeans and Americans now lived in Hong Kong, and everywhere there were signs of a flourishing social life. Isabella Bird characterized it as a life of cliques, boundless hospitality, extravagances, quarrels, gaieties, picnics, balls, regattas, races, dinner-parties, tennis, amateur theatricals, afternoon teas – the classic imperial social arrangement, in fact, 'with all its modes', as Miss Bird coolly added, 'of creating a whirl which passes for pleasure or occupation'.

As always, sport was important. A fine cricket field had been laid out beside the City Hall, with its pavilion on the waterfront; the great game of the season was the annual match against Shanghai, but another popular fixture was Monosyllables v Polysyllables (captains, 1885, D'Aeth and Holworthy). Besides the snipe and duck shooting they had always enjoyed, sportsmen could now go rabbit hunting, Mr Phineas Ryne having lately established a colony of rabbits on Stonecutters Island. There was a Yacht Club, and a Regatta Club, and a golf course at Happy Valley, and although lawn tennis had been invented only in 1873, Hong Kong bungalows already came with their own courts.

[1] When for instance Private George Stevens, asked to pay another three cents for a bunch of carrots, assaulted the shopkeeper, the *Hong Kong Daily News* described the action as 'making up the difference by giving the complainant a cosh over the head with a stick and a blow on the face with a disengaged fist'.
[2] Who was indeed to become world-famous as Sir Patrick Manson (1844–1922), one of the great pioneers of tropical medicine.

In the afternoons ladies would be carried out in their wicker sedan-chairs for promenades, along Kennedy Road to the place they called Scandal Point, after the Simla original, or into the fine new Botanical Gardens; and there they would sit and read in the fresh air, still in their chairs, looking out across the harbour while their chairmen sat gossiping on the grass beside them. In the evening, with luck, there might be a play to see. The amateur dramatic society had long moved out of its mat-shed auditorium into a more solid Theatre Royal within the City Hall; although the actors all used stage names – the taipans objected to the names of company employees appearing in theatre programmes – there was strong competition for parts, and capacity audiences were guaranteed.

As for Happy Valley, by now the racecourse was very different from the easy-going track of the 1840s, and a meet there no longer looked much like a Galway point-to-point. The Jockey Club came into being in 1885, and a picture of the Hong Kong Derby three years later shows a most elegantly ordered scene. The long row of cast-iron grandstands was gay with flags and flowers, the course was lined with flower-pots, and soignée ladies strolled here and there with parasols, escorted by sun-helmeted beaux.

The owner of the winning horse, Leap Year, was listed on the race card as John Peel, Shanghai, but this was only a pseudonym for Jardine, Matheson, who were as interested in horse-racing now as they had been forty years before. 'The Princely Hong' was still an emblematic force in Hong Kong life. It had outlived both its great original rivals, it had outstayed nine or ten governors, younger merchant houses had not discountenanced it, and it had a finger in a multitude of pies. William Keswick its chairman was also chairman of the Hongkong and Shanghai Bank, as well as a Legislative Councillor, while the company largely controlled the Hong Kong dockyards, and as owner of the sugar refinery was the colony's biggest industrial concern.

In this mercantile city it seemed only proper, especially to merchants, that Jardine's town office should be the very first building to greet the new arrival at Pedder Wharf, with its house flag flying and its liveried watchmen at the door. The taipan's No. 1 House was supplemented now by The Mount, a luxurious summer retreat on the Peak, augmenting the merchant-prince effect; and when, at noonday every day, a gun resounded across the colony, it was not a salute from the Royal

Artillery, or the Commodore's flagship, but the customary firing of Jardine's cannon at North Point.

But the 1880s being the years they were, the balance of circumstance had swung towards Government, and there had been in recent years a triumphant embellishment of the colony's official display. For the moment at least the Governor was palpably grander than any taipan. No longer did His Excellency live in rented accommodation, or, so to speak, in rooms above the shop. By the 1880s he had moved into a palace. It was modest perhaps by the standards of the British east, offering nothing like the magnificences of Calcutta or Madras, but it did possess a sovereign consequence unattainable even by the Princely Hong.

It stood on a plateau beside Upper Albert Road, on what used to be called Government Hill, opposite the Botanical Gardens, not far from military headquarters and the Anglican Cathedral, and looking down to the harbour in a posture of unmistakable authority. Every view-picture showed it. It was neo-classical in style, pillared all around, with a flight of ceremonial steps leading steeply down to the garden. It had a stately *porte-cochère* and a handsome pair of guardhouses, and it was lit throughout by gas, a convenience not appreciated by all its residents, who found it exceedingly expensive and not very efficient ('smoke and heat with very little light', thought Sir Richard MacDonnell, complaining to the Colonial Office in 1866 about his annual lighting bill of £500).

Its roof was flat, offering its occupants a quiet retreat in the sunshine and a lovely view over the harbour, and there were five tennis-courts, three grass, two asphalt. Its domestic staff were dressed in long blue gowns and white gaiters, and wore pigtails so long that they reached almost to the ground. When the Governor formally received guests he did so in a pillared hall the height of the house, Hong Kong's equivalent of a Durbar Hall, with a band playing in the garden outside. When he left the building on an official visit he was conveyed out of the grounds, wearing his gorgeously embroidered jacket, white breeches and cocked hat, in a sedan-chair carried at a jog-trot by eight Chinese bearers in red. When he went to sea he travelled, like a Doge, in a twelve-oared official barge.

A constant procession of grandees now passed through Hong Kong, and nearly all experienced the hospitality of Government House. Some of course were grander than others. The sociologist H. J. Lethbridge tells us[1] that even visiting authors could expect to be invited for a chat

[1] *Hong Kong: Stability and Change*, Hong Kong 1978.

with His Excellency, while H M the King of the Sedangs, who turned up wearing a uniform of his own design in 1888, was actually an engaging French adventurer named David de Magrena. But there were real swells too. There were the admirals of the world's fleets, nearly all of whom sent their vessels to Hong Kong at one time or another. There were the royal princes Albert ('Eddy') and George, and foreign potentates more genuine than the King of the Sedangs, and inspecting politicians from Westminster, and eminent financiers, and Ulysses S. Grant, and George Curzon the future Viceroy of India, who arrived in time for Queen Victoria's Golden Jubilee celebrations, during which three men were killed by celebratory salutes and two by firework displays – 'No Englishman can land in Hong Kong,' wrote Curzon none the less, 'without feeling a thrill of pride for his nationality. Here is the furthermost link in that chain of fortresses which from Spain to China girdles half the globe . . .'

Beneath this lordly aegis Hong Kong was far more structured than it had been in its pioneering days. The colonial statutes book had grown apace, and hardly a week went by without some new regulation in the Government Gazette. There was the Preservation of Wild Birds and Game Ordinance, the Child Adoption and Domestic Servitude Ordinance, the Married Women's Disposition of Property Ordinance, and there were decrees about the siting of Chinese cemeteries, and orders about the treatment in prison of First Class Misdemeanants (they were to be allowed their own food, plus half a pint of wine and a pint of malt liquor every twenty-four hours). Rickshaws were regulated, hawkers were regulated, even brothels were officially licensed now.

Calmness, aloofness of authority was the Empire's criterion, and as if to give physical expression to the ideal, Hong Kong was now equipped with its own exclusive hill station. A hill station was essential to your compleat colony. In India the archetypes had been built on high ridges of the Himalayas, or in the rolling Nilgiri hills, but less majestic possessions also had their examples. In Malaya there were the Cameron Highlands, in Ceylon there was Nuwara Eliya, and most pertinently another small island colony of the east, Penang off the coast of Malaya, possessed a hill station on the very doorstep of its town, with a bungalow for the Governor on top.

Victoria, Hong Kong, also had a mountain at its back door, and successive Governors had toyed with the idea of creating a hill station on the Peak. Despite the thick mists and the pervasive damp, it would provide healthy relief from the humidity down below, in summer the temperatures up there being five or six degrees lower than the temperatures at sea-level. It would also offer Europeans a retreat from the pushing Chinese community with its queer tastes and unhygienic habits – the hill station always was an epitome of imperial separateness.

The Government had made a start in 1867 by acquiring a former Army sanitarium, 1,700 feet up, and renaming it Mountain Lodge as a summer resort for the Governor himself. Though not all incumbents made much use of the place, and some of them intensely disliked it ('a damp and gloomy prison', Sir William Des Voeux called it) nevertheless it had become the nucleus of a settlement. Paths had been cut up the mountainside, the white speckles of villas appeared more frequently in the water-colours of each successive year, and in 1887 one of those ordinances reserved the whole of the Peak district for European residence (Chinese were not excluded in so many words, but were effectively kept out by a combination of building regulations and innuendo).

Until then one went up the Peak on foot or on pony, by camel perhaps if you were Mr Belilios, or most probably by sedan-chair, carried up the winding narrow tracks by teams of two or four Chinese chairmen – every Peak house had its chair-shed, the Hong Kong equivalent of a coach-house. The arrival of so many prosperous new householders, though, and the Promulgation of the Peak Residence Ordinance, led to the opening in 1888 of the steam-powered High Level Tramway, the first cable railway in all Asia and one of the steepest in the world.

This became one of the sights of Hong Kong. A tram left every quarter of an hour, the ride took eight minutes, and at its steepest point the gradient was one in two. It was a spectacular demonstration of British technique, for everything was made in England, put together by Scottish engineers, and run by British employees – drivers, brakesmen, conductors and all. In those days the Peak tram ran from its lower terminal near St John's Cathedral almost entirely through undeveloped hillside, and from far below in the harbour people could see its unwavering line precipitous up the mountain, and the shapes of its trams crawling so daringly up and down – an image of imperial accomplishment in the benighted East.

Beside the upper terminal stood the Peak Hotel, which soon became one of the colony's chief social centres. Unassuming enough at first, and intended chiefly as a way-station on the way to the summit, it had been amply extended, and people went there now for tea and dinner in the cool evening. Valetudinarians retired there, and there were summer balls and dances. So, with the Governor in his lodge, the rich Europeans in their villas (Cloudlands, The Eyrie, Tor Crest, Strawberry Hill), an Anglican chapel-at-ease for Sunday service, the Peak Club for bridge and gossip, a police station for security, the trams bravely trundling up and down, cucumber sandwiches at the hotel and the natives well out of sight, up there among the China mists of Victoria Peak the colonial aesthetic was fulfilled.

Far below, very early every morning, eleven filthy junks tied up at the Praya, and were filled to the gunwales with human excreta, tipped out of tubs by smeared coolies. Brown and stinking these nightmare craft lurched away through the harbour shipping and made their way to Guangzhou, where the colonial night-soil was sold as manure. They were instruments of private enterprise in the classic Hong Kong kind, for the public lavatories of the colony were run by private contractors, who first charged for shitting, and then sold the shit; but they were also a reminder of the squalor that still, despite first appearances, defied all colonial improvement.

Hong Kong's Chinatown, said the British traveller Henry Norman,[1] was 'probably about as insanitary as any place in the globe under civilized rule'. Those public lavatories, for example, were uniformly nauseating, while most Chinese households drained their effluence into open cesspools – if it was drained at all, for much of it, too, was bought for re-sale by freelance scavengers. Living conditions in the poor quarters were fearful. An officially commissioned report in 1882 – in effect the first Hong Kong social survey – showed that Chinese houses were generally divided by partitions into many cabins, each a dwelling about ten feet square. In one row of eight such houses 428 people were living. Hardly any houses had running water (and water from public fountains was available only in the small hours of the morning). Many had no chimneys, the smoke from their fires issuing from the windows, and in many pigs lived among the humans upstairs as well as down.

[1] *The Peoples and Politics of the Far East*, London 1895.

The smells were terrible, the dangers all too obvious. The author of the report, an engineer named Osbert Chadwick, warned that one day it would all erupt into frightful epidemic, and he was right – in the next decade bubonic plague fell upon Hong Kong, killing more than 2,500 people, nearly all of them Chinese but including the Governor's wife, and forcing scores of thousands to flee the colony. But even without the plague, in 1882 the mean life expectancy was eighteen years and four months; if you survived to the age of twenty, you could expect only another twenty-three years of life.

Directly, of course, most of these horrors affected only the Chinese community, which now numbered at least 150,000, and contributed virtually the whole of the colony's proletariat. Even in the most bigoted eyes, this was no longer a community entirely of riff-raff. Though it included all those slum-dwellers, and some 29,000 boat-people, it included too many wealthy businessmen, shipowners, agents and compradors. It was said that 90 per cent of the colony's revenue was contributed by Chinese; in 1885 eighty-three British property-owners were rich enough to pay property tax, 647 Chinese, and seventeen Chinese were among the eighteen richest of all (the eighteenth was Jardine, Matheson). There were many scoundrels still, but many Chinese professional men and craftsmen worked in the colony now. Lamqua the Handsome Face Painter had been succeeded by six professional portraitists, four daily newspapers were printed in Chinese, and the Tung Wah hospital was already active. In 1884 there were seven Chinese Justices of the Peace, and a barrister of Lincoln's Inn named Ng Choy had been appointed the first Chinese member of the Legislative Council.

Nevertheless European prejudice against all things Chinese remained incorrigible, in matters legal as in social attitudes. Racial segregation was as absolute as the Europeans could make it. Chinese were not only barred from the Peak, they were also kept out of most central residential districts, and they were freely insulted by the cruder of the European colonists. 'You cannot be two minutes in a Hong Kong street', wrote Isabella Bird, 'without seeing Europeans striking coolies with their canes or umbrellas.' There was no chance, of course, of even the most distinguished Chinese joining the Hong Kong Club; Major-General Edward Donovan, commanding the garrison in 1880, said that Chinese people gave 'ocular, auricular and nasal demonstration how unfitted they were for the neighbourhood of Europeans'.

The Chinese were often arrogant too, and could certainly be

annoying. Their concern for hygiene was vestigial, and to European ears the noise they made was indescribably awful – it was estimated that if every Chinese street-hawker uttered his street cry only once a minute, that would amount to a million raucous cries a day. Chinese could also be frightening. Violent crime was common still among them, and the local Triads were now said to have enrolled 15,000 members. If you took a sampan to dine aboard a ship in harbour, the pier-side constable took a note of its number, the sampan people having a habit of cutting their passengers' throats, robbing them and throwing them overboard. Nor had the British forgotten the affair of the poisoned loaves. Xenophobia periodically flared up into violence in China itself, and the possibility of a rising was never entirely absent from European minds in Hong Kong. Kowloon City, just across the border, was notoriously full of toughs, and Henry Norman made his readers' flesh crawl with the reminder that in a few hours 20,000 more could easily come down from Guangzhou.

Thus though the merchant community depended upon Chinese compradors, clerks and agents, and frequently liked them as individuals, distrust of the Chinese as a race seemed ineradicable; an element of fear and resentment, compounded by racial bigotry and reinforced by horrible social contrast, lay behind the grand imperial appearances of Hong Kong.

It was the ethnic injustices that chiefly offended the most remarkable Governor of the period, Sir John Pope-Hennessy, who came to the colony from the Windward Islands in 1877, and left in 1882, pursued by furious controversy, to be Governor of Mauritius. We may catch something of his personality from a picture taken in 1881, on the occasion of a visit to Hong Kong by King Kalakaua of Hawaii.[1] Having snatched this recondite monarch from the care of Jardine, Matheson, who represented his kingdom on the island, Pope-Hennessy entertained him handsomely, and sat with him in a garden somewhere for an informal celebratory photograph.

Framing the picture are the European worthies of Hong Kong, British and foreign, official and unofficial, stiff and self-conscious in

[1] Who was making a royal progress around the world before going home to crown himself at his very elaborate Coronation. Aged forty-five (he died in 1891), he was a hot poker player, revived the *hula* dance in Hawaii and wrote his own national anthem.

their whiskers, bowler hats, topees and cravats. In the front row, centre, sits the King, bewhiskered himself, wearing a straw boater and thickly suited. And beside him sits His Excellency the Governor, looking something like an Irish bookie, and something like Isambard Brunel the engineer, and a little like the Mad Hatter. He is very small, perky-looking, beardless with a beaky Roman nose, and he sits in an attitude of almost comical concentration, one hand holding a cane, legs elegantly crossed. On his head he wears a very tall pale-coloured top hat, tilted eccentrically over his eyes like the hat of a tipsy man-about-town, or an entertainer about to begin a soft-shoe shuffle; and all in all he projects a persona so sharp, so ludicrous, but yet so fascinating that the eye slides immediately over all those notables, over the King of the Sandwich Islands himself, to alight upon his peculiar presence.

He was an Irishman, and despite his profession a born rebel. Wherever he went in the colonial service he antagonized British settlers with his liberal views, especially on race, and infuriated the Colonial Office with his high-handed and often preposterous attitudes. His reputation had preceded him to Hong Kong, and a song in the colony's Christmas pantomime, just before he arrived, hoped the coming year would be

> Free from disasters, typhoons and tornados,
> Or 'rows' like they had in Barbados . . .

In the event from start to finish of his Hong Kong governorate Pope-Hennessy was never without some flaming squabble on his hands. He upset his own subordinates as readily as he infuriated the business community, and could seldom resist a gibe. Even his honoured guests might feel the sting of him: even in his speech of farewell to King Kalakaua he made an unfortunate joke about the 'trifling incidents' which had in the past damaged relations between Hawaii and Great Britain, 'such as the killing of Captain Cook by His Majesty's pre-decessors . . .'

This strange but compelling administrator had come to Hong Kong with a beautiful young wife and a baby, and had instantly upset the business community by his partiality towards the Chinese. He was forgiving to Chinese criminals, advocated better education for Chinese children, and even tolerated the Chinese practice of *mui tsai*, the sale of young girls into domestic servitude. He outraged loyalists by proposing to call the new astronomical observatory not after Queen Victoria, but after the Qing Emperor Kang Xi, who had built one in Beijing. He arranged full British nationality for eminent Chinese residents, he resisted racial segregation in the central town districts, he insisted that Chinese should have an equal right with Europeans to use the City Hall museum and library. It was he who appointed Ng Choy to the Legislative Council.

But it needed tact and understanding to lead the British community into more enlightened attitudes, and nobody could be less fitted for such a task than pesky Sir John. He had a genius for rubbing people up the wrong way, and unfortunately his idealism was hardly matched by his ability. He would accept no advice. He lost papers. He failed to answer letters. He quarrelled with the Colonial Secretary, because he insisted on handling everything himself, with the headmaster of the Central School, because he insisted on interfering with the educational processes, with the Registrar-General, whom he accused of immoral practices, with the Harbour-Master, whom he charged with dereliction of duty, with General Donovan, whose rival dinner-party in celebration of the Queen's Birthday he forbade (there being only one band available), with the taipan of Jardine, Matheson about almost everything, and more or less as a matter of principle with virtually the entire British commercial community, who all hated him, and whom he thoroughly detested in return. To cap everything, in 1881 Sir John Pope-Hennessy attacked with an umbrella, in a public place, the leader of the Hong Kong bar, whom he claimed to have caught *in flagrante delicto* showing a book of indecent engravings to Lady Pope-Hennessy.

So he achieved little in the end, and failed to make Europeans and Chinese much better friends: even the promising Ng Choy presently left Hong Kong for China, changing his name to Wu Ting Fang and becoming Chinese Ambassador to the United States. At the same time Pope-Hennessy compounded the old enmity between officials and un-officials. When the irrepressible Governor left Hong Kong in 1882, on his way to create havoc in the Indian Ocean, he was given many presents by the Chinese community, assured that he 'embodied the mind of heaven and earth', and awarded (at least by his own account) the sobriquet Number One Good Friend; but few Europeans came down to the wharf to see him off.

Out at sea the ships perpetually lay. This was a sea-Empire, those were the years of Rule Britannia, and Hong Kong's imperial status was best exemplified by the spectacle of its harbour.

The China trade had not proved quite so lucrative as the merchants hoped, but Hong Kong had become an entrepôt serving a wider region, and it was primarily as a place of shipping that it was famous – after London and Liverpool, the Empire's third port. Opium (its export to China now legal), sugar, flour, salt, earthenware, oil, amber, cotton goods, sandalwood, ivory, betels, vegetables and grains passed endlessly through the colony's go-downs, and the papers were full of ship arrivals and passenger lists – the Rev Osborne Chestnutt, M A from Liverpool, Misses Whiteworth and Button from Shanghai . . . At any one time there were likely to be at least 1,000 seamen ashore in Hong Kong; it had become one of the most familiar of all sailor-towns, abounding with seamen's boarding-houses and brothels, where merchant seamen (merchant Johns) got into fine old brawls with Royal Navy men (Johnny-haul-tauts), and well-loved grog-shops beckoned:

> We'll go down to Mother Hackett's,
> And we'll pawn our monkey-jackets,
> And we'll have another drink before the boat goes off . . .[1]

No wonder Press announcements warned that ships' captains and agents were not responsible for debts incurred by their crews in port.

Any Briton would be gratified to see the majestic variety of craft that now frequented the Crown Colony of Hong Kong. Centre-stage was the Royal Navy's Receiving Ship, the massive old black-and-white troopship *Victor Emmanuel*. Hugely flagged and covered with white roofing, which made her look like an immense elongated oyster, she lay in the harbour as the Commodore's headquarters, with her paddle dispatch boat, HMS *Vigilant*, usually alongside. She had been there since 1874, and was now one of the best-known vessels in the world. Every visiting admiral was entertained in her wardroom, and it was her guns that saluted the arrival of visiting warships (also the Queen's birthday, the anniversary of Her Majesty's accession, the anniversary of Her Majesty's coronation, United States' Independence Day, and the birthdays of the Prince of Wales, the King of Spain and the late George Washington).

In the naval anchorages around the *Victor Emmanuel* were sure to be other warships of the British China Squadron: the steam gunboats

---

[1] Quoted in *Sailortown*, by Stan Hugill, London 1967.

Firebrand or *Flying Fish*, *Linnet* or *Swift*, or perhaps the 6,000-ton ironclad *Iron Duke*, which was rigged as a three-masted barque but had a lumpish funnel abaft the foremast, and was chiefly famous for having rammed her sister ship *Vanguard* in 1875. Wandering ships of the far-flung fleet might sail in from Trincomalee, from Singapore, from Sydney; often foreign warships came too, and were ceremonially welcomed by the *Victor Emmanuel* whatever the current state of diplomatic relations.

By now there were as many steamships as sailing ships out there, with a Conradian variety of coastal freighters, British, German, Japanese (but mostly with British officers). There was an endless shifting mosaic of Chinese craft, 52,000 a year even in those days, fishing-boats from the outer islands, harbour sampans, great ocean-going junks with high poops and ribbed sails. There was a constant scurry of steam launches: many were privately owned – to possess a steam launch was already a sign of status in Hong Kong – many more flew the flags of the hongs, or of foreign consuls, or of hotels. There were the neat white paddle-steamers, like pleasure-boats on lakes, which maintained the ferry services to Macao and Guangzhou, and which the Chinese picturesquely called 'outside-walkees'.

Grandest of all were the big ocean liners which now made Hong Kong one of their regular ports of call: Messageries Maritime ships from Marseilles and Indo-China, Pacific Mail ships from Japan and San Francisco, and pre-eminently the ships of the Peninsular and Oriental Steam Navigation Company, at the last extremity of the all-red route from England – the liners of the P. & O., Kipling's Exiles' Line, which were part of the very ethos of Empire.

Coming as they did to Hong Kong past the Rock of Gibraltar itself, through desert sands of Egypt and phosphorescent Indian seas, they lay there under their sun-awnings as a reminder to every resident of Hong Kong, every visitor too, that though the sun might set over the hills of China, it never set upon Queen Victoria's Empire. One might doubt, said Des Voeux, leaving the colony at the end of the decade, whether any other spot on earth was 'more likely to excite, or much more fully justify, pride in the name of Englishman'.

7

MEANS OF SUPPORT

I

THE SHIPS ARE STILL COMING. ONE AFTER THE OTHER
they loom out of the West Lamma Channel. In the distance they
look no more than shimmery hulks, shapeless and intangible, but slowly
they resolve themselves, as they pass Lamma on the starboard side,
Cheung Chau on the port, into the huge ungainly forms of container
vessels, like floating warehouses, their decks piled so high with grey
boxes that their bridges are almost hidden. All through the day they
slide by, much faster than you expect and almost silently, a few crew
members hanging over their rails, the Chinese pilot just to be glimpsed
in the wheelhouse, the flag of Japan, or Taiwan, or Korea, or Panama,
scarcely stirring in the clammy breeze over their sterns. As long as the
Chinese have been in Hong Kong, so have the ships; the first purpose
of Hong Kong island was fishing, and for many centuries deep-sea
sailors have known about the shelter of its harbour.

It is the only deep-water harbour between Singapore and Shanghai,
and is by common consent one of the most spectacular sights on earth.
Nowadays it presents probably the greatest concentration of merchant
shipping to be seen anywhere, and since most of the ocean-going ships
lie at buoys in mid-channel, and are thus spread out across the water

for seven or eight miles, it is like a stupendous marine exhibition, through which a multitude of smaller craft, now as always, weaves, plods, circles, skims, loiters, swooshes or diffidently wavers.

When the early foreign merchants spoke of Hong Kong, they generally meant not the island, but the anchorage on its southern side, in the lee of Lamma. There are pictures of Hong Kong before the British acquired it which show this haven already crowded with foreign shipping, opium clippers and China-coast traders waiting for tides or monsoon winds, sheltering from bad weather, exchanging commercial information or picking up water from the waterfall at Pokfulam.[1] Captain Elliot at first intended to make his original settlement on the island's south shore but in the event it was the harbour to the north that became the port of Hong Kong. A strait really, through which the traffic from Guangzhou had always passed towards the more northern Chinese ports, it was sheltered by hills on both sides, and especially after the British had acquired the tip of Kowloon on its northern shore, was easy to defend from sea-attack.

The first British official appointment in Hong Kong was that of Harbour-Master, and the port has always been an allegory of order in chaos. It sometimes seems impossible that so many ships, of so many different flags, so many categories, can safely move in and out of such a jam-packed waterway; for some years the capsized and burnt-out hulk of the largest of all liners, the *Queen Elizabeth*, lay off Stonecutters Island, and it used to greet every ship entering from the west like a *memento mori* to navigators.[2] In earlier times the traffic looked even more uncontrollable. In the last chapter we surveyed the harbour through the proud eyes of the High Victorians, and recognized only its majesty, but actually in photographs of that time it can appear almost anarchic. Quite apart from the tumult of junks, sampans, ferry-boats and launches, the big ships appear to be in a state of confusion, facing this way and that, some steaming cross-channel, some making for the open sea, some apparently sinking with the weight of the lighters moored at their flanks, or about to collide with that queer old hulk in the middle of them, the *Victor Emmanuel*.

But if there was one thing the imperial British knew how to do, it was to organize a port, and there was no disorder really. In those days

[1] Which still flows, by the way, though in reduced circumstances, beside a pleasure park at Waterfall Bay.
[2] To insurers, too. Bought by Chinese owners for conversion into a floating university, the ship was burnt out in ill-explained circumstances.

the vast majority of the ocean ships out there were British, their masters well understanding the system, and anyway the whole idiom of the harbour was familiar to mariners in a period when everything to do with the eastern seas was dominated by British practice. You sailed your ship from Port Said to Aden, from Aden to Bombay, from Bombay to Penang or Singapore, from Singapore on to Hong Kong, and everywhere there were British charts to guide you, British pilots to see you into port, British harbour-masters to accommodate you, British agents to reprovision your ship, British shipwrights to make your repairs, and ships of the Royal Navy, swinging at their anchors in the roadsteads, to protect you on your way. Hong Kong was the last link in a familiar and well-tried chain.

The harbour-master's original office was a pretty pillared villa with a signal mast in front. Today his officials are housed, as you might guess, in electronically state-of-the-art control-rooms on top of a waterfront high-rise block, and are linked by radio with a series of harbour signal-stations. Their charge, though, has not much changed. Much of the port's tonnage is now handled at the container complex at Kwai Chung in the New Territories, the busiest in the world, and there are visionary plans to create another container terminal on an artificial island off Lantau; nevertheless most of the ships must still be loaded and unloaded at the mooring buoys, as they have been since the day of the clippers. The last P. & O. passenger liner, *Chitral*, 13,800 tons, set sail on the long voyage home in 1969; but the big cruise ships still berth at the Ocean Terminal at Kowloon, flying their streamers in the old style as they leave festively for Kobe or Shanghai. Yesterday's high-funnelled Liverpool freighters are today's Panamanian-registered container ships. Even the old Receiving Ship survives, in petrified form, as the Royal Navy shore establishment HMS *Tamar*, and still in the narrows the warships often lie.

The Port Authority which runs it all is like a Ministry of Shipping for this City-State, and its rules are as strict as were Lieutenant Pedder's at the beginning. Every ship over 1,000 tons must have a pilot. Every sampan must be licensed. No tanker may pass through the harbour, and ships using the eastern entrance, the Lei Yue Mun Channel, must report their proposed time of arrival to the minute, to allow coordination with take-offs from the nearby Kai Tak runway. The Authority has the power to license and inspect ships, too, but Hong Kong being Hong Kong, it has an incomplete hold upon the territory's own merchant fleet. By ownership this is the third largest in the world, after the Japanese and the Greek, but it flies many flags; of its 1,281 ships in 1986, only 188 flew the Hong Kong ensign, the others being registered in Argentina, the Bahamas, Denmark, Gabon, Honduras, Liberia, the Netherlands, Panama, St Vincent, Singapore, Taiwan, the United Kingdom and Vanuatu.[1]

Once a week the *South China Morning Post* publishes a Trade and Transport Supplement, ten pages long, and here at random are a few items from an issue I have before me. The Hanyin Container Line is offering a new all-water service to Long Beach, Savannah and New York City, Lloyd Triestino is accepting cargoes for Yugoslavia and South Germany. The Atlas Line offers a service direct to Chittagong, the Traverway Maritime Line sails to Famagusta, the United Arab Shipping Line is closing for Kuwait and Dubai. *River Ngada* is accepting cargoes for Monrovia. *Ming Energy* is loading for Jeddah and Le Havre. *Bold Eagle* sails for Felixstowe tomorrow. Cargoes for Kabul are being accepted by the Trans-Siberian Container Line. A Zim container ship leaves shortly for Eilat and Venice, and Burma Fire Star Shipping is loading for Rangoon.

The whole world indeed is loading in Hong Kong – on an average day there are 140 ocean-going ships in port, and during 1986 they came from sixty-eight countries. Seeing them moored, bunkered, provisioned, stacked and insured, arranging their freight rates, paying their crews, remains the territory's most obvious means of support.

2

Sometimes on the promenade outside the Regent Hotel, on the Kowloon waterfront, a virtuoso line fisherman practises his craft. So brilliantly sharpened are his instincts and so quick is his eye, with such a fierce exact intensity does he cast his hooks into the shadow of the shoal below, all the while glaring ferociously into the water as if he can see into its darkest depths, that a little crowd always assembles around him to watch the performance, and even rival fishermen sometimes abandon their own pitches to observe his technique.

I think of him as a living logo, because fishing was the first of all Hong Kong trades, and thousands of its residents live by their nets. This is the largest fishing-port in East Asia, and you cannot be long in Hong Kong without seeing a fishing-boat sail off to sea, whether it be a

[1] Though the one ship registered in Vanuatu, being of 48,000 tons deadweight, was far too big ever to have docked there.

high-pooped junk all black with age, or one of the blunt-nosed trawlers that always suggest to me sea-going bull-terriers, or possibly vintage Saabs. Off it trundles to its fishing-grounds with a dour kind of resolution, its engines thumping heavily, its crew working away unsmiling on its decks, and far out at sea you may later see it, among its scattered colleagues of the fleet, tossing and rolling in a web of nets as though it has been fishing there for ever. And taking the early-morning ferry yourself to the fishing island of Tap Mun, in the north-east of the archipelago, as the ship's cook warms up your canned breakfast noodles behind a canvas windbreak in the stern, and the fishermen on their passing sampans huddle themselves in hoods, scarves and anoraks against the dank – sailing on a winter morning out to Tap Mun, its houses battened down among the waters of Mirs Bay in a miasma of drizzle and dried fish, is a reminder that Hong Kong shares this sea-industry with peoples far, far up the coast of China, away beyond the Tropic of Cancer to the Yellow Sea and Manchuria.

Then nothing in all Hong Kong seems more permanent than one of its traditional junk-building yards, which sometimes build their craft in much the same way, to virtually the same designs, as they were built when the colony was young. One such yard stands on Cheung Chau, not far from the Pak Tai temple, and is a delight to visit – its craftsmen never mind your wandering around the slipyard, and generally offer the ultimate courtesy, indeed, of taking no notice of you at all. There is a fine smell of wood and varnish in the yard, a whine of saws sometimes, a flash of oxyacetylene from the dark workshed, in whose doorway a noble retriever often stands half in, half out of the sunshine. Let us watch now, as a junk is winched out of the water to have its hull cleaned.

On the deck of the vessel the whole junk family is assembled, as for holiday, with the washing hanging on its line behind; grandmother in black trousers sitting in a wicker chair, mother in a white silk blouse, two or three excited children crowded in the prow as the chains are attached and the elderly diesel engine beside the workshops begins its slow haul. It is a long job, as the boat is winched inch by inch from the water, but nobody's attention flags. Grandmother, mother, all three children hardly take their eyes off the chain, while the men of the junk crew, leaning over the gunwale with long poles, gently prod the boat in the right direction.

The yardmaster is on the slip, controlling everything with blasts of his whistle, and a couple of workers are poised in boats alongside, waiting to push chocks under the hull as it emerges slowly from the water. Watchfully the winchman waits, ready to ease his chugging engine at a whistle-blast. Earnestly, like mathematicians, the two men in the water calculate the right moment to push another chock in. Minute by minute, whistle by whistle, the craft is eased meticulously out of the water, until at last it is high on its chocks with all barnacles revealed, and from dog to grandmother everyone relaxes. The yard-master blows a final liberating blast and allows himself a single glance, almost a showman's glance, at the solitary European watcher by the workshop door.

A maritime tradition more radically sustained is that of the Macao ferry, which has been running in one kind or another since the colony was founded. The proximity of Portuguese Macao, neutral in time of war, jolly with food, wine and gambling halls in peace, has always been an inescapable fact of Hong Kong life. Sometimes it has been politically convenient to go there, sometimes it has been econ-omically handy. Villains have fled to refuge, unmarried couples have found solace, escaped prisoners have been succoured, and in the early years of Hong Kong rich merchants still possessed pleasure-houses in Macao, as they had in the day of the Guangzhou hongs. Even during the Second World War the Macao ferries still sailed. As we have seen, they have been in their time oared galleys and paddle-steamers, and large conventional ferry-ships still make the run; nowa-days though most people go to Macao in more startling kinds of vessel.

The ferry-station is startling enough. Part of a twin-towered Cen-tral complex which also contains a hotel, a shopping centre and the port's main control tower, it is more like an airport than a dock. Visual display screens tell you the times of sailings, when the next craft is boarding, the number of your departure gate. Along air-con-ditioned corridors the passengers make their way, most of them in-congruously clutching just the same shapeless packages they would have carried aboard the steamers a century ago, until crossing a glass-enclosed walkway they see their vessels waiting at the slips below.

Jet-foils or hovercraft, they are hardly like ships at all, but more like fantasies of adventure fiction, waiting there in their cavernous docks – themselves like submarine pens, or contemporary versions of Hong Kong's old pirate lairs. It is with a futuristic roar that today's passengers for Macao are carried in a furious rush to sea.

3

In a small Chinese shop on Cheung Chau I once bought myself a packet of candies made in Athens, and even as I opened it I marvelled at the chain of logistics that had brought it from the shadow of the Acropolis to be chewed by me on the corner of Tung Wan road. One can hardly name a commodity that does not pass through the mill of Hong Kong. Some things, like my Attic sweets, are Hong Kong's own imports coming to be consumed, others are Hong Kong's manufactured exports going out, but many are simply in transit, from one country to another, pausing only to be serviced by Hong Kong's expertise.

This, the re-export trade, was the original economic purpose of the colony. Hong Kong was a clearing house through which Indian and European goods could pass conveniently into China, and all the produce of China, including its emigrants, could be processed on its way to the rest of the world. The territory still fulfils that function, but now it offers services of altogether other kinds. Sometimes it acts as a back door to China; for example, since neither South Korea nor Taiwan maintains relations with Beijing, they send their exports to China through Hong Kong. Often its activities have nothing to do with China at all; many transactions between third parties, legitimate or clandestine, can be better achieved in Hong Kong than anywhere else in the east, so experienced and worldly-wise is this free port, and so dedicated to the principle that the customer comes first.

Hong Kong's economy has been described as 'a transformation economy', accepting things, changing them in one way or another, passing them on. This applies even to commodities like money, stocks and shares, so that far more complicated service industries now augment the port's original agents and chandlers. The colony is claimed to be the world's third-busiest financial centre, with its chief offices around the punch-drunk relics of Statue Square. More than 140 different commercial banks, from many countries, now have offices there, together with countless merchant banks, insurance companies, design firms, public-relations agencies, advertising people, accountants and lawyers specializing in trade and finance. The Hong Kong Futures Exchange is internationally important, and so is the Chinese Gold and Silver Exchange. Hong Kong having no exchange controls, the foreign-exchange market is served by a cosmopolitan multitude of currency dealers.

Central to it all is the Hong Kong Stock Exchange, a post in the line of speculation that connects Tokyo with London and New York. This was symbolically unified in 1986 in one of the more interesting new office complexes, Exchange Square in Central, which was designed by the Swiss architect Remo Riva, and stands silvery and elegant beside the water. The utterly computerized Stock Exchange is claimed to be (of course) the most modern in the world. It looks very like a space mission control station, with its massed banks of VDUs, and so smooth and calm is its atmosphere that for a time they considered playing background tapes of the old exchange's noisy clatter, to prevent alienation among the brokers.

During the 1980s the development of the port into a financial metropolis, and a base for business with a newly accessible China, brought to all these activities a new influx of opportunists, Chinese, British, American, Australian. In certain parts of town, at some times of the day, Hong Kong seems to have been taken over by regiments of young brokers, insurers, and in particular merchant bankers, a breed which is now part of the Hong Kong fauna.[1] Many of them might be classified, in the varying slang of the 1980s, as yuppies, Sloane Rangers or Hooray Henries, and seem to spend their time either telephoning the other side of the world to discuss exchange rates, or zooming around in Porsches from one cocktail party to another. Others carry more weight. For example in his office high above the harbour there sits an American who knows as much as anybody alive about the contemporary Chinese legal system. A member of one of the most eminent New York law firms, he more or less commutes between Hong Kong, Beijing and Manhattan, often flying to China from Hong Kong three times a week. He plays an almost unique role in the opening of the People's Republic to American business; he also arranged the loan to the Bronx Zoo of the giant pandas Ling Ling and Yong Yong.

4

He is in Hong Kong partly because he can so easily get in and out of it. The prosperity of this colony, once so far away at the end of the trade routes, has depended always upon a mastery of communications.

In the 1920s it became the only British overseas possession from

[1] But is apparently unlikely to progenerate – if expatriate debutantes call a man 'a merchant banker', according to the *Hong Kong Tatler*, it means he has 'proved to be totally inept in the arts of love'. E.g. (I extrapolate): 'God, what a wet, he's a right merchant banker.'

which you could book a through train ticket to London. You left from the Kowloon waterfront station on the Guangzhou train, perhaps the streamlined railcar *Canton Belle*, decorated all in green and silver and equipped with cocktail bar; you travelled via Beijing and the Trans-Siberian railway to Moscow, Berlin, Paris and Calais; and from Dover the Pullman coaches of the *Golden Arrow* took you on to Victoria Station, London. The line was, grandiloquently declared Sir Henry May, Governor at the time of its opening, 'the first tentacle, the first artery through which the red blood of trade would flow to and from the centre of British interests'. After several interruptions the service is available again now, and British expatriates with time to spare sometimes choose to go home on it.

Hong Kong's first air link was necessarily with London, too. Before the Second World War Kai Tak airport was hardly more than an airstrip reclaimed from the water, and I can remember myself when flying into it on a blustery day, even in the 1950s, seemed an all but suicidal exercise, the aircraft lowering itself crab-like, wobbly with gusts of cross-wind, nervously racing its engines and feathering its propellers, on to the small runway that ran parallel with the sea. In 1936, when the first scheduled flight arrived, the runway crossed a main road, controlled by gates like a railway crossing, and the Imperial Airways De Havilland 86 biplane was, in the imperial manner, escorted in by nine aircraft from the carrier *Hermes*.

One passenger was aboard, plus sixteen bags of mail, and it was the start of a weekly service to Penang, where people could join the flying-boat service from Australia to Britain. It took ten days to get home by way of Karachi, Bahrain, Alexandria, Brindisi and Marseilles. Soon the Chinese opened a thrice-weekly service from Shanghai, and flights began to Macao, and Pan-American flying-boats arrived from San Francisco, and by the end of the 1930s the drone of aircraft engines, the bus-ride to the shed-terminal of Kai Tak, the sight of the flying-boat crews, checking in at the Peninsula Hotel, were all familiars of the Hong Kong scene.

During the Second World War the Japanese extended Kai Tak, using prisoners-of-war as labour, using the walls of the old Kowloon City as rubble, and breaking in the process the memorial stone to the Song boy-emperor. But when peace returned the airport was very soon outgrown, and in 1956 French engineers began work on an audacious new runway protruding 8,000 feet into the harbour. This created an airport like no other, in the heart of the city as Berlin's Tempelhof used to be, and as London's City Airport would presently be, but forming an integral part of the seaport too. The work entailed demolishing a range of low hills, shifting eleven million tons of material to make the runway, and reconstituting the Song stone in a nearby park, where it remains.[1]

The result was an electrifying new approach to Hong Kong. An American airline pilot once told me that he never made the landing without a clenching of the stomach, so demanding is the flight-path, and no passenger who has ever flown into modern Kai Tak, especially at night, is likely to forget the excitement of the experience, as the harbour unfolds itself around one's windows, as the myriad lights glitter, as first the mountains, then the skyscrapers rush by, and one lands mysteriously on the runway among the waters, the deep dark blue of the seas on either side, the starry blue of the sky above, as in the middle of some fabulously illuminated bowl of glass.

In 1987 nearly 13 million passengers passed through Kai Tak, flying on thirty-seven international airlines. Naturally they are planning to replace it, and are searching around for engineering solutions sufficiently sensational.

5

Time itself is a commercial commodity in Hong Kong, and the speed of the colony's financial intelligence was always famous – even in 1843 the merchants of the hongs knew about Charles Elliot's dismissal from office before he knew it himself. Now, in the days of electronic money movement, the quick tip is more important than ever. When it is eight o'clock in the morning in Hong Kong it is midnight in London, seven p.m. in New York. This gives the speculators and exchange brokers of Hong Kong several hours to make the most of the market, and Hong Kong is as extravagantly computerized, electronically networked and visually displayed as anywhere on earth.

The Victorian Empire was obsessed with the security of its intelligence, and Hong Kong was thought to be especially vulnerable to foreign interference. The cable to Singapore, laid in 1894, was routed via Labuan especially to avoid the French in Saigon, and the line to Shanghai was worked from a hulk in the middle of the Min River, to keep it safe from the Chinese. Even so for years the colony depended

[1] Haunted incidentally by Mr Tse Pui-ying, whom we met on page 70, and who lives on the adjacent sidewalk.

for its links with Britain upon the Danish Northern Telegraph Company, and it was only when an All-Red Route to London was opened through Singapore and India that the colonists breathed easy – 'moored to England', as Isabella Bird phrased it, 'by the electric cable'. Today Cable and Wireless, the British telecommunications company which used to be as essential to the imperial ambience as the Club itself, is the largest employer in the colony, except only the Government. It is a major shareholder in the telephone company, runs all international telecommunications, and with its signal-station at the very summit of the Peak, and its vast satellite disks on a headland near Stanley, still plays a truly imperial role – eleven of the fourteen daily pages of *Singtao*, the London Chinese newspaper, are sent ready-made by satellite from Hong Kong.

Telephones came early to this colony, in 1882, and exactly suited the talkative genius of the Cantonese. By 1939 there was a telephone for every ten inhabitants (you dialled H for Hong Kong-side, K for Kowloon), and so efficient was the service that during the chaos of the Japanese invasion in 1941 it provided much the best means of communication for the embattled British army. Hong Kong taxis were among the first anywhere to have radio telephones for their customers' convenience, and cellular telephones which work even in the middle of the cross-harbour tunnel are essential to your really on-the-ball Hong Kong businessman. Since local calls are free in Hong Kong telephones are deposited casually in supermarkets, cafés and fast-food shops, for customers to use.

Television is also ubiquitous. The four channels, two in Chinese, two in English, are commercially owned, but the Government television service also transmits programmes on them all. Their audience is estimated at 5.1 million, which means that virtually all Hong Kong families, even those living on board sampans or in shanties of plyboard and corrugated iron, possess a television set. TV presenters are celebrities, like all public personalities in the goldfish-bowl that is Hong Kong, and after a week or two in the colony you may well find yourself gawping like everyone else when you see one of the European or American newsreaders (getting practical experience in Hong Kong, very likely, as a step to bigger things at home) striding star-like into Jimmy's Kitchen.

Behind the scenes a thousand less obtrusive electronics media are humming and stirring and bleeping through the hours. Important office blocks in Hong Kong nowadays are built, as it were, around their electronics. The territory has borrowed an idiom from the Americans as it borrows so many, and calls them not merely 'high-tech', but actually 'intelligent' buildings, able to think. They can think through the circuits that are laid between their storeys, through the aerials and dishes on their roofs, through laser beams and TV systems. The Hongkong and Shanghai Bank thinks constantly about the state of the Hang Seng financial index, displaying its conclusions on VDU screens all over the place. The Exchange Building on the waterfront will think also, if you pay it a fat enough subscription, about the day's races at Shatin and Happy Valley, and present the runners' names, the odds and the form through display units on your executive desk. It also talks: its elevators announce their progress in a sepulchral, very English male voice, like a butler's.

At night, however late, there are always lights burning in such office blocks of Central, and when I see them it gives me a not unpleasant tremor of the uncanny, as though they are lights from another world. I do not imagine people at their desks in there, only banks of computers, walls of flickering screens, tapes electronically whirring, cursors moving up and down, all bathed in the pale green light of the computer age. Nowhere is more inextricably enmeshed in electronics than is Hong Kong, and if we could see its myriad lines of inner communication, as one sees laser beams, the skies would be criss-crossed, the streets would be festooned, and we would be tripping over percentages wherever we went.

6

When the First World War was about to start, this is how the *South China Morning Post* commented on the prospects: 'Leading businessmen regard the present deadlock with some little satisfaction. Provided that it is not unduly protracted, they consider it a splendid medium for reducing the huge accumulation of stocks .. which have glutted the market for many months.' When the Second World War was about to start, Hong Kong entrepreneurs made lots of money by buying up silk for parachutes, camelhair for British Army overcoats.

Like it or not, there was never anywhere quite like Hong Kong for instant opportunities. It swarms with speculators of every sort, building properties and selling them, buying into one another, selling each other out, plotting joint ventures or coordinating takeover bids. It is like a mammoth game of Monopoly, tinged with enigma – for what is an outsider to make of news items like this?:

Yesterday's 100% support, on an undisclosed percentage poll of Hongkong Electric's share of capital, for Hutchison-Whampoa's purchase of 52% of Cavendish International Holdings was a Pyrrhic victory ... no one really wanted to defy Li Ka-shing, one of the most powerful players in Hong Kong's oligopolistic share market ...

It all makes for a constant nervous brio. A sort of universal *frisson* runs through the town, when the newspapers announce a suspension of stock-dealing, for instance, or a dashing new development by an Australian millionaire, or for that matter a shift in Chinese policy, a passage of words between Moscow and Washington, a threat of protectionism, or anything else which may, for better or for worse, affect the sensitive balance of the Hong Kong economy. When, in 1961, Jardine's shares were for the first time offered to the public, the offer was over-subscribed by fifty-six times; and when in 1980, in a move to thwart hostile takeover plans by Chinese magnates, Jardine's bought 40 per cent of Hong Kong Land, and Hong Kong Land bought 40 per cent of Jardine's, it was like the climax of a soap opera.

Nowadays the ups and downs of the volatile share market keep the investing classes constantly on their toes. Playing the exchange has become a vastly popular form of gambling in Hong Kong, and there are always knots of Chinese at shop-windows displaying the Hang Seng financial index, like the little crowds that assemble around television shops in London when a Test match is being played. Successive economic crises have given many people nasty shocks, especially the great world crash of 1987, which closed the Stock Exchange for three days and very nearly wrecked the Futures Exchange; but so far Hong Kong has always proved its resilience by bouncing back and keeping most of the punters out of bankruptcy.

Land is the cause of much excitement. Since the foundation of the colony all land on Hong Kong has been vested in the Crown (the only exception is said to be the site of the Anglican Cathedral, which was bestowed upon the Church as freehold in 1847). The original leases were for as long as 999 years, so permanent seemed the prospect of the imperial sway; as the realization of 1997 dawned more clearly, they were limited to seventy-five years, while in the New Territories they were always sold to expire in 1997, like the lease of the territories themselves – 27 June was the standard completion date, giving the lessee three days to pack up. The matter of leases was crucial to the 1984 agreement with Beijing – even the wildest gambler was reluctant to invest in a colony where tenure had become so brief and uncertain.

They can now be granted until 2047, the year in which, under the terms of the treaty, Hong Kong capitalism may legally be abolished.

But leasehold could be as profitable as freehold, and from the start land speculation played a large part in the development of Hong Kong. In the original auctions of the 1840s some people bought far larger tracts than they needed, in the hope of prosperity to come, and others made themselves rich by acquiring small lots all over the place. Long before the acquisition of the New Territories astute investors were buying land in the peninsula: they included several members of the Navy League, an organization vociferously demanding cession of the New Territories for strategic reasons. Every now and then there has been a sudden eruption of land prices – between 1975 and 1980, for instance, rents for offices in Central rose by 500 per cent, and the price of luxury flats by even more. There are frequent killings to be made, and a whole new class of investor, from many parts of the Pacific world, has put its money into Hong Kong properties.

On the most popular level, far below these mighty transactions, the gusto of capitalism is just as apparent – more so, because more of it happens out of doors. From one end of Hong Kong to the other markets are seething. In the New Territories the old market villages have been metamorphosed into overwhelming concentrations of tower-blocks, but still at their feet the open marts carry on as always in canvas-roofed enclaves among the concrete, selling vegetables and fruit from the remaining local farms, fish, pigs from China, herbs, crafts, oysters, ducks. The village of Lau Fau Shan, on the west mainland coast, is in effect one large seafood market. Its unlovely alleys are lined with tanks full of eels or garupas, trays of crabs and twitching prawns, and are all but permanently blocked by men pushing huge barrows of oysters, their wheels squelching horribly through the mixture of mud and fish-scale which surfaces the streets.

Up the steep slopes of west Central, around Hollywood Road and the stepped tumultuous passageway called Ladder Street, the stalls have an established air. They have been there almost since the foundation of the colony, and are supplemented by secondhand shops of all kinds. Like most Chinese markets they sell almost anything, but they specialize in old-fashioned bric-à-brac, silks sometimes, pictures and antiques of varying worth. Scholars still sometimes find valuable books and manuscripts around here, and tourists are happily deceived by the prevailing air of Confucian integrity.

On the other hand the vast market area which comes to life each evening around Temple Street, in the Yau Ma Tei area of Kowloon, is nothing if not contemporary. Interspersed with hundreds of al fresco restaurants, bubbling and steaming beneath their bright lights, and with shops stacked with cages of twittering birds, the stalls of Temple Street sell everything to do with modernity: everything to do with radios, calculators, computers, car engines, videos, televisions, telephones – every chip and plug and junction box – every distributor head, every kind of cable – new and secondhand, sham and genuine, legal and illicit, pristine, chipped, dented and re-built. Juvenile electronic geniuses wander here and there, inspecting circuits through thick spectacles. Housewives rummage through boxes of light-plugs. A Pekingese is curled up fast asleep upon a doorstep, and a man composedly watches TV on a chair outside his shop, and a woman is selling fish soup out of a huge cauldron, and a butcher is offering bloody eviscerations of sea-turtle, together with yellow-dyed segments of chicken; and through it all the radios blast, the transformers wink, the woman yells recommendations of her soup, the birds deafeningly twitter, the dog sleeps, and a huge good-natured crowd ambles and surges by.

Nearby there is a place called the Golden Shopping Arcade, which is famous for its counterfeit computerware. The counterfeit has long been a Hong Kong speciality, though nowadays, as the territory grows more sophisticated, many of its counterfeit merchants are moving on to Thailand, the Philippines, Indonesia and even China. In 1895 Henry Norman complained about counterfeit editions of English books. In 1986 Cartier watches, Dunhill lighters, Cussons Imperial Leather Soap, well-known brands of wine and dish-washing liquid were all being faked in Hong Kong, sometimes under not very subtly misspelled names: the Japanese Sharp Elsinate calculator, for instance, a favourite device of the 1980s, turned up in copyright-evading pseudonyms as the Shrap Elsmate, the Eisimate, the Spadb and the Spado (the Shrap 838 sold especially well in China because of its lucky number – two eights and a three).

The Golden Arcade is gloriously brash about it. It is a bright emporium, on three floors, divided into multitudinous premises like the old Chinese tenement houses and stuffed to the ceiling with all-but-authentic goods bearing all-but-accurate names. They sell often for a tenth of the original price, sometimes for a twentieth, and there are dealers who will, for a couple of dollars, copy almost any program onto your own computer disk.

From time to time the authorities clamp down upon this place, seize the more outrageous infringements of copyright and issue stern warnings: but the instinct of the Golden Arcade, which is to a heightened degree no more than the instinct of Hong Kong itself, is impervious to such pedantries, and business soon returns to normal.

7

Lounging in the shafts of their ancient vehicles, outside the Star Ferry terminal at Central wait the very last of the rickshaws. They remind me of the very last of the Bath chairs, antediluvian outside the Great Western Railway station in the Somerset of my childhood.

For a hundred years and more every Hong Kong memoir has made reference to the rickshaws. Every Victorian globe-trotter went for a rickshaw ride as a matter of course, and generations of servicemen, British, American and doubtless Japanese, indulged their high spirits in rickshaw races, or were carried insensible to their ships and barracks by worldly rick-men through the night. Today the venerable survivors of the rickshaw men do not try very hard for custom, only half-heartedly bearding ferry-passengers who look sufficiently inexperienced; and if you ever see a rickshaw actually in service, conveying a doubtless just-arrived visitor through the streets of Central, the frail and stertorous rickshaw man is likely to look as though this really might be his last run, while the passenger almost certainly sits bolt upright behind him in a posture of acute embarrassment.

Tourism has long been one of Hong Kong's purposes, but this has never become a tourist city. Its tourist industry is all mixed up with everything else, and those rickshaws are almost the only touristy thing to be seen downtown. There is a reconstructed Song Dynasty Village in the New Territories, and a huge pleasure compound, Ocean Park, above the sea on Hong Kong Island, but in general tourism is incidental to the nature of the place. The shopping districts of Kowloon which cater largely for the tourist trade, with their endless shelves of radios and cameras, their multitudinous tailors and their acres of toys, do not feel like tourist traps, as they would in most of the world's cities; they seem organic elements of a great merchant centre – more like medieval fairs of Europe than, say, duty-free shops at airports.

Nevertheless many of the greatest Hong Kong firms have concerned themselves, in one way or another, with the visitors' trade, whether as an extension of the transport industry, or a useful adjunct to real estate, or a source of foreign currency. Not including Chinese, more than four million visitors came to Hong Kong in 1987, 44 per cent of them from North America, Europe and Australasia, 40 per cent from Japan and south-east Asia; and although there are really not many sights to see, except the grand sight of Hong Kong itself, so stimulating is the pace of things, so various is the cuisine, so seductive are the bargains and so exotic the sensations that few tourists seem to go away disappointed. Every week the Tourist Association's magazine asks visitors what they have enjoyed most; buying a camera, they usually say, but often they mention the food.

To house this multitude Hong Kong never stops building hotels. Great fortunes have been sustained by the hotel industry, and several of the best-known hongs and merchant families have been hoteliers in their time. Today many of the greatest buildings around the harbour are hotels, from the dignified old Peninsula at Tsim Sha Tsui to the glassy palaces of the big international chains, with their preposterously accoutred doormen and their statutory indoor waterfalls; in obscurer sites behind, especially among the garish streets of Kowloon, thousands of lesser hostelries proliferate, ranging from modestly respectable family lodgings to houses of frank disrepute.

There have been good hotels in Hong Kong since 1866, when the Hong Kong Hotel was opened on the site of the defunct Dent and Company's offices, immediately beside Pedder Wharf. Its restaurant was nicknamed 'The Grips', nobody seems to know why, and it became at once a centre of local social activity, as well as the place into which every first-class traveller, escaping with relief from shipboard life, fell as soon as possible after disembarkation. It appears in many an old photograph, looking sombre but comfortable enough, rather like some of the old imperial hotels which still precariously survive in India, Pakistan and Burma, and described itself in 1892 [1] as being 'the most commodious and best-appointed hotel in the Far East'. It had bathrooms *en suite*, its bedrooms were gas-lit, its grill-room served chops or steaks at any hour, and it was equipped with 'hydraulic ascending-rooms of the latest and most approved type'. In later years it became almost a parody of the British colonial style; Chinese were banned from some of its public rooms, and when in 1926 fire broke out in the east wing, raging for two days and nights despite the efforts of fire brigades, army detachments and men from the warships

---

[1] By which time its telegraphic address was inexplicably KREMLIN.

in harbour, afternoon tea was served as usual in the west wing.

The Hong Kong Hotel survived into the 1940s, but by then had long been overtaken by the glamorous Peninsula and its sibling the Repulse Bay Hotel. The Peninsula flourishes still, but the Repulse Bay is perhaps the most universally mourned of all the buildings torn down during Hong Kong's relentless development of the 1980s. It was a dear old place, beloved by many for its view over the bay between Stanley and Aberdeen. Its famous teas, its wicker chairs, its string orchestras, its verandah above the beach – all these were a very epitome of British colonial life. Where it used to stand, now surrounded by high-rise apartment blocks, they have built a replica of its restaurant, scrupulous in architecture as in potted plants; but it can never be the same.

The top hotels of Hong Kong are among the best anywhere, and are repeatedly voted so in polls among readers of travel magazines. Competition between them is intense. As the launches used to outdo each other in smartness, when they went to pick up passengers from the ocean liners, so rival Mercedes and Rolls-Royce limousines nowadays attend the hotel guest arriving at Kai Tak. Ever more exclusive fashion designers show their clothes in the salons of the great hotels, ever more powerful companies hold their annual conferences there, ever grander chefs from Europe, from India, from China, from California are invited to display their cuisines. Except perhaps for Manhattan in the years between the world wars, I doubt if there has ever been a city in which the hotel has played so prominent a social role.

Some of these hostelries are quintessentially Hong Kong. The Peninsula, with its enormous lobby and chic French restaurant, figures in almost every description of the place. The Victoria sits above that Macao ferry station, the hydrofoils streaming out beneath it, and the carpets in its elevators are changed every midnight to display the new day's date woven into the textile. The Kowloon Hotel offers a computer in every bedroom. A plaque at the Hilton marks the table where Richard Hughes, an Australian journalist who was for years probably the best-known of Hong Kong expatriates,[1] liked to drink with his friends and brain-pickers. And there are few institutions more pungently characteristic of *fin d'Empire* Hong Kong than the Mandarin Hotel, in Central, which was opened in 1963 and has repeatedly been nominated the Best Hotel In The World.

---

[1] Especially after his immortalization as Old Crow in John Le Carré's *The Honourable Schoolboy* (London, 1977).

The Mandarin was the first of a new generation of *grande luxe* Asian hotels, but unlike the chain hotels which were to follow it, stood demonstrably in the line of the imperial caravanserai – the Peninsula across the water in Kowloon, Raffles in Singapore, the Galle Face in Colombo, the Taj Mahal in Bombay, Shepheard's in Cairo. It style is one of self-effacing but extremely expensive sophistication, rather like the style of your contemporary British taipan, and its roots in fact go back to the beginnings of British Hong Kong, for it was an offshoot of the Hong Kong Land Company, in which Jardine's held a powerful interest. The hotel looks one way across Statue Square to the Hong Kong Club, another across Des Voeux Road towards the Hongkong and Shanghai Bank, and a third across Connaught Road to the waterfront skyscrapers and the harbour. Once its front rooms all faced directly across the water, but since the buildings that have since interrupted the view were all built by Hong Kong Land too, there could be no complaining – and actually the Mandarin's present condition of enclosure, surrounded fraternally by such fabulously opulent neighbours, only enhances its cherished sense of Establishment.

Nobody could call it a beautiful building. Designed by the local architectural firm Leigh and Orange, who have been in Hong Kong since 1874, it looks rather squat and ordinary. However the moment its elderly Rolls drops you at its front door you know you have struck quality. Hardly have the doormen courteously opened the door for you than a most elegant young assistant manager, Chinese or European and tending only slightly towards the starchy, is welcoming you to the hotel as he might welcome a distant, well spoken of and by all accounts extremely wealthy relative. How glad he is to see you! How genuinely he hopes your jet-lag isn't too bad! How swiftly, giving you all his attention, he ushers you to your room – no need to check in, Good Lord no, we can see to all that kind of thing when you've had time to freshen up and enjoy a cup of Chinese tea!

The Mandarin is British-owned but cosmopolitanly run. Its manager, as I write, is Swiss, its concierge Italian, its public relations person extremely English, its front office manager Chinese and the four-piece band that plays gentle swing at tea-time is a family of Filipinos. It has five foreign chefs, 128 Chinese. It flies in its cheeses and hams from France, its steaks from the United States, and frequently has gastronomic festivals when it flies in chefs too from famous restaurants around the world.

It sees itself among the company of the discreet luxurious hotels that have their epitomes in Europe, and especially perhaps in London, and has no lounge-cataracts, fancy-dress doormen or revolving restaurants. Its interior décor, restrained and adult, is by the eminent theatrical designer Don Ashton; a running motif, appearing throughout the hotel, is the Seal of the Grand Secretary, mandarin of mandarins in the old Chinese Empire. Everything is just sufficiently orientialized to make you feel you might be sleeping in the guest quarters of one of the more traditional Anglo-Chinese hongs – a contemporary version perhaps of Jardine's old No. 1 House. A soignée White Russian widow has lived in the hotel since it was built (you can recognize her room from the outside by its profusion of potted plants), and moves about the building not like a customer at all, but absolutely like a friend of the taipan.

In short the Mandarin Hotel is an overt version of an inner Hong Kong style – the style of the loftier British of the China coast, tempered by long years of comfort and assimilation in the east. Once a month the Governor gives a luncheon party there, attended by a varying guest list of worthies; rather like the luncheons the Queen of England now and then gives at Buckingham Palace, though the victuals may be better.

8

Nevertheless buying and selling, even speculating and servicing, are no longer the chief functions of Hong Kong. Since 1950, when the United Nations clamped its embargo upon trade with Communist China, Hong Kong has turned itself into one of the world's great manufactories.

There were industries in the territory before. There were the traditional fishing, quarrying, shipbuilding and farming industries. There had long been industries making joss-sticks. In the nineteenth century Hong Kong preserved ginger was patronized by Queen Victoria herself, and was consequently to be found on all the most fashionable English dinner-tables. Sugar-refining flourished for a time, cloths and cottons were made, the Do Be Chairful Company were well-known makers of rattan furniture. There was a wolfram mine in the New Territories – once the miners had been persuaded the earth-spirits would not be angered, they made themselves an underground town, complete with shops, houses, markets, cafés, bars and even brothels. After the Second World War Hong Kong went in for cheap and nasty toys, and for electric torches, a speciality it has retained. The victory of the Communists in the Chinese civil war expelled to Hong Kong a powerful group of Shanghai manufacturers, who often brought their work forces with them – sometimes even their machinery – and established in the territory a vigorous textile industry.

But it was the Korean War embargo that sealed the development. Chinese Hong Kong, in particular, heeded the example of those astute and adaptable newcomers from Shanghai, who had been driven out of one profitable society, and had shown themselves determined not to be impoverished in another. The first sign of changing philosophies was the sudden emergence of an artificial flower industry, a trade until then dominated by the Italians; thereafter factories of all kinds erupted, especially in Kowloon, which now dramatically burgeoned.

To start with they were mostly hole-in-corner affairs, in lofts and backyards, in ramshackle warehouses, frequently in squatters' huts and sometimes even on board sampans. Hong Kong industries then were often Dickensian: sweatshop workers labouring terrible hours for miserable wages, small children assembling toys or picking at fabrics, makeshift machinery improperly protected, squalid conditions, ruthless methods, fantastic production levels and enormous profits.

It was an ugly thing to see in the enlightened 1950s. Though its exploiters, like its exploitees, were nearly all Chinese, the Hong Kong Government was repeatedly anathematized, in the House of Commons at Westminster as in the pages of newspapers around the world, for its slavish devotion to *laissez-faire* – for years it even declined to produce proper industrial statistics. But at however high a social cost, temporarily deprived of one function Hong Kong permanently acquired another.

Gradually that explosion of productivity was brought into some sort of order, and Hong Kong industry began to conform with international norms. Factory conditions became less awful, wages more humane, the exploitation of children less blatant. The *ad hoc* nature of it all gave way to more contemporary organization; by the 1970s Hong Kong industry was relatively respectable, and the colony was no longer an underdeveloped country with a sophisticated entrepreneurial superstructure, but one of the world's great productive Powers. The 418 registered factories of 1939, the 1,266 of 1948, had become by 1986 148,623. It was the most phenomenally rapid of all the world's industrial revolutions.

Now Hong Kong stands, they say, sixteenth among them all, exporting, with its 5.6 million population, more than India's 625 million. Its average wages are second only to Japan's in Asia. Critics say it is still too improvisatory or even amateurish of method, too dependent upon cheap labour and traditional management; three-quarters of those plants employ less than nine people, making them hardly more than cottage industries, and there is a growing shortage of sufficiently advanced technicians. Nevertheless the territory shows no signs of falling back. Every quarter a fat and glossy catalogue is produced, to show prospective customers what Hong Kong is producing, and it makes startling and curious reading. Such endless variety of ingenuity, given to the world by such splendid-sounding concerns – the Grand Dragon Universal Sales Company, the Ever-Rich Industrial Company, or the perhaps unfortunately named Flying Junk Industrial Company Ltd!

Here is a radio you can float in your bath, here an electronic studfinder. A hair-dryer is combined with an electric iron, a calculator with a paper-clip. There are electronic ashtrays. There are sonic ratrepellers. There are devices for the detection of counterfeit money. There are dolls of a thousand faces, and armouries of toy machineguns. Hong Kong is the world's largest exporter of textiles, toys and watches. It prints books in every language, and makes more films for the cinema than anywhere else except India.

The 412 square miles of the colony thus qualify as one of the most intensely productive regions of the world. Yet surprisingly little of it shows. There are few factory chimneys in Hong Kong, few great industrial complexes; it is as though all that work is done in secret, hidden away in back streets of the urban mass.

9

Even now much of this energy can be traced back, in one way or another, to the British hongs which we saw establishing themselves in the 1840s, congratulating themselves in the Victorian prime.

They used to adopt Chinese sobriquets, generally with the help of scholars and soothsayers, and these are still remembered, if only by the writers of company histories; for the most part though they have lost the grand corporate images they inherited from the days of the East India Company and the Guangzhou concessions. Their premises are mostly subsumed in anonymous skyscraper blocks, their interests are so diffuse, and spread through so many subsidiary companies, that their power has lost some of its old public impact. Countless newer houses, most of them Chinese, many of them American or Japanese, have joined and often superseded the senior firms. By the late 1980s Japanese and American investments had both exceeded British, Hong Kong's chief trading partners were, after China, Japan and the United States, and only one in twenty-five of the ocean-going ships that used the port flew the Red Ensign. Nevertheless much real power in Hong Kong, during these last days of its colonial status, remains in the hands of a few old British or Anglo-Chinese companies. In 1987 Hutchison-Whampoa published an advertisement demonstrating how widespread was its influence in Hong Kong throughout a working day: whatever you did, you were almost bound somehow or other to be contributing to its coffers, whether you were shopping at one of its 200 supermarkets, using one of the myriad products its agencies handled, buying an apartment, drinking a bottle of pop, having a drink at the Bull and Bear pub, switching on the electric light, using a cellular telephone or driving on an asphalt road.

Hutchison-Whampoa, though British by origin, is now Chinese-controlled. Other old companies remain in British hands, and under British management. They began often enough as furiously competitive shippers and port agents, but are often linked now behind the scenes, or rather in the pages of the Directory of Directors, in almost incestuous intimacy. Three institutions in particular form part of the fabric of the place.

The youngest has the Chinese name of Taikoo, Great and Ancient. In 1869 there visited Hong Kong a Yorkshire businessman of all the Yorkshire orthodoxies – John Samuel Swire, shrewd, steady, sarcastic, dictatorial, who frequently said 'I told you so' and was given to Yorkshire dicta like 'I write as I speak, to the point', or 'I aim to be strong enough to be respected, if not beloved'. He was the perfect businessman – 'a person', wrote an American contemporary in admiration, 'who lives by and for business alone' (besides being backed by 'practically unlimited supply of British pride and capital'). His partners called him 'The Senior'.

Together with a Lancashire mill-owner, Richard Butterfield, Swire and his brother William had founded a shipping and trading firm in Shanghai in 1866, and from there he extended his activities to Hong Kong. Butterfield was soon disposed of,[1] and the firm grew rich, in the

[1] 'Mr Butterfield retired from our firm at my suggestion,' wrote Swire succinctly, 'he was grasping and bothered me.'

classic Hong Kong way, as shipowners, ship repairers, agents, importers and exporters of many commodities. Its headquarters were always in England, it was active in Japan and China too, and John Swire did not himself stay long in Hong Kong; but by the time he died in 1898 the firm of Butterfield and Swire was one of the most powerful in the colony, with all the arrangements of the older companies, an office on the Praya, messes for the young gentlemen assistants and a house on the Peak for the taipan.

This hong was not always loved in the colony, partly because of its relatively liberal racial views. 'An undignified style of action,' commented an observer from Russell's ('The Flag Prospers'), when Butterfield and Swire invited Chinese freight brokers to a dinner, 'the Swire lot blustering away among the Chinamen . . . [hobnobbing] with every unwashed devil in the place.' Swire's helped to destroy Russell's in the end, as they had helped to drive the old and respected firm of Dent's ('Precious and Compliant') into bankruptcy, and were also considered rather too ruthless in their methods. They were, said a writer in the *Hong Kong Telegraph* in 1891, 'the everlasting Bugbears of Eastern commerce, the nigger-drivers, the sweaters, the Jews – worse than Jews, for no Jew was ever so full of hatred and persecution and intolerance of all others . . .' During the First World War the Governor himself, Sir Henry May, accused Swire's of reluctance to help the war effort – they were 'the most remiss in furnishing volunteers for the defence of the Colony'.

Certainly the firm seems to have lacked the easy-going style of the older British hongs. 'You are ruining your chance as regards advancement in our firm,' wrote Swire's taipan to one of his employees in the 1900s – '"American Women and Nips". We will not tolerate these vices, they lead the man into trouble, destroy his efficiency, & he sets a bad example to others.'[1] 'The Firm do not approve,' it was announced in 1900, 'of their Employees being interested in Race Ponies . . . to so interest themselves, in future, will certainly prejudice their chance of promotion.' 'I hope you will make that young nephew of mine work,' wrote Warren Swire when John Kidston Swire joined the Hong Kong office in 1914, 'he is *not* in China for his own amusement . . .' Nevertheless they have prospered ever since. The name of Butterfield was eventually expunged, but the firm remains ubiquitous in Hong Kong,

[1] From *Taikoo*, by Charles Drage, London 1970: but Mr Drage suggests that 'Nips' means not Japanese, but alcoholic measures.

controlling immense properties, running innumerable concerns. It flies its house flag (quartered in white and red, with a blue vertical stripe) on many vessels, and has a controlling interest in the colony's chief international airline, Cathay Pacific, one of the most important in the east. Listed as the third most profitable company in the territory, Swire's is really a world-wide conglomerate, with interests in tea plantations in Kenya, container terminals in Japan, oil in the Gulf, property in Florida, cold storage in Canada, hotels in Mauritius and bottling in Salt Lake City. Descendants of 'The Senior' are still prominent in its affairs.

Its great rivals were, and are, Jardine, Matheson, the first of them all, who have always been as inescapable in Hong Kong as they are in the pages of this book. They adopted their Chinese name, 'Ewo', State of Happy Harmony, in 1842, and officially resumed it in 1958 because the Chinese characters for 'Jardine' meant in English 'dumping ground'. Like Swire's, Jardine's had begun as general agents, buying and selling in China for clients in Europe, and had gradually diversified into shipowning, sugar-refining, banking, insuring, mining, railway-building and every imaginable kind of entrepreneurial activity in the east. Unlike Swire's, for 150 years their headquarters was in Hong Kong, and unlike Swire's again they depended very largely upon the personalities of their partners, who were almost invariably Scots.

Jardine succeeded Jardine in Ewo, Matheson followed Matheson, and in 1853 William Keswick, great-nephew of the original William Jardine, founded another related dynasty within the firm. By the 1980s the descendants of Andrew Jardine of Broadholm, Lochmaben, Dumfriesshire, had included fifty-one men, spread over seven generations, who were associated with the business. Among them were some remarkable people. William Jardine himself was called by the Chinese 'Iron-headed Old Rat' because of the insouciance with which, attacked one day in Guangzhou, he totally disregarded a blow on the head with a club. Then there was David Matheson who resigned to become chairman of the executive committee of the Society for the Suppression of the Opium Trade, and James Johnstone Keswick, a man of such unrebuffable tact that he was nicknamed 'James the Bloody Polite', and Alexander Dallas who went on to be Governor of Manitoba. James Matheson, who once called the Duke of Wellington 'a strenuous advocate for submissiveness and senility', bought the entire island of Lewis, considerably larger than Hong Kong, and built Stornoway

Castle on it. Henry Keswick, at the end of the First World War, bought an uncompleted Royal Navy destroyer and had it finished as his personal steam yacht.

Ewo always sounds more fun than Taikoo. On St Andrew's Day Jardine's used to take over Happy Valley for a celebration which culminated with the running of the Ewo Handicap, a mile race for ponies ridden by members of the staff. Men of all ages and all riding abilities entered the race. The winner got a cup, the last man in got a wooden spoon so large that it became a Jardine's custom to pass it around the company filled with whisky – 'Testing the Capacity of the Wooden Spoon'. I have a photograph of the jockeys who ran the Ewo Handicap in 1930, and a formidable crew they look: eight extremely healthy-looking Europeans, mostly Scots, ranging from the youthful to the grandfatherly, and eyeing the camera with expressions of unsmiling resolution, as if they were summing up the photographer's suitability for employment.

For Jardine's was stylish, but seldom reckless. Its partners set about things with a Scottish calculation. They owned the fastest sailing ships, with the best-paid crews and the most ambitious captains. They brought the first steamships to the China coast. They financed the first China railway. They set up a subsidiary in Japan as soon as the Japanese allowed it (Ei-ichiban-Kan = British Number One House). They moved swiftly into cotton, when the American Civil War cut off American supplies from Europe. They were agents for Armstrong the gunmakers, when China was rearming in the 1880s. They were local pioneers in insurance, in the use of the telegraph, in textile-weaving, in sugar-refining. They shared in the beginnings of the Star Ferry and the Peak tram. They acted as consuls for many foreign Powers, and their Chinese compradors often became great men in their own right – the rise to power of the Ho dynasty, long one of the most influential in Hong Kong, was founded upon the wealth of a Jardine's comprador.

By these means they became more than just a company, but an international power factor, with holdings and interests in many countries. When they first put their shares on public sale, in 1961, they described themselves elegantly as a company 'which participates widely in the commerce and industry of the Far East, in the merchanting [1] of imports and exports, the distribution and servicing of engineering products, the shipping industry, air transport business, insurance, invest-

---

[1] *Sic* – and there is such a word.

ment management, agency business and general merchant adventure'.

Though Jardine's is now listed only as the fifteenth most profitable public company in Hong Kong, its tentacles extend into many others, and it remains the most famous of them all. It is also still the most emblematic. For some years in the early twentieth century the company headquarters were moved from Hong Kong to Shanghai, where prospects seemed more exciting. They returned to Hong Kong in 1912, and when in 1984 it was announced that they were going to move once more, this time to Bermuda, a shock ran through the east. The future of Hong Kong was undecided then, confidence was shaky at best, and the news that the Princely Hong thought it wiser to shift its headquarters out of the colony had a devastating effect. Share prices slumped, and a hundred lesser concerns wondered whether it might not be wise to do the same.

The crisis of confidence passed, and within a few months Hong Kong had returned to economic boom, but in any case Jardine's move seems more legal than logistical. Most of the company's wealth is still tied up in its multifarious Hong Kong operations, and its Hong Kong office high in the modernistic World Trade Centre remains the biggest of all its branches. The noonday salute is still fired, by a Hotchkiss 3-pounder gun made in 1901, on the quayside near Jardine's old East Point premises, opposite the Excelsior Hotel. Eight bells is rung, too, on a ship's bell, and this is the ceremony which Noel Coward immortalized in *Mad Dogs and Englishmen*:

> In Hong Kong
> They strike a gong
> And fire off a midday gun
> To reprimand each inmate
> Who's in late . . .

Eminent visitors are sometimes invited to perform the ceremony, and once the Master fastidiously fired the gun himself ('I rather like loud noises').

The third historic old money-maker is 'Wayfoong', Abundance of Remittances, known to Hong Kong people simply as The Bank, and listed as the second most profitable public company in the territory. The Hongkong and Shanghai Banking Corporation was founded in 1864 by an association of local firms, and became a powerhouse of commerce and industry not just in Hong Kong, but all over the Far East – much of Japan's original foreign trade was financed by the

Bank, and much of China's railway development. Its presence is towering in Hong Kong, and it is a particularly masterful Chief Manager of the Bank, the Victorian Sir Thomas Jackson, who is portrayed frock-coated in the single surviving effigy of Statue Square.

The Bank has known its hard times – convulsions in China which paralysed its operations there, the Japanese occupation of Hong Kong, when its head office temporarily migrated to London, the batterings of the Korean and Vietnam conflicts and finally the traumatic agreement that Hong Kong was to revert to Chinese sovereignty. But like most such Hong Kong institutions, it has long since hedged its bets and stashed much of its assets far away. Besides its own branches around the world, generally in ports, it has acquired subsidiaries as prominent as the Marine Midland Bank of New York and the British Bank of the Middle East, as discreet as merchant banks in the Bahamas or Papua New Guinea. It owns investment management companies in New York, London and Sydney, it has its own satellite network, and whether you are taking out a policy with the Al Sakr Insurance Company of Saudi Arabia, buying stocks on the island of Jersey, or making a deposit with the Cyprus Popular Bank, you are dealing indirectly with HongKongBank (as its publicists vainly try to rename it). Its knowledge of China is profound – it is the largest foreign bank operating there, and its Shanghai branch remained open throughout the Cultural Revolution – and this gives it a unique and highly profitable status: in 1987 it was reckoned to be the sixteenth richest among the banks of the world, but its Scottish chairman announced that he wanted to make it the strongest of them all.

If Jardine's has been immortalized by Coward, the Hongkong and Shanghai Bank was immortalized by Auden – it was the Bank's new headquarters that the poet had in mind when he sneered at 'a worthy temple for the comic muse'. The history of The Bank is remembered, in fact, chiefly by its buildings. After renting property for its first decade, its directors built three successive offices of their own, all on the same site at No. 1 Queen's Road Central, and they have been pre-eminent in Hong Kong ever since, appearing on many of its banknotes, and in themselves forming an architectural index to the financial progress of the territory.

The first (1886) was a remarkable hybrid by the local architects Palmer and Turner, who had opened their office in Hong Kong in 1868 and are still there now. It was tropical Mediterranean on one side, monumentally domed the other; its main south door opened into

Queen's Road, its north door faced the grand new Praya along the waterfront. The second building (1935), was the one Auden commemorated, and was specifically commissioned, from the same architectural firm, to be 'The Best Bank in the World'. It was a skyscraper by the standards of the day, the tallest building between Cairo and San Francisco, with a pad for autogiros on its roof, air-conditioning of a kind and a squash-court in the tower. It was faced entirely in Hong Kong granite, the Bank buying its own quarry for the purpose, and its main banking hall was embellished with a magnificent mosaic ceiling, designed by a Russian artist from Shanghai, V. S. Podgoursky, and executed in a disused church in Venice. The building was thick with symbolisms, from Podgoursky's didactic murals, all about the blessings of trade and industry, to the Men of Vision, looking vaguely Assyrian, who gazed towards the waterfront from the façade. Outside the north doors reclined two heroic lions, one snarling, one merely looking cross, which were nicknamed Stephen and Stitt after senior officials of the day.

The Governor was in hospital with appendicitis on the day of this building's opening, so the ceremony was performed by his deputy, N. L. Smith, who was of the opinion that 'generations yet unborn will gaze at it with something of the same gasp of admiration that we today bestow on, let us say, Durham Cathedral'. Mr Smith must momentarily have forgotten where he was, for in the Hong Kong way scarcely a single generation had passed before The Best Bank in the World was torn down to make way for the third headquarters (1985). This is said to have been the most expensive office building ever erected, and manages to represent not merely the glory of profit and the sumptuousness of wealth, but also the hard intelligence of the financial life. It was designed by the Englishman Norman Foster. He made it a stunning centrepiece for the whole of Hong Kong, at least for the moment, and since for reasons more of legal advantage than of public spiritedness the whole of its ground floor is a public passage, all Hong Kong passes beneath its presence as beneath a frigid benediction.

We should spend longer with this building, because it was the first truly original modern structure to go up in Hong Kong. Among the slavishly trendy skyscrapers of Central, which had assiduously followed every architectural fashion from curtain-walling to mirror-glass, it erupted almost extra-terrestrially. Built of steel girders sheathed in grey, which gives it an erroneously plastic look, it stands like a upturned casket of glass and metal, bound about with massive girders and crowned with a ship-like miscellany of block-houses and aerials. It is entirely contemporary, except for Stitt and Stephen still recumbent outside its doors.

One's first impression, entering that open-sided ground-floor patio, is one of forbidding cloisteredness. Two long escalators, installed skew-whiff at the geomancer's insistence, crawl in steep diagonal through the open space to the working floors above, and riding up there feels like riding up to the gondola of a fairly unwelcoming airship. But just as Hong Kong itself combines the steely with a distinct note of the celebratory, so this remarkable building too gradually reveals to the visitor a kind of audacious endearment – a touch of devil-may-care. It is all so boyishly modern, so absolutely state-of-the-art, so piratically pleased with itself! Wherever you look there is something startling – mirrors to deflect sunlight into working areas, criss-cross escalators, vistas of bare steel. Through the enormous glass windows on the north side you can see the grand expanse of the harbour, and the ships lying there rank on rank look almost as though they are awaiting a signal from The Bank to sail away with their booty.

And turn your eyes the other way, over Queen's Road up the mountain behind: there on the ultimate building site stands the Chairman's official residence, itself almost grand enough to auth-enticate a banknote.

10

Such are three old corporate stalwarts of Hong Kong capitalism: but down the generations much of its fiercest entrepreneural energy has been provided by private citizens, remembered not just as the presiding names of institutions, but as individuals. Here are a few examples:
¶   George Duddell was Hong Kong's first master of the auction. In 1845 he successfully bid for the Hong Kong opium monopoly, paying $8,250 for it and re-leasing it to Chinese operators for $1,710 a month. Thereafter he never looked back. He became an auctioneer himself, and although in 1850 he was discovered to have knocked a ship down to his own bid at far less than its proper price, was appointed the official Government Auctioneer anyway. He also had a bakery, which baked much of the European community's bread after the affair of the poisoned bread in 1857, and at one time he was the third largest landowner of Hong Kong; he had bought four of his holdings, at $1 the lot, from the impoverished Colonial Auditor A. E. Shelley. By the mid-

1870s Duddell had left Hong Kong, having sold his handsome water-front office to Jardine, Matheson, and retired rich if not universally respected to live the rest of his life, it is said, in Brighton.

¶   'Captain' John Lamont, a self-educated shipwright from Aberdeen, Scotland, was the first European shipbuilder of Hong Kong. Arriving in the colony at its foundation, he set up a slipway immediately beside Jardine's go-down at East Point, and there he not only maintained Jardine's vessels for them, but also built Hong Kong's first foreign-registered ship, the yacht-like schooner *Celestial*. He became a famous figure of the east, as probably the best shipwright of the China seas, and ended up as owner of the Lamont Dock at the other Aberdeen, the one on Hong Kong's southern shore. When he died the Governor of the day, in the manner of the day, personally proposed a toast to this 'once common carpenter' who had made himself uncommon in Hong Kong.

¶   When the East India Company still maintained its concessions at Guangzhou, a Mr Edward Lane was a butler in its employ. When the first European shops were established in the new colony of Hong Kong, a Mr Ninian Crawford was a clerk in one of them. Today the names of their two families are household words in Hong Kong. Joining forces in the colony, between them the Lanes and the Crawfords ran, at one time or another, ships' chandlers, auction houses, hotels and bakeries. One Lane was involved in the *Keying* enterprise, one Crawford was secretary of the Hong Kong Club, and their memorial is Lane Craw-ford's, the oldest and most exclusive of Hong Kong's department stores, now Chinese-owned but still decidedly old-school.

¶   Douglas Lapraik, origins unknown, began his Hong Kong career in 1845, aged twenty-four, as an apprentice to a watchmaker, and ended it in 1866 a shipowner, a dockowner, and the principal hotel proprietor of the colony. He had invested in the *Keying*, too – some said he went in disguise to Guangzhou to buy the ship, the sale of junks to foreigners being forbidden. He was a partner of Lamont at the Aberdeen docks, his seven steamships held a near-monopoly of the trade with Fuzhou, Shantou and Xiamen, and he it was who gave to the city the Pedder Street clock. For years he lived with a Chinese mistress in an engaging Gothic folly, Douglas Castle, which survives to this day as a student hostel; but when he went home to England he married a bride from the Isle of Wight, and very soon died.

¶   In 1883 there arrived in Hong Kong from Baghdad a young man who preferred to call himself Kelly, perhaps supposing that the British

Establishment was fonder of Irishmen than it was of Jews. His real name was Ellis Kadoorie, and with his brother Elly he established a famous Hong Kong Jewish dynasty. They set up business as general brokers and agents, in the local tradition, but went into the hotel business and presently acquired control of the China Light and Power Company, which ran all the colony's power stations and distributed all the electricity. The Kadoories became, and remain, great powers in Hong Kong. They gave vast sums of money to charitable causes, were lavish patrons of Happy Valley, and were to be rewarded not only with a couple of knighthoods but also, as we know, with the first of all Hong Kong peerages.

¶   Paul Catchik Chater, a Christian Armenian from Calcutta, disembarked in Hong Kong in 1864, aged eighteen. Starting as a bank clerk, he soon had a finger in every kind of profitable pie – wharfing, electricity, rope-making, trams, ferries, banking, hotels, land. His Hong Kong and Kowloon Wharf and Godown Company became Hong Kong's chief dock operators, his most brilliant real-estate coup was the Praya Reclamation Scheme in Central, which created a slab of the most valuable building land on earth. An Anglophile and enthusiastic royalist, Chater threw himself into all the right activities (almost all – his young Scandinavian wife, extracted from Lyndhurst Terrace, was never accepted at Government House). He was a Mason, an art collector, a passionate racegoer. He became almost unbelievably rich, and built himself a vast and awful palace in mid-Levels called Marble Hall. When he died on a May morning in 1926 he left instructions that he was to be buried within twelve hours. The Stock Exchange, having opened as usual, hastily closed its doors again to prepare for the funeral, and by five the same evening the old millionaire was safely under the turf.

¶   The first Chinese to make a really great fortune in Hong Kong was Robert Ho Tung, chief comprador at Jardine's; born in 1862, he was a multi-millionaire by the turn of the century. Actually he was only half-Chinese, being the natural son it is thought of a Belgian merchant. Before he grew his mandarin beard he looked in some photographs distinctly European, with his long face, long nose and wide mouth, and the woman he married was Eurasian too – the daughter of a Jardine's partner. Ho Tung thought of himself however as Chinese, and as year by year he amassed his tremendous fortune he became one of the great figures of the Hong Kong Chinese community, ever more venerable, ever more generous in good causes, a founding father of the University of Hong Kong, now presenting a warplane to the Chinese Government for its fight against the Japanese, now giving a couple of fighters to the RAF.

He was knighted of course, a road was named for him, he was the first non-European to own a house on the Peak – four of them, actually – and he died in 1956 as patriarch of a whole clan of plutocrats, several of them millionaires and prominent still in Hong Kong life. When Oswald Birley painted his portrait in his old age, Ho Tung wanted to be shown wearing all his twenty-two decorations; Birley declined for aesthetic reasons, but painted the decorations themselves in a separate picture, to be hung nearby in its own frame.

II

Sir Robert was only the first. 'Do you wish your child to study in one of the oldest and most respected public schools in England?' said a Hong Kong press advertisement in 1986. 'If so, here is a chance not to be missed. The headmaster of Uppingham School will be in town from 6th to 12th April. Why not leave a message at the Mandarin, and Mr Bomford will contact you . . .?'

The Headmaster of Uppingham (founded 1584) had in mind children not of the English expatriate bourgeoisie, but of the ever-growing and ambitious Chinese moneyed classes. Today foreigners of many nationalities have joined the British in extracting the profits of Hong Kong, but it is the Chinese population that most spectacularly demonstrates the ideology of capitalism. The community's model and epitome might well be Chan Hon-wah, a rich Hong Kong businessman of the 1950s whose career has been recorded by the historian James Hayes. Chan had left Guangdong forty years before with four dollars in his pocket. One went to pay his fare, two he sent home as Lucky Money, as custom required, and upon the single surviving dollar he built so steadily expanding an enterprise that by 1953 his company had branches and agencies in most of the big cities of southern Asia.

If they are not all as successful as Mr Chan, on every social plane the Hong Kong Chinese are virtuoso money-makers. They are tireless workers. Kipling in *From Sea to Sea*, comparing the industrious in-habitants of Hong Kong with the languid natives of Bombay, said he had never seen a Chinese asleep in the daytime, and hardly ever seen one idling – 'let us annexe China,' he concluded. The Hong Kong Chinese are wonderfully astute: even among the villagers of the outer islands, before they were leased to the British at all, illiterate middlemen and financial organizers dealt with most intricate arrangements of loan and mortgage: illiteracy did not matter, James Hayes tells us, 'if other qualities required in this complex arena of money, chance, and human relationships were . . . demonstrable'.

And they are opportunists of genius. When communal lavatories were first installed in Hong Kong, Chinese entrepreneurs took to sitting on them for so long that people were obliged to bribe them to come off. When during the plague of 1900 the Government offered two cents for every dead rat delivered to the authorities, there was a brisk flow of imported rodents from the mainland. When the first tramlines were laid, Chinese manufacturers devised handcarts with flanged wheels to fit the tracks.[1] When the buses and trams themselves stopped running during the Second World War, Chinese operators pulled people about on flat-topped wagons.

Marine Department employees posted to the signal station on the otherwise uninhabited Green Island took to breeding goats as a sideline.[2] During the Japanese occupation the Chinese black market virtually took over the distribution of food. In the 1970s, when the future of Hong Kong first came into serious doubt, citizenship of a dozen foreign countries was offered by Hong Kong agencies, and one particularly persuasive operator even succeeded in selling people a World Passport, entitling them to go and live anywhere.

They are endlessly inquisitive and innovative. In the late 1980s Chinese salesmen from Hong Kong opened up a new trading route 2,500 miles across the breadth of China to Xinjiang Province, on the frontiers of the Soviet Union. They sold electric goods from air-conditioners to calculators (mostly Shrap 838s) for distribution inside the Soviet Union. Russian-Chinese middlemen paid for their goods sometimes in sacks of hard cash, sometimes in barter goods, sometimes in black-market US dollars, and the Hong Kong traders easily doubled their investments on every trip.

The Chinese magnates of Hong Kong are familiar figures of world

---

[1] They were soon made illegal, and the offence of building them is still on the statute books – maximum fine $HK 100.

[2] There are goats there still, presumably destined for Hong Kong restaurants. The snakes which proliferate on the nearby Stonecutters Island, however, though some may also end up in cooking-pots, are not the product of Chinese entrepreneurship: they are said to be descended from a snake-pit established there by the Japanese during the Second World War for the provision of serum.

finance, and those great Hong Kong companies which are not already Chinese-controlled are under constant threat of Chinese takeovers. Sir Run-Run Shaw, with his thin benevolent face and his wire-rimmed spectacles, his high brow and long fingers, looks like a Confucianist sage; he is the owner of two of Hong Kong's TV channels and one of the world's most successful film producers, whose sprawling studios above the sea at Sai Kung, in the New Territories, make far more films each year than Hollywood ever did. Sir Yue-Kong Pao, the greatest of the Hong Kong shipping magnates, presides over an empire that ranges from Star Ferries to Lane Crawford's. Stanley Ho, of the compradors' dynasty, owns the gambling concessions at Macao, together with many of the vessels that take the gamblers there, and has mansions in both cities. The richest Hong Kong resident of all is said to be the financier Li Ka-shing, who is not only chairman of one of the biggest ex-British hongs, Hutchison-Whampoa, with its many ancillaries and subsidiaries, but also controls the Husky Oil Company of Canada.

These are the local heroes of Chinese Hong Kong, together with rock singers and Sir Run-Run's film stars, and lower down the social scale a hundred thousand Hong Kong Chinese, even at the start of the uncertain 1990s, are hoping to emulate them one day. There are no class inhibitions in this place. Almost everyone shares the memory of old hardships, if only by heredity, and almost everyone has similar aspirations. Nor is there much sense of corporate purpose, as there is in Japan: the Hong Kong worker works above all for himself, with no nonsense about the sacred function of the Company, and is perfectly ready to change jobs at any time, if he can get more money or better prospects.

The 1850 report of the Hong Kong Education Committee remarked that the Chinese parent's attachment to education was 'secondary to his attachment to gain'. In fact the two enthusiasms have gone hand in hand, as they did in Samuel Smiles' self-helping England. Hong Kong's newly emergent middle class is immensely able and ambitious, and the mass of the proletariat, fastening its children's blazer buttons as it sends them off to school, is a living testimony to the ideological inspiration of free enterprise. There are said to be 30,000 restaurants in Hong Kong, and nearly all are family concerns. There are 4,700 fishing-boats, each in effect a private company. There are 16,478 taxis, and 15,654 of them are singly and privately owned.

12

Soon after the beginning of British Hong Kong there was a plan to build its chief town in Happy Valley, linking it by canal to the sea, and creating wharfs and go-downs within the shelter of the hills. There was a plan to import Australian sheep-farmers and cattlemen, with their herds and flocks; the southern slopes of Hong Kong Island would be turned into grazing-land, speckled with eucalyptus trees no doubt, with tin-roofed ranches above the China Sea, and Chinese cowboys riding about in floppy hats.[1] There still is, as I write, that plan to build a new container port, and a new airport too, on an artificial island off Lantau, to be spectacularly linked with Central by a viaduct across the western roadsteads.

But then almost nothing has not been proposed, at one time or another, for the making of money in Hong Kong. The chief strength of this economy has always been its flexibility. Because it has been relatively free from Government interference, it has been able to switch easily from idea to idea, method to method, emphasis to emphasis. If it is frighteningly changeable sometimes, it has proved resilient too, swiftly recovering its poise after wars, revolutions, riots, share collapses and even treaties about its future. As 1997 draws near we see Hong Kong still working at the furious pace to which the world has grown accustomed; contemplating its apparently irresistible momentum I find it hard to remember that within my own lifetime it was considered a dull backwater of Empire.

[1] Who would certainly have strengthened one of Hong Kong's more mysterious contemporary institutions, the Hong Kong Graziers' Union.

8

1920s: DOGDAYS

FOR THE BRITISH EMPIRE ALMOST EVERYWHERE THE YEARS between the two world wars were dogdays. The sacrifices of 1914–18 had exhausted the British people, and the fire of the imperial idea was fading. Imperialism's morality was widely questioned, self-determination was everywhere in the air, so that more and more the administrators of Empire approached their task in an apologetic, or at least conciliatory mood. Men of vaulting ambition or reckless disposition seldom looked for a career in the imperial service now; in India the Civil Service was steadily Indianized, in the Colonial Service the recruits most required, it was said, were steady, decent, diligent men, preferably with second-class degrees.

British capitalism seemed to be blunted. As a manufacturing nation Britain had been overtaken, as a commercial nation its supremacy was waning. No longer did the British merchant fleet have a virtual monopoly of the eastern trade. At home the General Strike of 1926, together with the subsequent great depression, seemed to many to signal the end of British prosperity – perhaps of British stability too.

Although the Empire did not reach its physical apogee until the 1930s, it was patently past its prime. Great Britain could not maintain its posture as the first strategic power of the world. All the forms of superbia were maintained, but the British formally acknowledged that they were no longer the sole arbiters of the sea; in the Washington Treaty of 1922 they agreed to parity with the United States in naval forces everywhere, to parity in the eastern seas with Japan.

All this affected Hong Kong more particularly than most other colonies. The ideal of *laissez-faire*, the very basis of Hong Kong, was out of fashion, as the conception of the Welfare State began tentatively to form, and strategically the colony seemed to be losing its meaning. At Washington the British also agreed to freeze the fortification of their strongholds east of the 110th meridian, which meant in principle east of Singapore, and in practice Hong Kong. The Furthermost Possession was no longer to be, it seemed, a link in Curzon's chain of fortresses, and the size of the China Squadron was progressively reduced. Hong Kong became something of a backwater once more – one of dozens of Crown Colonies, one of the smallest, by no means one of the richest, and rivalled by the growing cosmopolitan glamour of Shanghai, where 7,000 British 'Shanghailanders' already considered themselves much smarter. Imperial reference books of the 1920s give Hong Kong short shrift, and the fashionable tourists of the day, though they often dropped in during the course of their journeys through the Orient, seldom stayed for long.

It was only appropriate that visually Hong Kong seemed to have a completed air. Though it was still the third port of the British Empire, it was not in the condition of excitement, whether commercial or imperial, that we have noticed on earlier visits. It had calmed down. The Hong Kong dollar, worth 6s. 2d. in 1919, throughout the 1920s never rose higher than 3s., and this was no time for adventurous construction. The twin cities of the harbour remained the only substantial towns. The modernist styles about to fall upon Europe and America would not reach Hong Kong for another two decades, and people were still building much as they had been forty years before.

There had been great changes, of course, since 1880. Victoria had been transformed by Paul Chater's Praya Reclamation Scheme. The waterfront of the 1880s was now a block away from the sea, and on the extra land had appeared new premises for the Hong Kong Club, a new Supreme Court and sundry commercial blocks, all fronted by a new esplanade called Connaught Road. Statue Square, then called Royal Square, had doubled its size. It now contained a Cenotaph in memory of the war dead, and effigies of Queen Victoria, largely under a canopy in the middle, Edward VII, George V, Queen Alexandria and the eponymous Duke of Connaught on the esplanade. (The future Edward VIII had vetoed a statue of himself, suggesting that the money be put to better causes.) The Pedder Street clock-tower had gone, having been declared a hazard to traffic, and Jardine's had largely abandoned their East Point headquarters: the tea-chests in their go-downs there were full of archives, and in 1921 a last farewell had been said to No. 1 House with a sentimental candle-lit dinner. Across the water the Kowloon waterfront was now dominated by the towered terminal of the Kowloon to Guangzhou railway, and the four-square hulk of the Peninsula Hotel.

But all the new buildings remained sedately within colonial conventions – fan-cooled, teak-banistered, the Hong Kong Club with Moghul turrets over colonnades, the Supreme Court with a classical dome over arcades, the railway station in a sort of Indo-Byzantine style, the Peninsula perceptibly Chinoise, and most of the office blocks in varieties of tropical-Gothic. A quaint old Receiving Ship still dominated the harbour view – the former troopship *Tamar*, but looking much like the old *Victor Emmanuel* – and the fact that the Praya now extended further to the west, running in a wide sweep along the foreshore towards Possession Point where it all began, only seemed to confirm the sensation that this was the definitive Hong Kong, as it always would be. The French observer, Albert Demangeon, writing in 1925, summed it up, once and for all it seemed, as 'the proudest monument of England's commercial genius'.[1]

Over the hills behind Victoria the scatter of cool white villas now extended to the island's southern shore. The Repulse Bay had entered its delightful career of tea-dances and sundowners, and at Shek O, away on the island's western tip, a group of expatriate country-lovers were building themselves nice tiled bungalows, attended by gravel drives and ornamental flower-beds, almost as they might somewhere in the Green Belt of London. Even Kowloon, though it had grown explosively since the turn of the century, had developed in a seemly way, and the railway station tower was a proper substitute for the lost Pedder Street clock, guiding the ferry-boats, when the fog lay low, just as faithfully into their piers.

Colonial Hong Kong was set in its ways, too. It had been in existence as a British possession for close on eighty years, and the expatriate

---

[1] In *The British Empire*, London, 1925.

community had evolved its own values, rituals and conventions, soon picked up by newcomers and passed on to successors. It had its long-familiar pecking orders of race, function and residence. It had its naval balls and cricket tournaments. Going to see one's friends off on the P. & O., with all the well-loved festivity of gramophone music, streamers and popping champagne bottles, was part of life; so was the King's Birthday Party up at Government House, whatever you happened to think of the Governor.

Everyone in this society had his place – Lane Crawford's floorwalkers in their company mess, the corporal's wife in her married quarter at Murray Barracks, Lady Southorn the Colonial Secretary's wife in her stately drawing room on the Peak, Captain Wotherham, veteran of thirty years in the eastern seas, in his new retirement house overlooking the ships at Kowloon, Mr Kadoorie the vastly successful financier in his enormous house on Nathan Road, the harbour-master in the harbour-master's house, the general still in Head Quarter House, the Astronomer in his house beside the Royal Observatory, Ethel Morrison in Lyndhurst Terrace, Jardine's taipan well-fed as ever at The Mount, the Governor in his palace, electrically illuminated now, opposite the botanical gardens on Upper Albert Road.

By now the great business companies, once so agile and predatory, had acquired a portlier air – the air of Establishment. They had been on the China coast for several generations, and despite the uncertain times were at the apogee of their commercial supremacy, just as Hong Kong had reached its peak as an entrepôt of the China trade. The hongs held an economic stranglehold on South China, Guangzhou nationalists complained, and they were active everywhere else in China too. The Germans having been eliminated from the Far East – 'the impact of World War I on Jardine's', drily wrote one of the firm's directors in retrospect, 'was not disastrous'[1] – among their foreign rivals only the Japanese really counted, and their participation in China's affairs seemed by now no longer a great adventure, but simply business practice.

Their ships dominated the China coast, and provided the chief means of transport into the interior. Their money was behind railways, breweries, fur traders, hotels, textile mills, newspapers. Jardine's had offices

[1] Alan Reid, in *The Thistle and the Jade*, London 1982.

in all the main Chinese cities, and also in Japan, Manchuria and
Taiwan. The Hongkong Bank built itself, in 1923, a Shanghai office
even bigger and grander than its headquarters at 1 Queen's Road
Central – and it was only one of half a dozen great buildings on the
Bund designed by the Hong Kong architects Palmer and Turner.

But middle-age had set in, abetted by tradition. Asked to account
for a certain malaise at Swire's, one of its managers said that it was
becoming dominated by 'a lot of old crocks 50 to 55 years and upwards',
and J. K. Swire himself said there were 'too many deadheads at the top
out East'. The young John Keswick, arriving for his first job at Jardine's
Shanghai office, was handed the same pen that his father had used,
when he joined the firm, and was reminded that his grandfather, his
great-uncle, his father and his elder brother had all been in their day
Chairmen of the Shanghai Municipal Council. The representatives of
the Hongkong and Shanghai Bank were bigwigs too, great men in the
East. The blind Sinologue Guy Hillier, the bank's manager in Beijing
for thirty-nine years, was certainly one of the most influential people
in the capital, and when in 1925 his successor Mr Allen concluded an
interview with the then-dominant war-lord Duan Qi-rui, 'the Marshal
[saw] me to the door of the apartment himself, which my interpreter
told me was an unusual compliment for him to pay'.[1]

All this was apparent in Hong Kong, the source of so much power
and profit, but less in flamboyance than in accomplished routine. The
trading post had got used to itself. Taipans no longer hissed at
Governors, scandals were subdued, libel actions out of fashion. Some of
the flash had left the place, as it had left the Empire as a whole. When a
steamer of Swire's China Navigation Company sailed for Xiamen or
Fuzhou now, it sailed with immensely practised ease, drawn from long
experience; its brasses polished as ever, its black hull fresh-painted, its
house flag proudly flying, its awnings crisp and white, its dinner menu
offering roast beef and Yorkshire pudding as well as shark-fin and
pigeon-egg soup; but it lacked perhaps the old panache, either of High
Imperialism or of illegitimacy.

Almost as if in response to the flagging of public exuberance the
colonists of Hong Kong lived their private lives intensely. People
were living intensely all over the western world, in the days of the

[1] From *Wayfoong*, by Maurice Collis, London 1965.

Charleston and the cocktail, but it showed more in this minute enclave of western ways, set among its archipelago in the mighty flank
of China.

The European and American community was still dominated by its
Britons, but not quite so absolutely. The German colony had been
dispersed by the war, its memory besmirched by propaganda – as a
home-grown victory song had it,

> The Hun has got it in the neck,
> He's crawling in the mud,
> He's a nasty dirty thing,
> Though at fighting not a dud.[1]

On the other hand there were more Americans about – some 500 in
the later 1920s – more Frenchmen, more Dutch and far more Japanese,
while the Jewish, Indian and Portuguese communities had all produced
rich and eminent citizens to challenge the supremacy of the British.

But the British did not care, for the kind of Britons who lived in
Hong Kong still felt themselves to be at the apogee of their national
achievement. It took time for metropolitan attitudes to filter through
to this remote possession. Like Jardine's, Hong Kong had not suffered
much from the Great War, and for the most part people felt as privileged by destiny as they had forty years before. 'She had never', wrote
Somerset Maugham about one of his Hong Kong characters,[2] 'paid
anything but passing and somewhat contemptuous attention to the
China in which fate had thrown her,' and she doubtless felt almost as
superior to Dutchmen or Japanese (two half-Japanese girls, indeed,
particularly admired by officers of the Royal Navy, were thought
unsuitable guests by the loftier chatelaines of the day).

At the start of the 1920s much about the colony seemed to visitors
quaintly old-fashioned. The up-to-the-minute Hong Kong of the 1890s
had long been left behind. If you were invited to dinner at the Peak
from Kowloon, for instance, you took a rickshaw to the ferry-station, a
Star Ferry to Central, another rickshaw to the lower Peak tram station,
a tram to the upper station and a third rickshaw to your host's front
door – anachronism indeed to a traveller from post-war London. The
chief noises of the city streets were still the old noises, the cries of

---

[1] Quoted in Paul Gillingham's *At the Peak*, Hong Kong 1983, to which I am indebted
for much in this chapter.
[2] In *The Painted Veil*, London 1925.

Chinese hawkers, the clanging of tram bells, plus the hooters and chugging engines of the ships at sea.

In the course of the decade things changed. For one thing motor cars arrived in force – 'coughing, spluttering, honking demons', as a Chinese protest to the Governor called them. The Governor himself had ridden around in a car, rather than a sedan-chair, ever since the attempted assassination of Sir Henry May in 1912, and by 1929 there were 1,400 private cars in the colony, mostly American-built but including two Rolls-Royces, together with 247 taxis, 150 buses, 446 trucks and 460 motor cycles. The roads were beginning to be congested, and as early as 1925 Howard T. Werschul, an American flour merchant, got two months' hard labour for 'wanton and furious driving'.

European social life grew more sophisticated, as the years passed, but even so it sounds a sadly provincial society. It saw last year's films at the cinema (evening dress only in the Dress Circle), it played the gramophone records of the day before yesterday (*One Stolen Kiss*, or *Deep in My Heart, Dear*), it eagerly read the social news from London ('News and Gossip from the Metropolis'). It went to dinner-dances a lot, and to beach parties at Repulse Bay, where a row of 120 mat-sheds provided shelter for hamper lunches, and steam launches waited offshore to take the revellers home. It smoked a great deal, drank without much finesse – gin before dinner, whisky during the meal, brandy afterwards: Governor Sir Henry May, opening a drinking-water reservoir in 1918, had pointedly observed that because of the general preference for stronger liquids only one in two of the lower-rank European civil servants ever lived to draw their pensions. Sometimes the Tramway Company arranged evening excursions to the beaches at North Point, and parties got together to swim hilariously in the moonlight to the music of a band.

The community prided itself on its English idiosyncrasies, sometimes rather silly ones: the Governor Sir Reginald Stubbs, who attended Council meetings every Thursday morning and afternoon, said he might as well have tripe for his Thursday lunch too, and so instituted a luncheon club called the Victoria Tripe Hounds, with Master and Whips, which ate tripe and onions among comic flummery at Government House. At the same time, like most societies in the English-speaking world, Anglo Hong Kong was becoming slightly Americanized. The stars of Hollywood were the stars of its cinemas, the songs of New York were the songs on Radio Station ZBW (except on Sundays, when air-time was reserved exclusively for higher things).

'Cascade?' asked an advertisement for beer, and the answer was pure America: '*You Betcha!*'

In 1922 the Prince of Wales arrived for a three-day visit, with Lord Louis Mountbatten as his equerry: it was somehow characteristic of the place that when they walked for the first time into the apparently empty gardens of Government House there was a sudden blast of a whistle, and out of the shrubberies sprang a horde of boy scouts and girl guides, 'all yelling', we are told, 'shrilly'.

At the summit of expatriate activities stood the Peak, by now a snootier hill station than any of its Indian progenitors. It was officially defined by height – the Peak District constituted anything on Hong Kong Island above the 788-foot contour – and its allegorical situation up there among the clouds meant that altitude had become a kind of obsession. Peakites, as they were known, looked down not just topographically but socially too upon those with houses on lower contour lines.

> Before she arose to the Peak
>   (*wrote a contemporary lyricist*)
> Matilda was timid and meek,
> But now she offends
> Her Bowen Road friends
> With a smile that is cutting and bleak.

Bowen Road? Where was Bowen Road? Why, down in mid-Levels, at least 200 feet too low.

By now the Peak was a very beautiful residential area, its winding lanes half-hidden by trees, lined with ferns and shrubberies. No motor road ran up there yet, and the Peak tram, electrified in 1926, was busier than ever, and very obliging; if by any chance you missed the last tram up, which left Victoria at 11.45 p.m., you could order a private tram at any time up to three in the morning. The more traditional of the Peak's grandees, nevertheless, were still carried up and down in sedan-chairs; some went up by chair, down by bicycle, and Mr R. C. Hurley, whose house stood rather lower than the upper tram terminal, liked to complete his journey home on his 'motor-less motorcar', a four-wheeled carriage which enabled him to free-wheel all the way to his front door.

There were officers' messes on the Peak now, and a number of messes housing the young assistants of the great companies, so that the social life was lively. Dropping one's card at the Peak residences was an essential introduction to Hong Kong society, and every self-respecting household maintained a card-box by the gate; as Lady Southorn was to write,[1] the card-box was the very symbol of western civilization – 'the West has a box and the East doesn't'. Bridge sessions were popular. Crumpets at the Peak Hotel were excellent still. Dinner-parties were lengthy, six or seven courses being eaten, black ties worn, music sometimes provided by Filipino bands, additional young men courtesy of the Royal Navy.

A formidable Residents' Association kept up the tone of this Elysium, vetting even European governesses before they were allowed to accept employment (though it was up to the Governor himself, under the Peak Preservation Order of 1918, to decide who might be householders). The Chinese coolies who brought supplies up the Peak were forbidden to use the tram, and were obliged to labour with their heavy loads of coal, ice, food and building materials up the steep and often rain-washed tracks. In 1921 a compassionate clergyman discovered that one small labourer, aged six, spent twelve hours a day, six days a week, carrying fifty-eight-pound loads of coal from the waterfront to a house of lofty eminence.

A rung or two down the social ladder, many Europeans lived in the mid-Levels swathe of residential streets, between the Peak and the commercial waterfront, but by the mid-1920s there was a shift of social emphasis off the island altogether, across the harbour to Kowloon. Until the acquisition of the New Territories, twenty years before, such a movement had seemed inconceivable. Nobody then lived in Kowloon, it used to be said, except soldiers and Portuguese, and almost nobody respectable went there except to have a seaside picnic. There was nothing much to do there anyway, except for men of raffish tastes. In those days Nathan Road, the main thoroughfare, had degenerated after half a mile or so into a rutted country lane, and ended altogether at Boundary Street, marked by a bamboo frontier fence. Beyond were the mysteries of China, where superstition reigned, where bandits and tigers lurked, where ne'er-do-wells went to gamble with the natives, and unspeakable things went on in opium dens.

[1] In *Under The Mosquito Curtain*, Hong Kong 1935.

By the 1920s the New Territories had become the countryside of Hong Kong. People went hiking and picnicking there, looked at walled villages or collected wild flowers. Sportsmen shot duck in the Mai Po marshes, and the Governor had a country house at Fanling (much nicer, most incumbents thought, than Mountain Lodge). As the gateway to all these pleasures, Kowloon was no longer a disreputable enclave on a foreign shore, but was fast becoming a twin city to Victoria, and much of the colony's vigour had migrated there.

Old-fashioned ladies still asked of men 'Are you married or do you live in Kowloon?', but in fact besides many well-heeled Chinese, Indians and Portuguese, who often found it more congenial than the stuffier Hong Kong-side, a perfectly respectable British society was now settled in spacious and shady colonial houses on the edge of the town. Engineers, middle-rank officials, merchant-navy officers had settled there, and had formed a Kowloon Ratepayers' Association, like the more stately association of the Peak, to try and keep the Chinese masses out of their district too. And in 1927 the social balance was still further shifted by the opening of the Peninsula Hotel, much the grandest in Hong Kong, along the road from the railway station on the waterfront of Tsim Sha Tsui.

This was a world away from the now shabby corridors and old-fashioned saloons of the Hong Kong Hotel, long left high and dry away from the sea by the march of reclamation. Six storeys high and designed to international standards of luxury, the Peninsula was really a transport hotel, built to serve passengers disembarking from ocean liners, or arriving on the train from Guangzhou, Beijing, Moscow, Paris or London. But it became the smartest place of all to have a dance or give a party, the focus of young European social life, and for three decades the best-known building in Hong Kong.

Back across the water the Governors lived as Governors always had. Government House had undergone a metamorphosis. From the pleasant gentleman's villa we saw in the 1880s it had developed into a palace more on the Anglo-Indian pattern, with the addition of a large annexe, almost as big as the original house, containing a ballroom, a billiard room, a supper room, card rooms and smoking rooms. The first great guest to be entertained there was Grand Duke Nicholas, the future Tsar of Russia, who had found in Hong Kong, as we have seen, a fairly chilly public reception, and spent much of his time at

Solutions: *above*: expressway, 1980s; *below*: Peak tram, early 1900s

Central, 1980s: left, the head office of the Hongkong and Shanghai Bank;
centre, the Legislative Council building

Government House looking at his own ship through a telescope on the roof.

Two men occupied the house throughout the 1920s, and offered a pungent contrast in gubernatorial styles. The first was Sir Reginald Stubbs, a caustic and sometimes ferocious autocrat who spoke no Chinese and believed in corporal punishment for the natives. He was the son of a famous father, Bishop William Stubbs the constitutional historian, and he himself was an Oxford double-first, with a reputation for quick wits and no fooling about. Ironically he was to be remembered best in Hong Kong not for his despotic tastes, but for an act of reconciliation – The Return of the Kam Tim Gates.

These were the ancestral wrought-iron gates of Kat Hing Wai, the walled village at Kam Tin which we have earlier glimpsed. In 1898 they had been presented to the British Government by the Tang clan as a sign of submission to its authority, and whisked away to his home in Ireland by the Governor of the time, Sir Henry Blake. The Tangs had long regretted handing the gates over, and there were periodical requests for their return. Stubbs undertook to get them back. At first nobody could discover where they were, but they were eventually tracked down in Ireland and restored to the village at a cordial ceremony in 1925. Actually they were not a pair, Blake having simply selected for himself the best out of four, but they looked handsome enough anyway, and beside them a plaque was erected, in Chinese and in English, to tell the tale ('from this can be seen the deep kindness and great virtue of the British Government . . .').

This was not, in general, the Stubbs style. He believed all his life in the firm imperial hand. He went from Hong Kong to govern Jamaica, where according to the *Dictionary of National Biography* he was well-fitted to keep any strivings towards democracy 'within the bounds of realism', and then to Cyprus, where unrealistic subjects had lately burnt down Government House. Ending his colonial career as Governor of Ceylon – he was one of the few men ever to govern four colonies – during the Second World War he became the chairman, not a reassuring chairman one would imagine, of a conscientious objectors' tribunal.

The Old Hong Kong Hands must have loved Stubbs, for all his Oxford manner, and one can imagine him easily enough in the Hong Kong of the 1890s, or even at a pinch the 1840s. His successor was a much more modern man, and much less to the taste of the die-hards – a regular China-lover, a speaker of Mandarin and Cantonese, a skilled

Chinese calligrapher. The son of an Indian Army officer, Sir Cecil Clementi was a classicist too, and a fine linguist. He had family connections with Hong Kong, and had begun his own career there at the beginning of the century, but since then he had served in British Guiana and Ceylon, had made a famous journey across Central Asia, and had come back as Governor full of liberal notions. Unlike Stubbs, he was distinctly a man of the new, enlightened imperial times. He was a bold critic of racial prejudice, and declared quite openly that the division between Chinese and European communities in Hong Kong 'retards the social, moral, intellectual, and even the commercial and material progress of the colony'.

Dangerous words in the Hong Kong of the 1920s, where even the island of Cheung Chau had its own lesser Peak, forbidden to Chinese residents, and where European shop assistants would not dream of shaking a Chinese hand. Clementi, though, matched them with action, going so far as to appoint a Chinese to his Executive Council, the Cabinet of Hong Kong. Chinese now became frequent guests at Government House, and once the Governor even suggested abolishing the Hong Kong Club, that holy of colonial holies, and replacing it with a club open to the membership of all races.

Though Hong Kong did not recognize it, Clementi represented the way the British Empire was moving. As he frankly said, the day of European dominance in China, as in India, was coming to an end. By the end of the decade the British had renounced three of its concessions along the China coast, and had agreed in principle that all other extraterritorial privileges in China must gradually go. Among these they did not actually include the possession of Hong Kong itself. Even a Clementi could not yet imagine its return to China – 'I cannot believe that the British Empire will ever acquiesce in the retrocession of Hong Kong.' Nevertheless there were people alive in the colony then who really would live to see, never indeed the abolition of the Hong Kong Club, but plenty of Chinese members in it.

For like it or not – ignore it if you could – all around the 4,500 Britons of Hong Kong lived 725,000 Chinese.

Until now the Chinese of Hong Kong had been passive observers of its history. To visitors as to historians they figured only as an amorphous background, faceless and anonymous but for those few who, by adapting to western needs, had qualified themselves for notice. Very few Chinese names appeared in the history books, because very few Chinese had played public parts in the development of Hong Kong; and the mass of the Chinese population seemed to most observers oblivious to public events, intent only on making a living. 'The general indifference of the Chinese to all matters of public life,' Stubbs once said, 'was almost unbelievable.' But now, in this rather flat Hong Kong decade, for the first time the Chinese showed their strength. When the 1920s came to be remembered by those Old Hands, they would be remembered not after all for their ordinariness or their frivolity, but for their Troubles, the first Hong Kong had ever suffered, which came out of China to give the complacent colony early warning of things to come.

China was in a particularly confused condition then. The euphoria of the 1911 revolution, which had abolished the Manchu monarchy, had soon been dispelled by conflicts among the revolutionaries, by the emergence of the New Culture Movement which advocated the abolition of all tradition, by the birth of the Chinese Communist Party and by the marchings here and there of restless war-lords with their private armies. In 1921, Beijing being in war-lord hands, Sun Yat-sen, the father of the revolution, was elected president of the Republic in Guangzhou. He was repeatedly snubbed by the British, who regarded him as a rebel still, and preferred anyway to maintain, in the absence of any sensible policy, that whoever ruled in Beijing was the rightful ruler of all China. Sun Yat-sen further antagonized the British Empire in general, and Sir Reginald Stubbs in particular, by turning his regime sharply to the left, legalizing trade unions and welcoming help from the Soviet Union. Under its auspices a powerfully revolutionary and xenophobic movement arose, based upon Guangzhou, and inevitably turned its attention downstream to Hong Kong – that stranglehold of foreigners, the one corner of China where alien capitalists sat in sovereign state.

Within Hong Kong hundreds of thousands of Chinese, like the little porter of the Peak, still lived lives of terrible hardship, working cruel hours for miserable wages, often ill, often addled with drugs. Few of them had been born in the colony, but they were no longer fellow-pioneers, as the first Chinese settlers had been; they were mostly peasants from Guangdong Province plunged suddenly into the bewildering pressures of an advanced western urbanism. Poor people's housing was not much different from that described by Chadwick in 1882, and the Government was doing little to improve it. An absentee landlord of

Hollywood Road, it was recorded in 1924, sublet his tenement building to a middleman, who let it in separate apartments to other people, who rented out cubicles in each apartment – often twenty-five people in a single apartment, often far more. It was officially estimated, that same year, that about a quarter of the Chinese population smoked opium, and there were at least 2,000 opium divans. All the modernism of Hong Kong was designed to benefit the Europeans, not the Chinese: Station ZBW broadcast only an occasional programme in Chinese, and only one cinema provided a Chinese interpreter – who, sitting on a chair beside the screen, translated as he went along.

But the Chinese were by no means as impotent as they had been forty years before. As Clementi's dinner-table showed, there were many rich and influential citizens too – more every month, as refugees of substance fled the uncertainties of China. Educated Chinese had infiltrated many of the European residential districts, and Sir Robert Ho Tung had been lording it on the Peak itself for years. The University of Hong Kong, founded in 1911 by the personal efforts of the Governor Sir Frederick Lugard, was now producing a steady flow of Chinese graduates. The Tung Wah had developed into a powerful community organization. More ominously, there were active Chinese trade unions – not just old-fashioned guilds like the Firewood Dealers' Industrial and Commercial Association, or the Jinseng and Deer Horns Commercial Guild, with their roots in Confucian ideas of loyalty and order, but modern and militant unions with their roots in revolutionary Marxism, and their inspiration in Guangzhou.

The vast majority of foreign residents, as Maugham perceived, had not the slightest notion what was happening among the Chinese masses. The Chinese they met socially were all smiles and common interests, the Chinese they employed all charm and sycophancy. Social segregation kept the generality at a distance, and fierce punishments kept it in order – twelve months' hard labour and eighteen strokes of the birch, for instance, for stealing a handbag with $HK24 in it, three months' hard labour for taking a European's hat as he rode in a rickshaw. Though there had been localized riots about food prices in 1919, and a seamen's strike in 1922, it came as a shock to them in the middle of the decade to discover that the usual conspiracies of Triad and syndicate, the usual criminal activities in the congested tenements of Wanchai and Kowloon, the snatching of hats or handbags, could be directed to political ends.

Such a shock! The disturbances were hardly more than communal grumbles at first, almost undetectable upon the Peak; but after the death of Sun Yat-sen, in 1925, and following anti-foreign troubles in Shanghai, they erupted into a full-scale General Strike, together with a boycott of all trade between Hong Kong and the province of Guangdong, which included Guangzhou itself and provided most of Hong Kong's food. It was very nearly the rising that the British had feared, on and off, ever since the Indian Mutiny. For a few weeks the economic life of the colony was frozen. Seamen, students, hotel staffs, stevedores, domestic servants, bus and tram drivers all walked off the job. Even rickshaw men refused custom. Food prices soared, and there was a run on the banks.

There was much violence, and more violent talk. On the one hand the strike leaders terrified workers into striking, on the other an unofficial strike-breaking body, the Labour Protection Bureau, behaved just as thuggishly. In the middle stood Sir Reginald Stubbs, threatening intimidators with the cat-o'-nine-tails and advocating armed intervention by the Royal Navy, as in the old days. Frightening rumours swept the colony. Bolshevist bogeys loomed large. The Hong Kong Volunteers were mustered for possible action, and a State of Emergency was declared. 'Those who disturb the peace of the colony', announced Stubbs, 'will be treated, as is the way with the English, justly but sternly.'

The Peakites now found themselves obliged to undertake all manner of tasks they were not used to, such as ironing their own clothes, cooking their own meals, burying their own night-soil and even looking after their own children. Volunteers kept things going in hotels and cafés, drove the trams and distributed the mail, while the Royal Navy took over the Star Ferry service, not altogether successfully – as one of the local newspapers complained, the Navy's 'spotless uniforms and trailing impedimenta of silken hankerchiefs and lanyards' were hardly the gear for it. The strike leaders encouraged all Chinese to leave Hong Kong altogether, spreading rumours that the British were going to poison their water-supplies, and at the same time offering free train and steamer passage to Guangzhou. Thousands went, leaving the city half-empty and forlorn.

To make matters worse there was a spate of piratical attacks upon British ships. Sometimes the pirates boarded ships from junks, sometimes they sailed as passengers, attacking the crew when they were at sea, and forcing them to sail to some secluded and sympathetic haven on the Chinese coast. A ferry was actually hijacked on its way from

Cheung Chau to Central; relatives in Hong Kong were sent the amputated ears of three passengers, and a large ransom was paid. A special body of guards, many of them White Russian, was raised by the Government, and many ships went to sea with iron grilles isolating passenger quarters, bridges and engine rooms.

In these circumstances the strike leaders' demands do not sound exorbitant. They included an eight-hour day, the prohibition of child labour, the suppression of police brutality, an end to segregation on the Peak, a 25 per cent reduction in rents and labour representation in the Executive Council. These requirements were summed up in a *South China Morning Post* headline as LABOURERS' EXTRAORDINARY ATTITUDE, and they severely damaged economic confidence. Stocks, shares and land values dramatically fell, and there were many bankruptcies – twenty a day in September, 1925. A deputation of businessmen even asked Stubbs to arrange a $3 million trade loan from Britain to see them through the crisis. A loan, from Government to Big Business in Hong Kong – the times were topsy-turvy!

The cash was reluctantly provided by the Treasury in London, which did not however inconvenience the British taxpayer with the matter. This was still the Empire, and the money was raised instead from the West African Currency Board and the Straits Settlements of Malaya.

All in all the 1920s were not good years for Hong Kong, but they were not so bad either. They were dogdays after all. The political crisis did not last long, and the worst never happened. China's pattern shifted again. Guangzhou became less fiercely hostile. By the end of 1926 strike and boycott had both fizzled out, like the General Strike at home in Britain, and Clementi, now the Governor, made a friendly trip up the Pearl River to seal their conclusion.

Colonial life in Hong Kong resumed its style. 'We are constantly receiving,' announced Lane Crawford's catalogue, Autumn 1926, 'large consignments of Fascinating Creations for Evening Wear, all personally selected in London and Paris by our own representatives.' The Chinese returned to docility, and nobody had trouble with rickshaw men any more – 'you just go to the door and shout "Sha"', recorded an Englishwoman without malice, 'and they come running up, seeing who can get there first'.

9   CONTROL SYSTEMS

I

IN STATUE SQUARE THERE STANDS A DISTINGUISHED DOMED
and colonnaded building, with Ionic columns and red-tiled roofs,
which is a rare survivor of times lost. Designed in 1900 largely by Sir
Aston Webb, architect of the Victoria and Albert Museum in London,
it used to be the Supreme Court of Hong Kong, until that body moved
to its air-conditioned tower-building along the road. It was neighbour
to the Palladian City Hall, before that fine old structure was demolished, and to the Gothic Hong Kong Club, before the club's
metamorphosis into a skyscraper. It opened upon the cricket field,
until the stumps were transferred to a less valuable pitch. It looked
down upon the statues of Queen Victoria and her successors, until
Their Majesties were removed by the Japanese Army. For a couple of
generations it dominated the central ceremonial place of Hong Kong,
a stone's throw from the sea until reclamation took the sea away, and
its dome was one of the prime symbols of the island skyline.

Today it is dwarfed by the commercial structures around it, which
have reduced that once fine piazza into a finicky municipal garden,
trisected by roads. The one memorial remaining is the Cenotaph
honouring the war dead, the one statue still there is of Sir Thomas
Jackson the bank manager. Legend says the gardens themselves are

only spared, in one of the world's most valuable patches of real estate, because they are essential to the happy *feng shui* of the Hongkong and Shanghai Bank's headquarters at the head of them; actually they are spared because in 1901 the Bank agreed with the Government to keep an open space there 'for all time'.

But the old domed building survives, and has been meticulously restored, and is now the headquarters of the Legislative Council, Legco, the nearest thing the Crown Colony of Hong Kong has ever had to a Parliament. It is here, on a Wednesday afternoon when the Council meets nowadays, that one can best start an exploration of the systems by which this territory has been governed for the past century and a half; a Wednesday a few years back, in 1986, say, before the impending change of sovereignty began to alter everything, and made the British no longer their own masters in Hong Kong.

2

A session of the Legislative Council, in 1986, could be rather a comical affair. The Establishment of Hong Kong was there upon display. There was one double-barrelled Briton, there were Chinese with names like Rita, Lydia, Hilton or Donald, but no Japanese or Americans were present – this was still a British colonial assembly, run to its own rules. Hong Kong being what it is, a Florence of the art of public relations, television cameras were perpetually trained upon the assembly, while still photographs were taken through strategically placed windows on each side of the chamber – 'The Governor takes a sip of water during the debate,' said the captions next morning, or 'Miss Lydia Dunn adjusts her microphone . . .'

The unfortunate Governor presided, from his high mahogany dais – unfortunate because he must act not merely as Speaker, but also more or less as clerk, taking note of all proceedings hour after hour and only occasionally intervening himself. The British knights of the executive were ex officio there – Chief Secretary, Financial Secretary, Attorney-General, side by side on a front bench like Cabinet Ministers. The seven appointed officials were there, from the Secretary for District Administration (the Honourable E. P. Ho) to the Secretary for Transport (the Honourable I. F. C. Macpherson). The twenty-two appointed unofficial members were there – swells of the community most of them, bankers British and Chinese, businessmen, well-known public benefactors, all nominated to their seats by the Governor. And across the chamber sat the elected minority of twenty-four members, voted for not by the direct vote of the public, but by members of district, urban and regional councils, or by functional constituencies – this member representing the legal profession, that one industry, medicine or architecture. Of the fifty-seven members, forty-seven were Chinese.

This was the nearest that Hong Kong, while it was still really in control of its own destinies, had ever got to representative Government – the nearest that the British Government had ever thought suitable to the place. Hong Kong enjoys absolute freedom of speech and opportunity, but no freedom at all to choose its rulers. The basic principle of the Crown Colony system was that there should be a Government-appointed majority in the Legislature, and in Hong Kong that principle has always been maintained. The only direct elections are to local councils; it was only in 1985 that *any* kind of election to the Legislature first took place, and even then only a minute proportion of the population was qualified to vote – some 70,000 people in all. Any reforms that happen in the future can be construed as reforms under pressure: the Legislative Council, 1986, was the British Empire's own, voluntary summit of parliamentary democracy in Hong Kong.

It could be said then to be the summit of political aspiration among the Hong Kong Chinese, too. The prospect of 1997 has changed their views rather, as we shall later see, but until very recently most of them wanted nothing to do with politics. Bred as they were to the Confucianist conception of government by a specially trained élite, they were quite prepared to let the British do all the governing for them, while they got on with life. The Canadian social-psychologist Michael H. Bond, of the Chinese University of Hong Kong, has analysed [1] their attitudes thus: 'Social truth does not arise from the open clash of contending opinions, but is delivered by conscientious leaders after careful consideration of the issues. A grateful citizenry plays its role by repaying the efforts of the leadership with loyalty and acceptance.' Democratic, adversarial politics hardly come readily to such a citizenry. It is a step towards chaos, says a Chinese proverb, when argument begins.

The comedy of Legco, 1986, arose because now that the story was almost over, and any future constitutional changes could be made only with the consent, tacit or declared, of the Chinese Government in Beijing, the Legislative Council was conducted as a sort of solemn

---

[1] In *Inter-Ethnic Conflict: Myth and Reality*, Beverly Hills 1986.

parody of British parliamentary practice. Heavy were the courtesies, in the true Westminster style, laboured was the sarcasm, slight but ineffably Parliamentarian were the jokes. Those Knight Commanders of the front bench emanated genial power – three able but sufficiently ordinary Britons, to be encountered one might think any day on a stockbrokers' commuter train into Waterloo, transformed into Honourable Ministers on the other side of the globe. How the members laughed, when one of these mandarins offered a sally, and with what bridling modesty he resumed his seat amidst the amusement! The nominated members, heirs to generations of sycophancy or self-interest, generally addressed the Chamber respectfully, in all the convoluted usage of Westminster practice – 'Would the honourable member the Financial Secretary not agree . . .?' – 'I put it to my honourable friend the Secretary for Economic Services . . .' The elected members, while keeping within the bounds of Parliamentary propriety, demonstrated their independence with shows of defiance – they were after all the closest Hong Kong had ever seen to an official Opposition, and they had only been invented the year before. The speeches were nearly all in English, but with simultaneous translation into Chinese, and were for the most part earnest but pedestrian. The topics were generally innocuous. The vote of the assembly was, to put it bluntly, powerless.

For the Governor remained, in 1986, omnipotent. Anything Legco decided, he could cancel. Anything he decreed, Legco must accept. The authority of the Governor, sitting up here looking so bored, poor fellow, as the Honourable the Financial Secretary moved into the second phase of his argument about the relationship between inflation and exchange rates – the Governor's authority was derived 'from Letters Patent passed under the Great Seal of the United Kingdom', and was subject only to decisions of the Secretary of State for Foreign Affairs in London, or of the monarch. Like all his predecessors, he was not *just* the Governor. He might no longer be accredited to countless millions, as Sir John Bowring had been, but he was the titular Commander-in-Chief, the President of Legco and the representative of the Crown, 'exerting', so the official Hong Kong handbook said in a delicate periphrasis, 'a major influence over the direction of affairs'. He had an Executive Council to advise him, whose fourteen members were all ex officio or officially appointed, but he presided over it and decided what it should advise him about, and constitutionally he need not accept its advice anyway.

But there he sat, looking a little tired one thinks (as it happens he was the universally liked Sir Edward Youde, who was to die in office later in the year), courteously guiding Legco towards the next subject of its debate – whether or not discounts should be allowed on officially authorized leasehold transfers. It was a somewhat Carrollean sensation, any Wednesday afternoon towards the end of the 1980s, to stray into the protocol of this debating chamber out of Hong Kong's fantastic tumult.

3

Of course it was not comical really. Little in Hong Kong is very funny – this must be one of the most calculating and deliberate societies on earth. The degree of Legco's power, like its ration of democratic system, has been most carefully estimated and controlled, set against the unique circumstances of Hong Kong, and released or restrained as an engineer controls a steam valve.

If it had been situated anywhere else Hong Kong would long since have become self-governing, like almost every other British colony, to turn itself eventually I suppose into another such entity as Singapore. Standing as it does at the mercy of China, on Chinese soil, on Chinese terms, it has remained what it was at the beginning, a bureaucratic autocracy. Its constitutional situation now, as one of the most advanced financial centres in the world, is more or less the constitutional situation of Gambia or Bermuda half a century ago. It is the very last of the classic British Crown Colonies, even impotent dependencies like St Helena (population 5,147) or the Cayman Islands (population 22,000), now having legislatures with an elected majority. Hong Kong is an otherwise obsolete entity astonishingly preserved, or a preternaturally lively fossil: partly a British imperial relic, but in a more suggestive way an echo of a lost China too – it is very proper that the colony's crest is supported by a lion, sinister, but dexter a Chinese dragon.

The monarchical status of the place, like that of old China, hangs like a thin miasma over its affairs. Pictures of the Queen ornament offices, the Queen's Birthday garden party is one of the social events of the year, the Jockey Club, the Yacht Club, the Golf Club, the police force all enjoy the prefix 'Royal'. Having been graciously recognized in honours lists citizens are largely pictured in the local papers collecting their medals at Government House, or better yet at Buckingham Palace, still the fount of Hong Kong's chivalry. Royal visits are never forgotten. When Prince Alfred, the first member of the British royal family to come, arrived on board the warship *Galatea* in 1869, the event was described by a local historian, J. W. Norton-Kyshe, as unique in the history of the world – 'never before had a Royal Prince visited lands so remote from the centres of civilization'. Only one reigning monarch, Elizabeth II, has ever followed his example, but the future George V came in 1881, the future Edward VIII in 1922, and after Youde's sudden death in 1986 some people tipped the heir to the throne, Prince Charles, to succeed him – administrative experience, it was argued, knowledge of China and its languages, diplomatic expertise, all being less valuable in Hong Kong than a touch of the royal charisma.

During the spring blossoming of the azaleas the gardens of Government House, home of the Queen's Deputy, are open for one day to the general public. The occasion seems to exert an arcane compulsion upon many Chinese people of Hong Kong, and suggests to me some traditional festival of China under the Manchus, a day of chrysanthemums or lotus-blossom perhaps. On an average Azalea Day 100,000 people visit the gardens, and all day long the crowds hasten up the hill to the gatehouse where the sentry stands, in a mood partly festive (for they come in entire families, bringing their cameras) but partly in a spirit of awe.

Ostensibly, of course, the gardens themselves are the attraction of the day – still agreeable, with their shrubs and sloping lawns, for all the grim commercial buildings which now block their prospect of the harbour. Round and round their gravel paths the wondering throng meanders, taking flowered pictures all the way – small children dimpled among the blossoms, family groups posed in arbours – everywhere, at every splash of colour, the fixed smiles and the click of shutters. It is not however the foliage that is the real focus of the day, but the place itself, and the royal mystique it represents; when I was in the gardens one Azalea Day I saw a Chinese laboriously and reverently copying down in English, as one might copy Imperial Scrolls, the injunctions posted here and there, such as THIS WAY OUT, or DO NOT PICK THE FLOWERS.

4

A gubernatorial aide once showed me, in his room at Government House, how to affix the blue and white plumes on his ceremonial white topee (makers, Horton and Sons, London). They have their own Plume Box, and pushed into holes on the helmet's crown, are fastened with bolts below. The Governor, his entourage, and his armed forces, who are equipped still with many such fancies of the imperial tradition, offer the chief visible reminder that Hong Kong is still a colony.

We have seen that in previous decades, when Plume Boxes were far more common, the imperial factor was inescapable. It is only in the past half-century that Hong Kong has evolved into the condition of a City-State, half-autonomous, maintaining its own trade relations with foreign Powers. Before the Second World War it considered itself only another of the imperial departments, and officials saw their appointments to Hong Kong as steps in a career; just a glance at the roster of Governors down the years shows that they came from, or went to, possessions as promisingly varied as Corfu, Newfoundland, Gambia, New South Wales, Ceylon, Malaysia, India, Borneo and the colonies of the Caribbean.

The usual imperial transmigrations occurred. Ponies and eucalyptus trees came from Australia, indentured labourers went to South Africa, Mr Rynes' rabbits came from England, convicts were transported to Malaya (Pope-Hennessy indeed once suggested that Labuan might be attached to Hong Kong as its own penal dependency). Hong Kong Chinese, full citizens of the Empire then, travelled and settled everywhere under the British flag. For many years after its foundation, though, Hong Kong was particularly under the spell of British India. Every eastern colony was. The Empire in India was overwhelmingly the greatest of British possessions, the hub around which the entire Empire revolved. It was Curzon, who wrote so rapturously of Hong Kong, who declared that without the possession of India the whole Empire would lose its point.

The colony never had official links with British India. It had never been, like Aden or Burma, governed from Calcutta, and its defence was organized by the British, not the Indian Army – Kipling reported in 1888 that the commanding general talked about nothing but English military matters, 'which are very, very different from Indian ones'. Nevertheless the Anglo-Indian influence was profound. The ships from Calcutta or Bombay, the Indian soldiers so often to be seen, the Sikh policemen, the Hindustani words that had entered the vocabulary, the rich Parsee merchants, the generally Anglo-Indian style of living – all made British visitors feel they were still on the circuit of the Raj. Kipling, who thought Hong Kong 'beat Calcutta into a hamlet', nevertheless observed that even the richest of the taipans paid that city 'a curious deference'. At the end of the century surveyors brought from India mapped the newly acquired property of the New Territories; they named its high ground after hills of home, Mendips, Cotswolds, Cheviots, South Downs, but they called its chief rivers the Indus and the Ganges.[1]

Hong Kong even played a part in the Great Game, that prolonged shadow-boxing by which the British and Russian Empires struggled for control of the approaches to India; when its financiers lent money to the Japanese, in the early years of the twentieth century, it was partly to strengthen Japan's position against the Russians, and so to relieve pressure on the Raj in the remote marches of the Hindu Kush. The Indian connection provided a hint of glamour, and no doubt the presence of that mighty possession over the horizon offered the British some reassurance of security. How could their supremacy in the eastern seas be shaken, with such a power around the corner? It was in India that the colony raised its first military force – the Hong Kong Regiment, recruited in 1890 among Pathans, Punjabis and Bengalis, and uniformed dashingly in gold, scarlet, blue, and red stripes. When in 1941 the Japanese attacked Hong Kong, Rajput troops bore the brunt of their first assault, and a band of the Jaipur Guards welcomed the Governor back from imprisonment when all was over.

Another highly visible totem of the imperial factor was the Royal Navy. The size of its squadron in these waters varied down the years, but generally included ships of the most modern kind. 'Large crowds of interested visitors,' reported the *Navy and Army Illustrated* when the brand-new cruiser *Powerful* went into dry-dock at Kowloon in 1898, 'streamed every day to get a sight of the monster cruiser *in puris naturalibus*,' and those Hong Kong harbour views down the decades are like a register of naval architecture: now the black-and-white hulls of sailing frigates, now the bulky turrets of the ironclads – tall raked funnels of County-class cruisers between the two world wars, low-in-the-water gunboats (*Bee, Aphis, Ladybird*) from the Yangtze station, the war-torn task force, led by a battleship of the latest class, which restored British sovereignty to the colony in 1945.

In the last years of the nineteenth century Hong Kong was the Navy's largest naval station in the east, intended in combination with the base at Esquimault, on the western coast of Canada, to give the

---

[1] The names did not stick, and have long since reverted to the Chinese.

Royal Navy supremacy throughout the northern Pacific. Until the fortifications of Singapore in the 1930s the naval dockyard at Victoria was the Navy's only first-class repair base east of Malta. Hong Kong would not have been Hong Kong without the Navy then, for not only was it one of the colony's chief employers, it also set the social pace. An invitation to Government House might be the grandest, a taipan's dinner-table might be the most luxurious, but there was no party like a party on the Commodore's Receiving Ship, all white awnings and fairy-lights at its mooring in the harbour, and no ball like a naval ball, when the most elaborate and ingenious decorations enlivened City Hall, and there was always a new batch of spirited young officers to keep things going.

In later years there was for naval ratings, too, no club quite like the China Fleet Club. Built in 1933 just outside the dockyard at Wanchai, its hospitable bars and pool rooms were familiar to sailors from all over the world, and provided a beery, homely mirror of Britishness in the east. Generations of Royal Navy men knew Hong Kong; conversely generations of Hong Kong Chinese grew up with the Royal Navy. The dockyard workers were known to the fleet affectionately as 'mateys', the sampan girls who painted the warships had friends on every vessel. When the dockyard was closed in 1959, the Civil Lords of the Admiralty sent a message couched in the full glory of English naval language, recalling the loyal craftsmanship of the Chinese workers, and concluding splendidly: 'Their Lordships desire to express their gratitude for all the benefits thus bestowed upon the Royal Navy.'

The Army has been less munificent of style, but almost as intrusive, Hong Kong having been a military town from the start. Scores of British regiments, from Britain itself and from India, came to Hong Kong in the course of their imperial duties, sometimes to garrison the colony itself, sometimes on their way to fight the China wars, and they have left their mark. The general's house, so prominent in the early view-pictures, has been renamed Flagstaff House and is occupied by a museum of tea-ware, but is one of the very few old colonial houses left standing in Central. Nearby some of the old military quarters precariously survive too, and with their tall shady rooms, their twirling fans, their dark green gardens and their jalousies, provide covetably old-school accommodation for civil servants.

The garrison itself has long been shifted to barracks far from Central, but even now Hong Kong has a pervasively military strain. The commanding general is ex officio a member of the Governor's Executive

Council, and the armed forces maintain their headquarters on the site of the old dockyard; its high-rise building has a squeezed-in base which was modish among architects in the 1950s, but which is said by know-alls to be a security device, to keep intruders out of the upper floors. Flags still fly in Hong Kong, bugles sometimes sound, helicopters take off from the quay, and moored alongside are the five especially designed and enormously expensive patrol boats of the Hong Kong Squadron.

Hong Kong has always paid for part of its own defence – 70 per cent of it at the moment – and its forces spend most of their time keeping out illegal immigrants. Nevertheless it remains to this day a fragment of the imperial military system. The Hong Kong Squadron exercises with the Royal Navy far from home, and Hong Kong remains one of the few exotic postings available to the British Army. Three battalions of infantry are normally on station, supported by a service corps of 1,300 Hong Kong Chinese. Properly enough while one battalion is normally of British soldiers, based on the Victorian fort at Stanley, the others are of Gurkha mercenaries from Nepal, last heirs to the Anglo-Indian Army of the Raj.

Like George Curzon, the Empire used to think of Hong Kong as a fortress – it had a Fortress Commander and Fortress Artillery. It was a strongpoint from which the British could carry out their imperial duties throughout the East. The Second World War proved this nonsensical, and today nobody pretends that the place could ever defend itself against a powerful enemy. The Royal Navy dry-docks have been filled in, only their concreted shapes remaining to show where the gunboats and submarines once lay, and everyone knows that the garrison is there only to maintain the status quo for one more decade, until the barracks and the gun emplacements, even Flagstaff House perhaps, are handed over to the People's Liberation Army.

5

The imperial factor in Hong Kong reached its climax in 1897. It reached a climax then everywhere in the British Empire, for 1897 was that *anno mirabilis imperii*, the year of Queen Victoria's Diamond Jubilee, the crowning pageant of Empire, in whose celebratory parade Hong Kong Chinese policemen in conical hats marched through London with their comrades from all corners of the globe. Before the end of that same year the British raised with the Chinese Government the question of a lease in the New Territories, and the takeover of the new property

Treaty Ports and Foreign Enclaves in
CHINA, 1900

0   500   1000 km
0   500 miles

N

Beijing

Lushun (Port Arthur) (Russia)
Wei-hai-wei
(Britain)
Jiaozhou Bay
(Germany)

C H I N A

Shanghai
Ningbo

Fuzhou

Amoy   TAIWAN
(Japan)
Guangzhou
HONG KONG (Britain)
Macao (Portugal)
Qinzhou Bay (France)

in 1898 was the most conventionally imperialist event in the whole history of the colony.

For one thing it was the solitary example of military suppression, in the classic imperialist kind, during the presence of the British in Hong Kong. For another it was part of a general European grab in China – emulating, the more rabid expansionists hoped, the contemporary Scramble for Africa. People in Hong Kong had long been urging an extension of the frontier northward from Kowloon, partly because they thought the Chinese might one day attack the colony, partly because they saw prospects for land speculation. When the time came, however, it was in principle at least not for economic reasons, nor out of fear of China, that London authorized the acquisition of the New Territories; it was because the French, the Germans, the Russians and the Japanese were all getting their own colonies or Spheres of Influence on the China coast.

The British knew the New Territories, both mainland and insular, as a kind of exhibition of Chineseness in its pristine mystery, and as a good place for sporting expeditions. 'Proceed overnight to Deep Bay by steam launch', advised a sporting guide published in 1896 by R. C. Hurley, the man with the motor-less motor car, 'accompanied by a sampan or a small punt or dinghy. Follow the beaten track skirting the many villages . . . and with shooting all the way, you will, in a few hours, find yourself on the shore of Castle Peak Bay, where your steam launch should be in readiness to convey you back to Hong Kong.' The strategists coveted the mainland territory as a buffer zone, and the islands as a screen. As it was, they argued, a hostile army standing at Boundary Road, the northern limit of British territory since 1856, would be within artillery range of Hong Kong Island itself, while anyone could see what a nuisance could be caused by an enemy in the adjacent islands.

China being at that juncture half-prostrate before its various tormentors, the British extracted their concessions without too much difficulty. Under the Convention of Peking it was agreed that the new boundary should run some twenty miles to the north, where the mountain mass gave way to the flatlands beyond. It would cut off the peninsula from Mirs Bay to Deep Bay along the general line of the Sham Chun River (Ganges to the Anglo-Indian surveyors), both banks of which would be British. At the same time some 200 islands and islets, including Lantau which was twice as large as Hong Kong itself, would become British too. It was settled that the lease would run for a century, until 1997 – an eternity by British standards, a flicker of the eye by Chinese – and British and Chinese commissioners jointly surveyed the new boundaries, not always very accurately. Here and there you may still see the marker stones they erected.

Such was power! No rent was mentioned, or ever paid. The Chinese reserved their authority only within the walled Kowloon City, whose officials were allowed to maintain jurisdiction 'except so far as may be consistent with the military requirements for the defence of Hong Kong'. The British announced that henceforth the New Territories would be 'part and parcel of Her Majesty's Colony of Hong Kong in like manner and for all intents and purposes as if they had originally formed part of the said Colony'.

The Viceroy of Guangdong obligingly reassured the people of the leased territory. The British had promised to treat them, he said, 'with exceptional kindness', and he enjoined them to obey the laws of their new rulers. For their part the British assumed that their new subjects would accept the change of regime with pleasure – or if not with pleasure, as the Governor, Sir Henry Blake, himself qualified the thought, at least with equanimity. The Queen-Empress, he told them, hoped that they would be prosperous and happy, like her subjects everywhere else.

Things did not go so easily on the ground. Echoing the 'tremble and obey' injunctions of the Dragon-Emperor, Blake had gone on to warn the indigenes that, whatever their equanimity, 'all must render implicit obedience'. All, however, did not. The Viceroy of Guangdong might sanction the new arrangements, but the people of the 400-odd New Territories villages were profoundly suspicious of them. They had more or less run their own affairs for centuries, under the quavering but familiar authority of the Manchus. Their system of land tenure was infinitely complex, their clan system powerful. They were afraid that the British would play havoc with their traditions, and grossly damage the *feng shui*. 'We hate the English barbarians,' proclaimed a placard, 'who are about to enter our boundaries and take our land, and will cause us endless evil.'

An armed resistance was organized by the elders of the clans, led by the Tangs. Village militias were mustered by runner and by signal drum, until some 2,000 men were in the field. When the British began to put up a mat-shed at Tai Po, as a first office of their authority, it was burnt down by a mob. When they raised the Union Jack above it, they were attacked by the militias. Troops of the Hong Kong Regiment went into action, with artillery support, and warships were summoned to support their flank – so serious did the situation seem, for a day or two, that the Hong Kong Volunteers were mustered to fight off possible attacks upon Kowloon itself. What had seemed a loftily straightforward extension of British power turned out to be the one occasion, urban riots apart, on which the Chinese of Hong Kong physically resisted British authority.

They could not resist it for long, of course. The Governor was not much dismayed by the turn of events – such sudden accesses of irritability, he said, often happened in Ireland – and between them the troops and the Royal Navy soon settled the opposition. As a token of their submission the elders of Kam Tin, the chief Tang stronghold, presented to Blake those famous ancestral gates, no longer of much practical use to them because the British had blown up their supporting walls. The Union Jack arose from Tai O to Sha Tau Kok, and even the waters of Deep Bay and Mirs Bay were declared to be British. Another wedge of civilization, exulted the *Hong Kong Weekly Press* in best imperialist style, driven into China!

With the size of the colony extended ten-fold at a stroke, Hong Kong acquired an immediate new status and security. The second Convention of Peking was, however, ill-devised. Imposed by the British in the fullness of their imperial confidence, it unfortunately allowed for differing interpretations. The British considered their lease tantamount to a cession, giving them complete sovereign rights in the New Territories – 'part and parcel of Her Majesty's Colony'. The Chinese thought they were to remain suzerains, and that the inhabitants would remain Chinese, not British subjects. The Chinese later branded the Convention one of the 'Unequal Treaties' by which, they said, the West had bullied them into submission, and the differences of view were to rankle on until, nearly a century later, the impending end of the lease signalled the end of the Crown Colony too.

In the meantime the British soon extended their systems to the new districts. James Stewart Lockhart, the Colonial Secretary of Hong Kong, was charged with getting an administration going. For a time he advocated the expulsion of all those who had resisted – 'these men did not wish to enjoy the benefits of British rule, so it will be no great hardship to them to transfer their energies to a soil more congenial' – and he ruthlessly ignored all the rules of *feng shui* in establishing his police posts. So the resisting elders had been right, and if the disregard of cosmic forces did not bring bad luck to the villagers themselves, in the long run this little coup of Empire came home to disturb the imperialists.

6

Today the possession of Hong Kong is a doubtful asset to the British – some maintain it is a liability. Its imperial functions are vestigial, and in many ways it is hardly a colony at all. It is virtually autonomous in its internal affairs. Its currency is pegged to the US dollar, not the British pound, and its prosperity benefits the British economy only in the most indirect way, through the prosperity of British-owned companies. Strategically it means nothing to the British, diplomatically it has lately been a burden, industrially it is often in direct competition with Britain's own industries. The ideal of *civis britannicus sum* has long since gone by the board in the easternmost possession – successive parliamentary acts in London have ensured that very few citizens of Hong Kong are qualified to possess full British passports, or have the right to settle in Britain itself.

The very word 'colony' is almost taboo in Hong Kong now, and the Colonial Secretary was renamed the Chief Secretary in 1976. Since 1971 the Governors of Hong Kong have not been former Colonial Service officers, but diplomats with experience in China, and the presence on their staff of a Political Adviser from the Foreign Office is a reminder that in London Hong Kong's affairs are now seen more as a matter of foreign policy than of imperial duty. Governors nowadays rarely appear in their full plumed coxcombery; Youde, a former Ambassador in Beijing, preferred not to appear in it at all. It came as an anachronistic shock when, in 1982, the Executive Council committed Hong Kong to contribute £10 million towards the cost of the Falklands War – a last arbitrary echo of the days when Colonies rallied to the beleaguered Flag.

Now and then one comes across reminders of the old dominion. Even in 1987 one could read in the Press that the Deputy Chief Secretary was leaving to become Governor of the Cayman Islands. Administrators are still sometimes awarded the Imperial Service Order, which includes no more than 600 overseas members, and policemen are still proud to get the Colonial Police Medal, which is embossed with a truncheon. The Queen's head is on the postage stamps. The ships of the Hong Kong Squadron, their funnels emblazoned with coiled dragons, still project a little of the old superbia.

The police station at Yau Ma Tei, a stern and massive block all barbed and radio-masted, always reminds me of imperial police stations in Palestine long ago, and here and there are the unmistakable white houses of district officials, with flag-poles in their gardens. The best is Island House at Tai Po, built in 1906 as the domestic headquarters of the British Empire in the New Territories, which stands half-hidden by trees at the end of a causeway – once lonely among the waters of Tolo Harbour, like something in Venice, today with the tower-blocks of a New Town immediately at its back. It is no longer a residence of Government, but in its garden is a sad memento of its original purpose: the burial place of a young Englishman, only son to the District Commissioner, New Territories, who was killed in a car accident on Castle Peak Road.

And occasionally even now one may see, on a day of ceremony or celebration, an imperial exhibition of the old kind, bands and sergeant-majors shouting, every plume out of its Plume Box, judges in wigs and red robes, medals jangling on officers' breasts, swords, white gloves and His Excellency in full fig. I watched such a parade one Armistice Sunday. I was standing on the little balcony which projects above the main door of the Hong Kong Club,[1] and I looked down to the Ceno-taph, the Legco Building and the ceremonials below. All was as it always was. The commands were barked. The sad old hymns were sung. Trumpets trumpeted. Salutes were saluted.

Around the green a rope railing had been erected, and a handful of Europeans, mostly tourists I suspect, stood there in twos and threes watching. Just beyond them, in Statue Square, the Sunday multitude of Filipina women was settling down to its weekly jollities, chattering, laughing and fussing about with paper bags, and beyond them again the life of the great city proceeded altogether oblivious of the few score imperialists, with guards and musicians, pursuing their rituals at the war memorial.

7

In any case, though the mighty links of Raj and sea-power were signs of the wider grandeur, even in the imperial heyday Hong Kong was never quite like other colonies. It never had been. In 1842 Lord Stanley,

[1] Allegedly added as a saluting base for the Chairman of the Central Committee, when he arrives in 1997.

the Colonial Secretary in London, had sent Pottinger the first Governor a word of advice, the gist of it being that Hong Kong was geographically, historically and economically unique. 'Hence it follows,' wrote Stanley, 'that methods of proceeding unknown in other British colonies must be followed at Hong Kong.'

It was to become odder still with the acquisition of the New Territories, which turned it into the most peculiar hybrid among all British territories. Some of it was sovereign territory in perpetuity, some of it was rented until 1997, and in time it became clear that the one part could not survive without the other. Then nowhere else was so small a possession so intensely populated, so dominated by an ancient alien culture, and as years went by, so sophisticated and so rich – 'all this wealth,' as Kipling cried, 'wealth such as one reads about in novels!' In a sense too Hong Kong was always a pawn of foreign rather than colonial policy; not only did it exist in reaction to China, but it played an inevitable role in Britain's relations with France, Germany, Russia, Japan and eventually the United States.

'It is occupied,' it was said officially in 1843, 'not with a view to colonization, but for diplomatic, commercial and military purposes,' and in fact it was hardly a colony at all in the usual sense of the word. The British never exactly settled it – very few of them ever intended to stay there for long, and only a handful of Britons have ever made it their home. Nevertheless despite Lord Stanley the Colonial Service, and after it the Foreign and Commonwealth Service, was to govern Hong Kong conventionally enough.

The Crown Colony structure was more or less the same wherever it obtained, Fiji to Bermuda, and the standard grades, substantive ranks and pay rates applied in Hong Kong.[1] The District Officers of Hong Kong were very like D.O.s anywhere else in the Empire. Their duties were defined, by one of them, as being 'land court judge, magistrate, public auctioneer . . . director of small public works, country judge for small debts, land tax collector, registrar of land deeds, rates collector,

---

[1] The jargon too. In former times some colonial civil servants had a right to extra leave because of the long sea-passage home: when air travel came in they were invited to exchange this perk for educational privileges, and in Hong Kong those who accepted are still picturesquely classified as 'Old Terms Opted New'. To this day some expatriate officials retain the right to return home by sea at the end of their careers, and in 1988 a number of them astutely interpreted this as licence to take an expensive cruise on the liner *Canberra*, fetching up eventually at Southampton. Nothing sharpens an eye more keenly for the main chance than a lifetime in Hong Kong.

matrimonial disputes officer, forestry officer, agricultural "expert" (so called), land resumptions officer, and six or seven other things I can't now remember'.

The one administrative innovation, perhaps, was the idea of having *urban* District Officers, instituted in 1968. This did provide a curious rider to the imperial legend, replacing Carruthers in his pith helmet on tour in the bush with a young man in a business suit in an office above a shop. Otherwise all in the system was standard, except for size and extravagance: the official establishment was one of the largest of any Crown Colony, and the Governor was always among the highest-paid of colonial governors.

If his status has also sometimes seemed grander in Hong Kong than elsewhere, that is because in this colony it has been deliberately heightened. Most of Hong Kong's Governors have been career officials, men of the British middle rank; it has been the practice of the territory to make magnificos of them. Physical splendour has always been thought important to their function here; time and again I have been told of the particular effectiveness of Sir Murray MacLehose, Governor from 1971 to 1982, not so much because of his intellect or decision, but because he was 6'6" tall.

In the past, as we have seen, Governors went about in extravagant sedan-chairs; until 1949 the front seat of the Peak tram was reserved for them; today they are the only British functionaries anywhere, except only the Queen herself, to qualify for an official Rolls-Royce Phantom, besides having at their disposal a venerable gubernatorial yacht, the *Lady Clementi*. Their pay, in the late 1980s, is £93,000 a year – more than twice the British Prime Minister's. They no longer have Mountain Lodge, whose grounds were turned into a public garden when it was demolished in 1945, but they do still have Fanling Lodge in the New Territories, and as representatives of the Queen they command social precedence over almost anyone who visits the colony.

Until recent years the Governor was inescapable in Hong Kong. A survey of nouns, verbs and adjectives undertaken by the Department of Linguistics at Hong Kong University in 1973 found that the word 'Governor' was the third most commonly used in the *South China Morning Post*, so multifarious were the gubernatorial activities, and so fulsome was the attention paid to them. Governors and their ladies opened everything, presented everything, took every salute, presided over every ceremony, and there had accrued a ludicrous superfluity of streets, buildings, hills and institutions named for successive Their Excellencies.

There have been twenty-seven Governors of Hong Kong so far. One and all they have been knighted for their pains, even those who have not been unqualified successes, and while many have been sufficiently unremarkable men, some have been memorable. Sir Frederick Lugard, for instance (remembered in Lugard Road), the creator of Hong Kong University, developed the system of colonial administration he called Indirect Rule, and as Lord Lugard became one of the patriarch sages of British imperialism; he said of his time in Hong Kong that never in his life had he experienced 'such consistently hostile and sneering criticism'. Sir John Davis, that 'pleasant little gentleman' (Davis Street, Mount Davis), founded a scholarship for the study of Chinese languages at Oxford, still awarded to this day. Sir John Bowring (Bowrington Road) is said to have mastered thirteen languages. He was an MP for a time, edited the *Westminster Review*, wrote widely about every aspect of European literature, from Finnish runes to Bohemian verse, and was the author of a much-loved hymn, *In the Cross of Christ I Glory*.

Sir Henry Pottinger (Pottinger Street, Pottinger Peak) made an adventurous journey through Baluchistan and Sind, and wrote a book about it. Sir Hercules Robinson (Robinson Road – and Rosmead Road, for he became a peer) was almost the archetype of a Victorian imperial administrator, holding governorates in New Zealand, Australia, and most importantly in South Africa, where he did his best to prevent the Boer War. Sir Matthew Nathan (Nathan Road) became Governor as a bachelor of thirty-two; the only Jew to hold the office, he was sadly infamous in later life as the Under-Secretary of State in Ireland at the time of the Easter Rising. Sir David Wilson, who arrived in 1987, had not only edited the *China Quarterly*, but was also a distinguished mountaineer; asked what he would like to have called after him, when the time came, he suggested a rock face somewhere.

Their job has never been a sinecure, but has varied greatly in significance according to the state of history. Bowen once wrote that 'the ordinary work of a civil governor in Hong Kong . . . is not materially different from the ordinary work of the Mayor of Portsmouth,' while Lugard said his role was to endure fools gladly, to sign his name perpetually, to agree to the suggestions of the Colonial Secretary and to ensure that the final outlet of the main China trunk railway should be at Kowloon. On the other hand Bowring personally precipitated a war against China, Sir Mark Young was the first British colonial governor ever to surrender a colony to an enemy, and in recent years, as the future of Hong Kong became a great diplomatic issue, the office of Governor assumed an immense sensitivity – a wrongly chosen word could cause a crisis of confidence, dangerously antagonize Beijing or send the financial index disastrously slumping. It is a curious irony of the imperial story that the last Governors of this, the last great British colony, should be in some ways the most important Governors of all.

8

They speak of 'Government' in Hong Kong, rather than 'the Government', allegedly to differentiate it from the United Kingdom Government in London, and this gives the administration to my mind an appropriately amorphous feeling. It is supported by an enormous civil service, its lower ranks almost entirely Chinese, its highest largely European even now. Its senior expatriates are very well paid, and comfortably housed. In 1986 the Financial Secretary was paid about £6,500 a month, plus £450 expenses, and was given a large furnished house, a car and the services of two domestic servants, a cook and a driver; his electricity bill that year, paid by Government, came to about £15,000, and on retirement he was due to get a gratuity of about £72,000 in lieu of a pension. Once again I am reminded of old China, for this privileged official cadre is rather like the Celestial Empire's celebrated bureaucracy, which formed a layer of society complete unto itself, severely detached from the ordinary people.

For many years the senior administrators of Hong Kong were randomly selected. Government was administered by a mixed assortment of army men, ships' officers and miscellaneous adventurers, often wandering up from Australia in search of fortunes, among whom a knowledge of the Chinese language was liable to be regarded not as advantageous, but as suspect. Some of these fortuitous appointees were diligent and able men – they included Eitel the historian and J. R. Morrison, who was said to be the best Sinologue of his day, and whose death at Macao in 1843 was described by Pottinger as an irreparable national calamity. Others were mere place-getters, using their official positions frankly to enrich themselves, and of these the archetype perhaps was William Caine.

Caine dug himself into Hong Kong even before it officially became a colony. A captain of infantry with an undetermined past (he is said to have been a boy soldier in India), in 1841 he was appointed Magistrate, with powers over English settlers under English law, over Chinese under Chinese law. Although he seems to have established a precedent by being totally unqualified to administer either legal system, he never looked back. He was superintendent of the gaol as well, he was a member of the first Legislative Council, he became Colonial Secretary of Hong Kong and eventually, in 1854, Lieutenant-Governor of the colony. – thirteen years from obscurity to consequence.

But he had achieved far more than mere importance. He had become exceedingly rich, having made himself landlord to a large part of the expatriate community. He bought and sold property at enormous profits, and developed as a private speculation an entire new street – originally frankly called Caine's Road, now softened to Caine Road (there is a Caine Lane, too). Caine retired and went home to England just before the appositely named Sir Hercules Robinson set out to clean the Hong Kong stables. He was fondly seen off by the many local people who had shared in his success, and presented by Chinese businessmen with an inlaid mirror: 'doubtless', remarked the *Illustrated London News* ambiguously, in reporting this gratifying gift, 'Colonel Caine has done many a good turn for his Chinese friends.'

Caine was one of many. Their Hong Kong was a frontier town, and its methods could hardly be officially tolerated in the sober heyday of Victorianism. When Robinson arrived in 1859 he was horrified to find that not a single senior administrator spoke any Chinese language, and two years later a cadet scheme was founded, to provide the nucleus of a properly professional civil service. Candidates were chosen by examination in England, as they were for the Indian Civil Service, that paragon of imperial system. They were given two years of language training, went to Hong Kong first as interpreters, later as administrators, and gradually transformed the standards of its Government. For nearly a century they were all British, nearly all public school and Oxbridge, and they formed a caste of their own, distinct even within the Hong Kong Civil Service – often scholarly, always gentlemanly, usually honest, but inclined to be clannish and conservative – they usually spent their whole lives in the colony, and in each others' company.[1] After the Second World War a few Chinese had time to become Cadet Officers, before the system was abolished, and there are

[1] Their Hong Kong was described by a Colonial Office official, in 1934, as 'the most self-satisfied of all the colonies, except Malaya'. (Quoted in *Hong Kong under Imperial Rule, 1912–1941*, by Norman Miners, Hong Kong 1987.)

senior administrators in Hong Kong now who are products of the scheme, and who still fondly assume that you know what they are talking about, when they say they began their careers as Hong Kong Cadets.

Even so the expatriate civil servants have remained a remarkably mixed bag. Today's officials, from senior executives to police officers, are drawn from many origins and many administrative and technical disciplines. They may have been inherited from lost colonies elsewhere – many moved on from Africa in the 1960s, many more from Singapore and Malaysia in the 1970s. They may have been recruited across the divide from private enterprise. Some have just turned up, in the old way, and many are on short contracts: those who are making a career of the administrative branch are, in the British colonial tradition, expected to prove themselves as jacks-of-all-trades.

In 1986 the Financial Secretary was a former chairman of Swire's, while the Chief Secretary, having started life as a merchant seaman, had served as a colonial officer in Malaysia and was one of the few foreigners to speak both the Cantonese and the Hokkien dialects. The Attorney General, previously a counsel to the Ministry of Defence in London, was the co-editor of *Temperley's Merchant Shipping Acts*. The Chief Justice, a former Attorney-General of Gibraltar, was the author of *The Bones of the Wajingas* and *How to Dispense with Lawyers*. The Deputy Director of Trade had spent time on attachment to the Royal Visit Office, and the Staff Officer (Hawkers and Markets) had previously been Coordinator of the Festival of Asian Arts. Half the Government lawyers seemed to be Australians or New Zealanders.

There are at least 170,000 servants of Government in all, 98 per cent of them Chinese, making it much the largest Hong Kong employer. The Government Telephone Directory is 367 pages long. The Government Land Transport Agency has more than 6,000 vehicles, seven and a half for each mile of road. And the most heterogenous of all Government branches is the Information Services Department, the front of it all, which is headed by twelve Chief Information Officers, twenty-four Principal Information Officers, seventy-five Senior Information Officers and eighty-four Information Officers plain and simple. It is rumoured to act sometimes as a *dis*-information department: a Conservative Member of Parliament, Robert Adley, alleged in the 1980s that because of his heretical views on the future of Hong Kong the ISD had deliberately set out to besmirch his reputation, and reformist citizens of Hong Kong, too, have felt themselves to be the victims of its expertise.

In the main though it is a vast and skilful publicity instrument. It publishes a myriad books and pamphlets, from economic abstracts to architectural guides. It brings a ceaseless stream of overseas journalists, politicians and businessmen to Hong Kong, chaperones them carefully and sends them home to disseminate the received truth about the place. It shepherds foreign correspondents through their assignments, it briefs Government officials on their images, it produces every year the annual review of Hong Kong, almost as rich in colour plates as it is in statistics, which sells more copies in the territory than any other book. It publishes a daily digest of the Chinese Press. It is very kind to people writing books.

An astonishing gallimaufry of people has found jobs in this organization, from many parts of the world. Distributed among Government offices all over Hong Kong, with representatives in London, Brussels, Tokyo, San Francisco and New York, between them they constitute a most powerful engine of propaganda: for the size of the colony, I would guess, the largest, most active and most aggressive of all State publicity machines – so important is image to this system of control.

9

Hardly less varied are the officers who administer the Common Law in Hong Kong. They are no longer called upon to administer Chinese customary law, and are not obliged to understand any Chinese language – except in special hearings of trivial offences, the language of the courts is English, laboriously interpreted into Cantonese, Hakka, Hoklo or Tanka. There are four degrees of court, from magistrates' court to Court of Appeal, and in serious criminal cases juries of seven people are required to reach a verdict. I have spent many days, over many years, haunting the courts of Hong Kong, from the High Court to district magistrates' courts, and I have never seen, anywhere in the world, such a variegated assortment of jurists.

There are judges of a truly awful Englishness, the very embodiment of the Common Law, rigged out of course in full paraphernalia of full-bottom wigs and buckled shoes, and fluent in the circumlocutions of their trade. There are learned Chinese, similarly accoutred, just as bewigged, and hardly less as to the manner born. There are the inevitable Australians. I remember with affection a small neat judge, Scottish I think, who seemed to be in a condition of perpetual fidgety motion, never still, never at repose – now twitching his head this way and that, now suddenly removing his spectacles, now moving his pen, rearranging his papers, looking suddenly around the court, shifting his wig, putting his pen down, picking his pen up, for all the world as though he were some kind of mechanical toy, made in Hong Kong no doubt, and would presently run down into a recess.

It would be a miracle if all the legal men of Hong Kong were of high standard. For most of them the only true inducement to work in the territory is the inducement of money, and the quality of the law they administer seems to me distinctly variable. It is degrading enough, for my tastes, that after 150 years of British rule a population 98 per cent Chinese should have its cases tried in English. 'What's going on? What's happening?' judges sometimes irritably inquire, when interpreters are delayed by knotty points of translation, and the cry rings shamefully: how terrible to see, as I saw with pity one day, a young man from a refugee camp, charged with murder in the misery of his condition, tried before a European judge, British, Australian, Indian and New Zealand lawyers and a jury of five Europeans and two Chinese, all in a language he did not understand, below the crest of a monarchy resident on the other side of the world! I would not like to be defended by some of the lawyers appearing in the courts of Hong Kong. Nor would I happily appear before some of the magistrates. They are all professionals, members of the Civil Service, but some are both more professional, and more civil, than others.

Observe for example the magistrate, nationality immaterial, presiding over this morning's petty cases in one of the air-conditioned lower courts. He is a master of the legal cliché, besides being a stickler for every last nicety of the Common Law. The rules of evidence are sacrosanct to him, the pedantries of the court are as the bread of life, and sitting as he does alone upon his bench, hearing cases involving simple Chinese in a language he does not understand, he has long since perfected his techniques of brief authority. He bullies defendants mercilessly – 'Shut up, don't you open your mouth and blurt out.' He bludgeons witnesses – 'I'll ask you the question ten times, 100 times, 1,000 times if necessary, until it sticks into your thick skull.' He testily proclaims his own importance – 'This is a court of law, not a fish market, and I am presiding over this court. Do you understand that? Do you hear me? I am not speaking German or Greek to you.' And when at last he fines some miserable prostitute, or sends a bewildered hawker off to the cells, he does so without a flicker of regret, without a hint of understanding, only a petulant exertion of his own supremacy.[1]

[1] I have drawn and quoted this disgraceful man from life, verbatim, and I hope he recognizes himself.

10

Of course he stands very low in the hierarchy of imperial justice, which in Hong Kong still ascends, as it did in all the Empire once, to that ultimate court of appeal, the Judicial Committee of the Privy Council in London.

Once this was among the most august of all lawcourts, with a jurisdiction far exceeding that of the Roman Empire at its widest. It heard appeals from every part of the British dominions. Its judges were drawn from all over the British world, and its plaintiffs and respondents too came from anywhere the flag flew. Today its powers are sadly shrunken, few countries now recognizing its authority, but far away in London it still represents the ultimate hope of justice for appellants in Hong Kong.[1]

Cases seldom in fact reach the Privy Council – it is not easy to get leave to appeal there, and the cost is great. Among those that were heard in the past, some must have made Whitehall hearts sink, so peculiarly complex were the affairs of this possession. Cases of land tenure were always especially awkward, and all too often Hong Kong legal affairs impinged in one way or another upon international law. A piquant example was the case of The Attorney-General of Our Lady the Queen for the Colony of Hong Kong versus Kwok A Sing, which reached the Judicial Committee in 1863.

Kwok A Sing was one of 310 Chinese migrants who boarded a French ship in Macao, bound for a new life in Peru. They were indentured labourers, and were treated almost as slaves, kept below decks at night, and separated from the crew quarters by armed barricades. This was not what Kwok A Sing had expected, as he set off for his fresh start, and after a few days at sea he and several other men attacked the captain and crew. They killed some, and obliged the rest to sail the ship back to China. The mutineers disappeared, but Kwok A Sing presently turned up in Hong Kong. There he was arrested as a suspicious character, and when his identity was established the Chinese authorities applied for his extradition.

This was refused. The Chief Justice of Hong Kong maintained that the extradition treaty with China did not apply to political offences, which Kwok's arguably was, or to crimes like piracy which were justiciable in Hong Kong, while conditions on board the ship, it might also

[1] At least until the early 1990s, when it is due to be replaced by a Final Court of Appeal sitting in Hong Kong, with *ad hoc* judges imported from other Common Law countries.

be argued, were such as to make murder justifiable – part of 'the first law of nature, committed under the right of self-preservation'. Anyway, the Chief Justice ruled, since the crime was committed on board a French ship on the high seas, only the French could demand extradition.

The French had in fact considered asking for it, but perhaps preferred not to have conditions on board a French ship exhibited, and decided not to pursue the claim. Kwok was freed. The Attorney General immediately had him re-arrested and charged with piracy, a crime justiciable in the colony regardless of the nationality of the ship on which it had been committed; but the Chief Justice promptly ordered him released again, on the grounds that the facts had not altered, and an accused could not be placed in second jeopardy.

Unhappy Kwok! The Chinese wanted him, the French did and didn't, the British in Hong Kong could not agree. Six thousand miles away five eminent judges pondered the rights and wrongs of his predicament – Sir John Colville, Sir R. Phillimore, Lord Justice Mellish, Sir Barnes Peacock and Sir Montague E. Smith – far from the China seas, remote indeed from the slave ship on its way to Peru. What they decided was this: that on the one hand, the murder by a Chinese subject of a person who was not a subject of China, committed outside Chinese territory, was not an offence against the law of China, so Kwok was not extraditable there. On the other hand the Attorney-General was right, and he should indeed be re-arrested and tried in Hong Kong on a charge of piracy under the Law of Nations.

But the decision, though it found its way into the law books, was hypothetical anyway, for by then Kwok A Sing had sensibly left Hong Kong for ever, never to be heard of since.

II

Sad to say, one characteristic which set the Hong Kong administration apart from its colonial peers across the world was its tendency towards the sensational. From the beginning until our own times Hong Kong officialdom has been periodically rocked by accusations of corruption, and made notorious by quarrels and intrigues, sometimes venal, sometimes merely bizarre. By Asian standards they were untoward, by British imperial standards they were spectacular: Pope-Hennessy's umbrella attack upon the Leader of the Bar, pursued so the victim said 'with a fury quite inconceivable', was only the most farcical of a run of disgraces unique among British colonies.

In one period of ten years, between 1845 and 1855, the following

Between the World Wars: the Cenotaph and the Hong Kong Club,
with Queen Victoria bottom right

The Japanese invasion: *above*: the Jubilee reservoir, with the Shing-mun redoubt bottom right, below the pylon; *below*: Government House as the Japanese rebuilt it things happened: the Chief Justice was sacked for drunkenness; the Registrar-General was accused of associating with pirates; the Attorney-General was dismissed for calumniating a colleague; the Superintendent of Police was accused of having a financial interest in brothels; the acting Colonial Secretary was accused of accepting bribes; the Lieutenant-Governor (Caine) was accused of extracting rake-offs from market-men; the Governor (Bowring, whose son was a director of Jardine's) was accused of partiality in the award of contracts.

The advent of the well-paid and well-educated cadet officers improved matters, but scandals continued to erupt even among the hyphenated. In 1893 the most respectable N. G. Mitchell-Innes was sacked for alleged irregularities in his handling of Treasury accounts (though he went on to be an inspector of prisons in England). And in 1938 there arrived in the colony, as Director of Air Raid Precautions, Wing-Commander A. H. S. Steele-Perkins, a highly regarded expert in civil defence. Almost at once the colony corrupted him, and he became all too friendly with Miss Mimi Lau, secretary of the Chinese company that supplied pre-cast concrete blocks for his air-raid shelters. Unfortunately the blocks, though suspiciously expensive, were undoubtedly sub-standard. In the course of consequent inquiries into the conduct of Steele-Perkins' department, revealing all manner of peculation, its chief architect shot himself, one of its executive engineers tried to commit suicide, witnesses vanished and documents disappeared. Steele-Perkins himself was never charged, but his defective materials went for a time into the Hong Kong vernacular as 'Mimi Lau blocks'.

More recent scandals have generally concerned the Royal Hong Kong Police Force, whose senior officers are mostly British – in the years after the Second World War many came to the east after losing their occupations in Palestine, Cyprus and East Africa. The colonial police were often the weakest link in the chain of imperial probity, and in Hong Kong they have frequently been seduced by the general lubricity of life. The universal taste for gambling, the chance to smuggle, the immemorial habit of 'squeeze', the enormous profits of the drug trade, the display of great wealth, the familiar Hong Kong attitude of live-and-let-live – all these have been fatal to policemen of susceptible temperament, whether British or Chinese. In 1898 half the entire police force was dismissed for corruption.[1] Of the European police officers

---

[1] Those disgraced included Inspector Quincey, a Chinese foundling who had been taken under the wing of General Charles Gordon during his campaigns in China, and sent to be educated in England – 'a fine young fellow', thought the general, who fortunately died at Khartoum too soon to learn the truth.

who entered the force as sub-inspectors in 1952, four ended up in gaol. In 1966, at a time when Triad infiltration of his force was rampant. Hong Kong's Commissioner of Police admitted that there was corruption in virtually every walk of life, but added cheerfully that 'in terms of money the police force is probably not the worst'.

'Corruption,' snorts John Le Carré's world-weary Hong Kong police superintendent in *The Honourable Schoolboy*, set in 1974, 'they'll be discovering bloody steam next.' One after the other, through the 1970s, discredited policemen entered the headlines, first in Hong Kong's own newspapers, then in the London tabloids. A protracted sensation occurred when Inspector John MacLennan, found to be enjoying a homosexual relationship with a Chinese, was alleged to have shot himself, but was thought by many people to have been murdered in self-protection by his own colleagues. More celebrated still was Chief Superintendent Peter Godber, holder of the Colonial Police Medal for Meritorious Service, who was for a few years to enter the local demonology.

Having made very large sums of money by dubious practices involving the colony's crime syndicates, Godber fled Hong Kong just as investigations were catching up with him, and for some time lived comfortably beyond extradition in his cottage in Sussex, a perennial favourite of Fleet Street photographers. Charges of another kind, however, enabled the Hong Kong authorities to get him back again, and in 1975, on the evidence of two other confessedly crooked policemen, one British, one Chinese, he was convicted of corruption in the course of duty. He served thirty-one months of a four-year sentence, and retired to a villa in the south of Spain, where he found many colleagues, friends and sympathizers.

On the Hong Kong streets they were probably not much surprised: the lower ranks of the police force were, as everyone knew, almost without exception corrupt, so it was only to be expected that its senior officers would be too. The formidable Elsie Tu had been saying so for years. However the repeated exposure of police corruption made the venality of Hong Kong, whose economy depends so largely upon its good name, notorious throughout the world, and led to the establishment of the Independent Commission Against Corruption, the I C A C, whose chilling lights we saw at the Murray Road Car-Park that evening after dinner. Its first director of operations was a formidable imperial intelligence officer, Sir John Prendergast, who had previously served in Palestine, the Gold Coast, Egypt, Kenya, Cyprus and Aden, and the effect was immediate. Many a less prominent culprit was caught, and policemen with guilty consciences scooted away to bolt-holes across the world.

Petty corruption continues on many levels of Hong Kong life. In the passing of driving tests, they say, in the obtaining of houses, in the retention of profitable shoe-shine stands, in countless little matters of everyday life bribery can tell. I am told that firemen sometimes demand a bribe before they will turn their hoses on – or off. But it is nothing like as bad as it is elsewhere in Asia, and there has not lately been a major scandal in Government.[1] Even the police have stayed out of trouble – since the late 1970s, when 140 officers were arrested for involvement with crime syndicates, and in a last brave flourish of tradition some of them tried to break into the ICAC offices to destroy the evidence. 'This is certainly the right place to be a policeman,' I said one day to an expatriate officer at a well-known border smuggling point, thinking of the possibilities of excitement. 'Not since the ICAC it isn't,' he replied with a wink, thinking of the possibilities of graft.

12

Hong Kong has always lived by the freest of free enterprise. Government does regulate banking and stock-market standards, has lately stepped in to rescue several ailing banks, and was obliged to bail out the Futures Exchange during the great crash of 1987. It also manipulates the exchange rate for the Hong Kong dollar, pegging it to the US dollar. Nevertheless the essence of its economic policy is a determination to try anything once, coupled with the resolve to leave well alone, and the rigidly controlled economy of Singapore, Hong Kong's rival to the south, is held up as an example of how not to do it. Taxation is very low, there are no restrictions on the movement of currency, and as Hong Kong remains a free port only a handful of commodities (tobacco, alcohol, soft drinks, gasoline, cosmetics) are subject to duty. The energies of the market are left unshackled.

Economics apart, though, the official control systems are far from free-and-easy. Even today, among the apparently anarchic office blocks of Central, I fancy I can detect a heavy swathe of Authority running allegorically down the slope they used to call Government Hill: down

[1] Though as I write a Chief Government Architect is doing six years behind bars, and a judge has just resigned because he was found to have falsified details of his age and army record . . .

from the symbolical Peak through Government House and its gardens, through the Anglican Cathedral and its close, across the Government offices and the Murray Road Car-Park, the Supreme Court and the Legco building, to end at the military headquarters still at the old dockyard by the sea. It is like one of the energized ley-lines supposed to link holy places in England, or like the mystic route the Manchu Emperors used to follow, when they left the Forbidden City to commune with the gods in the Temple of Heaven.

Sometimes Hong Kong feels, in the British kind, excessively governed. In the 1950s and 1960s any sign of political protest was fiercely suppressed, and an ironic element of puritanism still tries to keep the place in hand – gambling illegal except at racecourses or betting shops, homosexuality illegal anywhere, prostitution illegal, exploding firecrackers illegal except on official occasions (but they are often exploded anyway), eating dogs illegal (though they turn up in restaurants pseudonymously as goats). On a very small country bus I once took note of the following instructions, pasted largely beside the driver: NO STANDEES, TENDER EXACT FARE, DON'T SPEAK TO DRIVER, NO SMOKING, DON'T STAND NEAR THE DOOR, NO DOGS ALLOWED. You need a licence to do almost anything, it sometimes seems: only the last few rickshaw men, dragging out the final years of their trade at the Star Ferry terminal, are ignored by the licensing authorities on the grounds that officially they no longer exist.

The police force numbers 30,000 men and women, and includes forces within forces. The Serious Crime Group is chiefly concerned with Triads, and employs 200 detectives, it is said, to observe and infiltrate the societies. The Special Branch is a political police force, concerned sometimes with Communist activities, sometimes with Kuomintang: its senior officers are nearly all British, Chinese preferring not to run the risks of reprisals after 1997. The run-of-the-mill force is never out of sight for long. Everywhere smooth-faced, robotic Chinese constables are riding about on immaculate motor bikes, sailing about in motor launches or signing the patrol books which are sometimes to be seen, unaccountably ignored by vandals, hanging from nails in public places. They are no doubt still corruptible on occasion, but look unforgivingly correct; one reads constantly of unauthorized market-stalls forcibly removed, unlicensed hawkers fined, and one can hardly look out across the waters of Hong Kong without seeing a police boat stop a passing sampan for inspection.

When in the 1950s a school charity wished to put up a temporary open-air stage for a fund-raising show, it entailed getting permission from the Secretary for Chinese Affairs, the Commissioner of Police, the Fire Brigade, the Urban Council, the Building Authority and the Accountant-General. The bureaucracy has a long arm still. 'Remote-controlled toy cars and other devices are strictly prohibited in the park area,' children are sternly warned in an announcement in Victoria Park; the penalty for non-observance could be twenty-four days' imprisonment, and the relevant regulations, so the infants are told, are to be found in Sections 17 and 18 of Pleasure-Ground By-Laws. At the Po Lin monastery I once saw a notice proclaiming REVISED EX-GRATIA COMPENSATION RATES FOR RESUMED LAND. In a dilapidatedly Chinese back street of Cheung Chau, all sagging wooden houses and sleeping dogs, I found an official announcement on an infinitesimal plot of overgrown ground, litter-strewn between two shacks: PROPERTY OF THE CROWN, it gravely said.

You would hardly know it from the dizzily scrambled appearance of the place, but strict zoning laws govern Hong Kong's development, especially in the meticulously planned New Towns. It requires a persuasive geomancer nowadays to bend a building regulation. Twelve storeys is the maximum height allowed in Kowloon, which accounts for a monotonous warehouse-look among even the most fashionable new structures, while Hong Kong-side restrictions vary from district to district. The Hongkong and Shanghai Bank building, at forty-eight storeys, is as high as one can build in its particular area; but fortunately for relations with Beijing, the new Communist Bank of China nearby, designed to be much, much taller, is situated on the other side of a zoning boundary.

Hong Kong is a place of Restricted Zones – Closed Areas, Security Areas, Correctional Centres, Drug Addiction Centres and an astonishing number of prisons. The Government has established Closed Camps to house refugees from Vietnam, the boat-people of the 1970s. Though cruelly cramped, and surrounded by barbed wire, they are generally run humanely enough, and their purpose is logical – to provide a home for refugees hoping for permission to re-settle permanently somewhere else, while making the experience sufficiently unwelcoming *pour encourager les autres*; but in the Hong Kong official manner they have a numbingly institutional air, with their fences, their bunk-houses and their blazered, royal-badged staff seconded from the Correctional Services Department, while as the years drag by, and nobody offers the poor inmates any happier sanctuary, they come to seem more and more like prisons themselves.

For one feels even there an instinct towards *punishment*. Punishment rather than reform has traditionally been the Hong Kong way of law and, order, and its methods have often been crude. Even in the 1920s people used to be put in the stocks, and hard labour then was hard indeed. In one form it meant shot drill and stone carrying, in alternate periods of half an hour each, not exceeding eight and a half hours a day; in another it meant turning a crank, with a resistance equivalent to twelve pounds, 12,500 times a day. Chinese strike agitators, declared Sir Reginald Stubbs the bishop's son in 1923, should be 'dealt with in a manner which will be likely to appeal to their deepest feelings, that is, by "the cat"'.

For a temple of *laissez-faire*, then, this is a very disciplinary place. Corporal punishment is practised, and capital punishment too is still on the statute book, though for many years the Governor has always commuted it to life imprisonment. An Englishman of military mien who once gave me a lift on Lantau, and who told me about his frequent experiences as a film extra, generally in authoritarian roles, turned out to be the hangman.

13

But in its final decade Hong Kong is also, belatedly perhaps, and un-expectedly to many, half-way to a Welfare State.

Before the Second World War official attitudes towards social pro-gress in the colony were extremely cautious, on the grounds that if con-ditions got too easy people would flood in from all the surrounding territories – the same argument that governs the camps of the boat-people now. 'Reforms based on western models,' said an official report in 1936, 'should only be introduced into Hong Kong in reasonable conformity with those enforced in neighbouring countries.' In the 1930s almost the limit of social services was the compulsory cleaning of Chinese premises, at least twice a year; thousands of people lived on the streets, as in Calcutta, and in 1937 a writer in the *North China Herald* went so far as to claim that half the population was starving – 'products of the social system of the colony, which does not provide wages at which the average Chinese family can subsist'.

Actually conditions in Hong Kong then compared quite favourably with those in other parts of the Empire, in India for instance, or in the terribly neglected Caribbean colonies, let alone with those in China; but it was not until the Chinese Communist revolution, in 1949, that matters were drastically to change. The influx of refugees into the city then dwarfed everything that had happened before, and placed Hong Kong under such social pressure as to be almost ungovernable. Not much more difficult than running Portsmouth, the sanguine Bowen had thought the running of the colony, but he could hardly claim it now.

For years after 1949 hundreds of thousands of Hong Kong people lived in ramshackle huts or mat-sheds, or were crammed hugger-mugger into stinking sampans, in a congestion that would have shocked even Osbert Chadwick seventy years before. In 1952 a survey showed that of 1,000 Chinese families, 687 lived in one room, and 120 in *part* of a room: twenty-three families lived on rooftops, only eight had a house. There was virtually no public housing. No-holds-barred was the rule among the new industrialists who proliferated in Hong Kong then, and in ghastly sweatshops, hidden away in tenements and dingy factories across the city, workers aged from eight to eighty worked fearful hours putting toys together, or making wigs, or operating dangerous machinery.

Arriving in Hong Kong myself late one night in the 1960s, and looking out of the window of my modest Kowloon hotel, I saw across the dark and rubbish-strewn pit of the place the slab of a gloomy industrial building beyond. Each of its windows was brilliantly lit, nearly midnight though it was, and in each a little Hong Kong cameo, distinct from all its neighbours, was joylessly displayed. Here four girls sat tense at their sewing-machines, silent and unsmiling, here a solitary shirt-sleeved man was hunched over his files, beneath the light of a naked bulb. Along the way eight or nine families seemed to be packed into one room, and I could see only flashes of infant limbs, waves of drapery, buckets, black loose hair, bedclothes. Every room was ablaze, every room was jam-packed, and across the intervening dark I could hear radios, clicking machines, shouts and children's screams.

In another city, I thought then, all that life out there might be a comfort, a reminder that all around me was the warmth of community. In Hong Kong it felt to me utterly indifferent, as though nobody was taking the slightest notice of anyone else. Hong Kong was certainly not noted then for social conscience, most of the Europeans preferring to ignore the miseries around them, most of the Chinese concerned only with their own families. Visiting liberals invariably went home horrified, demanding immediate reforms; but in the colony itself the purpose of Government was seen as being simply to govern, to provide the Confucianist order that enabled private enterprise to flourish.

Members of Parliament in London often advocated parliamentary institutions for Hong Kong, as the right cure for its inequities, and they were supported by a few modernists on the spot. Government though was reluctant to rock the boat, as a favourite Hong Kong idiom had it. Any move towards self-government might displease the authorities in Beijing, who would not fancy the idea of a capitalist Chinese City-State at the mouth of the Pearl River. Besides, many Hong Kong people distrusted the idea of an elected Government. Communists, or alternatively Kuomintang supporters, might accede to power, making life distinctly less comfortable for the other half, and anyway the British provided a reasonably benevolent kind of autocracy, enabling the rich to get richer and the poor at least less poor.

So let-do ruled, as much in social policy as in financial. It is one of the astonishments of British imperial history that before long this archaic colonial autocracy was to become the most socially intervention-ist Government any Crown Colony had known. It was foreseen at the end of the Second World War that cradle-to-grave public welfare in Britain would have to be reflected in the colonies, and London's directive to Hong Kong's first post-war administration spoke of 'a general plan for social welfare'. Nothing happened for years, and then it happened with an amazing suddenness.

It happened most obviously in housing. One year the myriad poor refugees of Hong Kong were herded into those unhappy squatters' camps, straggling over the hillsides in foetid grey muddles, and offering all the familiar symptoms of twentieth-century calamity: canvas-topped shacks, scavenging pi-dogs, pot-bellies and sunken eyes, old women scrunched in the corners of shanties, harassed defensive officials, good works by overworked volunteers, runny noses, festering open drains, flies, half-naked children and mud. Along the streets tin boxes were mounted, into which the populace might deposit dead rats; 13,000 a month was the average haul.

The passing of a couple of Governorates, the publication of five or six annual reports, and abruptly we find half a million people housed in brand-new Government-built estates, totally unlike anything seen in Hong Kong before. The Government had been forced into a vast pro-gramme of public welfare and civic planning – basically by the uncon-trollable flood of refugees out of Communist China, but in particular by a disastrous fire which, on Christmas Day 1953, not only made 50,000 settlers homeless, but brought to the notice of the world the terrible predicaments of Hong Kong's new proletariat. The colony never looked back. In what is claimed to have been the fastest building programme in history the twin cities of the harbour were transformed, over a few years, into a complex, multi-centred, State-organized metropolis.

'If you have massive problems, you must apply massive solutions,' decreed Sir David Trench, Governor at an early stage of this revolution. The population of Hong Kong doubled between 1951 and 1971, and the clumped and generally unlovely buildings of the public housing estates, some of them emblazoned with big numbers like barrack blocks, some embedded in parkland, some in jagged rock-like declension on hillsides, burst willy-nilly, as those resisting elders of the New Territories foresaw eighty years ago, through the general *feng shui*. Today's apotheosis of it all is provided by the seven New Towns of the New Territories, the first deliberately planned urban centres of Hong Kong, and prodigies of social intervention. Great new roads link them. Industries have grown up around their flanks. Ships moor alongside their wharfs, slinky electric trains slide in and out of their stations, and about as many people live in them as live in the original urban settlements.

The Government's Housing Authority is now one of the world's biggest public landlords, and the challenge of providing decent homes for all those hundreds of thousands of indigent fugitives seems to have affected the whole nature of Government in the territory. There are still sufficient social miseries, Heaven knows – what a Chief Secretary of the Colony once identified for me as 'rough edges of capitalism'. Housing remains desperately short, the population having increased, at a million each decade, faster than even Hong Kong can build. Dreary slums abound – the first hasty public housing of the 1950s is slummy itself now – and here and there that greyish nebulous stain upon a hillside still marks the presence of a squatters' camp. There are beggars in the subway stations, street-sleepers in alleys. A well-worked subject for visiting reporters is the survival of the Cage-Men, poor down-and-outs whose bunks in squalid doss-houses of Kowloon or Wanchai are screened with wire, like cages, to keep thieves out. No doubt in many a back-street factory working rules are still ignored.

But things have unimaginably improved, since I looked out that lonely night from my hotel window in Kowloon. Today almost half the entire population lives in apartments provided in one way or another by the State – horribly crowded very often still, especially in the older blocks, but at least with electric light, running water and probably a telephone. Nobody starves in Hong Kong, and there is enough in the way of public welfare to ensure that nobody need be utterly penniless,

even the street-sleepers and the Cage-Men. In the 1920s 90 per cent of
the population was illiterate; today 18 per cent of the Government's
budget, the biggest single proportion, goes in education. Schooling is
free and compulsory to the age of fifteen, illiteracy is unknown except
among old people, and even the children of the Tanka boat communities now have their own schools, courtesy of the Fish Marketing
Organization – as they sing in their dialect at the end of their annual
summer camp:

> Fish are the treasure of the ocean, knowledge is the treasure of books,
> For us, the children of the sea, industrious, hard-working and brave,
> So come, come together, children of the fisherfolk,
> Let us all sing together!

There are two universities, the University of Hong Kong whose first
language is English, the Chinese University whose medium is primarily
Chinese. A third is projected, and there are also two polytechnics, a
Baptist College, and sundry technical institutes. Even so, ten people
apply for every available place, and as I write some 30,000 students
have gone abroad for their higher education – about as many as have
stayed at home.

As for the health of Hong Kong, which for so many generations
made it notorious as one of the unhealthiest places in the British
Empire, it has been transformed. The fearful epidemics have long been
checked, and the sanitation is much less unnerving than it used to be.[1]
Medical care is not free, except to those in abject poverty, but it is very
cheap, and is probably as good as anything in Asia. The infant mor-
tality rate, 73.6 per thousand in 1953, is 7.6 per thousand today; while
according to the World Health Organization the territory's life expectancy – remember 1882? – is now the highest anywhere, promising
its male residents 75.1 years, its female 81.4, in which to make their
fortunes.

14

Nevertheless it is not towards benevolence that the systems of Hong
Kong are chiefly directed, but towards efficiency. Efficiency equals
wealth equals stability, still we are told what Chinese people chiefly

[1] Though foreign appetites are not always whetted by the washing-up at Chinese food-
stalls, still less at the simpler floating restaurants, where they simply swill the dishes in
the harbour's scummy swell.

want. For all its social betterments a pragmatized version of *laissez-faire* remains the ruling philosophy of this colony in its final decade: all possible techniques of twentieth-century modernity support the Victorian principles of Free Trade, Free Enterprise and the Open Door, re-defined by a Financial Secretary of the 1970s as 'positive non-interventionism'. [1]

Hong Kong's whole purpose, indeed, depends upon keeping a technical jump ahead of its neighbours. In previous times the contrast with backward Asia was much more pointed. To come from Guangzhou down the Pearl River a century ago was to move from one world to another. Guangzhou was still a pestilent walled city of narrow lanes and stinks ('Phew!' grumbled Kipling. 'I want to get back to the steamer'). Hong Kong was equipped with all the conveniences of steam, gas, electricity, telegraphs and artillery. The virtuoso Peak Tram clambered up the mountainside, the double-decker electric trams trundled along the foreshore below.

They trundle still, as a matter of fact – now the very last of their kind in the world, carrying 11 million passengers a month, swaying rather junk-like along their tracks with a creaking of slatted seats, and pressing so hard upon each other's wheels that often only a few seconds separate one from the next. The Hong Kong Tramway Company, now controlled like the Star Ferries by Sir Y. K. Pao, is the only surviving builder of wooden double-deck streetcars (though it does not exactly build them, but rather maintains them as palimpsests, constantly replacing parts, adding improvements, so that none of its 160 vehicles are exactly the same, and none can really be dated).

The trams are however almost the last mechanisms of nostalgia among the public services of Hong Kong, where as a rule nothing but the latest thing will do – there is not much nostalgia to the surviving rickshaws, and the very last of the sedan-chairs was found abandoned in a street in 1965. Today's public transport system is by common consent brilliant – Peter Hall the authority on civic planning has called it [2] 'perhaps the most modern and efficient public transport system in any of the great cities of the world'. [3] Besides those 160 trams, and those innumerable sampans, and the 11,000 buses, and the 16,478

[1] 'Of which,' comments one of my informants, 'Nero is the first recorded practitioner.'
[2] In *The World Cities*, London 1984.
[3] As an American remarked to me one day, disembarking from the dilapidated public sampan which had taken us to Lantau under the steersmanship of an elderly Chinese lady, 'We have nothing like it in Illinois.'

taxis, the underground Mass Transit Railway offers as good a rush-hour service as anywhere, so long as one has mastered the combination of snake-like weave and heave-ho necessary to get a seat.

Hardly had they built one tunnel under the harbour, now claimed to be 'the busiest four-lane facility in the world', than they started work upon another. Elaborate walkways and subways, served by countless escalators, link as in a web the offices of Central. In the New Territories a bay has been blocked, drained of sea-water and filled with rain to form the Plover Bay reservoir. A tunnel through the hills of Hong Kong Island links Central with Aberdeen. Another pierces the Kowloon massif south to north, and even as 1997 impends the Government has commissioned a second, east to west. Millions of dollars were invested a few years ago in a scheme to restrict traffic within the city areas; cars were to be fitted with automatic activators, totting up charges on wayside sensors as they passed, and only the implacable opposition of the business community put an end to the idea.

Everything must be slick, smart, shiny. The maps of Hong Kong are very fine, that annual report is sumptuous. I once saw a senior police officer arriving in his magnificent grey patrol boat on Cheung Chau, and as the craft swept in with a growl of diesels, and the officer stepped ashore to ramrod salutes, striding off into town head-and-shoulders above the bobbing elders and underlings, I thought the style of the event was less Empire than Hollywood. The Chief Secretary and the Financial Secretary of the Hong Kong Government are driven around in glamorous Mercedes limousines, dark blue and equipped with radio telephones – not the sort of vehicles one expects for British colonial officials, even Old Terms Opted New.

15

Penny-pinching was more common in the Empire as a whole: Hong Kong is as it is because its systems have been balanced always between private and public enterprise. The retired colonial officer Harold Ingrams, invited to write a Colonial Office book about Hong Kong in 1950,[1] concluded that Hong Kong should be regarded not as a colony like all the others, but as a department store, the board of directors being its leading citizens, official or unofficial. Often enough, as we know, there was not much love lost between the two sectors, but it is

[1] *Hong Kong*, London 1952.

true that the territory has habitually been run by a diarchy of Government and Big Business, British, Chinese and foreign. 'Hurrah for private enterprise!' wrote Sir Alexander Grantham, who had been appointed to his Governorship by the British Socialist Government of 1945.

Nothing is more absolutely Hong Kong than the entrance to the first harbour tunnel, completed in 1972. It is one of the major arteries of the entire territory, the chief link between its original twin cities, yet above its high portal are inscribed the words: THE CROSS HARBOUR TUNNEL CO., LTD. It always reminds me of Brunel's great inscription above the Great Western Railway Company's Tamar Bridge in Cornwall – I. K. BRUNEL, as tall as a man – so gloriously redolent is it of capitalist brag and energy. The Government sponsored the tunnel: The Cross Harbour Tunnel Co., Ltd (present chairman, Sir Y. K. Pao) took the risks and gained the profit.

Much of Hong Kong depends upon such compacts. It was Lugard, the Governor, who proposed the foundation of Hong Kong University, but it was the business community that paid for it. Today the Treasurer of the Chinese University is usually the chairman of the Hongkong and Shanghai Bank, and the third university is to be largely financed by the Jockey Club. Most of the land reclamation has been done by private enterprise: the very name of the reclaimed district called Kai Tak, where the airport is, commemorates its capitalist creators, Sir Kai Ho-kai and Mr A. Tack.[1] The mounted troop of the Hong Kong Volunteer Regiment was raised and commanded by Jardine's, and until 1922 there was no official fire brigade – the business houses each had their own. The buses, the trams, the Peak tram, the ferries, the telephones, the electricity services are all privately run; of the basic services, only water is provided by the public sector. The harbour pilots are members of a private cooperative, radio and TV are largely commercial, and many of the hospitals and clinics are financed by the Jockey Club or private enterprise.

Most telling of all, the Hongkong and Shanghai Bank is in effect the Central Bank of Hong Kong, one of the very few non-Governmental concerns to fulfil such a role in the modern world. It holds the colony's reserves, and together with the Chartered Bank, which is part of a London-based conglomerate, it issues all the colony's notes in denominations of ten dollars and above; they are ornamented with

[1] Not a misspelling – at least this is how Mr Tack's name appeared on the airport's original ornamental gates.

pictures of the Bank's offices, and signed by the Chief Accountant. Stitt the cross lion is featured on the $HK 500 dollar bill, Stephen the snarler on the $HK 1,000.

No wonder the Government, which has shares in several of the great companies, has adopted so many commercial styles and practices for itself. The auction for example has always been an instrument of its policy: it auctioned land leases from the start, it auctioned the opium concession, it used to auction the jobs of temple curators and it still auctions lucky car numbers. More recently the advertising industry has had a profound influence on official attitudes, too. The Government information service is in many ways no more than a huge public relations company, producing brochures and reports as extravagant as any private firm's, while the Royal Hong Kong Observatory, from its austere premises upon a Kowloon hillock, issues each year a calendar so glossy that one almost expects its monthly photographs to portray nubile girls, instead of View Across Mirs Bay, or Forest Activities in Guangdong Province. 'One Of The World's Biggest Homemakers', is how the Hong Kong Housing Authority describes itself.

It all seems natural enough, in this bastion of capitalism. It is the system that underlies everything. The public–private alliance is very old, and each side has gifts to bestow upon the other. In the 1980s six members of the board of the China Power and Light Company were Commanders of the British Empire, and it was soon after the company commissioned from British manufacturers the equipment for its new Castle Peak station, one of the largest single orders ever awarded to British industry, that its chairman became Lord Kadoorie.

IO   1940s: WAR AND PEACE

NORTH-WEST OF KOWLOON, BETWEEN THE BIG JUBILEE
reservoir and the southern coast of the New Territories, there is a
ridge called Smuggler's Ridge. Though it is bare itself, it looks
northward into wooded country, and southwards over the high-rise
blocks of Kwai Chung that creep year by year inexorably into the
higher ground.

A line of electric pylons crosses the ridge, a hiking path named for
Sir Murray MacLehose passes nearby, and not far away there is a
picnic site with explanatory noticeboards; but on the top, almost immediately below the electric cables, lies a place of distinctly unpleasant numen, where even on a bright sunny day, even with the
cheerful voices of walkers echoing through the shrubbery, one can feel
disconcertingly alone.

Scrabbled in the sandy soil up there, half-buried, all abandoned, are
the remains of a redoubt. There are steps leading into sand-filled
bunkers, gun-slits in concrete slabs, air-shafts protruding from the
ground, underground corridors which lead nowhere but are marked
with names like Shaftesbury Avenue or Regent Street. It is a very
haunted place. The wind blows constantly over the ridge and whistles
in the cables above. The derelict subterranean chambers are littered
with rubbish, foul with excrement, and sometimes your heart leaps

when, like a demon out of the earth, a scavenging dog suddenly appears from a dark tunnel and leaps crazily past you into the daylight. The rolling country to the north looks desolate. The familiar blocks of Kwai Chung, just out of sight, seem all too far away.

Fifty odd years ago, when Smuggler's Ridge really was a more solitary place, the Shing-mun redoubt was the key point of Hong Kong's military defence. It was here on the night of 9 December 1941, in the Crown Colony's centenary year, that the 38th Division of the Japanese 23rd Army, falling upon those bunkers, throwing grenades down those air-shafts, machine-gunning those staircases, in a few hours of fighting broke the British resistance, and so made it certain that the 1940s would be a decade apart in the history of Hong Kong.

Like nearly everyone else, the Japanese had been threatening and bullying China for years. In 1933 they had seized Manchuria, far to the north, and founded the puppet kingdom of Manchukuo under Pu-yi, the pretender to the Manchu throne. In 1937 they had taken Beijing and embarked upon a long and sporadic movement southwards through the Chinese provinces. Their advance put a temporary end to China's endemic civil war, and for a time the forces of the Kuomintang and the Communists fought together under the command of Chiang Kai-shek, with his capital at Chong-qing (Chungking). The Japanese had set up a second puppet Government at Nanjing (Nanking) under the former Kuomintang politician Wang Jing-wei; since the autumn of 1939 they had been ensconced in Guangzhou, just up the river from Hong Kong, and had stationed troops on the frontier with the colony (where they sometimes exchanged beers and civilities with the British sentries on the other side).

For years too the British military planners had been considering what best to do if the Japanese ever turned upon Hong Kong. Their views differed, and they kept changing their minds. The chief British fortress of the east was now Singapore, towards the cost of whose defences the Hong Kong Government had prudently offered £250,000, and the colony's own defences were slight. Nevertheless some strategists argued that at least it ought to be denied to an enemy as long as possible, and some thought it should be held at all costs until relief could come. Sometimes the plan was that the whole colony would be defended, sometimes that the mainland would be abandoned and the

to Guangzhou

Frontier

Mirs Bay

Chinese

Deep
Bay

Tolo Harbour

N E W   T E R R I T O R I E S

Shing Mun
Redoubt

Smuggler's Ridge

Golden Hill

Defence Line

KOWLOON

Lantau
Island

Power Station

VICTORIA

Victoria
Peak

HONG KONG
ISLAND

Aberdeen

Jardine's
Lookout

Repulse
Bay

Stanley

Stanley Fort

THE JAPANESE ATTACK
ON HONG KONG, 1941

➤ Japanese advances
— Roads ╫ Railway

0 ———————— 5 km
0 ———————— 3 miles

island held as a siege-fortress. Sometimes it was suggested that the place should be demilitarized, and not defended at all, and sometimes, perhaps most often, that it should offer a merely token resistance, for purposes of symbolism or example.

By 1941 the British Empire was at war with Germany and Italy, with whom Japan was in alliance, and Winston Churchill the Prime Minister in London seemed to have made up the planners' minds for them. If the Japanese did attack, Hong Kong was not worth defending with any seriousness. Its garrison consisted only of two British infantry battalions, two battalions of the Indian Army, some artillery fixed and mobile, a local volunteer force, a handful of small warships, two flying-boats and three venerable torpedo bombers without any torpedoes. 'If Japan goes to war with us,' decreed the Prime Minister, 'there is not the slightest chance of holding Hong Kong or relieving it.' The garrison could only be symbolical, and token resistance was the only sensible choice. 'I wish we had fewer troops there, but to move any would be noticeable and dangerous.'

There matters stood in the autumn of 1941. The general opinion in Hong Kong then was that, crazily though the Japanese were acting, they would not be so crazy as to attack this famous outpost of the British Crown. It had *never* been attacked, and was supposed to be impregnable anyway. Also it had old, friendly and profitable links with the Japanese. There was a prosperous Japanese community in the colony, and people often went to Japan for their holidays ('Oriental charms', as the travel advertisements said, 'are jealously preserved intact amidst the most advanced Oriental civilization').

The public attitude was defined by the *South China Morning Post* as a compound of reaction, faith, determination, nervous anticipation, evasion and simple fatalism. The conflict in Europe seemed remote indeed, but like all British possessions Hong Kong had officially been on a war footing since 1939. Adult British males were liable to conscription, and in June 1940 European wives and children were compulsorily evacuated to Australia (though some 900 women, many with children, had wangled a way to stay). Important buildings were sand-bagged against bomb blast. Beaches were wired. There were practice black-outs now and then, and publicity campaigns to raise war bonds or prevent careless talk – as the makers of Tiger Beer characteristically told the citizenry in one of their advertisements:

Scraps of information,
Jeopardize the nation,
TALK ABOUT TIGER INSTEAD!

But otherwise things were pretty normal. The ships still came and went, the Pan Am flying-boats still arrived, nobody went short of anything. A robber, we see from the *South China Morning Post*, September 1941, is sentenced to five years' hard labour and twelve strokes of the cat. His Excellency the Governor attends the All China Premiere of *Lady Hamilton*, with Vivien Leigh and Laurence Olivier. Jimmy's Kitchen advertises its tasty tiffins. The official Government Gazette invites tenders for the erection of dry latrines at Telegraph Bay Village, and publishes proposed new trademarks for the Wing Hing Knitting Family.

But that same month the Japanese occupied Indo-China, unopposed by the French Vichy Government there, and in response first the Americans, then the British imposed embargoes on all exports of steel and oil to Japan. This was a drastic blow to the Japanese – 'the most drastic blow', thought *The New York Times*, 'short of war' – and it instantly increased tension throughout the Pacific. Hong Kong now prepared more urgently for its own war. Major-General Christopher Maltby, Indian Army, the commanding general, was bullish about the prospects of defending the colony. He believed indeed that it could be turned into an offensive base, for attacks upon the Japanese in China, and he had faith in the line of strong-points, centred upon the Shingmun redoubt, which ran from east to west of the New Territories. There, he thought, some twelve miles south of the frontier, any invading force could be held long enough to allow an orderly evacuation of Kowloon and a build-up of strength on the island – which could itself hold out until help came from Singapore. Minefields were laid to protect the sea-approaches, and a network of seventy-two pillboxes was completed on Hong Kong Island.

Inexplicably Churchill, preoccupied perhaps with events elsewhere, was now converted to Maltby's view, and was persuaded that only a modest reinforcement would enable Hong Kong to put up a worthwhile resistance. As a result two battalions of half-trained Canadian troops, most of them French-speaking, disembarked in Hong Kong on 16 November, without motor transport, to help defend the indefensible colony. They were officially categorized in Ottawa as 'not recommended for operational consideration'. Just three weeks later, on 8 December, the Japanese, simultaneously attacking Pearl Harbor and invading the Malay Peninsula, crossed the border out of China into Hong Kong. Savagely bombing Kai Tak, where the Royal Air Force was instantly put out of action, they swept through the British advance guards in the northern New Territories, and on the following evening reached the Shing-mun redoubt.

It hardly delayed them at all. Maltby had thought it could hold out for a week, but it fell in a few hours, never to be remanned from that day to this. Many of its garrison died within their pillboxes, the rest abandoned the position. The Japanese did not pause. Bombing and shelling Kowloon, strafing ships and roads, they drove British and Indian troops alike helter-skelter down the peninsula and into ferry-boats, sampans, warships and lighters for the crossing to Hong Kong Island. In four days they were in full control of the whole peninsula. The last Star Ferry retreated to Blake Pier. The last exhausted rear-guards were brought back across the Lyemun Gap. The British on Hong Kong-side, terrified and aghast, could see the troops of the 38th Division massing on the Kowloon waterfront, and hear the eerie cries of their loudspeakers, interspersed with recordings of *Home Sweet Home*, booming across the familiar waterway – 'Give up, and the Japanese will protect you! Trust in the kindness of the Japanese Army!'

Before long the Japanese gunners were shelling across the harbour, the dive-bombers were screaming down on Central, and for the first time chaos struck the waterfront we have seen growing and enriching itself so steadily decade by decade through the chapters of this book. It was hardly to be imagined. It was like a dream, in which all things familiar were suddenly shattered or distorted. The *Tamar* was scuttled. Fires raged in Wanchai. Statue Square was thick with acrid smoke. At midnight one night bombs hit the Jockey Club stables at Happy Valley, and the horses escaped. Trembling and streaked with blood they raced in panic here and there through the dark streets.

By 13 December all the British forces were assembled within the thirty-one square miles of the island. 'We will hold off the enemy,' said an official communiqué, 'until the strategical situation permits relief. The simple task before everyone now is to hold firm.'

Behind the mountains grim and bare

(wrote a British soldier during the wait for the assault)

Like a wounded lion we lay,
Oh that the mother lion was there
To help defend her peaceful lair
And win the hard-fought day . . .

The Governor of Hong Kong was Sir Mark Young, a handsome and reserved Etonian, who had arrived from Barbados to take up his duties two months before. The Colonial Secretary, his right-hand man, was Franklin Gimson, who had arrived from England, never having been in Hong Kong before, on the very day of the invasion. Far away was Winston Churchill, Prime Minister, war-lord and imperialist, who had spoken of the British Empire lasting a thousand years, and who had now changed his mind about the futility of resistance. 'There must be,' he said in a message to the Governor, 'no thought of surrender . . . Every day that you are able to maintain your resistance you and your men can win the lasting honour which we are sure will be your due.'

The War Cabinet in London had been advised that, even after the loss of the New Territories and Kowloon, Hong Kong Island should be able to hold out for at least four months. It held out for rather more than a week. Far from fighting to the last man, seven out of ten of the servicemen under British command survived to surrender, and they handed over to their enemies enormous quantities of material. The control of the defence was ineffective, the troops were generally road-bound and inefficient, the equipment was inferior and the attitude to war was anachronistic. The defending force included Indians and Canadians who spoke no English, engineers fighting as infantry, in-fantry battalions without transport, RAF ground crews and Royal Navy seamen. It was a campaign summed up by the opposing boots – on the one side the British ammunition boots, heavy hobnailed things of coarse leather, their pattern unchanged since the Boer War, on the other side the light Japanese combat boots, supple, rubber-soled, silent. Clumping, unimaginative and archaic was the British conduct of the battle; swift, audacious and innovative the Japanese.

Yet the failure was understandable. This was the first armed conflict ever between the Japanese and the British, and the British were taken fearfully by surprise. Frozen in their attitudes of imperial complacency, they had come to believe that no Asian could be their match. The Japanese had been enormously admired for their fighting abilities half a century before; they had performed better than anyone during the siege of the Beijing legations in 1900, and Admiral Heihachiro Togo, victor of the Battle of Tsushima in 1905, had actually been made a member of the British Order of Merit. Now however, for reasons unclear, they were thought to be hopelessly inferior – short-sighted, poorly equipped and incapable of fighting at night. It had come as an appalling shock to the British when the tough and wonderfully enterprising Japanese regiments threw them with such appalling ease out of the peninsula and across the harbour strait. Maltby and his soldiers never really recovered their confidence. The battle for Hong Kong was lost on Smuggler's Ridge.

The 38th Division's intelligence was good. The large Japanese community in Hong Kong before the war (of whom eighty remained even on the day of the invasion) included many spies – the well-known barber of the Hong Kong Hotel, whom we met briefly in an earlier chapter, turned out to have been a naval commander all the time. The division was well supplied with maps of the British defences, and was never short of local guides. Equipped with these advantages, the Japanese prepared a plan for the capture of Hong Kong Island that was simple, decisive, and worked perfectly. Heavily shelling and bombing the island first, they landed their first trooops at East Point, not far from the old Jardine's headquarters, on the night of 18 December. Next they advanced straight across the middle of the island, over the high country east of the Peak, to divide the British forces into two parts, east and west. Finally they turned upon those separate parts, each cut off from the other, and mopped them up.

In the course of the battle the Governor, from his bunker under Government House, echoed the Churchillian style in a message of his own – 'Fight on. Hold fast for King and Empire. God bless you all in this your finest hour' – and Churchill himself signalled to say that every part of the island must be fought for, if necessary from house to house. There were repeated reports, officially sponsored for the sake of morale, that Chinese armies were on their way to relieve the island. Until the reality of Pearl Harbor became clear, it was hoped that the US Navy might come to the rescue; until the sinking of the Royal Navy's capital ships *Repulse* and *Prince of Wales* in the South China Sea, it was still hoped that something might arrive from Singapore. But it was all illusion. The British had no chance. Their forces were irrevocably split and scattered, and were presently reduced to isolated units fighting on more or less ignorantly of each other. They evolved no coherent strategy of resistance, but merely fought back wherever the enemy dictated, in a helpless series of defensive actions and half-cock counter-attacks. The poor half-trained Canadians, so recently disembarked in this totally unfamiliar environment, never did get their motor transport, and seldom knew exactly where they were. Even the Royal Scots, one of the most famous of British infantry regiments, fought with a sad lack of conviction. For nearly everyone it was a baptism of fire – only a few individuals had seen action in Europe or Africa, and a handful of veterans had fought, in very different circumstances, in the First World War. They never had a hope, and anyway their resistance made not the slightest difference, one way or the other, to the course of the war; it was an effect of grand tragedy that so much rhetoric was expended, and so many lives were thrown away, to demonstrate so desolate a point.

The British gave up on Christmas Day, to the gratified surprise of the Japanese, who had expected to be fighting for at least a month. Casualty figures have never been properly established, but the British side are said to have suffered about 2,000 killed and 1,300 seriously wounded, the Japanese rather more. At least 4,000 civilians died, nearly all Chinese. Some 9,000 British Indian and Canadian soldiers were taken prisoner. The defence had not been a disgrace, but it had certainly not been the epic Churchill seemed to want; the loss of Hong Kong was a humiliating event for the British Empire, and a curtain-raiser to the far more dreadful calamity of Singapore.

Still, in the face of this astonishing and terrifying new enemy, fighting with such sneaky subtlety and courage, some on the British side did respond with the old flair. In particular many of the men of the Hong Kong Volunteers, British and Chinese, set heroic examples. They knew the place and had a stake in it, and whenever the British armies scored a temporary success, or so it seems from the records, Hong Kong men contributed. At the North Point power station, by the northern waterfront, one of the most determined of the rearguard actions was fought by four officers and fifty-five men of the Volunteers' Special Guard Company, organized by an insurance manager named A. W. Hughes. They were all over fifty-five, were variously nicknamed the Hugheseliers and the Methuseliers, and were led by J. J. Paterson, taipan of Jardine's and a veteran of the First World War. One of the privates, aged seventy, was a nephew of Governor Des Voeux; another, aged sixty-seven, was taipan of Hutchison's (later Hutchison-

Whampoa). For fourteen hours these elderly gentlemen, very pillars of the Hong Kong Establishment, held out at the power station against repeated Japanese attacks and unrelieved mortar barrages, surrendering only when all their ammunition was expended.

The Royal Navy, too, faithfully honoured its traditions. We read of the old river gunboat *Cicala*, under her one-armed captain John Boldero, rushing here and there throughout the battle zone, now off the New Territory bombarding the Japanese with her 3-inch gun, now ferrying people across the harbour, now storming into the Japanese invasion flotillas, undaunted for all her thirty years, until at last, after surviving sixty-four bombing attacks, she is sunk in the Lamma Channel. We read of the five motor torpedo boats of No. 2 Flotilla hurling themselves past Green Island, all guns blazing, at full speed into the junks, barges and sampans that were taking the Japanese armies across the harbour, sinking ships right and left until two of the boats were lost, one was crippled and half the crews were casualties.

A handful of soldiers and sailors escaped to the unoccupied part of China. For the rest, on Christmas Day, 1941, Sir Mark Young the Governor and Commander-in-Chief handed them over, together with all his authority, to Lieutenant-General Takashi Sakai of the Imperial Japanese Army. It was the first time a British Crown Colony had ever been surrendered to an enemy. 'I had believed,' said a Portuguese officer of the Hong Kong Volunteers, 'and had been told to teach my troops that we would fight to the last man, to the last bullet. So to be told to capitulate was a serious blow to me.'

The British having almost all been locked up, the soldiers in prisoner-of-war camps in Kowloon, the civilians in an internment camp beside the sea at Stanley, the Governor for a few weeks in a suite at the Peninsula Hotel, before he was shipped away with other important captives to Manchuria – the British having been put away, the Japanese were left to do what they would with Hong Kong. In February 1942 a military Governor arrived. He was Lieutenant-General Rensuke Isogai, a Chinese specialist. He was said to be a gifted calligrapher and a master of the tea ceremony, but his first proclamation, put up in permanent form on the pedestal of Queen Victoria's statue in Statue Square, said: 'For those who transgress the path of right and do not keep within their correct places, I will deal with these according to military law, without mercy.' It was a warning ironically like Blake's threat to the newly conquered natives of the New Territories, forty-four years before.

The Japanese had said they would incorporate Hong Kong into their Greater East Asia Co-Prosperity Zone. They pointedly set up their administrative headquarters in the Hongkong and Shanghai Bank building (Isogai had the chairman's flat on the ninth floor), and ship after ship of booty sailed home to Japan, taking most of Hong Kong's cars with them – an American journalist,[1] crossing the harbour that January, counted twenty-six ships with deck-loads of cars. But as it turned out Hong Kong brought few other benefits to the Co-Prosperity Zone. It was not much use to the Japanese militarily, either, and in the long run was probably far more a nuisance to them than an asset. On orders from Tokyo it was not incorporated into the administration of Japanese-occupied China, which held sway up the river in Guangzhou, and it was never offered to either of the two puppet Governments which now ruled so much of China under Japanese auspices. It remained a military governorate, 'The Captured Territory of Hong Kong.'

They did very little with it. Even their monuments of conquest were few. Government House was rebuilt by a twenty-six-year-old railway engineer, Seichi Fujimura, redecorated by a firm from Osaka, re-landscaped by a gardener from Kyoto, and Nipponized with a tall eaved tower. On the summit of Mount Cameron, above Central, the foundations were ceremonially laid of a crowning victory memorial, the Temple of the Divine Wind. Shinto priests presided, and a sacred sword was embedded in the masonry of the monument, which was to be eighty feet high, supported on twelve concrete legs, and engraved with fifteen feet high Chinese ideograms meaning 'Heroic Memorial'. Otherwise the new rulers of Hong Kong built practically nothing, but merely used what they found as if it had always been their own: Japanese wrestling teams were awarded medals engraved, as it might be with depictions of their club-house, with a bas-relief of the Hongkong and Shanghai Bank building.

By and large the conduct of the Japanese in Hong Kong was despicable. During the battle they repeatedly bayonetted prisoners, after binding them hand and foot, and murdered doctors, nurses and patients in military hospitals. Immediately after the surrender they

[1] Gwen Dew, *Prisoner of the Japanese*, New York 1943. The Japanese also took a number of books from the library of the Hong Kong Club, found on the quayside at Yokohama after the war and returned to their stacks.

deliberately let their troops run wild, raping and looting everywhere. Their treatment of prisoners, military and civilian alike, was cruel, dishonest and apparently capricious – poor General Maltby was once beaten for allegedly having dirty fingernails. If the Japanese regular army, and more often the Japanese navy, sometimes behaved honourably, the unspeakable Kempeitei, the military police, tortured victims as readily and as brutally as any Gestapo.

Inasmuch as this ugly occupation had any logical aim, it was to replace one empire by another, and the Japanese did their best to discredit their predecessors. They deliberately destroyed British records, and replaced the British administrative system with a hardly less elaborate bureaucracy of their own. But there was no consistency to their methods. On the one hand the Chinese population was treated with vicious arrogance – for example passers-by who failed to bow to Japanese sentries were at best slapped on the face or hit with a rifle-butt, at worst thrown into jail. On the other hand the Japanese tried hard to win Chinese cooperation. Which was the better, they used rhetorically to ask, the corrupt alien way of the British, decadent, materialist and selfish, or the Kingly Way of the Imperial Army, the Confucianist way common to Japanese and Chinese alike?

Throughout the occupation the Japanese printed an English-language newspaper, the *Hong Kong News*, which had belonged to Japanese owners before the war. In retrospect the files of this publication give a chill insight into the life of the captive colony – so recently dominated by Stubbses, Pattersons and Lady Southorns, now in the hands of Isogai and the Kempeitei.

Of course it was a propaganda sheet, presumably intended to circulate among those who could read neither Chinese nor Japanese – the few neutrals left in the colony, collaborating Indians and the prisoners in their camps. One of its concerns was to give an impression of normality. Its language remained quite literate English. Its tone, at least in the early years, was jaunty. 'The Onlooker', for instance, in his column 'Looking at the World', offered the familar bottom-of-the-page quips, perhaps left over from stock ('Many a man today is living by the sweat of his frau'), while the column called 'About Town' tried to maintain an air of soigné gossip ('In contrast to the days immediately after the local hostilities, many pretty girls are now seen in town, beautifully dressed and generally without male escort').

The small advertisements also exude an everyday air. There are cameras for sale, rooms to let, a Japanese tutor is required by English-Speaking Neutral, Chinese Gentleman Requires Japanese Partner in Enterprising Import Business. Jimmy's remains The Place to Eat. Though the Hong Kong Hotel's snack-bar has been turned into a tempura grill, George Pilo-Ulski the Accordion Virtuoso plays during tiffin. Harry Roy's Tiger-Ragamuffins may still be heard on the radio and Frau A. Steinschneider, former member of the Vienna State Opera, continues to offer singing lessons.

But gradually a sinister strain surfaces even in the *Hong Kong News*. Though the form was familiar, and the style assiduously maintained, day by day the paper became a reminder that Hong Kong was utterly at the mercy of its conquerors, utterly beyond the reach of friends. What could be more depressing for the imprisoned British, than to learn that 'high German and Italian officers' had been 'inspecting' their colony? The news from Europe came only from the neutral countries, Portugal, Spain, Sweden, or from Vichy France, and as the years passed Britain was portrayed more and more dismissively as a vassal of the United States. Allegations of Japanese atrocities were dismissed with a cynicism hardly worth disguising, since everybody in Hong Kong knew the truth: they had been invented by the British propaganda machine, a Tokyo spokesman was reported as saying, and were 'utterly fantastic'.

Even Britain's supposedly loyal subjects, the newspaper constantly suggested, had deserted her. Leaders of the Chinese Rehabilitation Committee have sent a message to the Emperor, on behalf of the population of Hong Kong, congratulating him on Japanese victories. The Chinese Representative Council decrees that, the next day being Navy Day, commemorating the Japanese victory over the Russians in 1905, all business firms and residences must fly the Japanese flag. Mr P. A. Krishna, chairman of the Indian Independence League, has handed over 20,000 Yen to the New War Weapons Fund . . .

And sometimes the sense of cold triumph was more frankly revealed. 'Woe to all those who break the law!' an editorial warns, and every now and then hard chill decrees are printed in full. Heavy penalties would be inflicted on the owners of dirty premises, said the *News* one day in 1942, after the coming inspection of all residents' houses.

Readers are warned that while English may have been the dominant tongue when Hong Kong was British, Japanese was the most important language now; and there was a daily Japanese language lesson in the paper, together with a selection of Old Nippon Proverbs, sometimes rather gnomic.

The impression meant to be given by the *Hong Kong News* was of an occupation assured, efficient, stern but generally benign. It is true that the Japanese administration had a few merits. Its delegation of responsibility to local elders theoretically took the people closer to self-government than the British ever had. In the towns its merciless house inspections did keep disease in check. Its engineers extended the airport and put the first electric cable under the harbour, to restore the island's power (ships kept dragging it with their anchors, though, and it was not renewed until the 1980s).

But in general the three years of the Japanese presence were utterly wasted years, and the conquerors showed themselves only at their worst. The British were paragons by contrast. Pompous the old Governors may have been, but at least you were not thrown into the cells for failing to stand stock still at their passing. The British police were sometimes bullies and often crooks, but they were angels compared with the men of the Kempeitei, with their terrifying network of informers and their torture cubicles erected contemptuously on the verandahs of Sir Aston Webb's Supreme Court.

Much of the Japanese energy went into changing the forms of the place. Superficially at least everything was Nipponized, the stores, the banks, the hotels, the Jockey Club and even its horses, which were renamed with Japanese names, and supplemented with Japanese ponies. Lane Crawford's became Matsuzakaya, and its staff were photographed, just as they had been in the old days, grouped formally outside the front entrance around their Japanese managing director. The Peninsula Hotel became the Toa, Jimmy's Kitchen became the Sai Mun Café, Queen's Road became Nakameiji-dori. The military governor did not in fact move into his newly orientalized Government House, preferring requisitioned quarters at Repulse Bay, but Japanese sentries stood at the old guardhouses on Upper Albert Road, and the Rising Sun flew largely, of course, above the new tower. The Star ferry-boats were requisitioned, and some of them were used on the Guangzhou run – the first time they had ever sailed outside the harbour.

All the royal statues were eventually removed from Statue Square ('a logical step', observed the *News* obsequiously), and were shipped to Japan to be melted down.

What was it all about? The Japanese must surely have sometimes wondered, as they kept guard on their prisoners down the years, and watched Hong Kong decline into misery at their hands. For bombed, shelled and burnt during the fighting, the place certainly did not recover under the auspices of the Great East Asia Co-Prosperity Zone. The New Territories became more or less anarchic, fought over by gangs of bandits and pirates, by Communist liberation groups, by supporters of the Nanjing puppet Government, riddled with agents of the Kuomintang, the Communists, the absent British and the Japanese themselves. The towns became dingier, poorer, emptier, sadder. The schools emptied. Food and fuel became desperately short, and the Japanese resorted to all-but-compulsory evictions, packing as many Chinese as possible back into mainland China, and sometimes it is alleged dumping old people, women and children on barren islands or unfrequented Chinese shores. They aimed to reduce the Chinese population by a thousand a day, and they managed a figure of 23,000 a month throughout the occupation.

How nightmarishly sudden, how sterile, and as it turned out how brief, was this metamorphosis! It was as though all the century of Hong Kong's colonial history had been negated at a stroke. The famous exuberance of the place was all quashed, and gradually its vitality too wasted away. As the fortunes of war turned against the Japanese, and perhaps it dawned upon them that Hong Kong was proving a perfectly useless acquisition, the third port of the British Empire sank into destitution. Money lost its meaning and a black market, run by Triads, virtually took over the feeding of the populace. By 1945 the twin cities of the harbour were half-deserted.

Even the *News*, as the months dragged on, came to reflect this sense of abject failure. A whining, self-justificatory note crept into its prose. The Japanese had not been fighting for themselves, said an editorial in May 1945, but for the thousand million inhabitants of Great East Asia. 'Around Town' had long lost all its cockiness, and was reduced to a string of bureaucratic handouts – a forthcoming inspection of bicycle licences, a rise in telephone charges. Hitler was still glorified from time to time, and *Mädchen in Uniform*, a UFA all-women production, was advertised at the Meiji Theatre, but now there were reports of German defeats in Europe, and even references to the horrors of the concentration camps. When the nuclear bomb fell on Hiroshima the news led the paper; 'the Enemy's Last Card', the *News* called it, but not with much conviction.

The final issue, almost at the moment of Emperor Hirohito's surrender, contained an editorial entitled 'Health is Wealth', about Japanese medical achievements in Hong Kong, an essay about factors in the formation of the Japanese national character, a report headed Sumatra Appreciates Japan's Benevolence, a Want Ad for a 'lady golf set', and the last, and not the least enigmatic, of the Old Nippon Proverbs ('An east wind to the horse's ears').

When the British military prisoners were marched off to their camps, at the start of the occupation, they found that Chinese bystanders were perfectly ready to carry their bags for them, and throughout the occupation Chinese hawkers managed to sell foodstuffs and the odd luxury through the wire to the European prisoners. Sometimes their prices were outrageous, but often they were willing to accept cheques or I O Us redeemable only when the war ended, if it ever did, in a return to normal circumstances. It was only to be expected that in these wretched times, as in all others, they would display their usual commercial buoyancy; what was more surprising was their frequent genuine loyalty to a colonial Power which had not always been, as we have seen, very considerate to them.

Many, of course, were compromised. The Fifth Column which guided the 38th Division in its swift advance was mostly Chinese, and after the defeat the Japanese found their inevitable quota of collaborators. There were three principal puppet bodies, the Rehabilitation Advisory Committee, the Chinese Representative Council and the Chinese Co-operative Council, and some of the best-known Chinese citizens joined them, abandoning their British titles to do so; Sir Robert Kotewall, before the war the senior member of the Executive Council and one of the best-known men in the colony, became Lo Kuku-wo. In the New Territories there was the Asia Prosperity Institution, whose members were known colloquially as *shing lei yau*, 'victory fellows'. Some Chinese, at least in the beginning, supported the Japanese simply as fellow-Asians, and some believed in the puppet Government in Nanjing, which was in fact truly dedicated to Chinese traditional interests – it was said to include more poets than any other Government in the world – but saw the Japanese as less of a threat than the Kuomintang or the Communists. Some became informers and agents of the Kempeitei as they had been of the British colonial police before.

But in general they were not traitorous. If in those days there was hardly such a thing as a Chinese Hong Kong patriot, most people undoubtedly felt a loyalty towards China, so barbarically assaulted by the Japanese, and many revealed a staunch personal affection for the British. 'It may be assumed,' said an American intelligence report of the time, 'that the British must have rather a strong hold on many of these people,' and it was true that many Chinese ran terrible risks to help their colonial masters. They smuggled messages and medicines to the prisoners, they helped escapees, and they maintained a constant link with the British military forces in unoccupied China. Agents who worked for the British included a former chauffeur to the Governor, a garage assistant at Government House, a hospital cook, a dockyard clerk and several students. One of the great heroes of the war was a medical student, Ha Chan, who escaped to China when the Japanese invaded but repeatedly returned to Hong Kong, though twice arrested by the Kempeitei, on terrifying intelligence missions for the British – a slight bespectacled figure, like thousands one sees in Hong Kong today.

Even some of the more prominent collaborators may have thought they were morally justified – Kotewall and several others claimed that before the surrender they had been specifically asked by senior British officials to cooperate with the Japanese in the interests of the Chinese community. For the rest, they were seldom politically motivated, but were simply concerned for their own survival. For the vast majority of the population the alternative was no more heroic, but was simply to plug along as best one could, looting a deserted European house if the occasion arose, or taking its timbers for firewood, making full use of the black market which was active in every locality, and depending as always upon quick wits and family connections.

Almost all the British and their imperial soldiers were imprisoned, but some were freed and a few were left at large. Chinese servicemen were soon released, while many Indian prisoners-of-war opted to join the Indian National Army, the independence force sponsored by the Japanese, and served the occupying authorities as guards and auxi-liaries. During the first months of occupation a number of bankers and their families were put up at one of the obscurer hotels in Victoria, so that their expertise would be available to the Japanese, and a Government doctor, Selwyn Clarke, was also retained by the military. (The University's Professor of Pathology, instructed to continue his work at the Bacteriological Laboratory, killed himself instead.)

Inevitably a few adventurers managed to keep their freedom, by pretending to be neutral subjects, or just by lying low. A handful escaped to China, and some of these, led by the University's Professor of Medicine, the Australian Lindsay Ride, were formed into an intelligence unit, the British Army Aid Group. Among its sponsors was John Keswick, formerly of Jardine's, now an intelligence agent at the British Embassy in Chong-ging. The BAAG operated from unoccupied Chinese soil, but sent emissaries frequently into Hong Kong, and kept in contact with the prison camps. At one time it cherished an epic plan for a mass escape of all the prisoners, and it remained throughout the one direct line of contact between the British held in Hong Kong and the world outside.

Inside the wires things went on very Britishly, though with decreasing conviction as malnutrition and sickness weakened authority and enterprise alike. Several thousand of the soldiers were sent as labourers to Japan (but more than a thousand of them died when their ship was torpedoed by an American submarine), and many of the others were made to work on projects like the extension of Kai Tak airport. There were sporadic attempts to escape to unoccupied China, a few of which succeeded, and several officers and men were shot because of their contacts with the British Army Aid Group. Otherwise their long period of imprisonment followed the standard pattern of misery, common to all prisoners-of-war in Japanese hands – boredom, hunger, ill-health, sporadic cruelty and constant humiliation.

In Stanley Camp things were rather different. There the civilians reproduced among themselves, in grotesque microcosm, nearly all the characteristics of peacetime Hong Kong. Gimson, as the senior official internee, never for a moment relinquished his Governmental authority over his fellow-prisoners. 'The British Government in Hong Kong,' he proclaimed, 'is still in being and functioning except where prevented by the Japanese'; indeed he claimed that as chief representative of the Crown he should conduct the Government-in-captivity's foreign policy – that is to say, its relations with its captors. He resisted all proposals that British civilians should be repatriated, as the Americans presently were, on the grounds that this might prejudice the status of Hong Kong after the war, and when some of the internees signed a petition

China in Hong Kong: *above*: a visit from a Mandarin, 1907;
below: the walled city of Kowloon, 1890s

On the waterfront, 1980s and 1920s

asking him to change his attitude, he called them disloyal to the British cause.

The internees behaved much as you might expect them to behave. They were after all colonial Hong Kong concentrated, men, women and children, people of all ranks, deprived of their servants and thrown into each others' intimate society. They squabbled about hierarchy and precedence. They formed committees. They put on plays. They remembered the happy old days. They bowed as required when they passed a Japanese and they became far more resourceful, as the years passed, in looking after themselves. The businessmen grumbled, as was the Hong Kong tradition, about Gimson and about the Government, which many of them blamed for its failure to declare Hong Kong an open city. Gimson no less traditionally grumbled about them – 'they cannot appear to consider any other world than that in which they can make money and retire'.

And secretly, within their ranks, some heroic souls fought on. Links were maintained with the city still – with the bankers at their hotel in the first few months, with Selwyn Clarke who maintained a running supply of medicines into the camp until he was arrested, tortured and imprisoned. Now and then messages of boyish panache arrived from Ride and the BAAG. 'It is the Empire that needs you, not Stanley,' said one urging young internees to escape. 'How many guests would be interested in Liberty Bonds?' asked another. Sir Vandeleur Grayburn, chief manager of the Bank, was accused of espionage and imprisoned with appalling ill-treatment. In October, 1943, seven civilians were beheaded on Stanley Beach, almost within sight of the camp, for possession of a radio; they included the colony's former Defence Secretary.

One by one, we see in retrospect, the signs of tragedy sobered and matured the community within the wires. The sad little makeshift gravestones multiplied in the graveyard above the camp. Now one internee, now another, was taken away to torture, imprisonment or death. 'It is with the utmost regret,' said a notice signed by Gimson, 'that I have to report that the death of Sir Vandeleur Grayburn occurred at 7.30 a.m. on the 22nd instant in the Stanley Prison Hospital' – and everyone knew the horror that lay between the lines. D. W. WATERTON, said a mis-spelled graffito in a cell, with the days on a calendar scratched off beside it, ARRESTED STANLEY CAMP JULY 7TH 1943 COURTMARTIALLED OCT 19TH AND NO DEFENCE CONDEMNED DEATH EXECUTED DATE CALENDER STOPS...

*

Through it all the indomitable Gimson maintained his claim to authority, and when news of Japan's unconditional surrender to the Allies reached Stanley on 16 August 1945, he immediately exerted it. By then everyone in the camp was exhausted. The Japanese were demoralized, the internees were half-starved. There was nobody to object when Gimson declared himself Acting Governor and representative of His Majesty King George VI in the British Crown Colony of Hong Kong. It was not until eleven days later that a message from London, conveyed via Macao by an agent of the BAAG, authorized him to do so, and by then Gimson had already set himself up with an administrative staff in offices in Queen's Road, meaningfully close to the Bank. On 30 August the *South China Morning Post* reappeared on the streets of Hong Kong, after an absence of nearly four years. It consisted in its entirety of seven paragraphs on a single sheet. It was endearingly headed EXTRA, and this is how it began:

> The first communiqué from the Hongkong Government to the people of Hongkong since December 1941 was issued this morning at 11 o'clock as follows: 'Rear Admiral Harcourt is lying outside Hongkong with a very strong fleet. The Naval Dockyard is to be ready for his arrival by noon today ...'

Gimson's action may have changed the course of history. It had been agreed among the Allied Powers that liberated territories should be surrendered to those who had liberated them: since nobody had actually liberated Hong Kong, logic suggested (and the Japanese themselves assumed) that it should be surrendered to the supreme commander of the war zone in which it was situated. This was Chiang Kai-shek, who as we know disputed the legality of the British presence in Hong Kong. Handing the colony over to him, backed as he was by an America distinctly unsympathetic to the British Empire, might well mean that the British flag might never go up above Government House again.

But Gimson created a *fait accompli* which nobody felt able to reverse, and when two weeks later the Japanese formally surrendered Hong Kong after three years and seven months of occupation, they handed their swords to Admiral Sir Cecil Harcourt, R.N., who had sailed into the grey and desolate harbour, littered with wreckage, in his flagship the cruiser *Swiftsure*, attended by the battleship *Anson*, two aircraft carriers, eight destroyers, eight submarines and a flotilla of minesweepers.

*

Captain Shadwell, R.N., of H M S *Maidstone*, was among the first to get to Stanley Camp. He was described by one ecstatic internee as being 'so lovely and cheerful, plump and priceless', and the arrival of the Royal Navy certainly did wonders to restore morale and confidence. It was almost like old times! The Navy provided films for the cinemas, dance bands for celebratory reunions, and after three years without much fun the city was, we are told by the *South China Morning Post*, introduced to jitterbugging 'under the expert tuition of rhythm-minded members of the Fleet'.

In an astonishingly short time Hong Kong recovered its bearing – sooner perhaps than any other occupied territory, in any theatre of the Second World War. A British military administration took over from Gimson, handing over eight months later to a restored Colonial Government; very soon almost every aspect of the territory's life was back to normal, and the British had expunged nearly all traces of their humiliation.

They left the railway-station tower on Government House. They had been planning to build an altogether new mansion higher up the hill, but the Japanese had rebuilt the old one so thoroughly that they abandoned the idea, and the tower became one of Hong Kong's most familiar architectural images: its rooms proved popular among Governors' wives – sunny little chambers, reached by steep wooden staircases and just as suitable for embroidery as for calligraphy. However after several attempts the military blew up the Shinto-blessed Temple of the Divine Wind, which the Japanese never had time to complete; today only its cyclopean foundations can be seen, acting as podium to the three apartment blocks called Cameron Buildings, above Magazine Gap, and commanding still one of the most triumphant views in Asia.

They tried several Japanese officers and men for atrocities, executing some with a dreadful rightness at Stanley, sentencing some to imprisonment, finding some innocent. They hanged as a traitor one Hong Kong Chinese, a particularly vile creature of the Kempeitei, but decided that only those who had directly helped the Japanese in cruel acts against the populace should be punished for collaboration with the enemy; in the end about fifty of all races were found guilty. They replaced the Japanese military currency with new notes flown in from London within the month. They honoured the so-called 'duress notes' – Hongkong and Shanghai Bank notes which had been issued by the Japanese without proper financial backing; there had been much speculation in this strictly illegal currency, and its official recognition in 1946 was the foundation of several fortunes. They also honoured most of their wartime IOUs, even sometimes to the most blatant profiteers.

They commemorated their dead in a beautiful war cemetery above Chai Wan, on Hong Kong Island, looking across the water to the east, where their soldiers of all origins were honoured side by side, Winnipeg Grenadiers beside Rajput infantrymen, six drummers of the Middlesex Regiment beside a host of poor fellows with no known names. They put up a headstone to the only grave within the precincts of the Anglican Cathedral, that of Private R. D. Maxwell, Hong Kong Volunteers, killed 23 December 1941.

They rescued some timbers from the *Tamar*, and made new doors for the Cathedral out of them. They found the looted statues of the kings and queens of Statue Square, still intact in Japan; but times had changed, and only Queen Victoria's was re-erected – far from the centre of things, in Victoria Park at Causeway Bay, where under the Pleasure-Ground By-Laws children are forbidden to steer their remote-controlled cars around its plinth.

They confirmed Gimson in his Colonial Secretaryship, and he went on to be Governor of Singapore. They restored Sir Mark Young to his interrupted Governorship. They gave his Professorship back to Lindsay Ride, and he became the University's Vice-Chancellor. They awarded Ha Chan the Military Cross. They were never quite sure again about Sir Robert Kotewall, but since he was a very old friend of many of them, besides being one of the richest men in the colony, on the whole they gave him the benefit of the doubt.

For a striking thing about this aftermath was its swift decline of recrimination. Getting back to business was everybody's only aim. The territory was desolate. Bomb damage was everywhere, the harbour was full of sunken ships, everything was dingy and unpainted. Only 150 cars were left in the entire colony, and the 17,000 telephones of 1939 were reduced to 10,000. There was no time for reproach, as Government and business community alike, British and Chinese, civilians and military, set about repairing the damage. Admiral Harcourt himself had defined his task, when his ships swept into harbour that day, as being to return to Hong Kong 'freedom, food, law and order and a stable currency'. So successfully was the job done, and so quickly was confidence in the colony restored, that by the end of 1945 the population was back to 1.6 million – just what it had been at the beginning of 1941 – and Sir Robert and Lady Ho Tung were able to celebrate their Diamond Jubilee quite in the old style, in the presence of His Excellency at the Hong Kong Hotel.

As the liberated soldiers and the surrendered Japanese departed on their troopships, and many of the Stanley internees sailed home to recuperate, in flooded a new wave of Hong Kong opportunists. They came not only from China, where war was now resumed between Kuomintang and Communists, but also from Europe, Australia and America – a new generation of traders. merchants, speculators and entrepreneurs. In the prevailing post-war climate of liberal imperialism there were plans to give the people of Hong Kong a measure of self-government, but the public response was apathetic, and they were soon shelved. All Hong Kong's reviving energies went into the accumulation of profit. Within a couple of years all the docks were restored, the wrecks in the harbour were salvaged, and 46,000 vessels cleared the port in a single year. The Bank resumed its glory, the old hongs bounced back, and even the Japanese community was presently flourishing once again. Already we detect, so soon after the calamity, the first tentative outline of the skyscraper City-State that was to come.

Yet Hong Kong was profoundly and permanently changed by the experience of war. The pageantry of Government was soon restored, but this was never again to feel quite like a British colony. Its balance had been permanently shifted. Ride said in 1942 that the British had become known as 'the run-away British', and when Admiral Harcourt's fleet of liberation arrived it found itself greeted only by multitudes of Chinese flags, with hardly a Union Jack to be seen on junk or housetop. After the war the colonists were not, it seems, often taunted with their military failure – they had after all come back in triumph, and there is bound to be a Chinese saying about those who laugh last – but inevitably the relationship between the races had been altered by events. No longer could the British feel themselves in all ways superior to Asiatics, and though the manners of racial prejudice were to linger on, its forms disappeared.

The last vestiges of segregation were renounced – by the end of the 1940s anybody who could afford it could live on the Peak. The Hong Kong Club moved reluctantly towards the admission of Chinese. Old residents returning after a war away were astonished by the new free-

and-easiness of racial relations, and the social life of the expatriates was never quite the same again – the tea-parties never quite so ineffable at the Repulse Bay Hotel, the Club never quite so inexpressibly club-like, the bathing beaches, once so comfortingly reminiscent of Bournemouth, now swarming with Asians. Very soon Chinese had broken into every sphere of life, social and economic, and were challenging the British for the financial dominance of Hong Kong.

More and more, too, Hong Kong began to behave like a semi-autonomous State. The British Empire was now moving towards its swift disbandment, as colony after colony gained self-government or independence, but Hong Kong stood apart. None of the usual standards of aspirations, it seemed, applied to this peculiar territory, Curzon was proved right, in his prophecy that when India was lost the rest of the Empire would go too, but Hong Kong did not count. Hong Kong marched to a different drum. Hong Kong ran its own economic affairs, Hong Kong soon evolved a new and even more glittering image of itself, and was indeed the one territory of the dependent Empire, presently to be reduced to hardly more than a ragbag of indigent islands, which was able to stand on its own feet. As the years passed, and arrogant Empire faded into generally amiable Commonwealth, successive Governments in London learned to make Hong Kong a perpetual exception to everything.

The end of the imperial era, in fact, was leaving Hong Kong high and dry, but at the same time another mighty historical progression was about to toss the territory in its wake; for in the last year of the 1940s the Communists came to power in China, and everything changed again.

II

THE LANDLORD

I

AS I WRITE (FOR IT WILL NOT BE THERE FOR LONG), IF YOU walk up Tung Tau Tsuen Road north of the airport, just over the line between Kowloon and the New Territories, you will discover on your right-hand side a row of establishments curious even by the standards of this recondite place. One after the other, glass-fronted to the street, they are the surgeries of unqualified dentists. Their windows are full of pickled abscesses, illustrations of impacted wisdom teeth, grinning rows of dentures, and in the background of each shop a dentist's chair stands waiting, sometimes with the dentist himself reclining in it between customers while his ornamental goldfish (good for patients' nerves) circumnavigate their illuminated tank in the background.

Unqualified doctors and dentists practise all over Hong Kong, but these particular practitioners are there for a historical reason. They believe themselves to be beyond the reach of Government regulations and inspectorates, because that side of that stretch of Tung Tau Tsuen Road once formed the rampart of the old Kowloon City. This was the place, you may remember, which the Manchus maintained as a fortified headquarters before the British ever came to Hong Kong, and in which they reserved their authority when the New Territories were ceded in 1898.

In their time it was a walled city, rebuilt in 1847 specifically as a defence against the British across the water. It had six watch towers, walls fifteen feet thick, a garrison of 500 soldiers and a *yamen*, the administrative office, securely in the middle of it. Its guns were black with red muzzles, and its demeanour could be fierce: there are pictures of convicted criminals crouched outside its gates with placards round their necks, and of pirates, apprehended by the Royal Navy, decapitated on the nearby beach courtesy of the *yamen*.

When the British took over the New Territories they very soon got rid of the Chinese officials at Kowloon, relying upon loose wordings in the Convention of Peking, and subsequent legal quibbles never quite settled the status of the place. It became a sort of no man's land, known simply as The Walled City. The Chinese objected whenever the British proposed to pull the place down; the British never applied to it all their usual municipal regulations, and as late as the 1970s it was said that its only real administration was provided by the Triads.

For as the city grew around it, the Walled City became a famous resort of villains. Never being absolutely sure what their rights were, the British generally let it be, hoping that it would wither away of its own accord. It very nearly did; in 1933 there were only some 400 inhabitants, and by 1940 almost all its houses had been demolished. However it revived remarkably after the Second World War, when squatters by the thousand moved in, and by the late 1980s it was thought to house some 30,000 people.

By now the quarter bears no resemblance to the fortified town of the Manchus. Its walls were all torn down by the Japanese, to be used as rubble for extensions at the airport, and very few of its structures are more than thirty years old. Nevertheless it still feels like an enclave within the city, extra-territorial and even slightly unreal. It is a frightful slum. No vehicle can enter it – there are no streets wide enough – and its buildings, rising sometimes to ten or twelve storeys, are so inextricably packed together that they seem to form one congealed mass of masonry, sealed together by overlapping structures, ladders, walkways, pipes and cables and ventilated only by foetid air-shafts.

A maze of dark dank alleys pierces the mass from one side to the other. Virtually no daylight reaches them. Looped electric cables festoon their low ceilings, dripping alarmingly with moisture. It is like a bunker. Sometimes you seem to be all alone, every door locked around you. Sometimes the lane is suddenly bright with the lights of a laundry or a sweatshop factory, and loud with Chinese music. In the one airy space of the labyrinth still stands the old *yamen*, a low wooden building now used as a school and a community centre, and one gets the impression to this day of a close-knit, cohesive and homogenous community, altogether separate from the colony outside. The Hong Kong sanitation laws are still not applied. Fire risks are disregarded. The only planning restriction ever enforced concerns the height of the buildings – as it is, aircraft landing at Kai Tak come screaming disconcertingly low over the rooftops.

Like the British, down the years Chinese Governments have viewed the Walled City ambivalently. On the one hand they have never abandoned their claim to authority within it, and from time to time have made a minor issue of it. On the other they have felt that to make too much fuss about the Walled City in particular might imply recognition of British rights over the territory as a whole. The slum has accordingly remained a strange reminder of China's stake in Hong Kong, and of the subtle, patient, cat-and-mouse way in which the Chinese have viewed the progress of the colony.

Well before 1997 the Walled City of Kowloon is going to be demolished at last, the British and the Chinese no longer being at odds about it.[1] With it will disappear from Hong Kong an ancient thrill. Though in my own experience everyone within the Walled City has been kindness itself, and though in recent years Hong Kong policemen have been patrolling it, still even now tourists are warned against entering the place, for safety's sake, and are sometimes to be seen enjoying an anachronistic *frisson*, a last shiver of the Mysterious Orient or the Inscrutable Chinese, as they peer past the preserved abscesses into its unenticing purlieus.

2

I say a last shiver of the inscrutable, because in theory at least the 1984 agreement brought frankness for the first time to Anglo-Chinese relationships on Hong Kong. Until then nothing had been straightforward, and the hazy difference of views about the status of the Walled City could be taken as a paradigm for attitudes about the colony itself.

At least since the fall of the Manchu dynasty the Chinese have

[1] Some 4,500 of the residents have already submitted false demands for compensation: many have moved into the Walled City for that very purpose.

denied any British right to be in Hong Kong. They have maintained that both the cession of Hong Kong and Kowloon, and the lease of the New Territories, fall into the category of Unequal Treaties: that is, treaties unfairly forced upon a temporarily debilitated China by the ruthless military power of foreigners. The Unequal Treaty reached its apogee at the end of the nineteenth century, when Britain, Germany, France, Russia, Portugal and Japan all had their territorial concessions on the coast of China, and together with the United States enjoyed all manner of privileges in Treaty Ports and Spheres of Influence.

It was impossible to deny, though the British consistently did, that the treaties *were* unequal. The Chinese really had been obliged to make these concessions by *force majeure*, and they were given nothing in return. As China revived, one by one the foreign rights were abrogated. Most of the settlements were wound up between the two world wars – the British left Wei-hai-wei in 1930[1] – and in 1944 foreign rights in all the Treaty Ports were formally relinquished. The great international settlement at Shanghai came to an end in 1945. By the second half of the twentieth century there remained upon the coast of China only the two foreign enclaves that had started it all: Portugal's Macao, which had been there for 400 years and was so small as to be almost meaningless, and Britain's Hong Kong.

It seems slightly comical even to talk of relations between Hong Kong (population 5.6 million) and the People's Republic of China (population 1,000 million) – rather like the captive Gimson's foreign relations with the Empire of Japan. But the relationship is not just between a minute colony and a colossus, but between two immense historical forces – between cultures and traditions, systems, races and values. It was the irresistible energy of the modernist West, approaching the climax of its supremacy, that placed the colony of Hong Kong upon the edge of China; it was the impotence of the traditional Chinese civilization at its nadir that allowed this to happen; it is the gradual equalizing of the two, and the spread of technology absorbing them both, that is now bringing the association to its climactic denouement.

---

[1] Its villagers beseeching the British Government, so *The Times* reported at the time, 'to postpone the return of the territory till better times'.

3

One-nine-thousandth the size of its gigantic host, Hong Kong has often been likened to a parasite upon the skin of China. Sometimes looking across to the mainland from the top of the Peak, sensing the almost infinite landscapes of China which start beyond the Kowloon hills and stretch inconceivably away towards Tibet or Mongolia, it does occur to me that Hong Kong must seem to the leaders of China no more than an irritating itch on the skin. The simile, though, is false. Hong Kong's role has never been passive, or merely extractive. The colony has been the agency of far greater powers, and in its dealings with China has given as much as it has got.

For much of its history it was far more threatening than threatened. From the start it defied the laws and the traditions of China, whether they concerned the divinity of the Emperor or the ban on the export of Chinese technology to foreigners. It repeatedly served as a base for attacks on the Chinese mainland, culminating in Lord Elgin's humiliation of the Manchus in 1860, and the destruction of the Summer Palace in Beijing. Throughout the nineteenth century indeed the colony treated China with general contempt. 'I do not know,' observed Keswick of Jardine's in 1895, at the end of China's most miserable and humiliating century, 'that it can be good for China to be treated generously; for then the lessons of adversity and of supreme misfortune might be forgotten.'

From Hong Kong, in good times and in bad, the West has kept a monitory eye upon China. The colony has always been a base for intelligence and propaganda activities on the mainland. Today some of those great electronic aerials and dishes probing the sky above the territory are outposts of the Government Communications Headquarters at Cheltenham in England, part of the Anglo-American system of eavesdrop which spans the world, and others beam the Chinese services of the BBC to the remotest corners of the People's Republic. Even now the most thorough reportage of Chinese affairs is that in the Hong Kong press, in Chinese as in English: many pages are devoted to sessions of the People's National Congress in Beijing, and innumerable items are recorded that never see the light of day within the People's Republic.

Here too the opponents of authority in Beijing or Guangzhou have habitually prepared their subversions under cover of the British flag; republicans against Manchus, Communists against Kuomintang,

Kuomintang against Communists. Zhou Enlai took refuge in Hong Kong in 1927, early in his rise to ultimate power in China, and the Kuomintang authorities in Taiwan, still dreaming of a return to the mainland, have always used it as a base for mischief-making in southern China. Many a vanquished war-lord has retreated to Hong Kong to plan his come-back – the well-known 'General' Pipe Lee, for example, who for years held flamboyant court, together with his nine wives, in a fiercely fortified mansion in the New Territories.

But western imperialism was always an engine of development as well as of exploitation, and Hong Kong constantly projected new vitality, too, into the moribund mass of China. For better or for worse, its constant pressure for access to China's business gradually opened up the country to modern realities. Even the trade in opium at least instructed Chinese financiers in modern methods of exchange, demonstrated the advantages of contemporary ships and armaments, and helped to open the eyes of the mandarins to the fact that foreigners might be barbaric, but were not invariably fools. The middlemen who dealt with the Hong Kong hongs, and later the Chinese compradors who served them, were among the first truly cosmopolitan Chinese, and acted as agents of enlightenment as well as of greed. Western techniques were usefully grafted on to oriental bases: a first symbol of an awakening China was the design of the hybrid junks called *lorchas*, which had a Chinese hull with a western rigging.[1]

Later the merchants and bankers of Hong Kong played leading parts in China's own Industrial Revolution, such as it was. They envisaged gigantic new markets opening there to western exports, and immense opportunities for investment. Groping as they always were through miasmas of Chinese corruption, obstruction, ignorance and misunderstanding, they were constantly urging the purblind Manchu authorities towards progress, and Hong Kong became less like an itchy parasite than like a wasp, buzzing and stinging the lethargic giant into awareness.

It was largely through the agency of Hong Kong that steam, the prime instrument of nineteenth-century change, reached China. The sturdy river steamboats of Russell's, Dent's, Jardine's and Swire's became the chief means of transport into the interior, and Hong Kong

---

[1] And one of which, the *Arrow*, Chinese-owned but Hong Kong-registered, appositely became the cause of the 1856 war which finally took the armies of the west into the Forbidden City itself.

steamers dominated the coastal trade. The first of all China's railways was built by Jardine's. A quaint narrow-gauge line between Shanghai and Wusung, opened in 1876, it did not last long, the Manchu Government being unsympathetic to the initiative, but it was the beginning of the immense railway explosion which was to transform China in the last part of the nineteenth century. It was only proper that in the end a consortium between Jardine's and the Hongkong and Shanghai Bank should finance and develop the greater part of the system.

Money poured in from the colony to the sub-continent. Quite apart from investment money, repeated loans were made to Chinese Governments, and the Hongkong and Shanghai Bank became one of the most powerful forces in Beijing. For some years it was the one Bank into which all Chinese customs dues were paid, and when China went off the silver standard in 1935 all the silver surrendered to the Government was stored in the Bank's vaults. War-lords also came to Hong Kong for the wherewithal to fight their campaigns, and in the 1930s some 70 per cent of China's war needs, in its fight against Japan, reached it by way of the colony.

Engineers from Hong Kong helped to curb the perennial floods of the Yellow River. The first elevator in China was installed by Jardine's. Hong Kong contributed power to China's electricity grid. There were even times when the minuscule colony helped to alleviate China's food shortages. F. D. Ommanney, who lived in Hong Kong in the 1950s, when China's agriculture was in chaos, reported [1] that when his amah visited Guangzhou she took with her, for her hungry relatives over the border, two chickens, a duck, packages of fruit, sausages, eggs, tea and sweetmeats, large quantities of dried bread and three sacks crammed with burnt rice, scraped from the bottoms of cooking-pans.

4

'A celestial palace in a fairyland,' is how the nineteenth-century Chinese scholar Wei Yuan described Hong Kong. They have often expressed themselves in poetical hyperbole and politesse, but there is no doubt that the Chinese have always been astonished by Hong Kong, by its technical virtuosity and its speed of change. As early as 1845 a senior Guangzhou official wrote an ode to the colony describing it as a royal white city built on a rock, its buildings glittering in the morning

[1] In *Fragrant Harbour*, London 1962.

sun – 'yet on this spot ere-while were only to be seen the hovels of the roving fishermen. Where are they? – gone like the swallows of departed autumn!' The poet Wang Zuaxian, in 1870, said the colony was 'embroiled in a sea of music and song, its mountains overflowing with meat and wine'. The politician Wang Dao likened it to a row of flying geese, and the political reformer Kang You-wei, who much admired the ruling strategy of the colony, wrote about 'the splendour of the buildings, the orderly array of the roads, the solemn appearance of the police . . .'

Hong Kong has been a potent example to the Chinese across the frontier and up the coast. They see the colony as they might see an exhibition of modernity, and the mere contrast of material achievement, between the little colony and the immense republic, can only be stimulation of a kind – one car for every twenty-two people in Hong Kong, one for every 10,220 in China! China looks to Hong Kong for models managerial, constructional, architectural, financial. The computer age is reaching the People's Republic very largely through the medium of Hong Kong, and the concept of company law, unknown in Communist China but essential to satisfactory contracts with the outside world, is seeping into China by way of Hong Kong's legal community.

When Lugard founded the University of Hong Kong, he saw it specifically as an intellectual example for China – a British lighthouse whose beams would illuminate all around it. Hong Kong was always a base of Christian evangelicalism, too, and even in Mao Zedong's time Christianity was projected into China via this not very Christian colony: couriers of New Life Literature, a proselytizing organization, took Bibles into the mainland, and the Chinese Research Centre expressed itself concerned, like so many missionary groups before it, by the fact that 'many Chinese hearts are empty'.

Above all the whole ideology of capitalism, now fitfully reviving within the People's Republic, finds its nearest exemplar in Hong Kong. It could hardly be disregarded. Millions of Chinese comrades have relatives in the colony, many more have seen the place for themselves, and anyway history has proved that the patterns of Hong Kong can never be excluded from China. It was from here that Sun Yat-sen, a medical student in the colony, took home the ideas that were to overthrow the monarchy and impel the Celestial Kingdom at last towards the status of a contemporary Great Power. He was banished from Hong Kong for a time as being dangerous to its peace and good order, but twenty-five years later he told an audience at Hong Kong University that the source of his revolutionary inspiration had been

Hong Kong itself – he had been deeply affected by the orderly calm and security of the colony, compared with the disorder and insecurity of his home in Guangdong Province, only fifty miles away. 'The difference of Governments impressed me very much . . .'

Except I suppose for the simplest or remotest peasants, all Chinese know about Hong Kong. It is a metropolis of the Greater China which extends in communities large and small all around the world. Every corner of that vast informal empire maintains family or economic connections with the colony. Its remissions of money to the homeland are channelled through Hong Kong, and so often are its citizens, so that the territory has become an ante-room, or perhaps a pressure-chamber, through which a perpetual flow of Greater Chinese, Overseas Chinese as the People's Republic classifies them, passes on its way to the mainland.

I once took passage in a Chinese ship from Hong Kong to Shanghai, and found the vessel itself a microcosm of the Chinese world. It was like a reunion, as we passed from the threshold that was Hong Kong into the grand presence of the mainland. The crew were citizens of the People's Republic, cheerful, able, always ready to serve you a scraggy leg of duck wrapped in grease-paper from the snack bar, and obligingly disposed to turn a blind eye when you passed through a gate marked CREW ONLY. The passengers were of all Chinese kinds. They included elderly people returning from visits to relatives abroad, and rich Overseas Chinese from Taiwan and the Philippines, and Hong Kong students, and Chinese-American businessmen on trade missions, and a couple of academics returning from studies in Europe.

For three days we sailed through the South China Sea. We were never alone in it, for there were always fishing-boats about, and we were seldom out of sight of the shore whose landmarks the passengers excitedly pointed out to each other. By the time we entered the estuary of the Yangtze and steamed up-river to Shanghai, the experience had become doubly allegorical to me. I felt myself to be among a company of wanderers returning to their family; but I also felt I had been sailing in the wakes of all the ships that ever sailed up the China coast from Hong Kong, all the opium smugglers, tea clippers, Swire's and Jardine's steamers, all the multitudes of junks and sampans which have linked colony with mainland through all the pages of this book. Even as I write these words, looking out from my window across the harbour of Hong Kong, there I see the very same vessel, the *Shanghai*, flying the red flag at her stern and loading her attendant lighters for the next voyage home.

5

Still, if the 412 square miles of Hong Kong cast a surprisingly long shadow over China, the presence of the People's Republic's 3.7 million square miles looms decidedly larger over Hong Kong. Physically there is no escaping it, anywhere in the colony, or ignoring the fact that Hong Kong is geographically and geologically part of China, dependent upon its vast neighbour for most of its water and nearly all its food. When I survey that view from the Peak I find it hard to work out, contemplating its jumbled panorama of land and sea, which islands or hills are British, which Chinese.

To the Chinese Hong Kong has never been anything but part of China. China is China to them, traditionally every Chinese can only be a citizen of China, and the mere occupation by foreigners of a patch of Chinese territory does nothing to alienate it from the motherland. From start to finish the Chinese of all regimes have acted upon the assumption that in the fullness of time the foreigners would lose control of Hong Kong. Their attitude has generally been evasively temporizing. They have seldom lost their tempers over Hong Kong, but have allowed the last of the Unequal Treaties to wither away organically – it was the British, not the Chinese, who initiated the 1984 negotiations.

When Hong Kong was taken from them in 1842 their firm and crazed conviction was that China was in all ways the centre of the world. The very ideogram for 'Centre' stood for China too, and the title of Middle Kingdom was a reminder that everything else revolved around the heartland that was China. Western envoys were treated like menials or juveniles. Queen Victoria herself was severely reprimanded by Lin Ze-xu, Imperial High Commissioner in Guangzhou, for allowing the opium trade to continue – 'on receipt of this letter', the mandarin counselled her, 'let your reply be speedy, advising us of the measures you propose to adopt. Do not by false embellishments evade or procrastinate . . .'

Reading the history of Hong Kong, I sometimes get the feeling that the colony was ceded to Britain rather as a toy might be handed over to a recalcitrant child, merely to keep him quiet. Certainly for long periods the Chinese simply let things lie, without it seems much worrying about the status of Hong Kong. Often they were physically incapable of doing anything else, but at other times they seem to have exercised indifference as a matter of policy. When they did interfere in the affairs of the colony, they generally did so obliquely, but not always ineffectively. It happened first in the 1860s, with the so-called Blockade of Hong Kong. This was mounted because the Chinese resented the vast amount of contraband conveyed into China from the colony – as the British Minister in Beijing admitted at the time, Hong Kong had become 'little more than an immense smuggling depot'.

The British maintained that, Hong Kong being a free port, it was up to the Chinese authorities themselves to stop illicit trading. The Chinese accordingly bought some new (British-built) gunboats, set up new customs posts in the islands all around (sometimes commanded by British officers of the Imperial Chinese Customs), and for nineteen years stopped and searched Chinese ships coming and going from Hong Kong. This protracted and sometimes lackadaisical action succeeded, and in 1886 the British officially admitted their responsibility for controlling contraband moving in and out of the harbour. Here and there in the archipelago one may still find the remains of the customs posts established during the blockade, and the name of Smuggler's Ridge, where the Shing-mun redoubt stood, remembers the dispute too.

After the 1911 revolution, when the Manchus were overthrown and nationalism rode high in China, there was a spate of Chinese intrusion, official and unofficial, into Hong Kong's affairs. The colony had tried hard to stay clear of the various subversive movements, which is why Sun Yat-sen had been expelled in 1896 – he expostulated that he had only been trying to 'emancipate my miserable countrymen from the cruelty of the Tartar yoke', but it cut no ice with the British. After the fall of the monarchy, though, Hong Kong found itself far more deeply embroiled. A large proportion of its Chinese population was enthusiastically on the side of the revolution, rather thinking indeed that it ought to be consummated by the overthrow of British colonial rule too, and the end of the Manchus sparked off Hong Kong's first real political disturbances. Europeans were attacked in the streets, policemen were stoned, European shops were boycotted. Soldiers with fixed bayonets patrolled the towns, and reinforcements were brought in from India. It was then that Sir Henry May suffered his attempted assassination. The British were outraged by the event, one of the very few occasions on which one of their colonial governors had ever been physically assaulted, but the Chinese population of Hong Kong seems to have been less shocked, and the only Chinese-language newspaper of the day preferred not to report the incident at all.[1]

[1] A letter from the would-be assassin's landlady, intercepted by the police, mentioned only in passing that her lodger had tried to murder the Governor, 'and most unfortunately missed'.

Then there was the damaging series of strikes and boycotts in the 1920s, and in 1949 the Communist Revolution in China altered the nature of the relationship once again, sent the cadres swarming into Hong Kong with their Little Red Books, and set the scene for the colony's prolonged and confusing last act. Although the British Government was one of the first to recognize the new Communist regime, provocations of many kinds were practised upon the colony during the People's Republic's uneasy years of confrontation with the West. In May 1962, when things were particularly hard in China, 70,000 refugees were suddenly let loose across the border without warning, terrifyingly straining the colony's resources of food and housing. And in 1967, when the British Embassy in Beijing was sacked by activists of the Cultural Revolution, the most violent riots Hong Kong had ever known were incited by events across the frontier. Mobs roamed the streets waving red flags, brandishing the Thoughts of Chairman Mao and massing in their thousands outside the gates of Government House, which were stuck all over with propaganda leaflets.

Bombs were exploded then. Cars were burnt. Ominous messages, it was said, reached the Governor from the Politburo, and there came into being a famous and resilient legend of Hong Kong – namely that, as every visitor used to be told, Mao Zedong had only to lift a telephone in Beijing to get the British out of the colony. Nervous expatriates thought the end was near, and for a time it seemed probable that when the dry season arrived the Chinese would refuse their supplies of water to the colony, and so drive it into abdication. One of Hong Kong's great moments of historical relief occurred when, punctually on 1 October as usual, the telephone rang from across the frontier and the usual calm engineer's voice asked if the colony was ready for the turning of the stopcocks.

It was not the time. The Chinese had no desire to take over Hong Kong at that moment of their history, and their proxy intervention had been no more than a demonstration. Perhaps they hoped to force the Government of Hong Kong into some humiliating gesture of appeasement, as they did indeed force the Government of Macao, but if so they failed. Government House remained loftily immune to the goings-on outside its gates, and the crisis was ended largely by the stern and swift actions of the police, supported for once by a generally sympathetic public – it was no coincidence that after the events of 1967 the force joined the monarchical ranks of sportsmen and astronomers, and became the Royal Hong Kong Police Force.

Things returned to their peculiar normal. For another decade China remained forbidden to almost all foreigners, and one of the great excitements of travel was afforded by a visit to Lok Ma Chau, a hillock crowned by a police station which overlooked the flatlands of Guangdong to the north-west – utterly peaceful, placid, pastoral country it appeared in those days, and it made China seem a place of the Last Innocence, remote and forever unattainable. At souvenir stalls beside the nearby track hawkers sold not only the usual fans, straw grasshoppers and ceramic goddesses, but also copies of Chairman Mao's Little Red Book; and I remember vividly the queer and tantalizing unease the place left in me, the stall-holders one by one thrusting this text into my face, while behind their backs lay the vast silent compulsion of the homeland.

6

Along the road from the Hongkong and Shanghai Bank building rises the tallest building outside the United States, high above the old dome of the Legislature, monumentally dominating the view from Government House on the slope of the hill above and thus, one might surmise, finally spoiling its *feng shui* too. This is the Hong Kong headquarters of the Communist Bank of China, seventy storeys high as against the Hongkong and Shanghai Bank's forty-seven, for even before the Communist revolution it was axiomatic that the Chinese bank must be symbolically taller than the British, and preferable that it should be the tallest building in Hong Kong. Its designer I. M. Pei was one of the first Chinese-American architects to accept commissions in Communist China; [1] he has created it in a style which, while certainly not arrogant or overbearing, is nevertheless a declaration that Hong Kong is not only geographically, but functionally part of China.

In some ways Hong Kong is like an assistant Chinese capital – a financial capital perhaps to Beijing's political capital, like Rotterdam to The Hague. Lord Kadoorie once likened it to a Free Zone of the People's Republic, under British management, and certainly the Chinese Government itself has powerful financial stakes within Hong Kong, where it has long mastered the capitalist way of making money. The Bank of China, first established by the Kuomintang, is the People's

[1] And his father had been the Bank of China's first manager in Hong Kong, back in the 1930s.

Republic's chief agency for foreign financial dealings, and is the richest and most worldly of all Chinese Government banks. Something like 35 per cent of all the Republic's foreign currency passes through its hands, on its way to Beijing, and it also looks after the interests of hundreds of Hong Kong enterprises now owned or part-owned by Communist China.

These are sometimes hard to pin down, so ill-defined are China's activities in Hong Kong, and so entangled not only in murky inter-changes of politics and diplomacy, but also in the web of capitalism at its most dense. They are however undoubtedly immense. They are said to include at least thirteen banks, many real estate companies, airlines, hotels, stores, petrol stations, cinemas, warehouses, factories of several kinds and some say brothels. They are often indistinguishable from capitalist-owned concerns – so committed indeed to western manage-ment systems is China Resources Holdings Ltd, the vast State-owned hong which supervises all of China's overseas economic activities, that in 1987 it appointed an Englishman to be its local managing director.

This economic coalition is nothing new. Whatever the public atti-tudes of the British during their days of supremacy, privately even they were always aware that the colony could never be detached from its origins – this was the one British possession where the Mother Country was not England. In effect Hong Kong was hardly more than the greatest of the Treaty Ports, happening to fly the British flag. Just as many of the most enterprising Chinese took their talents and their investments to Shanghai or Xiamen, where they could deal with en-trepreneurs whose economic language they understood, and whose aims they generally shared, so many of them came one further, and crossed the frontier into Hong Kong. Until 1940 they could come and go as they liked – access from China was uncontrolled.

So the successive waves of immigrants who have peopled Hong Kong have in their own eyes hardly been immigrants at all, but merely migrants from one part of China to another. Hong Kong has been like a pressure-valve for China, and every convulsion there, every change of policy or regime, has brought another few thousand migrants over the Sham Chun River. The xenophobic Boxer troubles of 1900 sent a wave of prudent newcomers – it was dangerous in China then even to have associated with foreigners, and many Chi-nese who had worked for foreign firms thought it wiser to come and live under a foreign flag. Many more came in the aftermath of the 1911 revolution and during the Japanese wars of the 1930s, and vast numbers fled, as they are fleeing still, from the effects of Chinese

Communism: the main function of Hong Kong's armed forces nowadays is keeping out illegal Chinese immigrants, which they do with helicopters, speedboats, electronic detectors and 65 million candle-power searchlights . . .

When the times demand it the migrants move back again – 80,000 went in the plague year of 1894, 60,000 in the First World War, and at the Chinese New Year of 1986 500,000 re-crossed the border just to visit their relatives in Guangdong. For they have not often come for purely ideological reasons – not out of principle, so to speak. Businessmen and industrialists came because they could make money better in Hong Kong. Landowners came in the wake of the capital they had habitually stashed away in the colony. Religious people came to escape the secularization of Chinese society, whether under the Kuomintang with its bias against superstition, or under the Communists with their preference for atheism; the Buddhist monasteries of Lantau were mostly founded by migrants from the mainland, and just as Hong Kong used be a Rest and Recreation Center for battle-weary American soldiers, so it was too for spiritually exhausted Christian missionaries.

Often politics brought them. There have always been Chinese political presences in the colony, the various factions of the day supporting their own agents and manipulators, and often extending to Hong Kong their complex mainland feuds. In our own time the chief competition has been between the Communist Party and the Kuomintang. The Communists see Hong Kong simply as their own, and are waiting to take it over; the Kuomintang leaders in Taiwan, while they consider the off-shore islands of Quemoy and Matsu their front-line military bases against Communist China, regard Hong Kong as their political frontier. Each side has many and fervent supporters in the colony, together with loyal newspapers and trade unions; for years local Communists have participated in the People's Congress in Beijing, as delegates from Guangdong Province, while the seashore hamlet of Rennie's Mill, in the New Territories, has been inhabited since 1950 entirely by pro-Kuomintang refugees. Even now, so near to 1997, the rivalry is fierce. On 1 October, the anniversary of the 1949 Revolution, Hong Kong flutters with the red flags of Communism, everywhere from the Bank of China building to the offices of obscure labour unions or the high tenement windows of activists; nine days later is the Double Tenth, 10 October, the anniversary of the 1911 revolution, and out come the flags of the Kuomintang.

Straddling the ideologies, blurring the boundaries between politics and crime but powerfully representing China in Hong Kong, have always been the Triads. In earlier times the British feared them not merely as criminal organizations, but as xenophobic agitators too, and in their time they have been active in many kinds of political action – economic boycott, strikes, riots, anti-Japanese activities during the Second World War. They are often said to be in cahoots with the Kuomintang, and are certainly no friends to the Communist Government in Beijing, which treats them with no mercy; in the 1960s they helped the Hong Kong police to control the spill-over of the Cultural Revolution, a liaison easy enough to arrange because they have always supplied the force with some of its best-placed informers.

But then many kinds of Chinese villains have found it convenient to come to Hong Kong, where the rules are less draconian than they are in China, and the arm of the law has traditionally been at least as easy to bend. As late as the early 1950s pirates from the mainland were still active in the colony's waters, and Hong Kong fishermen were allowed to carry arms in self-defence against them. Nowadays anyone in China with a taste for smuggling, especially drug-smuggling, is likely to look ambitiously towards the Crown Colony. There are criminal groups specializing in illegal emigration from China, and the biggest of all Hong Kong robberies, the hold-up of a bank armoured car in 1975, was done by former Red Guards, bringing their talents to the colony after the collapse of the Cultural Revolution.

As for diplomatic representation of China in Hong Kong, formally there has never been any – no consul, no High Commission. Zhou Enlai once suggested that Beijing might open a diplomatic mission in Hong Kong, but the British declined the offer – there was no room in the colony, Sir Alexander Grantham is supposed to have said, for *two* Governors. In the 1940s there was, however, an official representative of the Kuomintang Government in the colourful person of Admiral Chank Chak, Chinese Navy. This engaging officer, very small and very entertaining, had lost a leg during an action against the Japanese on the Yangtze, and he bore himself with a Nelsonian style; when Hong Kong fell to the Japanese he escaped with great *élan* on a Royal Navy motor torpedo boat, and lived to become Mayor of Guangzhou and an honorary Knight of the British Empire.

He has had no successor in Hong Kong, but disguised in shadow-boxing and feinting for many years an official presence of the Communist Government has been tacitly recognized all the same. For long it was assumed to inhabit the Bank of China building, and during the long estrangement from Beijing all sorts of sinister things were supposed to go on there – when one saw its night-lights burning, one rumoured them to be the lights of plotters, subversives or indoctrinators. Today, though, welcoming smiles are *de rigueur* at the Bank of China, and I find it a most convenient place to cash my traveller's cheques – there are seldom queues, and the rates are favourable.

Later the unofficial chief representative of China in Hong Kong was the local manager of Xinhua, the New China News Agency, whose offices stood rather less prominently near the Happy Valley racecourse, and included dormitories for its staff. Over the years this functionary gradually came into the open. In the tense days of the 1960s he became the messenger by which Beijing's warnings were conveyed to the colony, and by the 1980s he was making official pronouncements on behalf of the People's Government, attending functions in a quasi-diplomatic role and generally behaving like an all-but-Commissioner.

When Beijing wished to drop a hint to the colony, it was likely to be dropped in the columns of *Mirror Monthly*, Xinhua's Hong Kong magazine. When Beijing felt it necessary to make a half-veiled gesture of authority, it was Xinhua's manager who was photographed edging a gingerly passage through the rat-infested corridors of the Walled City. And when, during the nervy months of the early 1980s when the whole future of Hong Kong was in doubt, and share prices showed a fragility as worrying to Beijing as to Jardine, Matheson, as often as not it was Xinhua's manager who was delegated to make some soothing declaration about the prospects of peaceful agreement.

Communist China, then, is deeply entrenched in the mass of Hong Kong, and plays a sophisticated and sometimes decisive part in all its activities. Yet even now China sometimes shows itself, in this relentlessly modernist territory, curiously naïve and old-fashioned, and occasionally as I consider its presence I feel just these sensations of nostalgic yearning that I felt on the hillock of Lok Ma Chau in the days when the frontier was closed. If there is anywhere in Hong Kong where you may still find solid old-fashioned workmanship, peasant craft and homely tableware, it is in the department stores of the Chinese Products Company or the Chinese Merchandise Emporium, where prices are low, stock is slightly dusty, service is leisurely, and I am reminded paradoxically of country drapers' shops in Britain long ago, or Middle Western hardware stores.

And sometimes a junk sails by from China, a real sailing junk without an engine, stealing noiseless among the freighters of the harbour. How infinitely old it looks! Its sails are like the very thin membranes of some ancient flying creature, and on its deck raggety Chinese with bony elbows obliviously recline.

7

On hilltop outposts, camouflaged and sandbagged, looking not at all unlike lesser fortresses of the Khyber in the great days of the Indian Raj, soldiers of the British Empire are still on guard, even now, above the frontier between Hong Kong and China. They may be Gurkha mercenaries, they may be Britons, and before them the frontier is marked for the twenty-five miles of its length, between Mirs Bay at one end and Deep Bay at the other, by a thick double row of coiled barbed wire, nine or ten feet high. Through it, for much of its length, a narrow road uncomfortably runs.

A drive along this peculiar thoroughfare, hemmed in on either side by its tangle of metal, is one of the oddest of Hong Kong outings. Even at the end of the 1980s, with Anglo-Chinese relations at their easiest, and the colony pledged to the Return, the whole frontier zone is sealed off to visitors, and this particular road, following the actual line of the border, is even more strictly prohibited. As your Land Rover weaves its way down the corridor you are unlikely to meet much other traffic within the wire; only a few British soldiers, perhaps, riding to their posts on tall old-fashioned bicycles, like village policemen in Agatha Christie stories, or Gurkhas, being of smaller build, riding the sort of BMX bikes that children like for gyrobatics. Through the mesh the gorge of the Sham Chun River still looks like an archetypal frontier.

In general it seems, as frontiers so often do, a dead or sterile country. Along the road on the other, Chinese side of the river you sometimes see cars and drab brown trucks; in the no man's land that lies beside the stream farmers in wide straw hats are at work, and a couple of women sit languidly on a small bridge, perhaps, to watch you go by. In general, though, it is an empty place. You pass down your caged thoroughfare as you might pass through a safari park without any animals, or perhaps a landscape emptied of life by some catastrophe. Here and there concrete Chinese watch-posts are embedded in the earth, sometimes just outside the wire; always you feel the presence of the British sentries, out of sight in their dug-outs on the hills above.

Well you may, for there are troops perpetually in 'ambush position' on this border, and they are linked by an electronic listening system called Vindicator, which records every sound along that corridor, the merest snip of the wire, the most cautious shuffling of feet. At the crossing posts all the paraphernalia of a frontier is still maintained, the police guards, the customs posts, on one side a silken Chinese flag flying elegantly in the breeze, on the other a Union Jack of bunting limply hanging.[1]

If the frontier at large seems deserted, the crossing-places feel as though half China is squeezing incessantly through the barriers, one way or the other. At Lo Wu the railway line to Guangzhou crosses on a steel bridge. The fastest trains go straight through, but passengers on the slower ones have to change here, and stream in their thousands through a cluster of buildings that feel, at least when you are being shunted through them yourself, remarkably like cattle-sheds. At Man Kam To endless convoys of lorries pass over the road bridge. At the village of Sha Tau Kok China-England Street demarcates the frontier as it has since 1898. It is like a little Berlin. A row of stone posts, down the centre of the street, marks the exact line between British and Chinese territory. Only residents of the village may cross it, but a constant flow of foreign journalists, visiting MPs and Congressmen, miscellaneous bigwigs of all nationalities, peer across it from neighbouring rooftops, courtesy of the Government Information Service, and are briefed about the situation by crisp British police inspectors in well-ironed trousers.

All this is anachronism. There have been times when this border has stood to its arms against foreign attack, and when it really did possess the baleful allure of an Iron Curtain. Such times are long gone. Those strongpoints could not withstand a military attack for more than an hour or two, and a modern army could cut through the wire wall in a trice. The only point of the barricade now is to keep illegal immigrants out of Hong Kong. The ambush patrols are certainly not out to fall upon advance guards of the People's Liberation Army, and Vindicator merely tells the soldiers when another few poor Chinese from Guangdong Province, in search of higher wages or better opportunities, have cut a hole in the wire.

But the British border guards, police and military, cling rather touchingly, I think, to former attitudes, as though nothing has changed. Even now very few of them have ever crossed into China themselves,

---

[1] Though it was pointedly a flag of silk which the British originally raised over the New Territories in 1898.

and they pine for yesterday's dangerous mysteries. There was glamour to Sha Tau Kok in the old days, when one never knew what was happening over there, when mad revolutionaries were liable to snipe at police posts, or half-starved multitudes might appear all of a sudden out of the homeland. But the need for a frontier, its very existence indeed, is fading now, as the two sides prepare for 1997, and the whole apparatus of wires, police posts, security zones, briefings, Buchan-esque forts and Vindicator has a quaint and dated air. Except for Gibraltar, whose frontier is only a street wide, and Northern Ireland, whose frontier is abstractional, this is the very last land frontier of the British Empire, and those indefensible posts on the former Mendip Hills, looking down to the ex-Ganges, really are the last descendants of Attock and Gilgit.

8

Only once, in all the 150 years of Hong Kong's history, did it seem possible that the Chinese might be about to take it back by force. In 1945, at the end of the Second World War, two Chinese Kuomintang armies passed through Kowloon to embark in American ships for Manchuria, recently liberated from the Japanese. Column after column, day after day they marched through the streets to the quayside and the waiting troopships, and the colony watched them with bated breath, just as it had watched the arrival of the Japanese five years before. The British Government had agreed to their passage through Hong Kong, but even so there was always the possibility, at least in the minds of ordinary people, that they would never leave.

It must surely have crossed the mind of Chiang Kai-shek, too, but the times were against the notion. It might arouse, the Generalissimo admitted, 'allied misunderstanding'. There has never in fact been any serious threat of a forcible seizure. In the nineteenth century the Chinese were incapable of it, in the twentieth they have presumably felt it unnecessary. At any time since the Communist Revolution they could certainly have taken Hong Kong if they wished, not only by force of arms, but by cutting off its water supplies or by starving it out; for many years the British have regularly imported a proportion of Hong Kong's rice from Thailand, partly in case of Chinese famine, but partly in case of Chinese blockade. In 1949 the British garrison was reinforced against a possible invasion, to a level higher than ever before – 30,000 men, double the force that had resisted the Japanese; but the worst never happened, gradually the garrison was reduced to its usual level, and the interminable hunt for illegal immigrants remained the nearest thing to active service its soldiers and sailors ever saw.

They would not seriously have resisted, anyway. Whatever the generals thought, political opinion at home would never have allowed it. Even the most fervently Churchillian Conservative Government would not have gone to war for Hong Kong as Mrs Thatcher's Government went to war for the remote and useless Falklands. For one thing there would have been no possibility of success, and for another the principles at stake were less than absolute. Not only the Chinese considered those treaties unequal; many of the British themselves could not contemplate the existence of Hong Kong, however dazzlingly it spoke of British enterprise and even of British benevolence, without some tremor of vicarious shame. Most of them knew very little about Hong Kong, but they did know there was something disreputable about its possession. Wasn't it something to do with opium? Weren't the police supposed to be bent? Hadn't they read something in the *Guardian* about a disgraceful lack of democratic rights?

Indeed throughout Hong Kong's history there have been Britons to suggest its return to China, sometimes on moral, sometimes on purely practical grounds. Gladstonian Liberals of course believed it should never have been taken in the first place, and later in the nineteenth century people sometimes argued that its possession was not worth the trouble of it. In 1918 the British Minister in Beijing, Sir John Jordan, thought it might be wise at least to return the New Territories to China ('altruistic speculation', minuted Curzon, by then Foreign Secretary – 'out of the question'). In the 1920s a body of opinion in the Foreign Office advocated joint Anglo-Chinese control of the colony. During the Second World War the Colonial Office suggested, in its best Whitehall idiom, that His Majesty's Government ought to be ready to consider with the Government of China the future position of Hong Kong, and 'should not for their part regard the maintenance of British sovereignty of the Colony as a matter beyond the scope of such discussions'.

In the post-war years British socialists repeatedly urged the voluntary return of the colony to the Chinese, notably the Welsh Parliamentarian Emrys Hughes, who wanted it exchanged for trading privileges in China, and whose ideas inspired a characteristic flight of verse in the *South China Morning Post*:

> The vughes of Mr Emrys Hughes
> Provoke a wheen disgusted phughes!
> Wot, swap Hong Kong for I.O.Ughes?
> Out upon ugh, we refughes!

The Chinese, for their part, made no direct demands for the return of Hong Kong. That its possession by the British smarted we need not doubt – it had smarted ever since 1842. As we know the Emperor had signed it away, with his vermilion signature, only with incredulous sadness. The statesman Zuo Zong-tang had written four poems of grief about its loss to China, and was indeed so distressed by the event that he seriously thought of withdrawing to a mountain hermitage for the rest of his life – such was the sense of disgrace in a patriot mind.

But over subsequent generations the rulers of China realized that Hong Kong could be recovered only by guile and patience. Their pathos meant nothing to the iron-fisted West, and their wrath was not very terrible to it. They learnt to deal cautiously with the British Empire. Under the Treaty of Nanking they undertook no longer to refer to the British as 'barbarians' in official documents, and their general attitude developed from affronted arrogance through sullen acquiescence to watchful calculation – as Qi-ying had confided to his Emperor in 1843, 'with this type of people from outside the bounds of civilization one has to be diplomatic in the essential business of subduing and conciliating them'.

The Chinese made it clear enough that Hong Kong was theirs. As late as the 1930s they were still claiming mineral rights in the New Territories, while in 1967 a spokesman described Hong Kong as 'an inalienable part of Chinese territory', and in 1972 another announced that its future lay 'entirely within China's sovereign right'. However they protested no more forcibly about the status of Hong Kong than they had about the existence of the Treaty Ports, and in time established amiable enough relations with the British; unless you count the Korean War of 1950, when British troops fought against Chinese as part of a United Nations army, there have been no hostilities between Great Britain and China since the Boxer rebellion of 1900.

So even the advent of a Communist Government in Beijing, which seemed so ominous to people in Hong Kong, did not spell out the end of the colony. The Chinese did not demand it, the British did not offer it, and with its usual pendulum shifts from confidence to panic, disconsolance to hope, Hong Kong proceeded through the 1960s and

1970s putting the future as far as possible out of mind. It was not the narrow hostility of Chairman Mao's regime, nor the lunacy of the Cultural Revolution, but the emergence of the pragmatic and apparently benevolent Deng Xiaoping, at the start of the 1980s, that brought the destiny of Hong Kong into an exact and final focus.

9

By then the deadline for the expiry of the New Territories lease was less than twenty years off, and without the New Territories, as all but a few cranks or diehards recognized, the island of Hong Kong could not be maintained as a British colony. The Chinese were being no more than usually aggressive about its future, but the minds of the local capitalists were wonderfully concentrated, and the matter was brought to a head, by the difficulties that now arose over the renewal of land leases; so that it was on British initiative that negotiations were opened between Margaret Thatcher's Government in London and Deng Xiaoping's in Beijing. They dragged on semi-secretly for a couple of years, now in Britain, now in China. Wild rumours periodically seized the colony, financial confidence alternately soared and slumped, Jardine's alarmed everyone by precipitately moving their headquarters to Bermuda, half the population tried to forget the matter while the other half talked of nothing else.

Never were talks more entangled in historical nicety. Since Hong Kong itself was not represented, they were in effect talks between the very same Empires which had first clashed over the very same issue a century and a half before. Since then the whole Scramble for China had come and gone. The French, the Russians, the Japanese, the Germans had all abandoned their footholds on the coast. The entire paraphernalia of Treaty Ports, Spheres of Influence, International Settlements and Extra-Territorial Privileges had been disbanded. Only the two old Empires, which had here come face to face so long before, confronted each other still over the negotiating table – the one infinitely more formidable than it had been in 1841, the other infinitely weaker.

The Chinese refused to recognize the validity of any of the three Hong Kong treaties, so that they could hardly solve the problem by simply extending the New Territories lease – in their eyes there *was* no lease. The British on the other hand maintained that all three treaties were perfectly legal, not Unequal at all; they had a right to keep Hong Kong Island for as long as they pleased, and Mrs Thatcher pointedly remarked in public that people who did not honour one treaty were unlikely to honour another. The talks were almost conspiratorially confidential, and with reason; the slightest whisper of disagreement was likely to lower stock values in Hong Kong, something equally distasteful to both sides, and any suggestion of deadlock might send capital fleeing to more predictable investment markets elsewhere. British and Chinese alike were treading very carefully, smiling grimly whenever they emerged to have their photographs taken by the waiting Press.

Their aims were self-evident. The British, while they can never seriously have hoped to prolong their sovereignty in Hong Kong, wanted to secure the survival of its capitalist system and maintain profitable relations with China. The Chinese, while they wanted Hong Kong back, did not want to kill the capitalist goose which was laying them so many golden eggs, and perhaps also hoped that by a generous agreement they might lure the recalcitrant governors of Taiwan, too, back into the fold.

As for the people of Hong Kong, probably very few of them knew what to want. The business community naturally feared its extinction under a Communist regime. The refugees from China possibly feared retribution, and certainly viewed with dismay a return to Communist ways of life. There were many supporters of the Kuomintang who would prefer Hong Kong to join Taiwan in an anti-Communist federation of islands, and there were some who dreamed of an independent City-State, like Singapore. Some demanded a plebiscite, or the establishment of full democratic institutions, but probably most, if the truth were told, simply wanted things to be left just as they were.

So the months passed. Now and again Hong Kong entered the world's headlines, when another enigmatic progress report was published, or another rumour eddied through the exchanges. China threw open its doors ever more welcomingly to the world and its money. Deng spoke soothingly. Mrs Thatcher spoke Thatcherly. In London the House of Commons considered the future of the last great British colony for thirty minutes flat. The manager of Xinhua was frequently interviewed, and encouraged nearly everyone by turning up with half his staff to the opening of the new and very racy Volvo Club – 'the largest Japanese-style night-club in the world'.[1] The Governor of Hong

[1] Which employs a thousand hostesses, drives its patrons to their tables in a vintage car, is decorated with 200 images of female nudes, and is fervently disclaimed by the Volvo Car Company of Sweden. At the moment a former Secretary of Monetary Affairs in Hong Kong is disputing with the Government his right to become its chairman in his retirement.

Kong kept his mouth shut. The English-language papers of the colony raucously debated the issue. The Chinese-language papers, being mostly under Communist control, hardly debated it at all.

And finally, in 1984, just thirteen years before the expiry of the New Territories lease, agreement was reached, and everything was changed. Not only did Mrs Thatcher appear in the Great Hall of the People at Beijing to sign the fourth and last Anglo-Chinese treaty on Hong Kong, but the Governor of Hong Kong himself, for so long a non-person in Communist China, stood by her side. All was smiles, banquets, compliments and simple diplomatic jokes. Pictures show most of the aides, on both sides, bowing and laughing convivially enough, but here and there one notices a Chinese even then aloof and poker-faced, and one remembers Qi-ying's report to the Emperor about keeping the barbarians happy.

10

There has never been a treaty, in the whole history of diplomacy, quite like the Anglo-Chinese agreement on the future of Hong Kong. The Chinese held almost all the cards, politically and even perhaps morally. The British could only argue, in essence that Hong Kong in its existing form had been extremely useful to China, and that to destroy it would benefit nobody. This argument unexpectedly prevailed. The British agreed to return the whole of Hong Kong territory to China in 1997, the Chinese agreed that it should retain its social and economic systems, and its 'life-style', for a further half-century after that, until the year 2047. Hong Kong would be incorporated into the People's Republic, but as a semi-autonomous Special Administrative Region, to be called Hong Kong, China. Residents would revert to Chinese citizenship, the People's Liberation Army would move in, but expatriate officials would be allowed to stay if required, and the structure of Hong Kong commerce and finance, the stock exchange, the banks, the insurance companies, the property development schemes – the whole teeming mass of it would be given another fifty years' grace. 'One Country, Two Systems', Deng called this solution to an otherwise intractable problem.

For the Chinese it was almost as radical a concession as the original transfer of Hong Kong had been. There were already four Special Autonomous Regions within the People's Republic, but none of them had acquired their autonomy by international negotiation, and one of them at least, Tibet, seemed far more autonomous in the theory than in the fact. Hong Kong had been given its special status by an agreement with a foreign Power, and the People's Republic seemed to have bound itself for the first time to a particular course of conduct, ideological conduct at that, within its own frontiers. One cannot help feeling that Mao Zedong, like Zuo Zong-tang before him, might have written a grief poem or two.

For the British too the agreement was something new. It is not quite true, as was often said at the time, that they had never before handed over a possession to a foreign Power; they had returned Minorca to the Spaniards, the Ionian Islands to the Greeks, Heligoland to the Germans. But they had never surrendered a territory which was in effect their own creation, and more significantly, perhaps, they had certainly never before denied to so advanced a colony the alternative of self-government. They had not consulted the 5,000 island fisher-folk when they took possession of Hong Kong, they did not consult the 5.6 million people of the City-State when they agreed to relinquish it.

Not until after the event, anyway. To make at least a show of popular consultation, after the conclusion of the agreement but before its signing, the Government of Hong Kong established an Assessment Office to determine what the mass of the people made of it. Sir Patrick Nairne, Master of St Catherine's College, Oxford, went out to Hong Kong to monitor its work (staying at the Hilton Hotel, rather than the Mandarin, so as not to be thought in the pockets of the British), and he was joined by Simon Li Fook-sean, a Hong Kong judge. Among those institutions whose views were heard were the Hon Wah Middle School Old Pupils' Association, the Vegetable Food and Grocery Hawkers' Welfare and Fraternity Association, the New Territories Poems and Songs Club, the Sai Yee Junk Builders' Association and the Shatin Sha Kok Estate Bean Goose House Mutual Aid Committee. Every kind of opinion was recorded, from that of the Legislative Council whose members predictably endorsed the agreement almost unanimously, to that of the Sun Yat-sen Memorial Association which claimed that the negotiations ought not to have been with Beijing at all, but with the Kuomintang Government in Taiwan. There should have been a referendum, thought the Cotton Bleaching and Dyeing Free Workers' Union. 'My heart is not truly at ease,' declared an unnamed individual.

Sir Patrick and Mr Justice Li found that the response conveyed 'an overwhelming message of acceptance', but they knew better than that really. They knew that people were hedging their bets, and wisely

Expatriates, 1980s

Hong Kong, 1988

hedged theirs too. 'The verdict of acceptance,' they added in the final paragraph of their report, 'implies neither positive enthusiasm nor passive acquiescence. The response to the Assessment Office has demonstrated the realism of the people of Hong Kong.'

Quite so. As it had been at the start, so it was now that the history of this extraordinary outpost was approaching its conclusion. Warily the two Empires had regarded each other down the decades, as the sign of the one rose, of the other fell, and for 150 years the colony had lived by making the best of the confrontation. Realism was its stock-in-trade.

II

It is a Thursday morning as I write, in my air-conditioned hotel bedroom in Central. Outside my windows, as in a silent film, I can see but not hear all the mid-week activity of the City-State.

The inevitable jack-hammer is soundlessly punching a hole towards a new underpass. A crane is swinging, three bulldozers are trundling about a building yard and a number of men in hardhats and business suits are poring over a map. The usual crowd is swarming into the Star Ferry terminal. The usual interminable traffic crawls down Connaught Road, police bikes with flashing blue lights now and then weaving a way among the cars.

In each neon-lit window of the office block across the road I can see a separate cameo: a shirt-sleeved young broker at his desk, a secretary telephoning, three or four people bent intently over something on a table, a solitary executive staring out across the city. On the promenade beyond the Post Office people are sitting in twos and threes in the sunshine, or drinking coffee at the café at the end of the pier. Pedestrians in their thousands hasten over the road-bridge, into the subway, along the sidewalk, in and out of McDonald's, all down the walkway to the outlying island ferry station. I count thirty-five freighters moored within my field of vision, some of them so engulfed in lighters that they seem to be in floating docks. A white cruise ship lies at the Ocean Terminal, with a fruit carrier astern of her, and the inevitable armada of launches, barges, tugs and sampans moves as in pageant through the harbour.

Over the water I fancy a shimmer of heat, or perhaps exhaust fumes, above the mass of Kowloon, and through it the Nine Hills loom a bluish grey. A Boeing 747 vanishes behind the buildings to reappear a moment later on the runway at Kai Tak. There are flashes of sun on distant windows. I leave my typewriter for a moment, open the sliding glass doors and walk out to the balcony; and away from the hotel's insulated stillness, instantly like the blast of history itself the frantic noise of Hong Kong hits me, the roar of that traffic, the thumping of that jack-hammer, the chatter of a million voices across the city below; and once again the smell of greasy duck and gasoline reaches me headily out of China.

12 INTERIM

NOW FASTER THAN EVER HONG KONG IS SWEPT TOWARDS
its next incarnation. We are too soon for finale – I can only offer
a tentative or disposable interim – but I have to say that it is not at all
unlike contemplating the mysteries of death.

The 1984 Agreement was registered with the United Nations, both
in Chinese and English, giving it at least a veneer of international
approval. It was indeed generally regarded by the world as a triumph
of peaceable diplomacy, especially for the British, who seemed to be
withdrawing from their last great colony without ignominy and
perhaps even with advantage. Within Hong Kong, as those monitors
discovered, it was probably seen by most citizens as about the best that
could be extracted from an unpromising situation. Deng seemed honest
and benevolent. His declared policy of the 'Open Door' sounded the
very opposite of chauvinism, China was apparently moving towards a
free-market economy. The year 2047, when the Agreement would
finally lose all force, seemed almost as distant as 1997 had seemed,
when the British signed the second Convention of Peking.

Nobody *knew*, though. Nobody knew who would succeed Deng
Xiaoping, already an old man, or what kind of Government would be
in power in China when the colony was surrendered. Nobody knew if
the Cultural Revolution really had been the last such manic eruption

of Chinese history, or whether within another ten or twenty years ideological fanatics might not drag China back into xenophobic isolation. The Chinese themselves, I think it safe to say, did not know what they were going to do with Hong Kong. Neither side knew exactly what was meant by 'lifestyle' or 'Special Administrative Region', or other reassuring words and phrases of the 1984 Agreement. When the Chinese promised an elected legislature, did they mean it to be elected in the Westminster or the Beijing manner? When they committed themselves to the accountability of executive to legislature, were they thinking of an obligation to obey, or simply an undertaking to report? The Chinese were to draw up a new constitution for the Special Administrative Region, the Basic Law, to be added to the Republic's own statute books; but nobody knew whether it would work as a constitution in the western sense, guaranteeing the rights of the people, or a constitution in the Communist sense, entrenching the powers of the State. As an American Sinologist once expressed it to me, in the semantics of Chinese diplomacy 'words are like rubber', especially when they are expressed in two languages; and the more familiar the terms of the treaty became, the more elastic they seemed.

Still, for the first four years things went smoothly enough, by Hong Kong's endemically bumpy standards. There was, after all, something massively organic to the flow of events, as though Hong Kong's return to its motherland was ordained and inevitable. As we have seen, the colony had never really been detached from China, and had never lost its sense of unity with everything fundamentally Chinese. Even at its most breathtakingly modernist, it felt Chinese at bottom, and its *laissez-faire* philosophies might have been as congenial to Confucius, who believed very much in minding one's own business, as they would have been to Adam Smith or Jeremy Bentham. Hong Kong even retained a kind of political loyalty to the idea, as against the reality, of the Chinese State. It is unlikely I think that any British Governor will be deified in the Daoist pantheon of Hong Kong, but among the honoured gods of the New Territories, along with the earth gods and the gods of sea and heaven, were the two Governors of Guangdong Province who, in the nineteenth century, helped the coastal people to return to their homes after the Great Evacuation.

By 1988 many of the great magnates of Hong Kong had made their peace with Marxist China. Lord Kadoorie, that peer of Empire, had involved himself in China's first nuclear power station, at Daya Bay just over the frontier, which was to supply electricity both to the People's Republic proper and to the Special Administrative Region. Sir Y. K. Pao, the archetypal Hong Kong billionaire, whose family had come to Hong Kong as refugees from Communism, was fast becoming as influential in Beijing as he was in the colony; for so long familiar to everyone as Sir Y. K., a truly imperial colloquialism, he began to appear in the papers instead as Sir Yue-Kong Pao, and one wondered how long it would be before he forgot his imperial usages and honorifics altogether, and tactfully returned to the persona he was born to – citizen Yue-Kong Pao from Zhejiang Province.

He doubtless foresaw vast new fortunes to be made on the mainland. As China pursued its policies of economic liberalization and foreign cooperation, the prospects for such Hong Kong tycoons seemed to be good, and at their level the osmosis we detected near the start of this book appeared to be easing the transition towards 1997. Hong Kong money figured largely in the Joint Ventures by which Beijing was adjusting to capitalist methods, and some visionaries thought that only now was the original promise of Hong Kong to be fulfilled, providing its traders with the enormous Chinese markets they had hoped for in the first place.

The interlocking of the two economies was evident already, and the process was by no means one-sided. Immediately across the Chinese frontier, where once the paddy fields and meadows seemed to me an earnest of innocence, there now arose one of China's Special Economic Zones, Shenzhen, where foreign investment was encouraged and a kind of semi-capitalism already reigned. It looked almost indistinguishable from Hong Kong itself. No longer was one side all pastoral simplicity, all modernity the other. The same high-rise buildings stood north of the border now, and the Shenzhen skyscraper with the revolving restaurant on top was financed, as it happened, by the same millionaire who financed the skyscraper with the revolving restaurant on Hong Kong Island. Scores of Hong Kong companies had moved their plants to the Special Economic Zone, where wages were lower and future possibilities seemed illimitable.

Shenzhen was not, of course, Hong Kong yet. An indefinable air of hangdog disgruntlement, coupled with something grubby or negative about the ambiance, blunted the edge of enterprise, and let you know that you were within the People's Republic. It felt nevertheless like an extension of Hong Kong, very nearly a suburb, as though it was the colony that was taking over the republic, rather than the other way round. The frontier between the Special Economic Zone and the future Special Administrative Region was already withering (hundreds of trucks crossed it every day). The real frontier had moved further back into China, and separated with police posts and barbed wire the half-capitalist Shenzhen from the less corrupted countryside beyond.

I say 'less', because actually Deng's economic reforms, opening rural areas to market forces, were gradually making the whole of Guangdong Province a free-enterprise zone. Sharing the vivacity, the acumen, the keen eye for a main chance of their relatives over the border in the colony, the people of Guangdong were doing their best to enrich themselves, and their province felt far more akin to the spirit of Hong Kong than to the bleak immensities of Beijing and the north – in many ways still as remote from these spirited southern parts as they had been in the days of the Manchu.

Within the colony, as the mid-1980s passed, life apparently proceeded much as always, in the usual theatrical swings, swoops and revelations. Various financial storms were weathered, and in externals at least the place was as exuberant as ever. A succession of new office towers restored some of the monumental dignity to Statue Square, presided over now both architecturally and figuratively by the stupendous Bank of China, whose podium seemed vaguely related to the Great Wall, but whose shining superstructure, soaring far above the bourgeois mid-Levels to challenge the supremacy of the Peak itself, exuded an opulent modern power – especially when, as I saw one evening, a great plume of water from its cooling system cascaded from its still uncompleted topmost floor, shimmering down in the night to disperse in brilliant spray over the city streets.

The usual grandiose projects entered the headlines. A dramatic substitute was projected for Kai Tak, involving the construction of a causeway across the harbour, the longest suspension bridge in the world and an island airport beyond Lantau. The second harbour tunnel was opened, the Peak tramway was equipped with new Swiss-made trams, new hotels proliferated. A new terminal for ferries to China was clad in gold-tinted glass. The Chartered Bank, in a gesture of petty capitalist bravado, built its new offices, immediately next door to the Hongkong and Shanghai Bank, just a few feet taller than Foster's masterpiece. Shops, chefs and cruise ships came and went. Jeremiah Tower, the celebrated California restaurateur, bought the lease to the old Peak Café, beside the tramway station, and planned to make it lovely. The shoeshine man outside the Mandarin still asked $HK15 to polish a briefcase, and a High Court judge resigned after being caught reading a novel during the hearing of a case. In short, as the decade approached its end Hong Kong was still unmistakably Hong Kong.

Yet all was not as it might seem to the stranger. The fact of 1997 haunted the people, when they allowed themselves to think about it. Even at those times when Hong Kong was at its most euphoric – when prices were booming despite everything, when the skyscrapers were out-topping each other – even then at the back of the communal mind lay an image of Hong Kong depressed and degraded under Communism: reduced like Shanghai to dingy impotence, Exchange Square drab and decaying, Connaught Road without its traffic, the jolly popular restaurants deprived of sparkle and Kowloon's bouncy stores all dullened by bureaucracy.

Many of Hong Kong's brightest citizens had already decided, in fact, to leave the colony. Chinese plutocrats had long banked money in other countries, bought houses, arranged passports and visas, and taken all other precautions against ill fortune that enough cash could buy. Now less affluent Chinese, too, were finding their way to Australia, Canada or the United States – in 1988 alone, it was guessed in the absence of official figures, some 50,000 went. There were even comfortably salaried Europeans and Americans who thought the time had come to go. ('We can't bear to leave Asia,' as one of them said to me, 'so we've bought a retirement house in northern Thailand, but of course we've got a little flat in London too . . .')

The sad thing was that Hong Kong had only then, as it neared the enigma of 1997, escaped from the shadow of 1949. Until lately it had been above all a city of refugees, working to establish themselves as refugees must. The census of 1981 established, for the first time, that more than half the citizens of Hong Kong had been born in Hong Kong, so that the city-state was achieving normality at last. It was developing into a truly established community, a community in the round. Socially it was becoming more humane and civilized, historically it was acquiring an identity of its own, even architecturally it seemed to be past the worst, and there had come into being, only in the previous few years, that well-educated young middle class which was the true pride of the Crown Colony, and which would be a credit to any country.

Hardly was it reaching this fulfilment than Deng and Mrs Thatcher had signed away its future. Nothing in the story of the British Empire seems to me more moving than this conjunction of events. To think of all that energy, all that hope, subsumed in the gloom of Chinese Communism, or for that matter the hopeless rigidity of Chinese tradition! Those families, householders at last, returned again to the condition of numbered tenants of the State! That generation of young graduates, so quick and receptive, truly the wards of liberal Empire, condemned perhaps in their maturity to the straitjacket of totalitarian thought, or the deadweight of a five-thousand-year intellectual backlog![1]

A new Governor, the 27th and probably the best Chinese scholar among them all, arrived in 1988 to guide Hong Kong through these doubts. Sir David Wilson might not prove to be the last Governor, but he was generally assumed to be the last with any real power – after him, it seemed, all would be protocol.

It was ironic that he was not an Empire man, having spent his entire official career in the Foreign Service, for never did a satrap of the British Empire play a more allegorically imperial role. The early rulers of Anglo-India were like angels of wrath, storming across Asia with their vision of a new heaven and a new earth. The High Commissioners of Palestine were so many Pilates, washing their hands of responsibility, the late viceroys of India were icons of age and fading power. But it fell to Sir David Wilson of the Foreign Service to prepare a last reputation of Empire. The taste that Hong Kong left behind would be the last taste of the Pax Britannica, and upon his term of office would depend the legend of the British in China – whether it would be an ignoble or an admirable legend, whether they would be remembered with gratitude or with reproach, as upholders or as violators of the historical *feng shui*.[2]

[1] Recently likened, by the eminent Chinese writer Bo Yang, to 'a putrefying vat of soy sauce'.
[2] His Chinese name was not encouraging to a superstitious society – pronounced Ngai Tak-ngai in Cantonese, it was interpreted as meaning 'twin ghosts come a-knocking'. Felix Patrikeeff, from whose book *Mouldering Pearl* (London 1989) I learn this, adds that the cognomen was in keeping with 'Sir David's distant glance and pallor'.

Wilson was one of those who had negotiated the 1984 Agreement, and when I asked him once what he saw as his historical duty in Hong Kong, he said it was to ensure that the territory was handed over to China in good working condition. I suspect, though, that he was being deliberately ambivalent, and certainly many people thought his duty to be more profound than that. Inspired in particular by a boldly outspoken barrister and Legco member, Martin Lee Chu-ming, there was a growing opinion that he owed it to the conscience of the British themselves, and of their lost Empire, to help bring into being a Hong Kong with a Government of its own, composed of Hong Kong people, elected by Hong Kong people, which would be strong and experienced enough to stand up to the Chinese Communists when they formally arrived in 1997.

On the whole, with many lapses and exceptions, British Government in Hong Kong had been good government. It had risen, as the Empire itself did, from the opportunism of its origins, through the jingo pomp of its climax, to a level of general decency. It had ensured personal freedoms, it had given stability, it had even in its late years made a brave start with social welfare, and tried to live up to the British Empire's truest morality, the morality of fair play. It had demonstrated that in certain rare circumstances imperialism need not be oppressive, but could be a species of partnership, or a technical service. A dispassionate foreign observer must surely concede that the barren rock had been lucky to escape so many of the miseries and deprivations of the Chinese mainland, and the local population certainly seemed to think so; polled in 1982, 95 per cent wanted the political status quo to be maintained.

But in one great respect the British in Hong Kong had failed to honour their own best values. They had consistently declined to give political power to the people, or even to keep them properly informed. Secretive, paternalistic, often apparently aloof and superior, they had maintained even into the last quarter of the twentieth century the modes of benevolent imperialism. Government remained, as we have seen, Crown Colony Government in its most traditional form, its oligarchy scarcely tempered by any kind of popular representation.

This was not the imperial norm. Almost everywhere else in the world the British, when they withdrew from their dominions, left to the successor Governments the structure of parliamentary democracy. The most backward and illiterate tribal State was introduced to the sophistication of One Man One Vote, even if its electorate could only recognize pictures of frogs or crocodiles as emblems of the contesting parties. Feudal chieftains found themselves transformed into Speakers, wearing wigs and preceded by maces. Erskine May was learnedly quoted in the equatorial heat, and all the precedents of Westminster were honoured beneath the twirling fans.

It did not often catch on. From Grenada to Zimbabwe other political forms soon took over. But it was an honourable attempt by the departing British to leave with their former subjects the political rights they so cherished for themselves – a kind of peace offering, in a way, after so much bullying and exploitation. That the subjects soon rejected the gift was partly a sign, perhaps, that it had come too late, but was at least partly a reflection of temperament or historical circumstance. Not every people is best served by democracy.

Away at the eastern end of their world the British had created a community infinitely more sophisticated than those tropic colonies. Yet in this one possession, perhaps the most brilliant of them all, the old forms of autocratic Empire remained. In 1987 the British Government promised to publish its own ideas about the political condition of Hong Kong in the run-down to 1997, and it was only then that the full meaning of this imperial archaism struck home. For the first time Hong Kong was projected into a frenzy of political activity. Many people thought that any radical reform would be playing with fire. Not only might it antagonize Beijing, but the bitter give and take of adversarial politics, probably compounded by corruption, and possibly manipulated by the Communist Party itself, would weaken confidence in Hong Kong and frighten money away – through all the colony's history the chief argument for doing nothing.[1] Others maintained that the mass of the Hong Kong populace was simply not interested in politics anyway. Others again, though, both Chinese and foreign, believed it was still not too late to institute properly representative Government in the colony; on the contrary, only a Hong Kong practised in governing itself would be able to maintain its personal freedoms after 1997.

So one saw something new in Hong Kong; a community racked by political argument. Scores of political groups came into being, savage political cartoons appeared in the Press, real political debates began to

---

[1] 'Don't talk to me about democracy,' was a remark attributed to Ronald Li Fook Shiu, chairman of the Stock Exchange. 'That's a word that should be obliterated from the vocabulary.'

happen in Legco. Martin Lee became one of the best-known figures in Hong Kong, seen by some as the man who might lead Hong Kong into prosperous autonomy as Lee Kuan Yew had led Singapore. Already, though, the British would do nothing without first measuring the response of Beijing. Foreign relations and commercial prospects came before colonial ideals, and when the long-awaited White Paper outlined the Government's plans, it proposed merely the accession to Legco of ten directly elected members, replacing members elected by local government bodies, and that not until 1992. Ten publicly elected members out of fifty-seven; it would still be a long, long way from Westminster.

Doubtless the People's Republic would sanction no more – convergence with its own plans for the colony was the declared aim of Beijing, of London and of the colony's own Government. Hong Kong accepted the decision more or less fatalistically, as another symptom of Britain's fading sovereignty. The politicians were momentarily quietened, and the territory waited to see what China itself would offer when, in the spring of 1990, the National People's Congress promulgated its Basic Law for the Special Administrative Region of Hong Kong, China.

A pause then, an unspectacular drift, until in June 1989 Deng Xiaoping's Government shifted almost everyone's perceptions, threw Hong Kong into an unprecedented turmoil of emotion, by the massacre of Tiananmen Square in Beijing, when a student demonstration demanding more democracy and less corruption was brutally suppressed by the People's Liberation Army – the very force which, under the terms of the Anglo-Chinese Agreement, would have the right to garrison Hong Kong in eight years' time.

The demonstration itself, so prolonged and so courageous, had inspired hitherto unsuspected passions in Hong Kong. Hundreds of thousands of people had processed the streets in high fervour but absolute order, seeing perhaps in the students' movement the hope of a genuinely new China at last, a China released from its hopeless inhibitions – and a China which could quite feasibly converge with a democratic Hong Kong. The murderous sequel in Tiananmen Square threw the territory into despair. China, it seemed, was still the old China after all. Suddenly 1997 seemed terrifyingly close, and its implications terrible.

Theoretically Hong Kong's situation was not much changed by the suppression of the freedom movement. Nobody should really have been surprised. If Deng and his regime seemed to have betrayed their own reputation for reasonable behaviour, they had really only been reasonable by their own lights. Their system of justice, their system of life itself was still governed by an esoteric mixture of Communist and traditional moralities; thousands of people were executed in China every year, often for crimes that would hardly be crimes at all elsewhere, and the cruel suppression of nationalist movements in Tibet was perfectly well known to the world. As for the official corruption to which the Beijing students were objecting, much of it had been engendered by the very free-market forces of which Hong Kong was the champion. Everybody knew well enough, too, that the 1984 Agreement was a gamble at best, and that if, when the time came, the Chinese thought it expedient to ignore its provisions, they would do what they pleased. It was the most fragile of treaties, based upon a delicate balancing of advantages, and upon the momentum of history itself; nobody pretended that it had been reached out of generosity or fellow-feeling.

Yet while the people of Hong Kong, both Chinese and expatriate, understood all this intellectually, emotionally they had still hoped for the best, while making what preparations they could to escape the worst. Those who arranged residence abroad often came back to work in Hong Kong; there was calculation rather than panic to the flow of emigration. Financially Hong Kong had survived the Agreement reasonably well, and if many investors played safe by distributing liabilities or shedding superfluous loads, still money flowed into the territory and the thrust of capitalism seemed unblunted.

Tiananmen changed all this. For the first time a streak of hysteria seized the territory. At first it was manifested in revulsion. Vast crowds demonstrated against the Chinese Government, something that had never happened before in all the history of the colony, and the whole territory mourned the young activists who had died in Beijing. The Hongkong Alliance in Support of Patriotic Democratic Movement in China organized protests and processions, and the dignity and authority of Communist China was brazenly insulted. Dissidents escaping out of China were sheltered, like Sun Yat-sen and Zhou Enlai before them. A statue of Miss Democracy was erected, modelled on the one the Beijing students had made. The city's taxi-drivers sounded their horns for a full minute in elegy. In Victoria Park an anonymous artist ceremonially lowered his trousers over four spittoons, representing the Four Cardinal Principles of Chinese Communism, and invited bystanders to spit, urinate or defecate in the receptacle of their choice. Anti-Communist slogans appeared in the windows of the still unfinished Bank of China, the very symbol of the Communist presence in Hong Kong; its architect I. M. Pei, the most eminent Chinese-American to be persuaded to work in China by Deng's reformist gestures, wondered publicly if he could ever bring himself to work there again.[1] The Communist-financed paper *Wen Wei Po*, for forty years a faithful follower of the party line, called Deng and his colleagues 'a clique of criminals': its circulation promptly tripled, and when its editor was sacked some thirty of his staff resigned in sympathy. In Statue Square the Cenotaph, erected in memory of the dead of two world wars, became a shrine to the victims of 4 June, renewed each day with flowers, Chinese texts, banners and poems.[2]

Hong Kong had never exhibited itself like this before, allowed its pent-up fears and resentments to show so frankly, or declared itself so politically aware. Even the Governor publicly allowed himself shocked and saddened by the killings in Beijing. Even the Hong Kong branch of the venerable and strictly apolitical Royal Asiatic Society demanded firmer British attitudes towards China – Tiananmen, it said, had 'removed all confidence in any guarantee that might come from the present Chinese Government'. Nobody interfered with the gigantic processions of protest, so deliberately offensive to Beijing, and the police stood by while that artist in Victoria Park dirtied the Spittoon of the Fourth Principle ('Supremacy of Marxist–Leninist–Mao Zedong Thought'). In Statue Square the British flag was raised and lowered each day over the mourning emblems around the Cenotaph.

All perceptions changed, and the vision of the People's Liberation Army shooting at random in Statue Square seemed even more vivid than the older image of a Hong Kong merely wasted and depressed under Communism – it did not go unnoticed that the Tiananmen shootings flouted the constitution of the People's Republic itself. Day

[1] And the spectacular plume of water falling from its summit, which I marvelled at a few pages back, was alleged later to have been an act of sabotage – the turning-on of stopcocks by angry construction workers, who perhaps intended to make it look like someone pissing on the thing.

[2] One of which, I happened to notice, entitled Last Will and Testament of a Fifteen-Year-Old Boy Killed in Tiananmen Square, concluded with an authentically indigenous bathos: *Translation Copyright 1989*.

after day new schemes were proposed for the future of the territory. The 1984 Agreement should be abrogated and re-negotiated – or simply abrogated, said a few zealots. The territory should be evacuated, and its population should start all over again elsewhere: in the Falklands, in the Andaman Islands, in the Scottish Highlands (an idea supported by the Adam Smith Institute, a powerhouse of capitalist ideology), in the Northern Territories of Australia (an idea welcomed by the Lands Minister of that territory, who said that such a settlement would very soon replace Sydney and Melbourne as the economic centre of all Australia – 'they could close down Victoria and New South Wales'). Hong Kong Island and Kowloon, not being subject to the 1897 lease, should be excluded from the agreement and floated as private companies. The lease should be extended by arrangement with Beijing.

There were those who insisted that Great Britain had a duty, there and then, to arrange alternative homes for Hong Kong people, particularly for those 3 million who held British colonial passports. In the days of *civis Britannicus sum* these documents had been equal to United Kingdom passports, but their privileges had long been whittled away, and for years they had not given their holders the right to settle in Britain. Now a demand arose for an adjustment of the law, to provide Hong Kong British citizens the right of abode in what a few sentimental imperialists still liked to call the Mother Country. For weeks 'Right of Abode' became the great political demand of the day, pursued by a variety of pressure groups – Freedom of Movement and Right of Abode Ltd, People Saving Hong Kong, the Honour Hong Kong Committee, which was supported by some of the great hongs, British Citizens for Hong Kong, which was started by concerned expatriates, New Hong Kong Alliance, which wanted to sue the British Government for deprivation of citizens' rights. All argued (optimistically, to my mind) that what was needed was merely an insurance, giving people the confidence to stay in Hong Kong, and that very few citizens of Hong Kong would actually be fool enough to want to live in the United Kingdom. Even in Britain itself the campaign found many supporters; it was the first political issue for years so directly to involve the national honour, and rejecting the Hong Kong British, many people thought, would be a disgrace – the *Spectator* had a cover one week depicting the British lion and Britannia herself, shield and trident laid aside, kowtowing from Hong Kong in the direction of Beijing.

However neither of the main British political parties saw granting a general right of abode as necessary to the national self-respect. The Government in London merely pledged a certain flexibility to immigration arrangements, in effect ensuring that certain useful categories of Hong Kong citizens, knowing that there would be somewhere safe to go in the end, would stay on the job in the meantime. In the territory there was a rush to get visas for other countries instead, and scores of agencies and legal experts, some more expert than others, sprang up with advice. Those with enough money could still arrange things quite easily – even Britain would welcome an immigrant if he had £150,000 in capital; those without queued in their thousands outside the Canadian, Australian and American consulates. For years half Hong Kong had intermittently talked about emigrating; now, it often seemed, everybody was actually doing it – almost every multi-national office reported losing skilled staff, and there was hardly a well-off Chinese family, even among those who most assiduously courted the regime in Beijing, who did not make arrangements to move to the West if necessary. In its mercurial way Hong Kong had decided, for the moment at least, that 1997 would be the end of its particular civilization.

All in all, in the late summer of 1989 Hong Kong seemed to me rather like a city under siege – but at a bad moment of the siege, when the hope of relief is fading, when the bravado is losing its flair, when the sorties no longer seem so heroic, when the first despondent women are refusing to cook their victuals for the men on the walls and the first rumours are circulating of desertion, compromise or surrender. That the city looked much the same as ever, in all its virtuosity, only heightened the sensation of bitter crisis. Before Tiananmen I had noticed the advent of a quality that I had never felt in Hong Kong – the quality of poignancy. Now a new abstraction seemed to me apparent – fear.

Throughout all this British officialdom, in its last great overseas possession, maintained in public an attitude of regretful reserve. It was almost as though the flag had already been lowered. Gradually the apparatus of colonial Government seemed to be disbanding itself. The Governor's public appearances were less frequent and less publicized, the Chief Secretary was rather less visible at plutocratic receptions. Only the military garrison was maintained at full strength, in case public disquiet degenerated into public violence.

By now indeed the Chinese Government was addressing itself directly to the people of Hong Kong, and to their indigenous leaders, as though it were already the sovereign authority. The hunting down of dissidents within China was accompanied by veiled threats against Hong Kong people who had supported them, or helped them to escape. The Alliance in Support of Democratic Movement, whose founders included Martin Lee, was denounced as subversive to the People's Republic, and there were repeated warnings against precipitate democratic progress in the colony before 1997. Clearly Beijing was taken aback by the strength of public feeling in Hong Kong, and with some reason. It was estimated that 600,000 people, one in ten of Hong Kong citizenry, had marched in the protests after Tienanmen: if the same proportion had marched in China itself 110 million people would have been in the streets.

But it is not over yet. The Union Jack still flies above Hong Kong, there are eight years of Empire still to run and anything may happen. Deng's aged clique may after all be replaced by a regime of more genuinely liberal temper. The urge to emigrate may slacken. Hong Kong's mood, so notoriously fickle, may easily calm again as the outrage of June 1989 recedes into the historical memory. In a wider sense, after all, Hong Kong stands on the winning side of the late twentieth century: the capitalist side, which works best in collaboration with political freedom, and which is seeing its old Marxist–Leninist enemy collapsing before it from Estonia to – well, to the gates of Beijing at least.

Besides, nothing so concentrates the mind like the prospect of hanging in the morning. The dramatic crisis of perception which resulted from the Beijing massacre certainly sharpened the awareness of Hong Kong, and even more perhaps the awareness of the British who had summoned it into being, had governed it for so long, and were now consigning it to destiny without, it had sometimes seemed, thinking very hard about it – a last confirmation of the old saw that the British Empire had been acquired 'in a fit of absence of mind'. Now for the first time the British public concerned itself with the fate of Hong Kong, and British officialdom too, whether in Hong Kong itself or in London, found its courses of action newly clarified.

The British had been planning, it appeared, to let Hong Kong proceed towards 1997 under the principle of convergence – the gradual merging of British and Chinese intentions towards the place, sometimes alternatively called 'mirror-imaging'. British and Chinese officials met regularly, under the terms of the Agreement, to review progress; the British were kept informed about the development of the Basic Law, and devised their own plans for democratic reform to dovetail with it in the end. The idea of making dramatic unilateral changes in Hong Kong while the going was good, though perfectly legal under the terms of the Agreement, would probably have seemed to the British Foreign Office provocative and contrary to the spirit of the accord. Now, all of a sudden, the notion of converging with a system which murdered its own citizens in the streets must have seemed to even the most timid British negotiators a shameful prospect. Convergence itself became a dirty word, and though few seriously thought that the treaty could simply be abrogated, the British were confronted willy-nilly with a need for bolder action.

They could, of course, steel themselves to let Hong Kong sink or swim. To many their refusal to grant residence rights to all British passport holders seemed to show that this was indeed their decision, and some argued that in the eye of universal history it would be a correct one. One way or the other, Hong Kong was destined to be re-absorbed into China, of which for better or for worse it formed a part; it might be wise in the long run not to resist the inevitable, but to oblige its people to fend for themselves. The colony was not a charitable organization, ran this line of reasoning, it was not important to Britain's own well-being, and its inhabitants had not gone there in any spirit of devotion to the British flag, but simply to better themselves. The British had done their best to arrange for the future of the Hong Kong population, which must now resign itself to the realities of being Chinese.

Or they could continue more or less as before, dealing with Beijing pragmatically while ensuring that Hong Kong became more and more an international charge. On the one hand they could offer sanctuary themselves to some morally and practicably reasonable number of immigrants – 250,000, say – while trying to persuade other countries to promise refuge, if necessary, in 1997. On the other hand they could muster the support of particularly interested countries – Japan, the United States – in pressing the Chinese to keep to the spirit of the Agreement. It was in everybody's interest that Hong Kong retain its confidence and its ability; not least in the interest of the Chinese themselves, who would hardly want to take over a demoralized shell of a city in 1997.

Or the British could be bold and generous, take a chance, promise sanctuary somewhere to everyone if the need arose, and give self-government to Hong Kong before 1997. Chinese warnings against democratic reform were mere impertinences, from a regime which had forfeited all claim to moral judgement or tutelage. The British were perfectly free to do what they thought best in Hong Kong until 1997 – just as, it was often forgotten, especially in Beijing, they would have a perfect right to supervise the proper application of the Agreement until its expiry in 2047. The democratic lobby in Hong Kong was given a powerful boost by the events in Beijing, and the need for truly representative Government in Beijing, for so long a heresy, now became almost the received wisdom. The Foreign Affairs Select Committee of the House of Commons, visiting Hong Kong in the summer of 1989, recommended that a full democratic system, with universal suffrage for all members of Legco, should be in action by 1997: the unofficial members of Legco were almost unanimously in favour; it seemed just possible that out of the tragedy of Tiananmen Square, out of its own apparent timidities, the British Empire might yet snatch a grand conclusion.

For myself, like most observers of Hong Kong I find my judgements varying from one month to the next – this is already the second revised version of my book's final chapter, and I expect to write several more before 1997. Sometimes I despair, especially at moments when I sense that China itself can never in our times be extracted from its endemic and frequently malignant muddle, or when the British seem more than usually bloodless. There are times however when I feel that even now, so late in the day, and against such formidable odds, British Hong Kong may yet have a happy ending. Suppose now that, by magnanimous policies of their own, by mustering international support, the British manage to persuade the people of Hong Kong that it would be in their interests to remain in the colony, while having the right to go elsewhere. Suppose that, as a result, financial confidence were restored, and foreign investment sustained. Suppose that a truly democratic, universally elected Goverment were in control of Hong Kong by the middle 1990s. And suppose, as we well may, that by 1997 China itself were governed by some younger and less reactionary regime, trying to steer the addled Republic towards a more modern and liberal condition.

Imagine the situation then! Hong Kong would be the very lodestar of Chinese progress, the epitome of enlightenment! Then the story of this territory might prove in the end one of the best of all the tales of

Empire. To have created upon this improbable terrain, among an alien people, so far from home, a society not only stable, educated, prosperous and free, not only self-governed by the imperialists's own high principles, but also standing as a model and an inspiration to its mother China – that might be a last justification for the idea of imperialism itself. And even if that fulfilment were to survive only a generation, to be destroyed by yet another new brutalism, at least it would add a sad majesty to the aesthetic of Empire – a memorial to what might have been, as the shutters close upon the once exuberant colony. The British would have seized their last chance to give Hong Kong one characteristic it has always lacked: nobility, the balance of purpose and proportion that the geomancers strive for.

It would take nerve, skill, self-confidence, a robuster attitude than the British in Hong Kong have lately shown. It would mean standing up to Beijing and all its insolences, risking what would come after, persuading the people of Hong Kong that the very possibility of success is worth fighting for, convincing the democratic world that the territory, now really an international City-State, should be an international responsibility. But if the British succeed in this, their last imperial mission, they could look upon Hong Kong as a proud valediction to a tremendous historical adventure. That poet of China long ago foresaw the city glittering with lights like the stars of Heaven, and his prophecy has been fulfilled. Far away across China, or out at sea, one can see the great red glow, like the flow of a mighty furnace, that is the sum of them. On the ground they speak of riches and energies and entertainments, of all the vigour and enterprise that the arrival of the British 150 years ago fired in this improbable place; it would make a fine conclusion to a book, as it would to an empire, if in the end they spelled out a grander message in the reflection.[1]

[1] As it is, at least one Hong Kong hotel is offering packages for the final night under British rule (I have booked a room myself). The quoted price is true Hong Kong: $HK1997.

13   READING LIST

HONG KONG HAS BEEN THOROUGHLY WRITTEN ABOUT IN the detail, with books on everything from the currency to the trams, but not so definitively in the general. The books listed here are mostly contemporary, are easily available at least in Hong Kong, and are the ones I have most used myself; others are mentioned in the footnotes to my text.

The most complete history is G. B. Endacott's *A History of Hong Kong*, London 1958, but there is sure to be a replacement on the way. Two earlier histories, still available and rich in detail, are E. J. Eitel's *Europe in China*, Hong Kong 1895, and the two volumes of G. R. Sayer's *Hong Kong*, published separately in Hong Kong in 1937 and 1975. Nigel Cameron's *Hong Kong: The Cultured Pearl*, Hong Kong 1978, is a general study of the colony and its past.

For the historical origins of Hong Kong there is Maurice Collis' *Foreign Mud*, London 1946; for the acquisition of the New Territories, Peter Wesley-Smith's *Unequal Treaty*, Hong Kong 1980; for the period between the world wars, Paul Gillingham's illustrated album *At The Peak*, Hong Kong 1983. The best books about Hong Kong during the Second World War are perhaps *Hong Kong Eclipse*, Hong Kong 1978, by G. B. Endacott with additional material by Alan Birch, and *The Lasting Honour*, by Oliver Lindsay, London 1978. *The Royal Navy in*

Hong Kong, by Kathleen Harland, Liskeard 1985, records the naval connection since 1841.

Invaluable on the Chinese background are two books by James Hayes, *The Hong Kong Region 1850–1911*, Hong Kong 1977, and *The Rural Communities of Hong Kong*, Hong Kong 1983. Also instructive and entertaining are the three volumes of the series *Ancestral Images*, by Hugh Baker, published in Hong Kong between 1979 and 1981.

I have learnt much from two sociological studies by H. J. Lethbridge, a collection of essays called *Hong Kong: Stability and Change*, Hong Kong 1978, and *Hard Graft in Hong Kong*, a book about corruption published in Hong Kong in 1985. An academic study of administrative systems is Norman Miners' *The Government and Policies of Hong Kong*, Hong Kong 1975. Austin Coates' much-loved *Myself a Mandarin*, London 1968, is an administrator's personal memoir.

The origins of the business community are traced in *The Taipans*, by Colin N. Crisswell, Hong Kong 1981. A major history of the Hongkong and Shanghai Banking Corporation is now being written; in the meantime we have *Wayfoong*, by Maurice Collis, London 1965. Jardine, Matheson's story is sumptuously presented in *The Thistle and the Jade*, edited by Maggie Keswick, London 1982. *Taikoo*, by Charles Drage, London 1970, tells the story of Swire's, and *Power*, by Nigel Cameron, Hong Kong 1982, is about the Kadoories and the China Light and Power Company. Gavin Young's *Beyond Lion Rock* is a history of Cathay Pacific Airways.

There is no general architectural study, but much of the ground is covered in *Tall Storeys* by Malcolm Purvis, a light-hearted history of the architectural firm Palmer and Turner published in Hong Kong in 1985. Three architectural books published by the Government are *Temples*, by Joyce Savidge, 1977, *The Story of Government House*, by Katherine Mattock, 1978, and *Rural Architecture in Hong Kong*, a compilation published in 1979. The Hongkong Bank published a book about its own buildings, *One Queen's Road Central*, by Ian Lambot and Gillian Chambers, to commemorate the opening of their new headquarters in 1986. Peter Hall has a valuable chapter on Hong Kong in the third edition of his *The World Cities*, London 1984.

The best guide-book is the *Insight Guide to Hong Kong*, repeatedly republished. The best maps are in the Government's two-volumed *Hong Kong Streets and Places*. The official *Annual Report* is obligatory reading for anyone taking Hong Kong seriously, and so is the annual journal of the Royal Asiatic Society's Hong Kong Branch. Among many books of pictures, outstanding are *Fragrant Harbour*, by John Warner, Hong Kong 1976, *The Hong Kong Album*, published by the Hong Kong Museum of History in 1982 and *Old Hong Kong*, with a text by Trea Wiltshire, Hong Kong 1987.

Hong Kong has not figured much in English literature, as against ephemeral fiction, and I can suggest only four books: Somerset Maugham's *The Painted Veil* (1925), John Le Carré's *The Honourable Schoolboy* (1977), and two by Timothy Mo, *The Monkey King* (1978) and *An Insular Possession* (1986).

Finally, for students of the denouement, *Mouldering Pearl*, by Felix Patrikeeff (London 1989), and two books by David Bonavia: *The Chinese*, published in London in 1985, and *Hong Kong 1997: The Final Settlement*, published in Hong Kong in the same year and gracefully dedicated to the memory of Captain Charles Elliot – the man who started it all.

THANKS

Many hong kong friends, colleagues and acquaintances, Chinese and expatriate, have generously helped me with this book. In addition a number have spared the time to read the typescript for me, in part or in whole, saving me from many naiveties: they include (for one or two prefer not to be named) Bernard Asher, James Hayes, H. J. Lethbridge, Neil Maidment, Peter Moss and Tak-lung Tsim.

Frank Fischbeck kindly allowed me to use his picture of the waterfront, Ken Haas his picture of the two expatriates. The Hong Kong Public Record Office showed me much courtesy, as did the Hongkong and Shanghai Bank, the Government Information Services Department, the Hong Kong Club and the Foreign Correspondents' Club. And Beth Gubersky, her dogs, cats and birds most hospitably allowed me the use of their house in the New Territories.

I am grateful to them all, but have allowed none to sway my judgements.

TREFAN MORYS, 1989

INDEX

FOR THE BEST IN PAPERBACKS, LOOK FOR THE

A CHOICE OF PENGUINS

The Literature of the United States   Marcus Cunliffe

The fourth edition of a masterly one-volume survey, described by D. W. Brogan in the *Guardian* as 'a very good book indeed'.

The Sceptical Feminist   Janet Radcliffe Richards

A rigorously argued but sympathetic consideration of feminist claims. 'A triumph' – *Sunday Times*

The Enlightenment   Norman Hampson

A classic survey of the age of Diderot and Voltaire, Goethe and Hume, which forms part of the Pelican History of European Thought.

Defoe to the Victorians   David Skilton

'Learned and stimulating' (*The Times Educational Supplement*). A fascinating survey of two centuries of the English novel.

Reformation to Industrial Revolution   Christopher Hill

This 'formidable little book' (Peter Laslett in the *Guardian*) by one of our leading historians is Volume 2 of the Pelican Economic History of Britain.

The New Pelican Guide to English Literature   Boris Ford (ed.)
Volume 8: The Present

This book brings a major series up to date with important essays on Ted Hughes and Nadine Gordimer, Philip Larkin and V. S. Naipaul, and all the other leading writers of today.

FOR THE BEST IN PAPERBACKS, LOOK FOR THE 🐧

A CHOICE OF PENGUINS

The Second World War (6 volumes)   Winston S. Churchill

The definitive history of the cataclysm which swept the world for the second time in thirty years.

1917: The Russian Revolutions and the Origins of Present-Day Communism
Leonard Schapiro

A superb narrative history of one of the greatest episodes in modern history by one of our greatest historians.

Imperial Spain 1496–1716   J. H. Elliot

A brilliant modern study of the sudden rise of a barren and isolated country to be the greatest power on earth, and of its equally sudden decline. 'Outstandingly good' – *Daily Telegraph*

Joan of Arc: The Image of Female Heroism   Marina Warner

'A profound book, about human history in general and the place of women in it' – Christopher Hill

Man and the Natural World: Changing Attitudes in England 1500–1800
Keith Thomas

'A delight to read and a pleasure to own' – Auberon Waugh in the *Sunday Telegraph*

The Making of the English Working Class   E. P. Thompson

Probably the most imaginative – and the most famous – post-war work of English social history.

FOR THE BEST IN PAPERBACKS, LOOK FOR THE 🐧

A CHOICE OF PENGUINS

The French Revolution Christopher Hibbert

'One of the best accounts of the Revolution that I know . . . Mr Hibbert is outstanding' – J. H. Plumb in the *Sunday Telegraph*

The Germans Gordon A. Craig

An intimate study of a complex and fascinating nation by 'one of the ablest and most distinguished American historians of modern Germany' – Hugh Trevor-Roper

Ireland: A Positive Proposal Kevin Boyle and Tom Hadden

A timely and realistic book on Northern Ireland which explains the historical context – and offers a practical and coherent set of proposals which could actually work.

A History of Venice John Julius Norwich

'Lord Norwich has loved and understood Venice as well as any other Englishman has ever done' – Peter Levi in the *Sunday Times*

Montaillou: Cathars and Catholics in a French Village 1294–1324
Emmanuel Le Roy Ladurie

'A classic adventure in eavesdropping across time' – Michael Ratcliffe in *The Times*

The Defeat of the Spanish Armada Garrett Mattingly

Published to coincide with the 400th anniversary of the Armada. 'A faultless book; and one which most historians would have given half their working lives to have written' – J. H. Plumb

A CHOICE OF PENGUINS

Adieux: A Farewell to Sartre   Simone de Beauvoir

A devastatingly frank account of the last years of Sartre's life, and his death, by the woman who for more than half a century shared that life. 'A true labour of love, there is about it a touching sadness, a mingling of the personal with the impersonal and timeless which Sartre himself would surely have liked and understood' – *Listener*

Business Wargames   James Barrie

How did BMW overtake Mercedes? Why did Laker crash? How did MacDonalds grab the hamburger market? Drawing on the tragic mistakes and brilliant victories of military history, this remarkable book draws countless fascinating parallels with case histories from industry world-wide.

Metamagical Themas   Douglas R. Hofstadter

This astonishing sequel to the bestselling, Pulitzer Prize-winning *Gödel, Escher, Bach* swarms with 'extraordinary ideas, brilliant fables, deep philosophical questions and Carrollian word play' – Martin Gardner

Into the Heart of Borneo   Redmond O'Hanlon

'Perceptive, hilarious and at the same time a serious natural-history journey into one of the last remaining unspoilt paradises' – *New Statesman* 'Consistently exciting, often funny and erudite without ever being over-whelming' – *Punch*

The Assassination of Federico García Lorca   Ian Gibson

Lorca's 'crime' was his antipathy to pomposity, conformity and intoler-ance. His punishment was murder. Ian Gibson reveals the truth about Lorca's death and the atmosphere in Spain that allowed it to happen.

The Secrets of a Woman's Heart   Hilary Spurling

The later life of Ivy Compton-Burnett 1920–69. 'A biographical triumph . . . elegant, stylish, witty tender, immensely acute – dazzles and exhila-rates . . . a great achievement' – Kay Dick in the *Literary Review*. 'One of the most important literary biographies of the century' – *New Statesman*

A CHOICE OF PENGUINS

Fantastic Invasion   Patrick Marnham

Explored and exploited, Africa has carried a different meaning for each wave of foreign invaders – from ivory traders to aid workers. Now, in the crisis that has followed Independence, which way should Africa turn? 'A courageous and brilliant effort' – Paul Theroux

Jean Rhys: Letters 1931–66
Edited by Francis Wyndham and Diana Melly

'Eloquent and invaluable . . . her life emerges, and with it a portrait of an unexpectedly indomitable figure' – Marina Warner in the *Sunday Times*

Among the Russians   Colin Thubron

One man's solitary journey by car across Russia provides an enthralling and revealing account of the habits and idiosyncrasies of a fascinating people. 'He sees things with the freshness of an innocent and the erudition of a scholar' – *Daily Telegraph*

The Amateur Naturalist   Gerald Durrell with Lee Durrell

'Delight . . . on every page . . . packed with authoritative writing, learning without pomposity . . . it represents a real bargain' – *The Times Educational Supplement*. 'What treats are in store for the average British household' – *Books and Bookmen*

The Democratic Economy   Geoff Hodgson

Today, the political arena is divided as seldom before. In this exciting and original study, Geoff Hodgson carefully examines the claims of the rival doctrines and exposes some crucial flaws.

They Went to Portugal   Rose Macaulay

An exotic and entertaining account of travellers to Portugal from the pirate-crusaders, through poets, aesthetes and ambassadors, to the new wave of romantic travellers. A wonderful mixture of literature, history and adventure, by one of our most stylish and seductive writers.

Beyond the Blue Horizon   Alexander Frater

The romance and excitement of the legendary Imperial Airways East-bound Empire service – the world's longest and most adventurous scheduled air route – relived fifty years later in one of the most original travel books of the decade. 'The find of the year' – *Today*

Voyage through the Antarctic   Richard Adams and Ronald Lockley

Here is the true, authentic Antarctic of today, brought vividly to life by Richard Adams, author of *Watership Down*, and Ronald Lockley, the world-famous naturalist. 'A good adventure story, with a lot of information and a deal of enthusiasm for Antarctica and its animals' – *Nature*

Getting to Know the General   Graham Greene

'In August 1981 my bag was packed for my fifth visit to Panama when the news came to me over the telephone of the death of General Omar Torrijos Herrera, my friend and host . . .' 'Vigorous, deeply felt, at times funny, and for Greene surprisingly frank' – *Sunday Times*

The Search for the Virus   Steve Connor and Sharon Kingman

In this gripping book, two leading *New Scientist* journalists tell the remarkable story of how researchers discovered the AIDS virus and examine the links between AIDS and lifestyles. They also look at the progress being made in isolating the virus and finding a cure.

Arabian Sands   Wilfred Thesiger

'In the tradition of Burton, Doughty, Lawrence, Philby and Thomas, it is, very likely, the book about Arabia to end all books about Arabia' – *Daily Telegraph*

When the Wind Blows   Raymond Briggs

'A visual parable against nuclear war: all the more chilling for being in the form of a strip cartoon' – *Sunday Times* 'The most eloquent anti-Bomb statement you are likely to read' – *Daily Mail*